PERSON, BEING, & HISTORY

PERSON, BEING, & HISTORY

Essays in Honor of Kenneth L. Schmitz

EDITED BY

Michael Baur & Robert E. Wood

The Catholic University of America Press
Washington, D.C.

The paper used in this publication meets the minimum requirements of American National Standards for Information Science—Permanence of Paper for Printed Library Materials, ANSI Z39.48-1984.

∞

Library of Congress Cataloging-in-Publication Data
Person, being, and history : essays in honor of Kenneth L. Schmitz / edited by Michael Baur and Robert E. Wood.
p. cm.
Includes bibliographical references (p.) and index.
ISBN 978-0-8132-1857-1 (cloth : alk. paper)
1.Philosophy. 2. Schmitz, Kenneth L. 3. Hegel, Georg Wilhelm Friedrich, 1770–1831. 4. Catholic Church and philosophy. I. Schmitz, Kenneth L. II. Baur, Michael. III. Wood, Robert E., 1934– IV. Title.
B29.P41558 2011
190—dc22 2010042284

CONTENTS

FOREWORD

At the University of Toronto, where he is professor emeritus, Kenneth Schmitz was known as "the Educator." Earlier in his career, students followed him from Loyola Marymount University to Marquette University when Marquette began its doctoral program in philosophy. His teaching itinerary moved through Indiana University to the Catholic University of America, and finally back to his native Canada at the University of Toronto. Even at his advanced age, he still teaches in Washington, D.C., where students from the John Paul II Institute and the School of Philosophy at Catholic University continue to be drawn more deeply into philosophy through his inspired teaching.

The contributors to this long overdue Festschrift—eighteen in number—are mostly former students at Toronto and Marquette, but also include fellow colleagues in the philosophic quest. Three of the contributors focus direct attention upon Schmitz's thought: the first paper, by James Kow, presents a general sketch of his thought; the second, by Louis Dupré, attends to Schmitz's 1982 Aquinas Lecture at Marquette University (later published as *The Gift: Creation*); the third, by James Crooks compares Schmitz's and Heidegger's treatment of "the Thing." Schmitz's thought centers on the metaphysical quest for an understanding of being, but, contrary to exclusive focus upon the universal, he has given focal attention to the singular. And like his beloved Hegel, who taught us to study the history of philosophy philosophically rather than simply historically, he carries on that quest through a dialogue with thinkers across the history of philosophy. The honoree's great gift was to teach students how to read the history of thought sympathetically, as a gold mine rather than as a minefield. This bears fruit in the majority of the papers: thirteen out of the eighteen focus upon some thinker or some movement within the history of philosophy. Schmitz's own focus upon Hegel is reflected in the fact that five of the papers in the history of philosophy are dedicated to an exposition of Hegel. Finally, two of the papers focus upon particular themes: John C. McCarthy's "Seeing the Unseen" and Robert E. Wood's "Being Human and the Question of Being."

In addition to thanking Kenneth L. Schmitz for his years of inspired teaching and scholarship, the editors also thank the authors who contributed to this collection. Generous financial support from Fordham University (through John P. Harrington, dean of the faculty of Arts and Sciences) and from the University of Dallas (through J. William Berry, provost) made possible the publication of this volume. We are also deeply grateful to David Gadon for his painstaking work on the index for this volume.

PART I

THEMES IN THE PHILOSOPHY OF KENNETH L. SCHMITZ

James Kow

1. THE PHILOSOPHY OF KENNETH L. SCHMITZ

The Recovery and Discovery of Things, Being, and the Person

Why take up philosophy? Kenneth L. Schmitz recalls that, while returning from leave in wartime England and browsing in a bookstall, he was astonished to find a book entitled *Does the World Exist?* In his words: "Recall the times. *That* world, too much with us.... What a fantastic mind that could raise such a question! I bought the book and philosophy had trapped a new victim."[1] A gracious victim, entrapped maybe, but a unique person, who has liberated many of his students and colleagues with his breadth of spirit and mind since then.

This chapter is dedicated, albeit hesitantly, to exploring the thought of Schmitz. Hesitantly, since to endeavor to examine Schmitz's thought risks unraveling its careful, elegant weaving. To apply his own finely wrought philosophical phrase to his thought, it is a "contextualized singular," and its influence is due not only to its own intrinsic merit, but also to the personal presence of the man himself. But Schmitz would want me to concentrate on his thought. And so I will explore Schmitz's view of the "texture of being"—the natures of things, the transcendentals, persons, and being in its analogous diversity.

1. Kenneth L. Schmitz, "Philosophical Pluralism and Philosophical Truth," *Philosophy Today* 10 (1966): 3–18, 6.

Schmitz's vision has been described by von Balthasar as "widening" in its influence on others, and I would say deepening as well. The context of his thought as a contextualized singular is astonishingly comprehensive. It requires great breadth on the part of his interlocutors to respond appropriately to his challenge to dine at his feast of insights. One might wonder what practical impact the "widening" of Schmitz's thought has had on his philosophy. Indeed, after reading his work, some may gently judge that a little too much theology has intruded here. Schmitz suggests that we bypass this critical border-like mentality, which isolates disciplines in a way in which they are not isolated in human life. Drawing upon Blondel, he suggests that we think of philosophy and theology as a place (*locus*) of encounter.[2] This is the personal, spiritual space of the Greek and medieval view that disciplines are not made up of propositions marching down a scroll, assassinating interlocutors left and right. The old sense of discipline expressed the habit of the intellectual virtues integrated with a well-formed sensibility and spirituality. The truly intellectual, philosophical life is a life of crossings and meetings, and of personal encounters we share in as a community.

I will trace the elaboration of Schmitz's thought through different but convergent emphases. What is so unusual about it is that it advances on many fronts. In all of his articles and books he invokes the whole tradition of philosophy, or at the very least, significant stretches of it, and in addition pertinent areas outside of philosophy proper. This refreshing approach resists simplification.

How should we characterize his thought more precisely? In his address "The Fortunes of Philosophy Within the Association," Schmitz recounts that, although he was attracted by the "purity of the intellectual life" in Maritain, without rejecting Maritain he "turned more in the direction of Gilson's historical studies."[3] Schmitz further relates that he found himself challenged by Hegel's recognition of the historical character of philosophical thought. For him, Hegel is "the first philosopher . . . to take history seriously within philosophy itself."[4] Yet at the Pontifi-

2. Schmitz, "God, Being and Love: New Ontological Perspectives Coming From Philosophy," in *The Texture of Being*, edited by Paul O'Herron, 265–82, 279, Studies in Philosophy and the History of Philosophy 46 (Washington, D.C.: The Catholic University of America Press 2007); hereafter "God, Being and Love"; *The Texture of Being* is an indispensable anthology of Schmitz's writings.

3. Schmitz, "The Fortunes of Philosophy Within the Association," *Proceedings of the Catholic Philosophical Association* 66 (1992): 13–28, 23.

4. Ibid., 23; also see p.22: "I found myself drawn away from system and towards his-

cal Institute of Mediaeval Studies in Toronto Schmitz relates that in his studies of the Middle Ages:

what he found most distinctive and pervasive ... was a certain luminous density.... I want to remark the ... mediaeval sense of the concrete ... what I call a certain earthiness.... For mediaeval concreteness was a physical concreteness that made room within it for the symbolic and the vicarious; in a word, it was a sacramental concreteness.[5]

Against this background Schmitz grasped the opportunity to examine the nature of things and being (Aquinas), history (Hegel), and person (Marcel) in a unique manner. One might say tentatively that he has always been exploring the sacramental and incarnational character of things and persons in the context of an analysis of the principles and causes of the analogous and causal community of being. Is Schmitz a Thomist? As he has written with fine discrimination:

while I have always acknowledged my debt to the great saint, I have also avoided claiming the honorific "Thomist" for my own thought. Still, I must confess that I experience a certain uneasiness whenever my own thought seems to be in contradiction with the balanced and profound thought of St. Thomas.[6]

---

tory in the cultivation of philosophy." Taking this advice I intend to adopt the same approach to Schmitz's thought. Schmitz sees that Hegel's history is specified more as historicity. Moreover, there is a hardening in Hegel of opposing nominalist units, raising conflict to a transcendental status. In sum: negation is dialectical, not analogical. For a thought-provoking new reading of analogy by Schmitz, see "Naming God: Analogical Negation," in *The Thought of Louis Dupré: In Christian Spirituality and the Culture of Modernity*, edited by Peter Casarella and George Schner, S.J. (Cambridge, U.K.: Eerdmans, 1998), 159–75.

5. Schmitz, *What Has Clio to Do with Athens?* (Wetteren, Belgium: Universa, 1987), 12–13; See Schmitz, "Concrete Presence," *Communio* 14 (1987): 300–15. For Schmitz the Catholic sense of presence flourishes in medieval concreteness or earthiness. It is incarnated in a religious sensibility with an intimate sense of the presence of God, not only in nature, but in the experience of the form of a human life as lived sacramentally by Christ in his birth, life, crucifixion, death, and resurrection. Also see Marie-Dominique Chenu, O.P., "The Symbolist Mentality," in *Nature, Man, and Society in the Twelfth Century*, edited and translated by Jerome Taylor and Lester K. Little, 99–145 (Toronto: University of Toronto Press, 1997).

6. Schmitz, "Created Receptivity and the Philosophy of the Concrete," *Thomist* 61 (1997): 339–76, 341n6; hereafter "Created Receptivity"; this article reveals the profound influence Marcel has had upon Schmitz, who combines the fullness of metaphysical first principles and the plenitude of the Christian tradition, with Marcel's contemporary sense of the full; see G. Marcel, "On the Ontological Mystery," in *The Philosophy of Existentialism* (New York: Citadel Press, 1967): 9–46, especially 12: "provided it is taken in its metaphysical ... sense, the distinction between the *full* and the *empty* seems to me more fundamental than that between the *one* and the *many*." Schmitz shrewdly notes that for Marcel this is also "the appreciation of the mystery whereby the full permeates the empty"; "God, Being and Love," 274.

Schmitz has developed his own thought walking along the path of the history of philosophy. He acknowledges that we need a shift to the concrete in philosophy today. Is his philosophy the answer? We should know better. For Schmitz, "philosophy in its actual career is not to be identified with *any* system of philosophy, not even with *my* own philosophy." Is there then a danger of relativism? For Schmitz the diversity of philosophies expresses philosophy's abundance. He asks: "What, then, is the source of the diverse unities of thought we see manifest in each of the thinkers? We might better try to ground it in *personhood*."[7] Schmitz brings a philosophical piety and humility to his philosophizing that is rooted in a deep sense of gratitude before being in its history and eternity.

Schmitz's project originates in wonder, which has been a lifelong recovery of metaphysical realism, of being, but at the same time he acknowledges the important turn to history, which brings forth the history of being, providing for the new, the new freedom that ushers in new responsibilities regarding how we are to employ prudently and moderately the new powers available to us, not merely as individuals in an environment, but as persons in a mutual career with the dear beings and things with which we share creation. Schmitz's attempt to understand the nature of things, being, history, and persons has led him to a recovery of metaphysical realism, but as his thought has developed, it has become a recovery that is actually an advance in being itself. And so Schmitz's recovery of being is at one with the discovery of our being anew in the new freedom that recognizes the contribution of a well-formed subjectivity to being, which ultimately is the gift of a freely giving loving Source—we can say, with the correct stipulations, that it is a theological self Who is the root nourishing the human spirit.

In the next section I will look at the initial part of the development of Schmitz's philosophical voyage and develop his thought by reflecting upon Hegel, the philosophy of religion, and Aquinas. "Toward the *Gift* of Creation and its Implications" will examine the themes in and surrounding Schmitz's book *The Gift: Creation*. Subsequently, "Schmitz's Critical Encounter with Contemporary Thought" brings us to Schmitz's encounter with the main strands of contemporary thought. "The Contribution of German Idealism and Aquinas" is a necessary preparation for the thinking that occupies him to this day. In "Schmitz on Wojtyla/ Pope John Paul II and the Person," I discuss Schmitz's views on Wojtyla's philosophy and his own views of the person. In "*The Recovery of Wonder*

7. Schmitz, "The Fortunes of Philosophy Within the Association," 25.

and Reflections" I will briefly scrutinize his book the *Recovery of Wonder*. Finally I offer my conclusion.

The Project: The Recovery of Metaphysical Realism—Hegel, the Philosophy of Religion, Aquinas, and the Unfolding of Schmitz's Thought

In his article "Toward a Metaphysical Restoration of Natural Things" Schmitz lays down certain themes that will remain as the mainstays of his thought. He notes that, despite the modern view, human beings do not exercise unconditional mastery over nature. Instead, we have lost a certain "primacy of being"; being has lost its value; we have lost the medieval world of mysterious evidences. But despite being faced with the closed modern *principium* of subjectivity, Schmitz asserts: "Perennial principles are not static, they are enduringly permanent." Still, what is lost is the "subject-of-being" that is a "being-with-Him"—God.[8] In another remarkable article, "The Redemptive Role of the Knowledge of Nature," Schmitz describes the Christian attempt to understand the nonhuman world in a metaphysical-theological tradition.[9] In his view, "The fullest spiritual openness of the human understanding is accomplished in the intimate copresence of the being of the knower and the known.... The ontological structure of the thing is an invitation for understanding."[10] Being known makes an ontological and transcendental difference to the thing known.

Just so did Aquinas attend to the concrete character of human nature in its individual status. There is, however, something explicitly more for Schmitz—the transcendentals. For him metaphysics considers "all that belongs to being in any way whatsoever." The transcendental characters of being are the "unqualified context of meaning, in which the diversities of human persons and things are seen as members of the community of being."[11] Schmitz is intrigued by

> the transcendental concomitants of being ... it is to these that metaphysics needs to look, for they form the web within which the context of individuals—is constituted....

8. Schmitz, "Toward a Metaphysical Restoration of Natural Things," in *An Etienne Gilson Tribute*, edited by Charles O'Neill, 251, 259, 261 (Milwaukee: Marquette University Press 1959).

9. Schmitz's Freiburg im Breisgau article "The Redemptive Role of the Knowledge of Nature," *Franciscan Studies* 24 (1964): 223–60; note the nuanced references to Christ in a philosophical context: 232–34; 243–44, 256–60.

10. Ibid., 252–53.

11. Schmitz, "Human Nature, History, and the Transcendental Character of Being,"

We need to articulate the inherent worldliness of the individual, in a way in which the context enters into the very being of the individual.[12]

Or, St. Thomas emphasizes being, and roots the transcendentals in it, because of his focus on actuality. Moreover, he identifies the transcendentals with being.[13] Consequently, for Schmitz, we require an integral metaphysics in order to appreciate the concrete existence of human persons and human communities. This integral metaphysics of actuality must include nature and history. By intelligently registering all that is, the human spirit enlarges being itself.

Schmitz now develops his own thought through examining Hegel, the philosophy of religion, and Aquinas. Let me take them sequentially. Schmitz's encounter with Hegel is life-long, but a significant part of it occurs during the 1960s and 1970s and moves particularly in the area of the philosophy of religion. Schmitz observes that philosophical thought for Hegel is an overreaching activity that comprehends the other in conceptualization—*Begriff/Begreifen*. The finite and infinite are not separate; to the contrary, they constitute a complete systemic totality. Ergo, speculative reason is the one including the many. With this, the farthest transcendence of spirit for Hegel exists as nature in its objectivity, entailing that only like can oppose like: it is the same.[14] In other words, Hegel's central notion is *Geist*. It overreaches in order to recover itself through the interiorization of opposition. In the Hegelian world entities

Proceedings of the Catholic Philosophical Association 40 (1966): 124–34, 129, 131. His book *The Recovery of Wonder: The New Freedom and the Asceticism of Power* (Montreal and Kingston: McGill-Queen's University Press, 2005) is present here in the beginning *in nuce;* hereafter *The Recovery of Wonder.* Also see the initial Schmitz article, "Natural Wisdom and Some Recent Philosophy Manuals," *Proceedings of the Catholic Philosophical Association* 32 (1956): 181–90.

12. Schmitz, "Metaphysics: Radical, Comprehensive, Determinate Discourse," *Review of Metaphysics* 39 (1986): 675–94, 692–93.

13. Schmitz, "*Was heißt Philosophie?* One Hundred Years of German Catholic Thought," in *One Hundred Years of Philosophy,* edited by Brian Shanley, 133–55, 142–43n30, Studies in Philosophy and the History of Philosophy 36 (Washington, D.C.: The Catholic University of America Press, 2001). Through natural things and the concomitant properties of being—the transcendentals are being *per se,* not merely *ens commune (ens rationis).* See the discussion of transcendentals in the *Recovery of Wonder,* 125–26; see another discussion of the transcendentals in Schmitz, "Death and the Rebirth of Man," in *The Texture of Being,* edited by Paul O'Herron, 283–99, 296–99, Studies in Philosophy and the History of Philosophy 46 (Washington, D.C., The Catholic University of America Press, 2007); "in traditional metaphysics it is the transcendentals that make up the texture of being," for, "Suppose that being is a *gifted* texture that houses the transcendentals open to development, but not indifferent to finite conditions? And suppose that reason is receptive of that structure?" 298.

14. Schmitz, "Hegel's Philosophy of Religion: Typology and Strategy," *Review of Metaphysics* 23 (1969): 717–36, 729.

find their meaning and self-existence as co-constituting moments completing the system.[15]

Schmitz now poses a deeper question that appears to draw Hegel's *Geist* as close as is possible to the Christian God. Schmitz notes that James Collins admits a kind of religious mystery in Hegel, yet for Collins this mystery is involved in a completely self-realizing process. Why? Because ultimately, I suggest, Hegel's God is not jealous, and as Spirit he reveals himself entirely. So this is a very qualified mystery. Schmitz assesses that there is something more. He proposes that we consider that religious mystery in Hegel involves the "staggering thought of an absolute absence of an absolute presence from itself."[16] To wit, the absolute is absent from itself in its recognition of all its discursive movement—the developing logic of spirit that constitutes its momentary subjectivity. Reason has exhausted itself. Schmitz states controversially that "there arises out of the Hegelian dialectic the possibility of a non-dialectical presence."[17] Later Schmitz modifies this provocative suggestion by noting that "Hegel's sense of absence never reaches beyond *indeterminacy,* beyond the absence of determinations."[18] Conversely, for Schmitz, mystery is properly an excellent transverbal and transconceptual presence-in-absence determinate actuality of another order, not the Hegelian religious mystery of an indeterminate absence. Consequently, whereas the Hegelian Trinity serves the sentence of hard labor working toward its goal (by pushing differences to their ultimate, manifesting a tragic Greek sense of life), the Christian Greek Trinity finds the Father delightedly ensconced in the bosom of a family. Still, Hegel has

15. Schmitz, "Hegel's Attempt to Forge a Logic for Spirit," in *Dialogue* 10 (1971): 653–72, 668–69; see Schmitz's "Hegel on Kant: Being-In-Itself and the Thing-In-Itself," in *The Philosophy of Immanuel Kant,* edited by Richard Kennington, 229–51, Studies in Philosophy and the History of Philosophy 12 (Washington, D.C.: The Catholic University of America Press, 2001). Hegel criticizes Kant for tolerating the relationless *An-sich-Sein* of the thing-in-itself. For Hegel, no thing can be so completely indeterminate. This restricted Kantian self-relatedness also constitutes Kant's subjectivity, which, for Hegel, is an *a priori* synthetic unity that Kant does not take speculative advantage of.

16. Schmitz, "The Conceptualization of Religious Mystery," in *The Legacy of Hegel (The Proceedings of the Marquette Hegel Symposium 1970),* edited by Joseph O'Malley and Ken Algozin, 108–36, especially 128 (Hague: Martinus Nijhoff 1970). For more on mystery, see Schmitz, "Theological Clearances," in *The Texture of Being,* edited by Paul O'Herron, 245–64, especially 246–50, Studies in Philosophy and the History of Philosophy 46 (Washington, D.C., The Catholic University of America Press 2007).

17. Schmitz, "The Conceptualization of Religious Mystery," 131.

18. Schmitz, "An Addendum to Further Discussion," *American Catholic Philosophical Quarterly* 73 (1999): 277–90, especially 279–80, 280n3; hereafter "An Addendum."

sensed something novel, namely the dynamic of human spirit to release "a new trans-natural texture of meanings and values."[19] Indeed man is finite, but as finite he and God are participants together journeying toward self-discovery, wherein finite man discovers his infinitude, and the infinite God his finitude. This is the real Hegelian religious mystery of the eternal processes that involves creation *qua* estrangement and reconciliation.

Whence the central energy of the dialectic? Schmitz points to nominalism, which stresses the unit or individual entities in their enclosed simplicity. This stressing leads to a heightening of oppositions and contradictions. No unity between completely separate units is possible. Schmitz judges this to be the nerve of the power of the negativity driving the dialectic to system: "It is this demand for identity, as absolute selfhood that marks the distinctive presence of nominalism at work in the Hegelian logic. It is the demand for unadulterated and indivisible unity."[20] In consequence, Hegel has expressed the modern sense of conflict and made it as originary as the reconciliation (*Versöhnung*) achieved.

Schmitz's more specifically philosophy of religion articles date from around 1970 onward. Schmitz's goal is to philosophize out of all the concrete resources that life furnishes. The experience of religion is crucial due to the mysterious evidences it provides for life and philosophical thought. The importance of religious experience is noted by Schmitz in a slightly phenomenological way. I am not suggesting that he is utilizing a new phenomenology as such, but he is sensitive to experience in the generous breadth of that term. To this end he comments: "The third major source for an understanding of religion is the pre-philosophical phase of the phenomenology of religion."[21] This is not an immanentizing phe-

19. Schmitz, "Hegel's Attempt to Forge a Logic for Spirit," 655.

20. Schmitz, "On a Resistant Strain within the Hegelian Dialectic," *Owl of Minerva* (1994): 147–54, 150.

21. Schmitz, "Philosophy of Religion and the Redefinition of Philosophy," *Man and World* 3 (1970): 54–82, 59. See also Schmitz's favorable but not uncritical review of Dupré's *The Other Dimension*, in Schmitz, "Scrutinizing the Inscrutable," *Review of Metaphysics* 27 (1978): 346–70; for insightful critical remarks, see 362–70. For the prephilosophical phenomenology based in the metaphysics of being, see Schmitz's article "Natural Imagery as a Discriminatory Element in Religious Language," in *Experience, Reason, and God,* edited by Eugene T. Long, 159–76, Studies in Philosophy and the History of Philosophy 12 (Washington, D.C.: The Catholic University of America Press, 1980). Also see "Ritual Elements in Community," *Religious Studies* 17 (1981): 163–77; note the metaphysical discussion of the need for rituals as "the disclosure of a fundamental ontological order. They become symbols of limit" (173). See Schmitz, "World and Word in Theophany," *Faith and Philosophy* 1 (1984): 50–70; note the assertion of the rabbi to an experience of the sacred presence. In Schmitz's appraisal:

nomenology, for experience eludes exhaustive description, since it intimates a beyond. Schmitz's sense of experience, I submit, is akin to Marcel's kind of phenomenology and experience, but within the metaphysics of being.

Philosophy's conceptual form of meaning now encounters the mystery of religious meaning that dwells in symbol, rite, ritual, and many other rich forms. Philosophy employs concepts in the finite language of analogy; or more accurately, in speaking about God, the complexity of the *modus significandi* is inadequate to the simplicity of the *res significata*. Nonetheless, language as being analogously discloses some shred of conceptual meaning about the ultimate Being. Dissimilarity does not simply obliterate similarity. More, though, the speaker in his speech to and about God, in response to speech from God, undergoes a transformation. To this end religious symbols sustain us, since they bring to presence what they symbolize. This actuates the philosophical language of analogy. Consequently, we can "stammeringly" speak about and name God, as Catherine Pickstock has said in a liturgically philosophical note. Yet the initiative is all divine. Beyond philosophical speech there is only the silence that struck St. Thomas.

In the important articles of 1974–1980 Schmitz unfolds his own thought through a deep reflection on Aquinas. In his article "Enriching the Copula" his goal is to enhance the copula through reflection on the ontological side of knowing, which in unison preserves the integrity of the known. As the metaphysical judgment *ad rem,* thought is the *processus ad rem*. And so the focus of assertive judgment is a cognition terminating in the thing, which is resolved into its ontological situation of the community of being. Thought too is being; so thought comes into its fullness of being. Accordingly thought enjoys an ontological relation to the thing's being and to the being of its union with the thing. For Schmitz this is the copula's double nature or double presence—the unity of thought and being—as a limit, which functions onto-existentially to identify and distinguish in the comprehensive horizon of being and nonbeing.[22]

"If the Rabbi spoke truly, it is a fresh theophany, but not a bare immediacy" (52). Hence a mediated immediacy. Also for Schmitz: "It is a misreading of a nature-theophany, then, to place the interiority in the human psyche alone; for there is an interiority in the cosmos as well. A nature-theophany recovers a distinctive depth in nature, penetrating beyond nature as mere fact into nature as creature" (67).

22. Schmitz, "Enriching the Copula," *Review of Metaphysics* 74, no. 27 (1974): 492–512, 503–7; "Another Look at Objectivity," *Proceedings of the Catholic Philosophical Association* 48 (1974): 74–87; "Immateriality Past and Present," *Proceedings of the Catholic Philosophi-*

On the corresponding side we have specific factors of objectivity. As we know, knowledge occurs in the community of beings. First, such knowledge takes place, for Schmitz, in a "singular universality" and possesses a fundamentality of comprehension; there is an affinity between these beings. Second, knowledge in its respect for the thing discloses it in its own being. This is the radical imperative: that in philosophy we seek the truth. Third, truth is a letting be—a disclosure. Finally, the human perspective on things is selective. It expresses a noetic limitation. All these factors disclose objectivity to be an achievement.[23]

Schmitz in his "Immateriality" article maintains that there are resonances between classical and contemporary conceptions of immateriality. Classical properties of self-actuation, immanence, and transcendence find a not-incompatible resonance in contemporary conceptions of openness, totality, and limit. Of interest too is the "affinity" Schmitz descries between medieval and contemporary immateriality. To *incarnatio* there is situation; to *ratio,* totality; to *intellectus,* presence.[24]

Second, Schmitz affirms that the medieval and contemporary metaphysical principle of actuality is transcendental presence, a contemporary sense of presence that

> recovers, deepens and expands the mediaeval sense of actuality. It does this by redefining it in appropriately temporal and historical terms.... The immateriality of historical presence is the source of a new order, able to be congenial to the career of natural things, sensitive to the historical existence of men and their societies, and able to also disclose the spiritual resources that live at the origin of men and things.[25]

Recall that all this is for the sake of truth. Schmitz remarks that, according to Aquinas' De Veritate, truth precedes knowledge. Truth is the assimilatio, adequatio, convenientia, comparatio, correspondentia, and conformitas between knower and known. The fundamental adequatio is the processus ad rem, ad esse. Again, Schmitz articulates the process of truth in an ontologically determinate manner, not in the ontologically indeterminate manner of Heidegger.

Nevertheless, like Heidegger, Schmitz concentrates upon the tem-

---

cal Association 52 (1978): 1–15; "A Moment of Truth: Present Actuality," *Review of Metaphysics* 38 (1980): 673–88. The theme of immateriality comes out strongly in Schmitz's later work, "Purity of Soul and Immortality," *Monist* 69 (1986): 396–415.

23. Schmitz, "Another Look at Objectivity," 74–87.

24. For this rich discussion I refer the reader to "Immateriality Past and Present," 2–9, and 9–12.

25. Ibid., 13.

poral (which must always, for him, be understood as open to the eternal) dimension of truth. Correcting the absolutely immanentized internal-time-consciousness of Husserl, and the unstable future-oriented temporal structure of Heidegger's *Dasein,* Schmitz discriminates in the present between (1) the ordinary copresence of *simul et sequens,* which are successive, and (2) the remarkable copresence of *simul et sequens.* His breakthrough is his insight into this new sense of simultaneity and metaphysical reciprocity.[26] This new sense of copresence—grounding our ordinary experience of copresence—is a layered, textured sense of presence and temporality; it recognizes the gentle weight of time, in contrast to the dragging fleetingness of transiency alone.

Toward the Gift of Creation and Its Implications

In the year before Schmitz's 1982 Aquinas Lecture at Marquette University, which was issued as *The Gift: Creation,* Schmitz published an important article in Fordham University's journal *Thought,* bringing together Aquinas and Hegel at the deepest level of *creatio ex nihilo* and *Entzweiung.*[27] First I will discuss this article, then *The Gift.*

In "Transcendental and Empirical Pressures in Human Subjectivity," Schmitz comments on the twin demands of modern philosophy: in a rationalist vein it is the transcendental demand for system; in an empirical vein, the demand for evidence. How can these competing demands be satisfied, since they expose the divisions of our world? Hegel argues that through the achieved complete presence of subjectivity in the substance of modern life, *Geist* is enabled to recover all of the self's essentially spiritual moments in nature and history in a higher speculative unity. Schmitz judges that Hegel's turn to history is crucial in order to do full justice to being. If Hegel is correct, then his recovery entails that in our world, in his philosophy, we have attained the absolute world form.

In the next section of this article Schmitz probes the profound difference between Aquinas and Hegel in a discussion that clears the ground for *The Gift.* Both Aquinas and Hegel realize that we are encompassed in an *exitus et reditus.* Schmitz remarks of Hegel: "This going and coming that results in knowledge, this *exitus* and *reditus* is no mere metaphor, it

26. Schmitz, "A Moment of Truth: Present Actuality," 679n20, 681–86; Aquinas, *On Truth,* trans. Robert W. Mulligan (Chicago: Regnery, 1952); Aquinas, *De Veritate* in *Quaestiones Disputatae,* vol. 1, trans. and ed. Fr. Raymundi M. Spiazzi (Turin and Rome: Marietti, 1949).

27. Schmitz, "Transcendental and Empirical Pressures in Human Subjectivity," *Thought* 56 (1981): 227–86; Schmitz, *The Gift: Creation* (Milwaukee: Marquette University Press, 1982); hereafter *The Gift.*

is a real movement . . . it is a movement of the human spirit."[28] For Hegel the process commences as an *Entzweiung*. Primitively put, the indeterminate whole sets out to find its meaning, value, and truth in its journey of self-determination to self-determinateness. Need—the indeterminateness of the Father in the Hegelian Immanent Trinity—drives the negative labor of spirit to recover all its developing essential moments, which is the self-discovery of all that it has been. Schmitz deems Hegel to be seeking the same out of the same-and-other so as to ensure speculative unity. Hegel resolves the twin demands of the modern world by reconstituting subjectivity as momentaneous. Reconciliation, for him, is the exhaustive upwelling of the self from its depths without remainder. Unlike Marcel's humble ontological exigency, Hegelian spirit's own initial indigence demands all and remains restless with a self-definitive overcoming. Hegel's is a self-determining system, whose Baconian backbone, as H. S. Harris suggests, leads to a kind of holistic rational empiricism. But then what of Aquinas?

In Schmitz's view, Aquinas cherishes things from the viewpoint of creation. Chenu notes that the *exitus et reditus* movement is played out in the structure of the *Summa* as well as in the written order of being itself—creation as the Book of God.[29] Schmitz says of creation that Aquinas "reclaims the Other from the Other-and-same, beginning and ending his effort with the Other." This is the "Other beyond otherness." God! In sum: "*reditus in se ipsum et in Deum.*"[30]

Is Hegel vanquished? It would be imprudent to ever be so sure, but Schmitz makes another major point. He asserts that the Hegelian beginning is not a *Vermutung*, which posits nothing, but a *Zumutung*, which encloses an expectation.

> Yet . . . there is at least one pre-determination. It is what I have called the nominalist thrust that excludes otherness. For the demand does not simply suspend otherness, it insists on the pure self-determination of thought. It presupposes the concrete results of the *Phenomenology* only insofar as those results have brought thought to the demand for purity of self.[31]

28. Schmitz, "The First Principle of Personal Becoming," *Review of Metaphysics* 47 (1978): 757–74, 770.

29. See Maria-Dominique Chenu, *The Scope of the Summa of St. Thomas*, trans. Robert Brennan and Albert Landry (Washington, D.C.: The Catholic University of America Press, 1958); for *exitus et reditus*, see 15–21, 27–33.

30. Schmitz, "Transcendental and Empirical Pressures in Human Subjectivity," 284–87.

31. Schmitz, "On a Resistant Strain within the Hegelian Dialectic," 154; see also Schmitz, *The Recovery of Wonder*, 62n26.

In *The Recovery of Wonder* Schmitz notes that Hegel has the *Zumutung* for the project of *absolutes Denken* regarding his Science of Logic. At the vexed beginning there is for Hegel an immediacy that is burdened with an assumption. At the beginning with Aquinas we can say nothing—nihil—for all there is before creation is God. This nihil is executed uniquely. We should query whether the Hegelian negativity and its prominent historical derivatives in philosophy are not broken on the *nihil* of *creatio*.

In *The Gift* Schmitz employs St. Anselm's category of gift to explicate the sense of creation.[32] Schmitz's two tasks are to explain the absolute nature of creation *ex nihilo* and to reassemble a suitably rich texture of causality in order to better understand the nature of God's creative activity. In *creatio ex nihilo* we do not traffic in facts, givens, data, or the self-giving of Hegel's *Geist*. No, in *creatio ex nihilo* there is a donation from nothing. This causality is ontologically unique: it executes an absolute sense of privation, since before *creatio* no subject is present. If there is to be something, it will be a sheer receiving, sheer receptivity. *Creatio ex nihilo* is the gift of the creature even to receive freely all of the being that it is.

In reply to the objection that creation introduces an unwarranted asymmetrical relation, Schmitz long ago addressed this issue in his 1964 article "Weiss and Creation."[33] Opposing Weiss's radical pluralism,

32. Schmitz, *The Gift*, 29–34; Schmitz's explicit exposing of creation as a gift along Anselmian lines ties in with the Anselmian-inspired Christian distinction between God and the whole in Robert Sokolowski's work; see Sokolowski, *The God of Faith and Reason* (Notre Dame, Ind.: Notre Dame University Press, 1982; Washington, D.C.: The Catholic University of America Press, 1995), 12–40; citations are to the Notre Dame edition. Also see Sokolowski, *Christian Faith and Human Understanding* (Washington, D.C: The Catholic University of America Press; Notre Dame, Ind.: Notre Dame University Press, 2007), 38–65; and Schmitz, "Theological Clearances," 257–61. St. Anselm's prayer and spirituality are his creaturely starting point for *The Gift* and Christian distinction; see Schmitz's comments on Anselmian prayer in "Natural Imagery as a Discriminatory Element in Religious Language," 164–66. More generally, for Schmitz, Christian prayer leads us into the concrete; see "Concrete Presence," 307; see also "The Redemptive Role of the Knowledge of Nature," 256: "For a holy intelligence, sanctified by God, the effort to understand nature is not only an effort to spiritualize and thereby make it anew; it is also and above all an endeavor with Christ to liberate things from their fallen state, that is, to redeem them." For an interesting treatment of prayer, see Jean-Louis Chrétien, "The Wounded Word: Phenomenology of Prayer," in *Phenomenology and the Theological Turn: The French Debate*, translated by Bernard Prusak (New York: Fordham University Press 2000), 147–75.

33. See Schmitz, "Weiss and Creation, *Review of Metaphysics* 18 (1964): 147–69, especially 163–69. For Schmitz's examination of the most contemporary metaphysical work in the grand tradition of metaphysics, see Schmitz's article on the thought of Paul Weiss: "The Modes in Process," *Review of Metaphysics* 21 (1967): 310–42.

Schmitz maintained: "What a philosophy of existential act insists upon, however, is that at the deepest level of causal communication there is no reciprocity, precisely because there is no patient which can set the conditions for the reception of being."[34] In Marcellian fashion this is the gracious reception of what and who *creatio* endows us with. It is an investiture in beings. More beings, but no more being, since God is the fullness and plenitude of being. Still, Schmitz acknowledges that our "own being" is a hard question for the Thomist.

Unlike Sartre and others, Schmitz does not see this asymmetrical relation between Creator and creature as humiliating the creature. Schmitz is extremely aware of the importance of the integrity of creaturely being. As a result, he underscores that our being is our own being. We possess dignity in the very intimacy of our being related through *creatio* to the source of our being. Unlike what Schmitz understands as Hegelian emanationism, and unlike what occurs in closed systemic philosophies, we are not items integrated exhaustively into a totality. As creatures we participate intimately in a community of beings, in an open interplay of orders, that intimates and is oriented to a determinate mystery of light—both transcendent and immanent. Hence the shine of things reveals the luminosity of the immanent and transcendent Godhead.

For Schmitz the creatureliness of the creature does not nullify it, but is the manner in which it enters into being. Whereas the absolute *nihil* is the creature's meontological predecessor, the principles and causes (intelligibility) that constitute things and persons in their metaphysical interiority are gifted by creative causality. This is God's *relatio rationis* to creatures: God does not depend upon his creatures. The formula *relatio rationis* expresses the asymmetry of the Creator-creature relationship. On the other hand, creatures do possess a *relatio reale* to God because they metaphysically and causally do depend upon Him for their *esse* and essences.

Schmitz's reflection on *creatio ex nihilo* is a reinitiating project in order to animate anew the sense of creative causality that has been lost in modernity. Modernity has transformed the metaphysical principles and causes and forms of being into modern patterns, prime matter into elements, final causes into human conscious purposes, and efficient causes into physical motions. In consequence, the deep interiority of things and being has been supplanted by more pliable factors susceptible to human control, seen as so necessary by the moderns if we are to be powerful

34. Schmitz, "Weiss and Creation," 167.

enough to alleviate the ruinous human estate and thereby make it commodious. The Cartesian slogan for this is the human mastery of nature. Schmitz has repeatedly and eloquently discussed the loss and transformation of classical philosophical and metaphysical principles in modernity.[35] I submit that the natural-supernatural distinction, so obvious to us, arose out of a late medieval nominalist attack on the intelligible natures in creation. Due to the perceived threat that the intelligible natures of things—then seen through the disguise of an Arabic, largely Averroistic, necessitarianism—posed to the omnipotence of God (the *de potentia absoluta* and *de potentia ordinata* debates), nominalism, inspired by the simplicity of early Christianity, judged that the glory of God required the denaturing of intelligible natures, since such intelligible natures confronted, thus affronting, God's glory and omnipotence. With the nominalist ejection of natures, however, creation's orientation in the nature of things to the transcendent source was severed. What was a created unity was now cleft in two: a new pure state of nature (unlike the created nature hitherto understood) and a new detached separate supernatural. This late medieval nominalistic dualism has served since then as the template for the future entrenched dualisms and multiplicities that have plagued and still plague our world. That is why an integral metaphysics, such as Schmitz has achieved, is of such significance.[36]

The Aristotelian crux for thought, as Thomas Prufer referred to it, is

35. Why there has been little response to Schmitz regarding his analysis of the history of philosophy puzzles me. It may be due to the epistemological and political nominalism that rules the day, despite many people desiring to belong to a greater whole. Schmitz notes that the seventeenth and eighteenth centuries bypassed the metaphysics of the four causes. Knowledge is now to be found in the study of motion. For Schmitz, relations in our day have become very important. It would be wise to remember that Aquinas, in his *On the Principles of Nature,* understands natural motion as the reduction of the imperfect to the perfect, and he avers that relation is the "weakest" category. Take away the perfect, and is it possible that relation becomes even weaker? Look at the anti-system systems of postmodernism with their complete collapse into pure and impure contingency.

36. See also Henri de Lubac, *Augustinianism and Modern Theology,* trans. Lancelot Sheppard (New York: Crossroad, 2000), especially 145–233; also see Hans Urs von Balthasar, *The Theology of Henri de Lubac,* trans. Susan Clements (San Francisco: Ignatius, 1983), especially 63–73. The more famous medieval proponents of nominalism are Ockham and Biel. This doctrine has influenced the history of thought, from Leibniz's doctrine of possibles to Heidegger's statement that "Possibility is higher than Actuality"; see the following: Heiko A. Oberman, *The Harvest of Medieval Theology: Gabriel Biel and Late Medieval Nominalism* (Durham, N.C.: Labyrinth, 1983): 30–56; the important Oberman article "Some Notes on the Theology of Nominalism: With Attention to Its Relation to the Renaissance," *Harvard Theological Review* 53 (January 1960): 47–76; Armand A. Maurer, "Some Aspects of Fourteenth-Century Philosophy," *Medievalia et Humanistica* 7 (1976): 175–88; and Paul Vignaux, "Nominalisme," In *Dictionnaire de théologie catholique,* vol. 11 (Paris: 1909–1950), cols. 561–87.

the tart phrase "universal because first" in Aristotle's *pros hen* equivocation.[37] Schmitz recognizes that something important occurs in Aquinas when universality is identified with determinateness. This is not Hegel's *Geist's* move from indeterminateness through a self-determining process to self-determinateness. Schmitz knows that for Aquinas determinateness is present at the beginning. It is the first—*Ipsum Esse.* As *Esse* it is what is most actual, rich, complete, intimate, and full: it is the principle of plenitude. Whereas Hegel's *Geist* moves from the primitive to the primary, Schmitz sees Aquinas' first principle as eternally primary and full. Counterfactually, if Aquinas' first principle was primitive, it would stand in need, but it is not in need; rather it is an absolutely giving Who.

In addition, Schmitz comments that while the world is not an individual, it possesses "its own *mode* of being."[38] The ownness of creaturely being and creation is in its (in)dependence upon the loving being Who as the Trinity creates it. In Schmitz 's view, it is the development of the transcendentals that will fill out our philosophical understanding of the world more than the Kantian *conceptus cosmicus* (*Weltbegriff*), more than the true infinite of Hegel, more than Husserl's horizon, and more than Heidegger's *in-der-Welt-Sein.*

After *The Gift* there follows a more Catholic reflection on creation in his article "The Roots of Catholic Intellectuality," a reflection that situates itself in the Christian experience of creation and forgiveness and yields new resources for philosophical thought.[39] What changes for us is the song, the *Doxa* singing of a theodramaturgy, due to God's initiative, between God and man. What is pivotal is that a new unprecedented intimacy has been proffered by God to man in forgiveness, an intimacy intensifying our transcendence in relation to human limits. We break through Greek limits; we also break through finitude. For we are creatures *ad-Deum* in this freely forgiven opportunity of again sharing in the infinite divine life and love.[40]

37. See Thomas Prufer, *Recapitulations: Essays in Philosophy,* Studies in Philosophy and the History of Philosophy 26 (Washington, D.C.: The Catholic University of America Press, 1993). See Stephen William Laycock on Prufer's and Sokolowski's "phenomenological Thomist view of creation," where "God is essentially to be conceived independently of the world," in *Essays in Phenomenological Ontology*, edited by Stephen William Laycock and James Hart, 11–15, 13 (Albany: State University Press of New York, 1986) .

38. Schmitz, *The Gift,* 111.

39. Schmitz, "The Roots of Catholic Intellectuality," in *CCICA Annual* 1984 (Washington, D.C.: Catholic Commission on Intellectual and Cultural Affairs, 1984), 1–18.

40. Schmitz has drawn our attention to the difference between limit, finitude, and infinitude; see Schmitz, "Theological Clearances," 251–55.

For Schmitz it is no wonder that Henry Taylor Osborne should write of "Christian immoderation" at this news. I propose that philosophically we have to be aware that while creation happened, re-creation through forgiveness may be even more important. Why? Because for the Christian, *reditus ad Deum* is the proper response in gratitude to the free gift of beings and being. Such forgiveness, I suggest, is the authentic herald of the new freedom and new liberty offered to us. We experience a new sense of human freedom because we appreciate a new sense of divine freedom in the intimate experience of love as forgiveness. To appreciate this we have to rethink creation as Schmitz has done in *The Gift*. His philosophical thought of creation is a metaphysical re-creation of *creatio ex nihilo*'s metaphysical causality. Hear Schmitz's voice: "the creative principle is also a recreative principle."[41]

In two articles after *The Gift*, Schmitz more explicitly deploys the metaphysical and conceptual resources that have served him so well and will continue to do so.[42] These metaphysical principles are explained as having analogous diversity writ into the very principles themselves. Enlisting Aquinas' *On the Principles of Nature*, Schmitz comments that "principle" is a wider term than "cause." The character of being is analogous and is comprised of principles (*principia*). Strikingly, these compose the radical diversity of the various principles of natural being, even as in the *Doxa* we cited. As Schmitz asserts:

Even the matter, form, and privation considered in one category differ irreducibly from the same principles considered in another category. . . .

It is important, moreover, to recognize that the analogical character of being does not result from the gathering together of its divers principles into itself. On the contrary. Being is the principle of principles: and so, their ana-

41. Schmitz, "The Redemptive Role of the Knowledge of Nature," 233.

42. Schmitz, "Analysis by Principles and Analysis by Elements," in *Graceful Reason: Essays in Ancient and Mediaeval Philosophy Presented to Joseph Owens, CSSR*, edited by Lloyd Gerson (Toronto: Pontifical Institute of Mediaeval Studies 1983), 315–30. Schmitz admires especially one Thomistic work suffused in the light of transformal *esse;* see Gerard Smith, *The Philosophy of Being* (New York: MacMillan, 1961), esp. 276–367, on the transcendentals; Schmitz,"Gibt es für den Menschen Wichtigeres, als zu überleben?" ("Are There Things More Important for the Human Race than Survival? The Greek Heritage: Rationality,") in *Das europäische Erbe und seine christliche Zukunft*, vol. 16, edited by Nicholas Lobkowicz (Cologne: Hans Martin Schleyer-Stiftung, 1985), 95–104 (English text 348–56); hereafter "The Greek Heritage: Rationality." This 1983 paper was delivered at an important meeting of philosophers and theologians, including Joseph Kardinal Ratzinger/Pope Benedict XVI and R. Spaemann. It outlines a theory of the four discourses, with philosophy's own epistemic and noetic (Schmitz's) discourses.

logical character expresses the original diversity that characterizes being itself. . . . The analogical diversity is rooted *within* each principle itself.[43]

Hence each principle as the source and first item in its order discharges itself in opposite directions. For example, form is a principle both of specificity/definition and difference; and matter, a principle both of continuity and discontinuity.

Schmitz notes: "Von Balthasar has driven the sense of diversity even further, insisting that difference in the mode of diversity is to be found in the Source, whose plenitude includes positive difference (singularity) within the richness of its unity."[44] Here Schmitz refers to von Balthasar's use of the transcendentals. Schmitz has also employed the transcendentals, but more reservedly:

Personal dignity incorporates these formal directives, but these formal human values arise out of the concrete individual's unique presence, a presence whose particular value is situated within the context of non-specific values (what the Schoolmen called "transcendentals") inherent within being itself.[45]

With metaphysical principles and transcendentals, philosophy also employs a distinct discourse. As Fr. H. Carr, Schmitz's original philosophical mentor, said to his classes, "only the Greeks had a grammar," thus alerting Schmitz to something more here. We can say that grammar led the Greeks to objectification, to "partial distantiation," and to conceptualization. Language brings the world to concepts; *res* to *verum*. Schmitz delineates four kinds of discourse: philosophy, mathematics, history, and linguistics. But discourse occurs in the context of *Moira,* which sets a limit to human life, thus engendering Greek tragedy. But limit is not Christian finitude, as Hegel knew. The relation between limit and finitude/

43. Schmitz, "Analysis by Principles and Analysis by Elements," 319, 322.

44. Schmitz, "Postmodernism and the Catholic Tradition," *American Catholic Philosophical Quarterly* 73 (1999): 233–52, especially 251.

45. Schmitz, "The Geography of the Human Person," *Communio* 13 (1986): 27–48, 45. Von Balthasar relates the transcendentals and analogy as follows: "The One, the Good, the True and the Beautiful, these are what we call the transcendental attributes of Being, because they surpass all the limits of essences and are coextensive with Being. If there is an insurmountable distance between God and creature, but if there is also an analogy between them which cannot be resolved in any form of identity, there must also exist an analogy between the transcendentals—between those of the creature and those in God"; Hans Urs von Balthasar, "A Résumé of My Thought," *Communio* 15 (1988): 468–73, 471; see Angela Franz Franks, "Trinitarian *Analogia Entis* in Hans Urs von Balthasar," *The Thomist* 62 (1998): 533–59.

infinitude? Simply that Christian forgiving love overcomes the Greek limit, giving rise to a new sense of freedom and new possibilities of being, doing, and thinking. Why? Because the Christian divine is not part of the whole as the Greek divine is part of the whole cosmos.

Schmitz's Critical Encounter with Contemporary Thought

From the 1980s onward Schmitz contrasts his own metaphysical approach with contemporary thought. He declares: "Metaphysics is the most controversial and controverted of the philosophical disciplines … if it did not already exist … , then it would be necessary to invent it." Metaphysics uses language in a more selective way than ordinary language does. In focusing upon objectification and conceptualization, metaphysical language presses toward ultimate cognitive ends.[46] A fundamental philosophical, metaphysical divide is noted by Schmitz: when we consider the possibility of something we can either define actuality in terms of the possibility, or possibility in terms of actuality.

Such themes serve as an index of the pluralism of metaphysics. I would add that philosophical language is polyglot: analogical, dialectical, empirical, and deconstructionistic. Modally speaking, postmodernism has sprung us into the age of the impossible, as Derrida has so belabored, beyond the possible, necessary, and actual. Metaphysics has much catching up to do. Nevertheless, for Schmitz, we should not be moved by impatience. Mark that he still emphasizes first principles, not foundations, because foundations are ambiguous. As Hegel knew, a foundation can either be a *Grundlage* (base) or a *Grund* (ground)—either an indeterminate origin or a determinate result. In Hegel's perspective, the ground lies ahead as a result—*Wirklichkeit*. The opacity of foundations as indeterminate fails to account for the given to which they appeal for justification. They cannot provide the *logon didonai* that Plato adduced to be the defining characteristic of the true philosopher. For Schmitz there are metaphysical firsts—principles.

Now Aquinas's and Schmitz's first principles are sources, like the Greek *archai*. The primary ontological unity is complex in its constitution, the *tode ti* of Aristotle. For Aquinas it is this *hoc aliquid* as a unity as an *ens indivisum*. But what of firstness? For Schmitz a principle (*principium*) is "a firstness or primacy, from which consequences (*principiata*)

46. Schmitz, "Metaphysics: Radical, Comprehensive, Determinate Discourse," 676; Schmitz, "The Greek Heritage: Rationality," 350–53.

follow as from a source, and follows according to a certain order which is in keeping with the principle that establishes it."[47] Firstness furnishes the scope for possibilities. Moreover, a primary principle is full and possesses an inherent plenitude relative to its order. It is not a system, but rather an origin. As such it goes to the roots—it is radical. In addition, the principle forms a comprehensive universality that is analogous in its diversity. These first principles give rise to an unrestricted universality. The question is whether these first radical, analogous, and comprehensive principles and the analogous character of their terms can provide unity to Schmitz's inquiry. Because they are principles of actuality, they constitute contextualized/*ti*/*aliquid* individuals/*tode*/*hoc*. This occurs in a transcendental context, in which "even Thomas ... fell back ... upon an incomplete characterization of the transcendentals."[48]

In his article "Neither With Nor Without Foundations" Schmitz provocatively queries: *"Is it possible that entity has been forgotten in the question of Being?* Is it possible that the community of beings has been devalued in the search for Being?"[49] He proposes that we can again speak of the metaphysics of entity—the language of the *tode* (commonality) *ti* (singularity), and Aquinas' *hoc aliquid*. We have to concede the danger, though, that *substantia* as *ens per se* in Latin unduly accentuates the primacy of separate individuals maybe more than Greek *ousia* does, just as *actualitas* appears to reify *energeia*. As a remedy, Schmitz recommends that we recognize the individual as a "contextualized singular," with a new sense of commonality and context expressed through "language, technology, art, religion, science and philosophy."[50]

Schmitz rejects the Heidegger-Schürmann identification of firstness with coercive power.[51] By contrast, he declares that the firstness of principles generously communicates fullness. First principles are open

47. "Metaphysics," 685.

48. Ibid., 692. Conversely, for Schmitz, Thomas "does acknowledge that reality in another way." Through judgment as the grasp of the order of being Aquinas makes explicit "the context [*esse*] into which the principles are to be resolved as into actuality," 693–94. See Schmitz, "Enriching the Copula." "Indeed, the copula breaks open into 'is' and 'is not,' it breaks open into a transcendental value, a value which pervades both speech and things, which counts both in truth and in being" (508).

49. Schmitz, "Neither With Nor Without Foundations," *Review of Metaphysics* 42 (1988): 3–25, 4.

50. Ibid., 8; the sense of the context Schmitz refers to already arises in "Human Nature, History, and the Transcendental Character of Being": "Meaning-acts are historical, personal, ontological. What intervenes is the spirit in its intelligent freedom" (132).

51. See Schmitz, "Neither With Nor Without Foundations," 10–12, 22 for Schmitz's comments on Heidegger-Schürmann.

principles. So firstness is neither totalizing nor systematizing; to the contrary, it is a plenitude first in the good order that activates the spiritual freedom of that order. Firstness is the root of all that follows and branches out from it. It is transformal *esse*.[52]

At this stage, in the article "The Greek Heritage: Rationality," Schmitz reintroduces the distantiation and conceptualization the Greeks achieved in relation to the world. He informs us about veridical discourse that treats of assertions about the truth and falsity of things; on the one hand, epistemic discourse proceeds sequentially and with justifications: "In sum: epistemic discourse moves methodically within a semantic context of truth, argument and evidence." On the other hand, noetic discourse "is more or less open discourse that arises within the ontological truth-relation. It is an original spontaneous yet receptive discourse under the influence of the concrete situation."[53] We can see that, due to the forgetfulness of entity and metaphysics, philosophical discourse today is in fact epistemic discourse; it seems evident now that this is the proper discourse for a "radical, comprehensive and determinate" approach addressing the sources of our being. Foundationalism has been epistemologically seduced in its quest for certainty. If Schmitz is right, then talk of entity will be heard once more in philosophical circles.

In his article "From Anarchy to Principles: Deconstruction and the Resources of Christian philosophy," Schmitz further elaborates on the Heidegger-Schürmann rejection of metaphysical principles. Schmitz sees the critical challenge to be to "the very 'principle' of principle."[54] He responds that it is part of the vocation of Christian philosophy (Note: "shared in part by many who are not Christian") "to appropriate *by certain rational and properly philosophical means* certain insights first disclosed by Christian revelation." Most notably Schmitz holds:

52. See ibid., 13, on "roots"; it is remarkable how Schmitz recapitulates themes so as to develop and bring them forward in a new context. The discussion of truth (14–15) harkens back to the 1980 article: "A Moment of Truth: Present Actuality" with references to Aquinas's *De Veritate* again. But to look ahead for the important images of root and branch, see Schmitz, "The Root and Branch of St. Thomas' Thought," in *Thomas Aquinas and his Legacy*, edited by David Gallagher, Studies in Philosophy and the History of Philosophy 28 (Washington, D.C.: The Catholic University of America Press 1994), 1–15; see also Schmitz,"Postmodernism and the Catholic Tradition," 241. Regarding the history of philosophy, Schmitz remarks that "It is an oft-told story of how the tree of philosophy was stripped of its branches."

53. Schmitz, "Neither With Nor Without Foundations," 18.

54. Schmitz, "From Anarchy to Principles: Deconstruction and the Resources of Christian philosophy," *Communio* 16 (1989): 69–88; For an interesting reflection on Horkheimer and Adorno, see 79–83, 81n15, 84.

Nor need any apology be made for such a proceeding, since philosophy has never been exclusively conceived from within pure reason itself. . . . We must speak of a Christian *philosophy*—and not merely of a Christian philosopher—when, in important ways and in addition to other sources, the philosophy itself responds with positive interest and follows out lines of inquiry first suggested by Christian experience.[55]

In nuce Schmitz's rejoinder is that the Tri-unity of the Godhead provides a richer sense of unity than has been acknowledged. The Trinity is neither dominated by domination nor by a power *potentia absoluta Dei* (a nominalist theme). By comparison the Trinity is the self-surrendering and loving self-donation of three persons to each other. "The unstinting generosity and infinite abundance of the first principle will give room for all possibilities within creation—even, it must be remarked, for possibilities of evil."[56] God/Trinity/*esse* are more intimate to creatures than they are to themselves. God is both immanent and transcendent. And this loving first principle is the "mystery of presence, rather than of absence, not a hiddenness brought about by domination and reductionism, but a light too bright for clear sight."[57]

In "Postmodern or Modern-plus?" Schmitz deftly handles the postmodern strand of contemporary thought .[58] Postmodernism in indicating the historical character of norms seems to assume that it has thereby razed them. What postmodernism is essentially doing is privileging its own fragmented contingent formless way of life over the analogous diversity of being, and over the complex metaphysical unity of the tradition. The postmodernist does this because he fears that unity, in principle, leads to intellectual totalitarianism and political tyranny. Because postmodernism denies origins or first principles, it is ensnared in time, thereby lacking a genuine sense of eternity or transcendence. Most calamitous perhaps is the postmodernist's hardly new, but now more

55. Ibid., 83–84.

56. Ibid., 87. For discussions of evil, see Schmitz, "Entitative and Systemic Aspects of Evil," *The Polish Academy Quarterly* 2 (1978): 149–61; Schmitz, "Shapes of Evil in Mediaeval Epics: A Philosophical Analysis," in *The Epic in Mediaeval Society: Aesthetic and Moral Values,* edited by Harald Scholler (Tübingen: Max Niemeyer 1977), 37–63.

57. Schmitz, "From Anarchy to Principles," 88. Schmitz notes that postmodernists, in particular Derrida, tend to obstruct the mystery of light. For this impeding move Blanchot and Bataille are key; see the excellent work by Kevin Hart, *The Dark Gaze: Maurice Blanchot and the Sacred* (Chicago: University of Chicago Press, 2004); see also the engrossing study of Bataille, Peter Tracey Connor, *George Bataille and the Mysticism of Sin* (Baltimore: Johns Hopkins University Press, 2000).

58. Schmitz, "Postmodern or Modern-plus?" *Communio* 17 (1990): 152–66.

visceral, inversion of *theoria* by *praxis*. Schmitz somberly recognizes: "What is at stake is *the very definition of reason itself*."[59]

Schmitz discerns that we live in an increasingly postmodern milieu. It seems to me that Schmitz is warning us of the danger of the possibility of a contingency—ill-(in)formed—moodily overrunning modern life. Do we have the intelligible resources to do justice to contingency, while not permitting it to dominate and exercise a coercive power over natural things and human beings? As Schmitz comments: "Indeed, it took me some time to realize that the very notion of 'principle' (*arche*) had ceased to function in the premodern way, that is, as a source of being."[60] There has also been a redefinition of rationality, or we may say a loosening of rationality, an unraveling of it while postmodernly reveling in that unraveling? So Schmitz, who is not prone at all to exaggeration, avers: "I have come to realize that what is at stake in postmodern criticism is not simply the prolongation of modernity, but the broad sweep of Western thought and culture itself reaching back to its origins."[61]

We are now told in his 1999 article "Postmodernism and the Catholic Tradition," written after the *Recovery of Wonder* lectures of 1997, about

59. Ibid., 163. I have left out an interesting discussion of Derrida by Schmitz; see 157–63. Regarding a putative postmodern Christian, in my view, see Schmitz's book review of Marion's *God without Being*, "The God of Love," *Thomist* 57 (1993): 495–508. For Schmitz's more direct criticism of Marion's interpretation of St. Anselm's ontological argument, he writes: "Am I wrong in understanding that ... Anselm seems to have escaped Heidegger's onto-theological circle?" How? Because, for Anselm, God is no Marionian metaphysical idol: God is a "being than which nothing greater can be conceived"; Schmitz, "An Addendum," 287. For Schmitz on St. Anselm's ontological proof, see "Theological Clearances," 255–57. Regarding Marion's approach in the book generally, Schmitz's point is that Marion does not fully appreciate the metaphysical import of *omne agens agit sibi simili*, for despite the dissimilarity between creatures and God, there is some similitude, no matter how tenuous. (Marion in the Carlson English translation attempts to qualify his position, but only muddies the waters: "when he thinks God as *esse*, Saint Thomas nevertheless does not chain God either to Being or to metaphysics" [xxii]. Marion continues to cast a wary eye in the direction of the idols of metaphysics and Being.) I suggest that Marion has not taken seriously enough the classical axiom that affirmation about God cannot be separated from the deep negation that qualifies it. For a lengthier discussion of these metaphysical insights or the three "metaphysical axioms of causality," see Schmitz, *The Gift: "omne agens agit inquantum est actu,"* 118; *"omne agens agit sibi simile,"* 118–19; *"omne agens agit propter finem,"* 119. Again, for the transformation of metaphysical causality under the twin pressures of the modern rationalist transcendental demand for system and the empiricist demand for warrant, evidence, and satisfaction, see Schmitz, "Transcendental and Empirical Pressures in Human Subjectivity, 273–82; Schmitz, "Analysis by Principles and Analysis by Elements," 316–17, especially 324–30.

60. Schmitz, "Postmodernism and the Catholic Tradition," 235.

61. Ibid., 237.

the distinctive role that history will receive in his work. The turn to history has had an impact on philosophy's self-understanding because it now requires a new theory of meaning. In this move to concreteness, the philosophies of meaning have an even greater responsibility to take account of being, and philosophies of being have to conform themselves to the transcendental of truth. For Schmitz, meaning resides in the context of truth, which transcends it, and human meaning and truth are measured by divine truth. But this human truth companionate with the divine is intimately woven into the history of being in its newness. Yes, our being is indeed our own in its received integrity. This concreteness, for Schmitz, is not empirical, but the unity of a metaphysical singularity-commonality: singularity joins "the commonality of the universal and the determinacy of the particular."[62]

The most important part in Schmitz's article is section three, wherein he recommends that we need to pay more attention to the *nihil* in *creatio ex nihilo.*

> the creature is nothing short of an absolute *nihil* that is concomitant with the actuality of its whole being received in its entirety as a gift....
>
> [t]he creature is an actual being ... with a *nihil* that transpierces ... it more deeply than the metaphysical principles of the potentiality of matter and the possibility of essence, all of which are touched by this radical contingency. This metaphysical account is deeper than all other accounts of contingency.
>
> The *nihil* does not attend the creature as something in itself, but rather as the index of the freedom of its Creator. In sum, the nothing is not a mysterious antecedent stuff, but the cipher of the sheer gratuity of the Creator.[63]

In his "An Addendum" to this article Schmitz states that "the *nihil* looks back to the gratuity of the communication of being (*influxus entis*)."[64] Similarly we have to look back and also up to the overarching gift of creation, whose Creator, Schmitz holds, transcends it on all sides, while being intimately present to it.

While postmodernism identifies firstness with coercive power, Schmitz identifies firstness with loving being, upon which he meditates

62. Ibid., 247.

63. Ibid., 249.

64. Schmitz, "An Addendum," 283; see especially the remarks on the transcendental, 282n8, the remarks on *analogia entis,* and 285–86, 285n13. For Guardini and Przywara on the analogy so crucial to Schmitz's analysis, see Schmitz, "Postmodernism and the Catholic Tradition," 251.

via the persons of the Trinity. In addition, postmodernism, although rightly drawing attention to the contingency of life, overplays its hand, and collapses under its own nominalist contingency of the bottomless life. It fails to appreciate the *nihil* in *creatio,* as we will see.[65]

Together with the numerous works we have considered, Schmitz's has been involved with the intellectual and spiritual life of von Balthasar's journal *Communio.* This flourishing involvement developed a tempo regarding his publication of articles in it from the 1980s to the present. Here I would like briefly to note again a more explicitly Catholic intellectuality, not that Schmitz's work is not as a whole informed by such a sensibility, understood as a mind open to what is best *kath' holos.*

We must recognize in Schmitz's thought his clear insight that "an acceptable account of the sacred *as it is experienced* must recognize *prima facie* the experience of the sacred initiative and the basic receptivity of man."[66] The sacred is a mysterious *coincidentia oppositorum.* Hence, for Schmitz, Christianity's own "completeness-claim" has to be examined very carefully by Christians. To reach a balanced judgment we can have confidence and faith, because eternity—a divine person—has descended into time. This enables a restoration of the balance of the time

65. Here I have to note that Schmitz's metaphysical focus means that there is room for those inspired by his thought to develop the insights in his social philosophy. His most political work, in my judgment, is self-admittedly metaphysical; see Schmitz, "Is Liberalism Good Enough?" in *Liberalism and the Good,* edited by R. Bruce Douglas, Gerald M. Mara, and Henry S. Richardson, 86–104 (New York: Routledge, 1990). Actually, Schmitz performs a great service, since this metaphysical approach acts as a corrective to the many nonmetaphysical social and political philosophy works available. The "Liberalism" article is more an ontologic of culture and therefore speaks to the differential individual, although Schmitz does comment on Ackerman, Rawls, and so forth. What comes into play importantly in this article is the individual and the individual's good, and this takes us backward and forward to the ground that Schmitz thinks most crucial—metaphysics and natures and persons. But there is a bijou here: the penetrating insight that the preinstitutional liberal self's elective freedom is not so much the power to choose as the power to unchoose. In his book *The Recovery of Wonder,* is Schmitz, in talking about the asceticism of power, thinking about whether we have the power positively to unchoose some of the dangerous powers we bring to nature and ourselves today? Also see Schmitz's "Community: the Elusive Unity," *Review of Metaphysics* 37 (1983): 243–64. This article, with its insightful comments (244–50), takes advantage mostly of the metaphysical themes drawn from Aristotle's *tode ti,* which manifests the "trans-atomic latitude" or generosity of form that allows the concrete individual to transcend, and so as an individual not to be restricted to, his individuality (244). Metaphysical issues come to fore (250–56), as do more broadly cultural issues (257–64); see also Schmitz, "The Ontology of Rights," *Ave Maria Law Review* 3 (2005): 275–88. In sum: There is a return in a new way in Schmitz's thought to what he variously calls the concrete individual, the concrete singular, or the contextualized individual.

66. Schmitz, "Divine Initiative and Christian Praxis," *Communio* 5 (1978): 44–52, 46.

structure for Schmitz. This aforementioned eternity has been philosophically present as a theme in Schmitz's work from the beginning. He is concerned now that in our society "not only have we focused in recent times almost exclusively upon the present, but we have shrunk the span of the present to dangerously narrow limits."[67] By focusing on the present and with our huge expectations for the future, we have lost our living connection with the past—yes, even after our turn to history. The ballast of the past is jettisoned, and so we sail rather too precipitously and wildly into the uncharted future. It seems to me that the future is arriving faster than ever before (*eschatologica furiosa*), placing greater pressure upon nature and human nature, and upsetting their slower rhythms. The temporal structure of human life has become unbalanced: it is wobbling. The turn to history is no doubt an advance in being for Schmitz; but it unfortunately incites the nominalist dicing up of history into ideologically manipulable separate enclosed units so that we become unable to comprehend the continuity and unity of our own story regarding who we are—the stories and myths of our origins in the religion and poetry of our various cultures.

For Schmitz eternity is timeless, but it is also time*ful* as the measure of all times, and the eternal is actually personal, not impassible. It is a permanent, reliable, and faithful actuality (in "philosophical" Hebraic *olam*). Here philosophy does not reach its limits, as much as it is called upon to expand and deepen those limits interiorly, which, for Schmitz, is manifest in a transcendence like Marcel's—a greater immersion in this creation in which we find our abode. Genuine transcendence is a transcendental baptism. Now arises the question concerning the paradoxical relationship between the integrity of nature and the gratuity of grace. In his *Communio* intervention "Catholicism in America" Schmitz counsels us to shift "the discussion to deeper, more comprehensive, and more properly religious grounds. In calling for further reflection, *Communio* has drawn upon the works of the *ressourcement* theologians, especially that of de Lubac and Balthasar."[68] Schmitz commends that we should

67. Schmitz, "Traces of Eternity," *Communio* 15 (1988): 474–77, 295. Schmitz asserts that we "need a viable concept of eternity thought through in contemporary conditions. Without such a concept the current emphasis upon eschatology is liable to degenerate into a speculative case of historicity"; see Schmitz, "The Language of Conversion and the Conversion of Language," *Communio* 21 (1994): 742–64, 759n21.

68. Schmitz, "Catholicism in America," *Communio* 19 (1992): 474–77, 476. For an instance of the *ressourcement* Schmitz advocates, see Henri de Lubac, "Retrieving the Tradition: On Christian Philosophy," *Communio* 19 (1992): 478–506, first published in 1936 in French, but still valuable. What is invaluable is de Lubac's *Catholicism* (London: Burns and Oates

take this project in a religious direction, not in a moral or political one. His advice is sound; we are too prone to injecting moralizing and politicizing into all our discussions, leaving religion and theology without a voice in the public square. Schmitz is not opposed to moral or political debate; instead he is in favor of variety of voices in the liberal public square, particularly voices that have been hitherto sidelined.

How can we speak about such things, though? This requires a conversion of language, which has already been made possible by the Incarnation of a who, a who Who as Word has absolutely transformed human language. Simply put, the divine Word transmutes human words. Previously, in Schmitz's "The Roots of Catholic Intellectuality," we witnessed the transformation of Greek conceptualization and the breaking through of Greek tragic limits, a breakthrough to the finite creature in a new *Doxa* singing us to an intimate and interior creational relationship with an infinite Loving God. Therefore, with this conversion of language, the language of analogy takes on a new energy. A new sense of the concrete and interiority is given in the presence of the Word. If Christian life is the participating of the creature in the divine life, then life converts human discourse, developing a new sense of Catholic concreteness incarnated in an inclusive and intensive language, encompassing all its aspects.

Undeniably an incommensurability remains between the human word and the divine Word, but it is imbued with an unprecedented intimacy. We might dare to say that Schmitz's philosophy ultimately springs fresh from an analogy of intimacy and from intimacy as a previously unrecognized transcendental (with freedom) of being. Our participation in divine life reveals the mysterious Tri-unity, who is/are the transconceptual hyperdeterminate origin of Christian language. What is the hearer of the Word to do? To remain silent, or to receive this unique experience in the minting of new words? For Schmitz, the goal of language is "to place itself before the paradox of an infinite Determinacy, or a determinate Infinite."[69]

[Universe Book Editions], 1962). See Hans Urs von Balthasar, "Retrieving the Tradition: *Communio*—A Program," *Communio* 33 (2006): 153–69; "On the Tasks of Catholic Philosophy in Our Time," *Communio* 20 (1993): 148–87. Schmitz contends that there has been a "large scale loss of Christian tradition and the need for its retrieval in new forms. This requires the retrieval and growth of Christian tradition. In many respects we live in a post-Christian society"; see "The Language of Conversion and the Conversion of Language," 763.

69. Schmitz, "The Language of Conversion and the Conversion of Language," 758.

The Contribution of German Idealism and Aquinas

In the late 1990s Schmitz details the development of nineteenth-century German philosophy. In his study of Lessing, Schelling, and Hegel, among others, there appears to be a preparation already for revising the *Recovery of Wonder* lectures delivered in 1997 and published in 2005. As we ought to know, we are possessed by a historical consciousness more than possessing it. This is why the turn to history has oddly ruptured the living bond between the present and past. Ontologically, difference prevails; historically, historicity; temporally, finite time trumps eternity. And thus in modernity we dodge classical metaphysical claims. The turn to history was also a turn, however, to a rational freedom that became Gnosticism in late enlightenment German thought.[70] Two characteristics of this Gnosticism, for Schmitz, are the radicality of otherness and salvation through possession of speculative knowledge. These are tied into an energy of ambiguous promise. Schmitz detects in Schelling's Godhead first the character of "a *conatus* of a wildly turbulent sort" without any teleology, then, second, Schelling's desire to exonerate the freedom of God in his creative act.[71] Schmitz rejects this. Schelling's position misfires because it insists upon the continuity between God and creation, which denies the utter gratuity of God's *creatio ex nihilo.*

By contrast Hegel stresses the *reditus* of *Geist* in absolute knowledge. But Hegel has to begin (*Zumutung*) somewhere even in his attempt to avoid Gnosticism. He admits that God the Father is indeterminate and abstract in the aboriginal *othering* (*Entäußerung*) of the immanent Trinity. And for the *reditus?*

> In Hegel, however, it is the character of the exile and the nature of the return that signals a transfigured gnostic motif, for the human journey is a passage, not simply from evil to good, but from relative ignorance to absolute knowledge.[72]

Schmitz recognizes that neither for Hegel nor for Schelling is the mystery of an original plenitude of light present, the same as the light that

70. Schmitz, "What Happens to Tradition When History Overtakes It?" *Proceedings of the Catholic Philosophical Association* 68 (1994): 59–72; Schmitz, "The Transfiguration of Gnosis in Late Enlightenment German Thought," *Communio* 21 (1994): 691–712. For a discussion of the enlightenment, see Schmitz, "Enlightenment Criticism and Embodiment of Values," *Indian Philosophical Annual* 18 (1986): 33–53.

71. Schmitz, "The Transfiguration of Gnosis in Late Enlightenment German Thought," 698.

72. Ibid., 707.

inspired medieval life and theology. In addition, the love Schelling and Hegel refer to is a somber labor, hardly the gratuitous, generous love of the Christian God. Gnosticism ultimately, for Schmitz, emerges from a sense of power—the *conatus,* the *Wollen.* Ad quem? Before this, though, can we put a proper name to the rather protean motion of modernity? Lessing, it is, who underscores the importance of historical development and the primacy of motion—the principle of historical development—epitomized in his own endless searching.[73]

This *conatus* demands to be probed as an advance upon *ens divisum,* for its form is one of a new self-expression. And in his "The Idealism of the German Romantics" Schmitz rightly focuses upon the idealistic systemic totality and upon the *"part and power."*[74] A new sense of freedom arises here, but at the cost of the causal power of traditional things. In contrast to a metaphysics of *creatio ex nihilo,* the idealists advance a metaphysics of creativity. It appears as Kantian moral autonomy, Fichtean self-constitution, Schellingian free artistic expression, and Hegelian rational self-determination. The freedom of metaphysical creativity (in its epistemological/gnosticological values) overcomes *creatio ex nihilo.* This presupposes the inversion of thought over being and freedom, and modern cognition over things. It is also a new freedom that differs from the English and French freedom of individual free choice. Its character is to creatively redefine *creatio ex nihilo;* in Hegel's case it does so by inflating the power of negativity in nonbeing. With confidence it professes to satisfy the empirical demand for warrant and evidence; opening out historically to nature scientifically, it also claims to satisfy the rational demand for system in the concrete. Certainly it is a new interiority, but the interiority of infinite subjectivity, not the older interiority of ontological principles.

These articles furnish a fine analysis of the sense of (German) ontological freedom that contributes to the synthesis of the new freedom, just as will the elective freedom of free choice of the English and French in the 2005 *Recovery of Wonder* book, but a synthesis is effected there with Schmitz's insight through a furthering of his metaphysical analysis of things and the community of being.

73. Schmitz, "Lessing at God's Left Hand," in *Modern Enlightenment and the Rule of Reason,* edited by John McCarthy, Studies in Philosophy and the History of Philosophy 32 (Washington, D.C.: The Catholic University of America Press, 1998): 213–31.

74. Schmitz, "The Idealism of the German Romantics," in *The Emergence of German Idealism,* edited by Michael Baur and Daniel O. Dahlstrom, 176–97, Studies in Philosophy and the History of Philosophy 34 (Washington, D.C.: The Catholic University of America Press, 1999); for totality, see 179–84; for power and creativity, see 184–89, 192–97.

That very insight emerges in three articles on Aquinas in the 1990s. The turn to history implicates a rethinking of the traditional sense of experience in its integrity.[75] Briefly, the classical conceptualization of experience has given us the riches of the subjects of being (*supposita entis*) composed by their immaterial interior ontological principles and causes, which are the roots and sources of their luminous mystery. In modern understanding, human consciousness has replaced these factors as an unquestionable *"subjectum fundamentum inconcussum,"* as Heidegger intoned. But this is precisely, I submit, subjectivity as *conatus* (free choice), with its own version of a more diluted concreteness. Do not forget, though, that modern experience is a palimpsest. Reading carefully, can we not discern a residual (perhaps vigorously residual) concreteness ingredient in experience—like the resistance of Marcel's being? Josef Pieper and Thomas Gilby have noticed with Schmitz such a perduring concrete presence in the interiority of creatures, leading them back to their creative source.

But such a creative source is both "most actual and determinate" and "most common and universal."[76] Its name is *esse* as the root and branch of all that is. Before becoming too fervent about this convergence, Schmitz admirably cautions us, due to the danger of intensely stressing Thomas's metaphysics, neither to reduce all philosophy to metaphysics, nor all metaphysics to being, nor being to existence—even if Aquinas transformed the Aristotelian diversity of things and the equivocity of being into an analogous diversity of beings within the community of being with the transcendentals. In Schmitz's assessment, Pseudo-Dionysius has joined via participation unity, goodness, and beauty to *esse*—an *esse* reached by the judgment of *separatio*. This transcendental texture of being is woven into the creaturely participation in being communicated by God. The finite creaturely being is *habens esse*—it possesses *esse*. This is the root of its positive nobility.

Schmitz's remaining article on Aquinas owes much to Erich Przywara's contribution not merely to the metaphysical doctrine of analogy employed in speaking about God, but to the lived metaphysical analogy of being. While Przywara (and Guardini) reject Hegel's transcendental primacy of dialectical conflict and argued self-reconciliation, strikingly, Przywara, in his doctrine of polarity, recognized the negativity inherent

75. Schmitz, "St. Thomas and the Appeal to Experience," *Catholic Theological Society of America* 47 (1992): 1–20.

76. Schmitz, *The Gift*, 100–1.

in analogy, following the axiom that affirms that there is a greater dissimilarity between God and creatures than there is similarity. Or, in the Incarnation of Christ as man and God, the creature and Creator enjoy an analogy of intimacy in their extreme *Polarität* of mysterious love. Or, the vertical analogy between God and creatures supports the horizontal analogy between creatures. Put in Thomas's way, the causal community of being supports the analogous community of being.[77]

Schmitz develops this as a radical analogy of negation for, may I say, a *vacare Deo*? Although there is discontinuity in speaking about God, although there is more dissimilarity than similarity between creature and Creator—still there is a unique *influxis entis* in *creatio ex nihilo,* and so human language has a fragile wordhold in predication about God. This is Aquinas' analogical, not Hegel's dialectical, mode of negation, which Schmitz will mine.[78]

What is this new, yet old analogy? For Schmitz it is neither the analogical negation of ordinary adjectival modes nor the expressions of complexity (both of which involve differentiation), nor is it the analogical negation of indifferentiation of speech about God. The result? Philosophical silence. And out of this silence this threefold negation gives rise to a new mode, a new way of speaking to and about God, originating a fourth mode of analogical negation. As Schmitz says:

> We have been led to the classical distinction between the mode of signification (*modus significandi*) and the reality meant (*res significata*). It is a very curious negation, and a curious distinction. For it says: "What you mean to

77. Erich Przywara, S.J., *Polarity: A German Catholic's Interpretation of Religion,* trans. A. C. Bouquet (London: Oxford University Press, 1935).

78. Note Schmitz's observation that, like Przywara, "Guardini rejects the couplet 'above and below' in favor of 'above and within'"; Romano Guardini, *World and Person,* trans. Stella Lange (Chicago: Regnery, 1939), especially 35–60; see Schmitz, "*Was heißt Philosophie?* One Hundred Years of German Catholic Thought," 149n50. For Przywara this is *Ana-logie über-in* (149n50), or as in Schmitz's "An Addendum," *Analogia entis "anö in-über katö,"* 285n13. For Schmitz on Przywara, see *Was heißt Philosophie?* 148–51. For Przywara, see the article by the eminent James Collins, "Przywara's 'Analogia Entis,'" *Thought* 65 (1990): 266–77. For Przywara and von Balthasar, see "Hans Urs von Balthasar: A Portrait," by Medard Kehl, in *The Urs von Balthasar Reader,* edited by Medard Kehl and Werner Loser; translated by Robert Daly and Frederick Lawrence (Edinburgh: Crossroad, 1985), 17–22; also see Edward T. Oakes, "Erich Przywara and the Analogy of Being," in *Pattern of Redemption: The Theology of Hans Urs von Balthasar* (New York: Continuum, 1997), 15–43; Peter Henrici, "The Philosophy of Hans Urs von Balthasar," in *Hans Urs von Balthasar: His Life and Work,* edited by David Schindler (San Francisco: Communio), 149–67; more generally, see Edward T. Oakes and David Moss, eds., *The Cambridge Companion to Hans Urs von Balthasar* (Cambridge: Cambridge University Press, 2004).

say is not what you say." At the same time it recognizes that such a disparity is in principle unable to be remedied or overcome. Such a distinction presupposes that the mind can detect differences that are not separable, distinctions that are not separations.[79]

This is the distinction between the *modus significandi* and the res *significata,* which constitute, for Schmitz, a determinate inexhaustible mystery. In sum: *analogia entis* is unsurpassable!

Schmitz on Wojtyla/Pope John Paul II and the Person

Now a man appears who will draw Schmitz's thought. In his book on Karol Wojtyla, Schmitz probes Wojtyla's practical interest, more phenomenological in appearance than metaphysical, in the acting person. It is the sincere attempt of a Catholic personalist in our time to attend to the living of the person through his own subjectivity, and Wojtyla does justice to this basal human experience. But his is neither a subjectivistic nor an idealistic subjectivity, for he accents the reality of the causal efficacy of the human will in its relation to the Good. In other words, Wojtyla does not neglect the metaphysics of being; the good of the will is rooted in existential act; further, the ethical act's distinctiveness resides in the person's spiritual freedom. As Schmitz notes:

If I am correct then Wojtyla here has appropriated the primary value of much of German Idealism with its emphasis upon freedom and spirit, while ensconcing it within a traditional metaphysical horizon."[80]

Moreover, Aquinas' metaphysics is a vital part of Wojtyla's ethical analysis in *The Acting Person.* Notwithstanding Wojtyla's retention of the Thomistic metaphysics of being, he has promoted phenomenology's role in the philosophical enterprise. Wojtyla's phenomenology underscores the manifest reality of the human person as a free, responsible agent. An interplay exists between Wojtyla's phenomenology and metaphysics as he exposes the human person's interiority. In Schmitz's considered judgment: "what interests Wojtyla is not principally a general metaphysics of being, or even of existential act, but that metaphysics insofar as it is focused upon and plays a role in the analysis of human action."[81] With his phenomenological realism Wojtyla has judiciously infused subjectivity

79. Schmitz, "Naming God: Analogical Negation," 172.

80. Schmitz, *At the Center of the Human Drama: The Philosophical Anthropology of Karol Wojtyla/Pope John Paul II* (Washington, D.C.: The Catholic University of America Press, 1993), 55n32.

81. Ibid., 67n19.

into realism. To this degree, Wojtyla has departed from the prevalent phenomenological position, since his phenomenology supplies a personal interior opening to transcendence in response to the value of the Good. His phenomenology is not snared within the immanent phenomenological horizon.

On a more religious yet still philosophical level, Wojtyla's Christian personalism beholds the human person as a cell (*cellulam*) in the church. Lest one be concerned, this does not detract from the dignity or integrity of the person, since in Wojtyla's philosophical backgrounding, for Schmitz, there is an analysis that "discloses the human person as called to act in communion with others in the realization of his or her possibilities."[82] Reaching back to the beginnings of this communion or solidarity with others, it is not humanly indiscriminate because "the beginnings of that solidarity must pass through the duality of gender by passing through the intersubjectivity of masculine and feminine."[83]

In his 1992 article "Catholicism in America," Schmitz highlighted the need for *ressourcement,* drawing on de Lubac and von Balthasar. Here he mentions that Vatican II's intention, at which Wojtyla was a contributor, could be summed up in two words. One word we know: *ressourcement;* another word is coined for the Council—*aggiornamento.* The church will be brought up to date. Not that she is outdated, but the eternally inflected temporal rhythm that the church moves to differs from the cadence of rushing time. Yet, as Schmitz has pointed out, the trace of eternity that is genuinely Catholic is also time*ful,* and so embraces contemporary time. For this reason the contemporary world is a special part of the church's *missio.* Recall that in Schmitz's 1984 Catholic Commission on Intellectual and Cultural Affairs article he posed the challenge pointedly:

> To understand what is good and to sift out what is not in the complex ideas associated with the Enlightenment constitutes a challenge to Catholic scholarship in a variety of fields. It seems to me that Catholic learning and Catholic higher education is being called: It is being called to cultivate old roots, so that in Christ's garden new shoots of faith may grow.[84]

82. Ibid., 89.

83. Ibid., 105; I would suggest that the reader examine Schmitz's chapter 4, "From Peter's Chair: A Christian Anthropology," which continues with the themes in this paragraph and provides Wojtyla's theological context drawn from the Priestly and Yahwist accounts of Genesis that deepen philosophical reflection. There are astute comments, on solitude, solitariness, (100–4), the Church (109–15), and the Encyclicals (116–20).

84. Schmitz, "The Roots of Catholic Intellectuality," 17.

This [also] seems to be the view of Wojtyla who regards metaphysics as an explanatory science. His principal interest in traditional metaphysics is, of course, in the role it can play in the analysis of the human moral act. My [Schmitz's] own interest in metaphysics itself leads me to take it to be all that and more, at once abstract and concrete.[85]

Wojtyla's project focusing on the human act is, in Schmitz's estimation, not incompatible with the universality and utmost intimacy of Thomas's esse. Wojtyla calls for an advance in these discussions, and Schmitz comments in his judgment that "he [Wojtyla] has in mind a further development on the phenomenological side of the analysis rather than the metaphysical side."[86] Finally, Schmitz provisionally judges that, on the other hand, "such a universal ontological interiority is at least implicit in . . . Wojtyla's thought."[87]

In Schmitz's later thinking about Wojtyla, in both "God, Being and Love" and "The Witness of Beauty: The Profile of God," he finds in Pope John Paul II's *Fides et Ratio* a hale and satisfactory metaphysics of realism and being. *Fides et Ratio* appreciates the irreducibility of the human person in the existential dimension of human life as "the one who seeks the truth." All values flow from the truth. Pope John Paul II discerns the "existential connection between knowledge and freedom, between truth and love."[88] Wojtyla has undergone a metaphysical journey:

In the same *Lublin Lectures* ... Karol Wojtyla is concerned to formulate a philosophical anthropology of the human person as it plays itself out in the field of human action, as it integrates knowledge and love, truth and freedom, in a human search. As he passes from St. Augustine's linkage of love with the highest Good, Wojtyla arrives at St. Thomas Aquinas.... And it is in St. Thomas, with a deepened Aristotelian dynamic of human action that Wojtyla finds a recognition of the depth that secures love to existence as part of the realism that suffuses both the plays and the philosophical writings.[89]

The Lublin school's existential Thomism supplies the metaphysical mooring for Wojtyla's analysis of human action. Or, as the encyclical states, "Persona nominatim locum constituit praecipuum ut quis con-

85. Schmitz, *At the Center of the Human Drama,* 127n15.

86. Ibid., 137n28.

87. Ibid., 136; note that Wojtyla's project succeeds, for Schmitz, given the fulfillment of three metaphysical and two phenomenological conditions; see 143–45.

88. Schmitz traces this back to the Wojtyla's plays; see "God, Being and Love," 265, 268.

89. Ibid., 270–71.

grediatur cum actu essendi ac, propterea, cum meditione metaphysica."[90] To echo Marcel, being is not indifferent to the homo viator's personal quest. We are implicated in the logos of love. The encyclical's beginning in wonder is at one with Schmitz's *Recovery of Wonder.* To recover wonder, for Schmitz, has been not merely his life's project, but rather his vocation or *missio.* Essentially it is the recovery of the metaphysics of the community of being; it is not simply the recovery of the whole, but rather a rediscovery of creation; it is a rediscovery of the deep sense that we are gifted and that the appropriate response ingredient in this creaturely condition is the *esse posture* of gratitude. Schmitz recognizes that in subtle ways Christian revelation has outwitted us in amplifying the scope of the philosophical quest.

And what of today? Despite flogging the notion of difference, postmodernism has actually opposed the greater emphasis on the "relational" character of knowing just as much as it has rejected the notion of self or person. This is unsurprising, since the postmodernist position enthusiastically confirming the futility of desire cuts the threads of meaningful relations. But the person is relational, if nothing else. I suggest that, since truth is a person, then Schmitz is fully justified in asserting that the context for truth is the "*communio personarum.*"[91] For him: "what is at issue is human perfection, and that is served, not merely by abstract knowledge, but in a dynamic relationship of faithful self-giving with others."[92] Schmitz sees a profound advance in Wojtyla's thought. Wojtyla's turn to phenomenology has turned him, in *reditus,* to "the ontological interiority in the concrete and historical order of being itself"; or Wojtyla's realistic phenomenology of the subject occurs within being as an advance of being. Schmitz does observe that Wojtyla's "earlier philosophical work has been construed as indispensable, but [it] ... betray[ed] an unintended infection from the modern primacy given to the distinction of subject and object."[93]

God is God. Given our finite human estate, we receive the divine in a manner proportionate to our being. Owing to this, Schmitz notes that for Wojtyla beauty is a "profile of God." St. Thomas too reflected upon the "texture of being, the enduring presence of the true, the good, and

90. I have expanded on Schmitz's quote; "God, Being and Love," in *The Texture of Being,* 270n23; for other quotes from *Fides et Ratio* one can refer to this footnote.

91. Schmitz, "God, Being and Love," 278.

92. Ibid., 279.

93. Ibid., 281.

the beautiful," as Wojtyla did.[94] As Wojtyla, who experienced the darkness of war, Thomas realized that nature could be harsh in its lessons. No doubt, but beauty is eternally present in its clarity, radiance, light, harmony, and proportion. Beauty is a transcendental. Schmitz, in stressing the importance of the integrity of things, has all along been implicitly drawing our attention to their beauty, even when they may appear ugsome, to resurrect an antique word. Beauty is special, for in its genuine spiritual power it possesses "the integrative power to embody the companionate transcendentals of unity (*unum*) and relation (*aliquid*), and above all, to draw together the honesty of truth (*verum*) and the value of the good (*bonum*) and thereby give them a face."[95] These transcendentals differ *secundum rationem* (conception), not *in re* (being). For Schmitz, as for Wojtyla, it is "the task of each of us to unite these transcendentals within our own lives.... It is part of the task of personal integration and transcendence of which John Paul speaks in the *Acting Person*."[96] Sacramentally, beauty summons us to holiness, for it is the beauty of Love.

To sum up: in *At the Center of the Human Drama* Schmitz remarks on Wojtyla's encouragement for a development of his analysis on the phenomenological side, while not ignoring the metaphysics of being. There is simply at that point in 1993 a difference of emphasis. But from prior to *Fides et Ratio* forth there is a profound recognition by Wojtyla of being and love—the loving being who freely and generously gives to the created being in the mode of being of the world all that it is. The integrity of natural things, of contextualized singulars/individuals, of persons in love, and knowledge, is secured through ontological generosity.

What remains is to address Schmitz's understanding of the person that has been influenced by Marcel. From the 1980s onward, Schmitz extends his analysis of the person in a key set of articles, which converge in the 2005 *Recovery of Wonder* book. In "The Geography of the Human Person," Schmitz distinguishes three *sine qua non* features of the person: uniqueness, dignity, and intimacy. What is remarkable is that the language of persons has been applied to the interior life of the Christian Trinity (the Godhead) in an effort at *fides quaerens intellectum*. This most intimate of intimacies reveals itself as self-donating loving relations, (subsistent) relations who are persons.

94. Schmitz, "The Witness of Beauty: The Profile of God," in *The Texture of Being*, edited by Paul O'Herron, 300–15, 300–1, Studies in Philosophy and the History of Philosophy 46 (Washington, D.C.: The Catholic University of America Press, 2007).

95. Ibid., 307.

96. Ibid., 312.

In my shortened rendition of Schmitz's ample analysis, the modern understanding of the person edges out of a Protestant inwardness experienced as the anguish of sin—a negative intimacy of inner darkness. Thence stealthily stealing out from the faithful troubled individual believer, through secularization, surfaces the secular rational passionate individual. For Schmitz an introverted self-consciousness steeped in self-enclosed privacy then hides *out* in plain sight as the principle of subjectivity. In other words, the most distinctive feature of the modern principle of subjectivity is that it is a "process of inward uniqueness outwardizing itself."[97] Differing from the modern sense of privacy, the older theological *interiority* was due to an intimacy with God. This is astounding. We can enjoy, albeit creaturely, the viewpoint of creation, for being is not indifferent to the presence of persons. The constitutive actuality of the person—rooted in its own *esse*—guarantees his integrity. *Esse* is at the center of the communicability that pervades the spiritual realm.

In "Selves and Persons: A Difference in Loves," Schmitz highlights the theme of the "communicative incommunicability of personal existence."[98] While modern thought is seized by self-reference, self-identity, and Cartesian mental self-reflection, we initially have Aristotle's *tode ti* and the Latinate *substantia*. But the crucial contrast recoups Aquinas's sense of person. It is incommunicability that distinguishes the spiritual being of the person. Understand that person springs from *esse,* not essence. A person is a kind of relation, not a self-referential or self-identical relation, but a subsistent relation through its complete dependence upon God. When we turn to the Trinity, these are the subsistent relations of personal self-donating and self-surrendering in loving each other. These are the processions that are real relations in the Trinity. Schmitz proposes:

> Suppose that the Trinitarian life marks the world with its own character as *gift*.... Creation viewed under the light of that love which is self-donative, is read as the uncalled-for generosity that flows without compunction from within that divine communal Life.[99]

97. The same phrase is employed in Schmitz, "The Authority of Institutions: Meddling or Middling?" in *Communio* 12 (1985): 5–24. 12. The 1985 "authority" article foreshadows the themes of the 1986 "The Geography of the Human Person" article; see 8–14. This discussion of institutions, though, places them in a religious context, unlike the "Liberalism" and "Community: the Elusive Unity" articles; see 6, 17–24.

98. Schmitz, "Selves and Persons: A Difference in Loves," *Communio* 18 (1991): 183–206, 203. For Schmitz's discussion of the modern self, see 186–96; for an analysis of the person, see 196–206.

99. Ibid., 201. Also see "Created Receptivity"; Schmitz says that the creature is a "sub-

It is these relations of the Trinity, in whose image creatures are created, for it is properly the Trinity which creates. But this does not erase the legitimate self-reference and self-identity that belongs to finite creatures. What it gratuitously allows for is the "communicative incommunicability of personal existence" without any loss of substance; it is a metaphysical or spiritual communication without loss. Indubitably, there are sad spiritual losses in human life: the loss of meaning, suffering, and evil.

With Schmitz's article "The First Principle of Personal Becoming," we are informed that the traditional metaphysics of *Geist* (the systematic totality principle) may well be complementary with *forma* (the *specifying* principle). Does Lessing's primacy of motion and historical development then carry the day? No. Motion as Aristotle knew is "first to us" (*pros emin*), since metaphysical causes perform beneath the surface of things. Hence Schmitz can say: "Paradoxically, it was a mystery of intelligible light that shrouded each and every thing."[100] But the loss is severe: we lost the sense of the sacrementality of natural things; we lost transcendence; we lost natural metaphysical interiority; we lost immateriality and interiority. Spirit, however, as "communication without loss," remains, not merely as a possibility, but rather as an actuality, except for those who have conceded to Heidegger that possibility is higher than actuality, or to Derrida that only the impossible is now impossibly possible. But spirit as "communication without loss" is present in the concrete in the field of free activity, which Pieper has described as leisure, the leisure to worship. Other examples of "communication without loss" are surely parenting, friendship, teaching, and all the givings and receivings we are capable of.

In Schmitz's "Created Receptivity and the Philosophy of the Concrete," the theme of "communication without loss" grows into its proper Marcellian dimensions of availability and receptivity. This is, for Schmitz, a capability for nonpassive receptivity. Why do we need such a metaphysical sense of spirit? Schmitz comments that "If being is truly universal, then modern developments must have occurred *within* being, and be in some sense connected with the *history of being*."[101] To put this

sisting relation" (360, 363). This draws the creature very close to the subsisting relation of the Trinity; see Schmitz's stipulations at 360n59. Also Schmitz admits that "more needs to be said in order to offset the charge that substance itself is being dissolved in this radical relation. Such a sense is especially important today, if only because the metaphysical sense of substance is not readily understood . . . in the contemporary thought-world" (366).

100. Schmitz, "The First Principle of Personal Becoming," 762.

101. Schmitz, "Created Receptivity," 345.

in proper perspective, Schmitz counsels us to attend to the receptivity that serves as the principle of personal being. This receptivity is "an *integral mode* constituted of both act and potency."[102] Proceeding, Schmitz writes in a qualified way that "there is an integral mode of act and potency ... not entirely alien to Thomistic metaphysics." As active potency it is a receptivity "if it is deepened to mean the response to the primary institution of created being, its primordial reception, such active potency is enfolded within the integral mode of non-privative receptivity."[103] Is Thomas always this direct in his writings? Schmitz notes that there is a "not always explicit concreteness in his [Thomas's] Aristotelian vocabulary."[104] He is not criticizing Aquinas, but he is commenting that in Aquinas, Aristotle's equivocity of being has been transformed into a deep, yet implicit understanding of the transcendentals, a *separatio* of *esse,* and an understanding of the analogous community of beings, that Aristotle himself did not achieve. Now Marcel in relation to Thomas stresses, not simply being or *esse,* but the fullness (including receptivity) of being and *esse.* The more explicit sense of full and empty complements Thomas's metaphysical insights. Marcel insists that we avoid systemic claims. So here there is no conflict with Aquinas, for Aquinas appreciates the order of creation. There is no system of creation for Aquinas, Marcel, or Schmitz.

Whereas the concrete in Aquinas is found in the metaphysical composition found in creatures, in Marcel it is found in receptivity as the principle of personal being at the concrete level. Not only do human beings or persons possess interiority, so do things: they are *supposita entis:* "And this ontological interiority [of things] lends its character to all interior relations, including the spiritual interiority encountered in personal beings."[105] In relation to potency and act regarding the spiritual being of persons, Schmitz declares: "At the level of personal being this is more adequately expressed by receptivity than by passive potency."[106] More strongly:

> it is a genuine receptivity that transcends the gulf between activity and potency without destroying their real distinction. It does this by including them within what I have called an integral mode of being. The sense of receptivity has deeper ontological roots than either created act or potency considered in themselves.[107]

102. Ibid., 349.
103. Ibid., 365.
104. Ibid., 351.
105. Ibid., 366.
106. Ibid., 369.
107. Ibid., 370–71.

Does it then follow that receptivity also possesses deeper ontological roots than active potency considered in itself? Let us put this aside until the end of this section.

Continuing his reflection upon Marcel, Schmitz asks what personalism contributes to philosophical understanding. Schmitz comments that

> the personalism of a thinker such as Gabriel Marcel has played the part of a sort of "holding operation" for the values formerly associated with a traditional metaphysics of being and resonant with Christian faith: hence a Christian Personalism. I [Schmitz] still hold that view.

And another nugget from Schmitz:

> But I have lately come to see that such personalist philosophy surpasses its role as the treasury of traditional values, and that it realizes an *advance* in the progressive unfolding of being—mark this well: an advance, not only in our *understanding* of being, but a forwarding of the unfolding of *being itself* in its history.[108]

For Schmitz this new advance

> will not require of traditional metaphysics an alteration in the very sources (*archai, principia*) of being as articulated in a metaphysics of existential act. Nevertheless, the consolidation will manifest in concrete fashion a radical development in our understanding of the modern modalities of being.[109]

Schmitz is astounded that personalism has been birthed as a robust realism out of idealism. But Marcel's philosophy requires more, for it has not actualized the potential of the ontological freedom of German idealism.

Then Schmitz springs this upon us: "is it too daring to ask whether freedom itself may be considered a transcendental property of being as such? He adds: "If this expansion of freedom seems extravagant, we might reflect that the Source of all being is the absolute Freedom, Who is God."[110] To which Schmitz's answer is: "Freedom is the transcendental character of being ingredient in the intellectual and spiritual factor in man, and present throughout the hierarchy of created spiritual substances, and perfectly actual in the very center of divine life."[111] For human beings this is the call to the exercise of a receptive, responsible freedom.

108. Schmitz, "The Solidarity of Personalism and the Metaphysics of Existential Act," in *The Texture of Being*, edited by Paul O'Herron, 132–45, 134, Studies in Philosophy and the History of Philosophy 46 (Washington, D.C.: The Catholic University of America Press, 2007); hereafter "Personalism and the Existential Act."

109. Ibid., 135.

110. Ibid., 143.

111. Ibid., 144.

I understand Schmitz to accept and develop Marcel's view that receptivity at the personal existential level is analogously present in all being. Schmitz states: "It seems to me that with suitable analogous diversity such receptivity is characteristic of all creatures."[112] Consequently, Schmitz has consolidated the traditional metaphysics of being with contemporary personalism.

The Recovery of Wonder and Reflections

The Recovery of Wonder's goal is to diagnose what needs to be metaphysically rethought: the ontologic of our culture. In our reflection upon ordinary things we recognize their extraordinary complexity, a unity of singularity and commonality, which requires us to exercise a new discipline and asceticism. In other words, our hope for the future embraces natural things sheltering transcendence.

Schmitz begins his *Recovery of Wonder* with the same Wordsworthian passage of his 1966 article "Philosophical Truth and Philosophical Pluralism," which narrated how philosophy came to Schmitz: "The world is too much with us; late and soon."[113] So much so, that in this world being has become unbearably light, as Kundera has written. Schmitz proposes to recover for things their "rightful place in learned discourse and in reality."[114] Things have lost their ontological weight, thus compromising human freedom. Consequently we need to recover the real metaphysical constitution of things with their value.

Schmitz summons the article "The Greek Heritage: Rationality," which furnished an understanding of both conceptualization and discourses (mathematics, history, linguistics, and especially philosophy in its noetic form), making possible *theoria* about, or a transcending openness to, things. Yes, there is *creatio ex nihilo,* and so a nothingness accompanies creatures as their resident contingency, but things are not merely nothing, nor merely contingent. They are between nothing and being. They are creatures disclosing a radical contingency and dependency in being.

Schmitz applies Aristotle's leading insight anew to the *tode ti* (Aquinas's *hoc aliquid*) of natural things—their "real composite character." Unfortunately, history tells of the expulsion of the specific nature of things

112. Schmitz, "An Addendum," 284n17.

113. Schmitz, "Philosophical Truth and Philosophical Pluralism," 6.

114. Schmitz, *The Recovery of Wonder,* 7. See Schmitz, "Natural Value," *Review of Metaphysics* 38 (1984): 675–94, 692–93; this article discusses Aristotle.

in modernity. The moderns, understanding things to be composed of individual units (elements), saw no need for deep interior metaphysical principles and causes constitutive of complex unities of natural things. Thus, either depth merged into surface phenomena or disappeared into clouds of eccentric particles in the atom. In consequence, there is no need for the modern "thing" to inquire into its source or origin. Either it functions, or it is broken. This is the ontological destitution of Marcel's broken world. It is simply empirically given as data, or more ambitiously with idealism; it assumes the form of the self-giving of the infinite subjectivity striving to systemic completion and closure. The modern world in a sense functions frighteningly well, as Heidegger asserted. Technology is bereft ontology.

We live in a more ontologically deprived world without Hopkins' sense of "the dearest freshness deep down things." Things are dead. For Schmitz whither? The death of things as metaphysically understood by him can be explained as due to the influences of nominalism, voluntarism, and mechanism. Broadly put, nominalism denatures intelligible creation, reducing it to isolated individual units, whose motions (impacts and collisions) the mechanism then entraps in mathematical descriptions, thus making them disposable for a seemingly total manipulation by the human will in voluntarism. As the area of *praxis* expands, *theoria* contracts, since there is less intelligibility (the interiority of principles and causes) to contemplate. Crucially and simultaneously, the ascetic spiritual discipline (for philosophy was always a way of life and not merely an academic subject) that things were owed by a considerate cognition becomes unnecessary. This separates the intellect from spirituality. This is the loss that prompts Schmitz to call for an "asceticism of power." Devastatingly, for us, we survive in the wake of a rupture severing spirituality from intellectuality. One becomes mere subjective devotions; the other, arid impersonal argumentation.[115]

But Schmitz sees something of what may not look like a positive dimension, but maybe actually is: the will as *conatus,* the will as freedom. *Conatus* supplies a much needed energy and dynamism in a world

115. Louis Dupré and Adriaan Peperzak have stressed this theme as well: Louis Dupré, *Passage to Modernity* (New Haven: Yale University Press, 1993), especially 167–89, 190–220; Adriaan Peperzak, *Reason in Faith: On the Relevance of Christian Spirituality for Philosophy* (New York: Paulist Press, 1999), especially 71–129; Peperzak, *Thinking: From Solitude to Dialogue and Contemplation* (New York: Fordham University Press, 2006), especially 127–63; Peperzak, *Philosophy between Faith and Theology: Addresses to Catholic Intellectuals* (Notre Dame, Ind.: University of Notre Dame Press, 2005).

that might have overlooked its no doubt ambiguous advantages. Perhaps surprising to some of his readers, *conatus,* German idealism's ontological freedom, English and French elective individual freedom, pose an intriguing question for him.

As we survey these various understandings of freedom, the question arises whether we can embrace these different versions in a new synthesis. I think we can. And it is this synthesis I would call "the new freedom." What is new in modernity is not only the emphasis upon the conative aspect of freedom, the energy of choice and self-determination, but the developed appreciation of the value of freedom itself.[116]

But freedom has to emerge through the good of things as well, since they are our companions on the way and neighbors with whom we realize our freedom. Things provide the context of the community of being, enabling human freedom to assume a shape, and justly so, since we are not angels, but incarnate beings.

Schmitz accepts the merit of modern experience with its stress upon subjectivity, because it infuses its insight into freedom into the metaphysics of being. And for Schmitz this new freedom finds its root in genuine interiority and transcendence. The ambiguity of the new freedom tasks us with the recovery of things in their integrity, while the metaphysics of being, in turn, tasks us with recovering the best of modern subjectivity. Hence freedom is intensified and enlarged. A note of caution: for some this freedom has not stopped modern subjectivity from experiencing itself as the primary good—as infinite. Some also resist relinquishing the claim that the new freedom justifies itself as absolute autonomy.

Schmitz disagrees. We need things for freedom to be at home in being. Moreover, there is a metaphysical concept that has an affinity with *conatus:* namely, the orientation to the Good. This deeper freedom is present in all beings. As an ordered freedom it expands form; as a larger freedom it is the implicit form dwelling in the very constitution of things. It is modern experience itself that has alerted us to these new possibilities inherent in being. With being and this deeper sense of freedom, our creaturely freedom is, in turn, illuminated by the original freedom of love.

Because we are human creatures, we have to exercise moderation—what Schmitz calls *"a new asceticism of power."*[117] Modernity, which separates spirituality from the intellectual, is profoundly wanting in its

116. Schmitz, *The Recovery of Wonder,* 73; see the three conceptions of freedom, 92n19.
117. Ibid., 119.

self-understanding of its own power. Schmitz's asceticism is the call to such a self-knowledge of the limitations of power. But genuine knowledge is infused with a virtuous sensibility. And thus asceticism requires a unity of life, integrating spirituality and intellectuality. To paraphrase Kant, spirituality without intellectuality is too enthusiastic and gushing, and intellectuality without spirituality is too abstract and desiccated. Schmitz's asceticism of power is not born out of fear, but rather out of a respect for the integrity of things, and, we should mark, out of the respect we owe ourselves as well. When we lose things we lose all, including ourselves; when we respect things, we do not gain all, but we come into the presence of the greatest value—our new freedom in intimacy with things and God.

Conclusion

In recovering the things and being of yesteryear we are not simply restoring the *status quo;* rather, we are engaged in a recovery and discovery that are given graciously by being in its history (beyond Hegel's philosophy of history/historicity of finitized infinitude). This is the history of being.

Now the future opens to the synthesis of the new freedom on the condition that we practice an asceticism of power. In his 1959 article "Toward a Metaphysical Restoration of Natural Things," Schmitz contended that we are not given unconditional mastery of nature. A loving being beyond endows us with ourselves and the things we call our natural companions in our home of creation. This is the gift of love out of an originary fullness of persons—the inexhaustibly intelligible mystery of the light of excellence of *creatio ex nihilo.*

Where von Balthasar has affirmatively employed the transcendentals of being and the doctrine of analogy (analogy in a limited way) in order to give us a new vision of the Trinity in its immanent and economic dimensions, Schmitz has subtly turned analogy and the transcendentals to the person, while maintaining them in their traditional metaphysical context of the community of being.[118] If Norris Clarke is correct about person as a pure transcendental perfection, then this touches Schmitz's position. Schmitz, however, has said that freedom is a transcendental in a sense compatible with Thomas.[119] I submit that there cannot be a per-

118. See Antonio Löpez, "Eternal Happening: God as an Event of Love," *Communio* 32 (2005): 214–45.

119. "Personalism and the Existential Act," 143–44.

sonally responsible freedom without receptivity in loving and knowing. Going beyond Fr. Clarke, I wonder if Schmitz would agree with me that Christian philosophy stands or falls with its position on the actuality of receptivity being a transcendental, a transcendental that is applicable analogously to God as well. For I see divine receptivity as the loving source of the gift of creation. God in giving creatures and creation all is truly equally completely receiving of all creatures and creation given. At this stage we have reached a fruitful passage between Przywara's negative accent, but active emphasis, on analogy as polarity and von Balthasar's positive emphasis on the transcendentals.[120] Does Schmitz see the need for mediation here? What we can say is that neither the analogy between God and creatures nor the transcendentals has been broken. Schmitz embraces both the analogy of being and the transcendentals of being in a profound understanding of an *esse* open to the dynamics of history and freedom. And all this is due to the fact that God is, indeed, in his creating activity (the theo-human drama we live as spiritual persons), God.

So finally we have arrived at things of yesteryear, today, and tomorrow: from *pragmata, chremata, onta, res,* things with insides but no metaphysical interiorities, Kantian things as objects as phenomena, scientific things as particles and clouds, so many flourishing things. But then maybe the Marcellian singular of his concrete philosophy is still, though, not a fully metaphysically appreciated natural thing. Or may we say a Schmitzian dear thing, a contextualized singular? An old/new thing, an old/new freedom as a companionate advance in the now historical temporality/mysterious eternity of being. As Schmitz observes, forgiveness is not merely restoration; instead it is a recreation into a new state of love, intimacy, and liberty. Schmitz's vocation in recovering the tradition calls us to discover for ourselves, for our own persons, his radical and comprehensive and generous thought and sensibility.

120. See the illuminating articles on Przywara by John R. Betz: "Beyond the Sublime: The Aesthetics of the Analogy of Being (Part One)," *Modern Theology* 21 (2005): 367–411, and "Beyond the Sublime: The Aesthetics of the Analogy of Being (Part Two)," *Modern Theology* 22 (2006): 12–50; also see Thomas F. O'Meara, O.P., *Erich Przywara, S.J.: His Theology and His Word* (Notre Dame, Ind.: University of Notre Dame Press, 2002).

Louis Dupré

2. THE GIFT AND THE GIVING

Before beginning this essay I feel obliged to disclose its writer's prejudices. I have been a friend of Kenneth Schmitz for some forty years. We have shared discussions, panels, and, during one extended period, regular meetings in Boston and Philadelphia. We have read each other's writings, published and unpublished. We have enjoyed personal encounters in which we subjected private experiences to common reflection. I have learned much from my friend, from his uncommon knowledge of Hegel (I still continue to consult his unpublished commentary on Hegel's *Logik*), from his religious perceptiveness expressed in beautifully crafted essays, from his insight into the goals and functions of postmodern philosophy, to which he devoted some recent writings. But most of all, I admire his philosophical attitude: thoughtful, unrushed, open to ideas from all quarters, aiming at that ultimate form of philosophy, contemplation. Reading him or listening to him one feels he is in the presence of one who knows the joy attached to the examined life: he so obviously savors the beauty of ideas and the words in which we express them.

In the following pages I shall elaborate some of the ideas contained in the Aquinas lecture he delivered at Marquette University in 1982. This profound and dense treatise of 142 pages displays all of the qualities I have mentioned. It shows how profitably philosophy may be applied to a theological subject. Having read it, one can hardly conceive how theology could ever have survived without the aid of philosophical reflection. That critical reunion of philosophy and theology, lost since early modern times, has in twentieth-century thought shown new signs of life. *The Gift: Creation* is a marvelous fruit of that revival.

When Kant closed the doors that give entrance to metaphysics, he also closed them to theology, which had traditionally provided philosophy's fundamental concepts. In doing so he concluded a process that had started at the end of the Middle Ages, when nominalist theology divided reality into separate realms: a natural one, the factual result of God's decision, and a supernatural one, the inscrutable territory of God's absolute power. The former was to be ruled by philosophy and science, the latter by revelation. The two realms had nothing in common, even though philosophy soon felt the need to construe its own "natural theology." Theology proper either continued to feed on its past or restricted its domain to scriptural and historical studies.

Philosophy's subsequent slide into naturalism or scientific positivism continued unchallenged until the early twentieth century, when phenomenological philosophy initiated a comprehensive investigation of all meaning. To the religious believer, the content of faith constitutes the most fundamental source of meaning. Why, then, should this source not deserve to be investigated along with the foundations of positive sciences or of social structures? To be sure, not every object of religious belief is worth philosophical investigation. The unwarranted claims of religious emotion or the wholly unsupported "events" reported in popular legends need not be taken any more seriously in the area of religion than similar claims would be in other sciences. Still, those profoundly meaningful experiences of religion, unjustifiably neglected in early modern philosophy, deserve to be given full philosophical reflection.

Even of the primary experience of transcendence little was heard in philosophy until such phenomenologists as Heidegger, Jaspers, and Ricoeur made it a central subject of their speculation. The new philosophical attention given to that primary experience is not necessarily conducive to religious faith. Transcendence can be interpreted in many ways. But at least the content of religious faith thereby came to appear worthy of serious philosophical investigation. Religious mysteries have, despite modern resistance, continued to furnish conceptual paradigms to philosophy. Rightly so, because they yield a more profound insight into human existence than positivist or naturalist philosophies have ever done.

A basic question that has always occupied the human mind concerns the beginning of things. Neither science nor naturalist philosophy gives a complete account of the origin of the cosmos. Religion, without answering the question of origins which falls entirely outside its competence, concentrates all attention on the character of dependence inherent in finite reality as a whole. It views this dependence as a mystery revealed as *creation*. In *The Gift: Creation* Kenneth Schmitz philosophically explores what this revelation implies. He subjects it to phenomenological analyses of gift giving, such as Gabriel Marcel and Marcel Mauss have left us.

A first paradox we encounter in the concept of creation is that something is given without there previously being someone to receive it: the receiver himself is the gift. Another one is that all genuine giving consists in, or represents, a giving of oneself. But who in creation is the giver? We have simply named the giver by the gift. The gift is Being, and the giver we call total or absolute Being. This implies that all creation partakes of the Creator's own reality. Even the ability to *receive* forms part of the gift. The reciprocation, part of all gift-giving, takes place *within* the divine giver, for the creature's response is still a gift. Thus the idea of Being, central to ancient and medieval metaphysics, sheds light upon the mystery of Being, while the mystery illuminates the idea.

In Western thought, the naming of the Absolute as Being, that is, as source and foundation of all reality, combined the insight of the earliest philosophy with that of its earliest revelation. Parmenides declared Being to be one. The voice in the burning bush had also said: "I am the one who is." Mystics, Jewish, Christian, and Muslim, have interpreted this to mean that the Creator's presence in creation does not essentially differ from his presence to Himself. The Platonic tradition has supported this religious insight by teaching that the One is present on all levels of Being. The thesis, as transmitted by the Arabic commentator Avicenna, is ambiguous and could easily assume a pantheistic meaning, as it may have done in Amaury de Bène's theory that God coincides with the Being of all that exists: *Ipse Deus est esse existentibus* (though so it also appears in Pseudo-Dionysius).

Eckhart presents a more orthodox reading. His two major Latin works begin with the words *Esse est Deus*. Yet following an earlier, Plotinian understanding of participation, he so sharply distinguishes God's Being from that of created beings as to exclude even an ordinary analogy between the two. If God is Being, the creature is not; if the creature is, God is not. For him, God's *knowledge* (*intelligere*) is the source of Being, even as the Good, in Plato's *Republic*, is said to be "beyond Being" (*hene-*

ka teys ousias). As the source of Being God is totally present in each being, yet God does not share the created mode of existing.

I have mentioned Eckhart before the great Dominican theologian who preceded him, because his theory of participation appears to have followed an earlier neo-Platonic tradition (going back to Plotinus) than Aquinas did, whose early Platonism may be traced to the Proclian *Liber de Causis*. According to St. Thomas, all beings participate in God's Being, although their participated mode of being differs from God's substantial or essential Being. The fourth and longest part of *The Gift: Creation*, modestly entitled "A Thomist Justification," contains a learned report on how, in Thomas' thought, the Christian mystery of God's self-communication transformed the ancient metaphysics of Being.

The creature receives what God is *per essentiam*. Since this reception constitutes its very existence, one cannot claim that it *has* Being: it *is* what it receives. "In giving *esse* God in the same act produces that which receives it." The creature thereby becomes an entity in its own right, but it remains fully dependent on (and participating in) God's Being. In God, Being is simple; in the creature it is determined. Even though Being is the source of all determinations, Being itself has no determinations.

Needless to say, a divine Being without formal determination would have been meaningless to the ancients. Aristotle's notion of being is mainly predicamental—the copula in a proposition. Aquinas is not ignorant of this predicamental meaning of the term. But the idea of participation so totally determines his use of it that the copula becomes an assertion of Being, rather than a mere *symbol* of predicamental union between two terms. The Thomist idea of Being possesses an existential richness that is totally absent from Aristotle. Cornelio Fabro summarizes the difference in *Participation et Causalité* (Louvain 1961): the foundation of Being cannot remain outside Being, yet neither can it be articulated in the form of an entitative predication, as it was in Aristotle.

For Aquinas no less than for Eckhart, the term "Being" possesses a religious meaning and has a mystical connotation. At the beginning of the *Summa theologiae* (I, qu. 8, a.1), he raises the question of whether God is present in all finite things, and he answers: "Being is innermost in all things and most fundamentally present within all things, since Being is formal in respect of everything found in a thing. Hence God must be in all things and innermostly." This text refers to the quasi-formal causal presence of God in all things. Unfortunately that mystical presence is seldom mentioned by later Scholastics, because most of them applied the modern, predominantly efficient, and external notion of causality (which in Aristotelian thought belongs merely to the action of *techne,* the capacity for the employment of means) to the act of creation.

Yet another historical figure occupies a central place in the religious metaphysics of Being: Nicholas of Cusa, the spiritual giant of the fifteenth century. This distant follower of Eckhart most daringly formulated the mystical implications of the theology of Being. He interprets creation as an unfolding (*explicatio*) of the very Being that in an enfolded mode (*complicatio*) is God as God is in himself. The totality of all that exists or even could exist is God's own Being unfolding itself. Finite beings are distinct from God's Being only through their finitude. This makes them *other* with respect to each other as well as with respect to God's infinite Being. But God is *not other* than creation. Cusanus therefore prefers to name God *not-other* (*non-aliud*), the one predicate that is exclusively God's own.

The Absolute defines both itself and all the rest—provided we do not understand God as being *other* than "the rest." God grants creatures their own identity. God is not only cause of all things but the foundation of their self-awareness. The self-identity of a finite being for Cusanus (as for Eckhart) consists neither in those determinations that distinguish it from another (because *omnis determinatio est negatio*) nor in the contingencies of its private existence, but in its innermost Being, which coincides with God's Being. Despite this coincidence, creatures are not similar to God, as the theory of the image might lead one to believe. In Eckhart's theology, which Cusanus here follows, creatures, because of their determinateness, are totally unlike God. To call the creature an image of God refers to God's immanence in its very Being, as Origen and Gregory of Nyssa had earlier explained.

In Cusanus' theology of creation Being is absolute, act without potency. Whatever exists "besides" that Absolute can only be an overflowing of divine Being, not a different being. Potency is no more than the nothingness to which the divine act has conveyed a receptivity of Being. Thus, as Cusanus argues in *De possest* (the title combines *posse* and *esse*), God is the ground of possibility as well as of actuality. Possibility does not precede actuality as a vacuum within which God creates, as Leibniz assumed. Nor is there a need for a divine *sensorium* of absolute time and space, within which the physical world originates, as in Newton's *Principia*. In God, the possible coincides with the real.

The intimate union of God and creation in Being vanished when modern philosophy refused to consider causality in any other than an efficient way. Developed in the course of the scientific revolution, the modern notion of causality substantially differs from the more comprehensive ancient and medieval one. For Plato, Aristotle, and the neo-Platonists, efficient causality was by no means the only form of causality. Its primary meanings were *formal* and *final*. Mechanistic physics needed no other concept of causality for referring to the communication of power than the purely external efficient cause. Christians had always interpreted God's creative act as a causal one, but never exclusively as one of efficient causality. In efficient causality the cause remains external to the effect. The two never coincide. In the fresco on the ceiling of the Sistine Chapel, Michelangelo has represented God as having released Adam from his hand. In the older Christian tradition, however, creatures had always remained permanently linked to the Creator.

The change in the concept of causality largely deprived the mystery of creation of its specifically religious quality. In the philosophical theology of the seventeenth century, creation became a "making" and a "moving" of the cosmos—both purely external activities—whereby the weight of meaning fell entirely on the beginning divine activity. Once God had created and moved the cosmos, it was on its own. The role of the Creator was reduced to a one-time activity. Soon the question occurred as to whether even this one act was indispensable. Does the universe have a beginning? Thomas himself had conceded that reason alone cannot prove it. Moreover, is an external force needed to justify motion, the presumed source of the cosmos' functioning? Had Newton's principle of inertia not abrogated the assumed temporal priority of rest over motion?

Diderot argued that none of these questions required a theological answer. If the universe had always existed as a body in motion, no cause was needed to bring it into being or to set it in motion. Of course, that still left the existence of order and coherence unexplained. But why should matter not have possessed the power to move *itself* from chaos to order, especially over an infinite stretch of time? Biology and zoology had sufficiently shown that nature was endowed with more than the static powers of mechanistic physics. Diderot granted that we do not know the answer to these questions. But what do we gain, he wondered, by ascribing natural events to a force outside the world, of which we know nothing, rather than by assuming it to reside within the world?

When Kant in the *Critique of Pure Reason* refuted the argument for the existence of God based on causality and showed (in "The Antinomies of Reason") that it was impossible for reason to prove or disprove the beginning of the world, the idea of creation appeared to have become a dead problem for philosophy. Believers might continue to accept the idea, but they ought not to count on the support of reason. Thus matters stood at the end of the eighteenth century when two of Kant's most intelligent followers, Fichte and Schelling, directly attacked the notion of a cosmology conceived without absolute foundation. I mention them, even though they play no role in *The Gift,* because they strongly influenced Hegel, who prominently appears in Schmitz's discussion.

At the beginning of the *Logic* Hegel describes the concept of Being as so abstractly universal that the mind can hardly distinguish it from its opposite, that of pure nothingness. It certainly possesses none of the ontological richness characteristic of St. Thomas' idea of Being. Even so, it spells the revival of the metaphysics of Being. According to Cornelio Fabro, Hegel also describes the Absolute as *esse ipsum,* but in his dialectical philosophy an idea attains its truth only after it has gone through the full circularity of thought. Thus the all-comprehensive idea of Being attains its completion only in the final syllogism of absolute identity-in-difference. The same sources of Aquinas's theory of Being are also at the origin of Hegel's: Parmenides and the Bible.

At the end of the *Logic* Being discloses the qualities of unity and truth, which the indeterminate concept of the beginning had barely intimated. Hegel now clarifies that the abstract concept of the beginning had been no more than the immediate form of Being. Still, even that early concept had not been immediate, as sense intuition or representation is. It had the immediacy of thought, as its universality indicated. Nor was it static or lifeless: its very nature implied development both in thought and in Being. Hence its truth lies in the concrete totality at the end. Indeed, Hegel's thesis that Being may be called absolute only when it has become in-itself and for-itself is inspired by the religious idea that Being attains its full significance in the theology of the blessed Trinity.

In a note (*Zusatz*) attached to § 573 of the *Encyclopedia of Philosophy,* Hegel states that the speculative nature of his treatment is inseparable from its religious significance. Only through revelation has the metaphysics of Being been able to attain its full meaning. In the true sense of the term, *God* alone in his self-relatedness is *Being.* All finite entities participate in that divine Being. "The entire course of philosophy and more specially of the Logic has not only disclosed this distinction (between religion and philosophy) but also judged, or rather the nature of this distinction established in those categories through which it has developed and allowed itself to be judged."

The revival of the religious metaphysics of Being formulated by St. Thomas and his followers would not have been possible if twentieth-century culture had not expressed a metaphysical reawakening of its own. Even the philosophy of Hegel did not gain its full metaphysical impact until the middle of the nineteenth century. I believe that the new need for metaphysics in our time was at least in part a response to a vacuum of meaning left by the senseless First World War and by the horrors preceding and accompanying the Second World War. Yet new methods in philosophy had also made a deeper probing of existential meaning possible. I have mentioned the phenomenological movement. Eventually the "bracketing of existence" characteristic of its early period came to be seen as conflicting with the full analysis of meaning. Sartre rightly pointed out that there was a *phenomenon* of existence independent of the essence of things. Whereas for Husserl, the phenomenon of Being had, at least during the early period, consisted in the being of the phenomenon, for Sartre the fact of existence differs from the appearing essence. Being cannot be reduced to its being known, its *percipi*. *L'être n'est pas un apparaître.*

Influenced by his early studies of Scholastic philosophy, Heidegger initiated a more thorough exploration of the idea of Being. In *Being and Time* he reopened the way to Being through a reflection on the human condition. The human person is the one being that raises the question of Being. So Being ought to be disclosed in a reflection on the fundamental human experiences. In his later work Heidegger radically turned to an analysis of Being itself, away from the still subjective study of *Dasein* (existence) as reflecting Being. Yet both his later and earlier works forced contemporary thinkers to give full attention to questions of transcendence once reserved to theology. More than any other recent thinker, Heidegger was responsible for having removed the Kantian barriers on the way to Being, even though he himself rejected the "metaphysics" developed since Plato as an obstruction to Being.

In the meantime, Thomist philosophy also, stimulated by Leo XIII's letter *Aeterni Patris,* was revived and, with it, the cross-fertilization of philosophy and theology. Ironically, the new Scholasticism gained full momentum with thinkers who had been steeped in Kant's principles. They attempted to build their reinterpretation of traditional metaphysics within Kantian restrictions. Maurice Blondel, in his doctoral dissertation, *L'action* (1893), argued that all human activity receives its impulse from a desire that surpasses the object of choice. This transcendent aspiration of the will opened philosophy to theological insights, albeit under severe methodical limitations.

Moving in the same direction, Joseph Maréchal, in *Le point de départ de la métaphysique,* a five-volume reinterpretation of Western epistemology, showed that a similar aspiration underlies human knowledge. Still, with Kant, whose restrictions continue to rule his thought, Maréchal excludes any intellectual intuition of a transcendent reality. Instead he suggests that many philosophers do in fact recognize an *implicit* intuition in the self-surpassing drive of all thinking. The intellectual dynamism inherent in all acts of cognition points to a transcendent idea of Being, and thus indirectly reopens philosophy to metaphysics as well as to theology.

Many Thomists considered this epistemological reinterpretation incompatible with an essentially realist philosophy. Yet in meeting the challenge of the Kantian critique, Thomist philosophy had proven that it was not defenseless against the anti-metaphysical, anti-theological thought of the modern age. Metaphysics again came to occupy a leading place in philosophy. After the defensive strategy of transcendental Thomism had won this battle, it was no longer necessary to squeeze Aquinas's thought within the conceptual restraints of the Kantian critique.

That new openness enabled Kenneth Schmitz to write *The Gift* without feeling hampered by the negative rules set up by the critical philosophy of the modern age. That critique has given us a more precise understanding of the distinction between philosophy and theology. But it no longer forces us to maintain a total separation between the two, as it did a century ago. Metaphysics has come to recognize the profound existential meaning of religious ideas as well as the theological origin of some of its own fundamental concepts. Theology also has overcome its inhibition against metaphysical concepts, as we observe in such major religious thinkers as Rahner, Lonergan, and von Balthasar. *The Gift: Creation* may count as a model of the new approach.

James Crooks

3. "PRAISE THE WORLD TO THE ANGEL"

Heidegger, Schmitz, and the Liturgy of the Thing

Praise the world to the angel
not the unsayable
you can't impress him with sumptuous feelings—
in the universe where he feels things so fully you're just a novice.
Show him, then, some simple thing shaped by its passage through
generations that lives as a belonging near the hand, in the gaze.
Tell him of Things.
He'll stand more astonished than you did beside the rope-maker
in Rome or the potter by the Nile.

Rainer Maria Rilke, *Duino Elegies*

In the realm of abstract speculation that seems now to encompass all the discursive spaces of the academy—from the university senate to the faculty/student barbecue—one tends to imagine the future of philosophy either as a response to economic, technological, and ideological forces external to it or as the steadfast resistance of those forces.

More often than not, the proximate origin of the first option is the institution's planning process. For decades now, universities have been underfunded. When the money does come it tends to target disciplines and modes of research with evident market value. Under the pressure of this arrangement, deans and departmental chairs call on working philosophers to apply the lessons of their canon in demonstrably useful ways and to promote and shape those lessons in accordance with the expectations of their government masters and their market-savvy student client base. As disheartening as this call may be when we hear it from the mouths of administrators and/or bureaucrats, it has a deeper intradisciplinary resonance that extends back at least as far as the linguistic turn at the end of the nineteenth century. It stems from the idea that philosophy as traditionally understood has been surpassed as an instrument of discovery by other disciplines (mathematics, empirical science, and computer science, for example) and that it will remain relevant only to the extent that it approximates in its work the methods of those disciplines.

More often than not, the proximate origin of the second option is graduate study. It is there, not yet directly responsible for the education of others and the long-term care of the university but on the point of inheriting these duties, that we feel most keenly the hypocrisies and inequities of the culture around us; there, too, that we are charged seriously for the first time with bringing something new into the world and so of changing it. In contrast to the first option, the deeper intradisciplinary resonance of the notion of philosophy as resistance is readily apparent—especially for those trained in the tradition of continental Europe. After the Second World War that tradition has mounted an increasingly radical critique of culture, headquartered in France and led by a cohort of thinkers whose influence now extends far beyond philosophy itself (e.g., Foucault, Derrida, Deleuze, and Beaudrillard). The consensus of these thinkers (but not only these) is that the culture around us tends inevitably toward coercion and deception. The task of educators in general and philosophers in particular is, accordingly, to deconstruct its monuments.

And yet if we turn away from the projection of an abstract future—from the question of what form our discipline ought to take nowhere in particular as a result of courses offered by no one in particular—and look back concretely at what the best of our teachers have achieved, we see a third option. Beyond acquiescing responsiveness or thoroughgoing resistance, its defining gesture is consecration. The corresponding method, if I might travel to the frontier of this word's customary usage, is liturgical. Perhaps less obliquely: it has been my experience that the best teachers in our discipline somehow gather the entire world into the modest space of their classrooms—not in order to confirm the prevailing conventional wisdom about it or to reject it as mere human construction, but to set it before us as an unassailable wonder, a reality so textured and subtle that we acquire, from a comparatively fleeting taste of it, the sustenance of lifelong learning. I think of this as a kind of invocation or philosophical call to worship. Moreover—and this is equally important—it seems to me that these teachers also send us away (back to the lives we thought we knew) to ponder for ourselves and try to communicate to others the exhilarating sense of abundant life that comes with genuine insight. I think of this as a kind of commission or philosophical benediction.

Even at the beginning of his long career—indeed, perhaps especially there—Martin Heidegger was a master of these effects. Long before the sensation of *Being and Time* established his place in the pantheon of twentieth-century thought, his students at Marburg and Freiburg were promoting him as "the hidden king" of philosophy, auditing his lectures in numbers that would put today's academic stars to shame. By all accounts, his powerful classroom cocktail of Catholic erudition and Husserlian phenomenology had the effect of resurrecting before their eyes those works that the science-friendly consensus of the prevailing neo-Kantianism had long since buried; of invoking and accommodating the entire Western tradition in a dialogue on the question of Being that was at once both metaphysical (in a wide sense) and urgently existential.

For my generation of graduate students at the University of Toronto in the 1970s and '80s, Kenneth Schmitz cut a similar figure. His lectures on Hegel were legendary (I still have the course notes for his seminar on the *Greater Logic*). But his scholarship in all areas of the tradition provoked in us an astonishment at its depth and a desire to appropriate its wisdom. His capacity for nurturing that desire in dialogue was especially impressive. A contemporary of mine once remarked that Schmitz could make something philosophically interesting of virtually any student comment. He was right. Schmitz often found ways of re-presenting subtle insights of Aristotle, Aquinas, and Kant as generous transfigurations of our own commonplace or even wrongheaded provisional readings. Many of us felt commissioned to the arduous work of finding our own writerly voices as a result of that generosity.

I want to recruit Heidegger and Schmitz as spokesmen for my third option—the attempt to imagine the future of philosophy as a consecration of the world and the method of philosophy as a liturgy: Heidegger because of his expertise in the art of invocation, Schmitz because of his expertise in the art of commission. I should stress, however, that I am motivated in this by something stronger than the anecdotal evidence of admiring students. I propose to pair Heidegger and Schmitz in pondering philosophy's future, because, for both, teaching follows being. That is to say, the method they adopt instructing others is liturgical because for both—each in his own way—*thinghood* is liturgical. In what follows, I try to show this provisionally in relation to two texts: Heidegger's essay "The Thing"[1] and Schmitz's book *The Recovery of Wonder: The New Freedom and the Asceticism of Power.*[2] In advance of that it will be useful to sketch briefly the story of what Schmitz calls "the death of things." For it is the end of this story that he and Heidegger—each in his own way—aspire to write.

Heidegger and Schmitz on the Death of Things

For the better part of the past 150 years, philosophers in the West have been processing a crisis in representational thinking that reaches its apex in the works of Kant and Hegel. The problem, baldly stated, is that the trajectory of that thinking seems to call for a kind of sublation of thingly being in transcendental subjectivity that neither individual, cultural, nor (far more evident of late) environmental experience validates; that in the development of metaphysics between, say, the middle of the seventeenth century and the middle of the nineteenth, the subject somehow oversteps its bounds.

Proposed solutions to this problem have been ingenious and surprisingly diverse. For Nietzsche and subsequent kindred spirits (I think especially here of Foucault and Deleuze), the way forward lies in recognizing subjects and objects alike as manifestations of power. Their argument is that both the idealism of nineteenth-century German philosophy and the realism of the older Aristotelian tradition misconstrue what *is* by substituting superficial configurations of consciousness or physical nature for the deeper play of forces that produces them. The crisis of representational thinking affords us an opportunity to pierce that façade; to see to the bottom of nature and so to recast our view of the entire traditional range of philosophical concerns in terms of power relations.

1. Cf. Martin Heidegger, *Poetry, Language, Thought,* trans. Albert Hofstadter (New York: Harper and Row, 1971): 163–86.

2. Kenneth L. Schmitz, *The Recovery of Wonder: The New Freedom and the Ascetism of Power* (Montreal and Kingston: McGill-Queens University Press, 2005).

For Frege, Russell, Wittgenstein, and the founders of linguistic philosophy, the way forward lies in apprehending the deep structure of natural language. Their argument is that the tradition in general and late nineteenth-century neo-Kantianism in particular fail to distinguish clearly between the psychological and the logical. The latter, rightly understood, is an irreducible feature of the objective world. The crisis of representational thinking prods us toward an analysis of language capable of expressing that irreducibility that generates, in turn, a powerful new response to traditional problems.

For Buber and Levinas, the way forward lies in subordinating the world-constituting activities of the transcendental ego (which is really to say its very being) to the reality of Others. Here it is neither metaphysics nor logic, but ethics that holds out the promise of an antidote to the deep egocentricity of the modern period. Whatever we want to say about our capacity for self-consciousness in accounting for our place in the world, it is our consciousness of the Other that truly marks us as human. To ponder that consciousness is to restore and acknowledge the limitations of the overstepping subject; to put representational thinking in its place.

Talk about "the death of things" needs to be grasped as a propaedeutic for responding to this problem in yet another way. For both Heidegger and Schmitz, the folly of the overstepping subject is inscribed, like the sentences in Kafka's "Penal Colony," on the proverbial back of the thing. That is to say, for both, the ruined thing presents us with incontrovertible evidence that our philosophy has gone wrong.

What this evidence looks like and how it is to be interpreted constitute central questions for the later Heidegger—especially in his well-known assessment of technology. There, his claim is that the ruined thing comes to presence as *Bestand*—"standing reserve" in Lovitt's rather technical English translation, "stock" or "inventory" in common parlance. A remark on the transformation of the Rhine in the advent of hydroelectricity makes the point accessibly and clearly:

> In the context of the interlocking processes pertaining to the orderly disposition of electrical energy, even the Rhine itself appears to be something at our command. The hydroelectric plant is not built into the Rhine River as was the old wooden bridge that joined bank with bank for hundreds of years. Rather, the river is dammed up into the power plant. What the river is now, namely, a water power supplier, derives from the essence of the power station. In order that we may even remotely consider the monstrousness that reigns here, let us ponder for a moment the contrast that is spoken by

the two titles: "The Rhine," as dammed up into the *power* works, and "The Rhine," as uttered by the *art* work, in Hoelderlin's hymn by that name.[3]

In the work of technology, all things are reduced to the status of "something at our command." Earth, air, fire, water, and their permutations are essentially raw material for the willing subject. This condition erodes the nature of things entirely. They are and remain only as challenged forth. No thing whatsoever—even the kind of thing that we are—maintains ontological independence or dignity. Heidegger describes such a circumstance as "monstrous." And if we follow him in apprehending it as the condition for the possibility of the liquidation of cities and populations that sent Europe into convulsions a mere decade before his account of it, it's difficult to disagree.

All the same, the reduction of things to *Bestand* doesn't arise, as it were, "out of the blue," one day in the 1920s or '30s. It is itself an effect of the epoch-making project of modern mathematical physics. As regards our present concern, the key feature of that project is the homogenization of space. The scientific revolution of the seventeenth century obliterates the ancient conception of a layered *cosmos,* where the movement of a given thing is conceived as a kind of elemental homecoming (the things of the earth tending downward, for example, the things of the air or ether upward). As a result, things don't belong anywhere in particular. They lose their proper place. That, in turn, compromises their capacity to be familiar or intimate. It cancels what Heidegger calls their "nearness." "The Thing" begins by thematizing this cancellation:

All distances in time and space are shrinking. Man now reaches overnight, by plane, places which formerly took weeks and months of travel. . . . Yet the frantic abolition of all distances brings no nearness; for nearness does not consist in shortness of distance. What is least remote from us in point of distance, by virtue of its picture on film or its sound on radio, can remain far from us. What is incalculably far from us in point of distance can be near to us. Short distance is not in itself nearness. Nor is great distance remoteness. . . . What is happening here when, as a result of the abolition of great distances, everything is equally far and equally near? What is this uniformity in which everything is neither far nor near—is, as it were, without distance?[4]

3. Cf. Heidegger, *Basic Writings,* ed. David F. Krell, trans. William Lovitt (New York: Harper and Row, 1977), 297.

4. Heidegger, *Poetry, Language, Thought,* 165–66.

I'll follow the thread of Heidegger's response to these questions shortly. Here we need only consolidate the premises of the framing logic: the withdrawal of a thing's nearness, manifest almost paradoxically in the collapsing of spatiotemporal distances, is the condition for the possibility of its reduction to indifferent stock or inventory. Where space is entirely uniform, the things that occupy it become in principle undistinguished.

But even this relation isn't absolutely primordial. At the most basic level, the homogenization of space one sees in mathematical physics is a function of the metaphysics of subjectivity expressed decisively for the first time in the work of Descartes. The hallmark of that metaphysics is the disposition to take the world in advance—to re-present it—as the objective sphere of the self-securing/knowing subject. Where self-securing and knowing are closely identified, what gives itself in advance as firm and certain—what the Greeks called *ta mathemata*—acquires special privilege. Physics thus becomes mathematical in the service of a representational thinking that wants to project the essence of nature ahead of all specific encounters in order to establish its place in the midst of what stands over against it. The logic that concludes with the reduction of things to *Bestand* begins with the equation of nature and objectivity.

In its broad strokes as a history of ideas, Schmitz's account of the ruined thing is harmonious with Heidegger's. What the latter calls the metaphysics of subjectivity, the former calls "the new freedom." But the protagonists of its development—Descartes and Kant especially—are the same. Nevertheless, Schmitz fills out or saturates Heidegger's framing logic in at least three important ways.

First, he works out a subtler account of the shift in thinking that is consolidated in the *Meditations* and the *Discourse on Method*. The promotion of an epochal history of Being, every chapter of which must begin with an unexpected seizure (the displacement of theocentric medievalism by the sudden upsurge of the subject-object dualism, to take the most relevant case), tends to blot out a complementary layered and gradual accretion of intellectual trends. Schmitz argues convincingly that at least some of the circumstances that eventually produce the metaphysics of subjectivity—conspiring, as it were, in advance against the thing—are already present in the fourteenth century. There, for example, we see the rise of nominalism and voluntarism. Both enhance the constitutive role of mind—the former in its subordination of Aristotelian substance metaphysics to terminist logic, the latter in its promotion of the primacy of the will. Moreover—and perhaps more importantly—both encourage a kind of general disposition without which the later revival of atomism could not have occurred. However arbitrary its second coming, it is this postulate and its corresponding aesthetic that emerge in retrospect, having been absorbed across the disciplinary lines of Western intellectual culture, as the practical point of exit from the *via antiqua:*

> The root difference between the old and the new way revolves around the different concept of the unit. In the older, ontological way, the primary unit (*tode it, hoc aliquid* = *res*) is inherently complex though undivided (*unum est ens indivisum*); while in the new way, each ultimate basic unit is not only undivided but allegedly indivisible . . . since they are in principle utterly incomplex, absolutely simple, supposedly the ultimate units of reality. [T]his has proven to be a powerful motive for scientific research . . . for the past four hundred years, until our own century and even now to some degree, much of basic science has been propelled by the search for ultimate particles, the indivisible atoms that are the "building blocks" or basic units of the scientific understanding of the physical world.[5]

We might say that the method modeled by atomism is the inside or engine of the self-securing that culminates, in Heidegger's framing logic, with the devastation of twentieth-century technology.

Granting this, a second way in which Schmitz saturates that logic is by showing its engine humming under the proverbial hoods of some of the classic vehicles of modern thought. If we retrace, for example, the steps along the famous circular path of Descartes' *Meditations,* what we see above all is the reduction of external reality to its building blocks. Descartes begins in the world of multiple and complex Aristotelian substances; he concludes with the world of uniform extension in which things themselves are essentially other than and opposed to the *cogito,* or objects. His method amounts to sifting the first domain to the point where only the second remains. Here the possibility of Heidegger's *Bestand* already looms—all the more so because, extending the volutaristic trend of the late Middle Ages, the collapse of all nonmental substances in pure extension is coupled (in *Meditations* IV) with the claim that the scope of the will is infinite. In Kant's first and second *Critiques,* these transformations are radicalized. His analysis of theoretical reason reduces our knowledge of extension to knowledge of appearances. The Cartesian object is now a mere phenomenon utterly dependent, by definition, on the structures of consciousness. At the same time, his account

5. Schmitz, *The Recovery of Wonder,* 57–58.

of practical reason allots to the free or self-determining rational agent a power of legislation that outstrips anything to be observed in nature. "The autonomy of Reason," Schmitz concludes with typical incisive simplicity, "triumphed over its alleged heteronomy to things."[6]

In the spirit of exposition and comparison, think of this more finely detailed account of the thing's ruin—first by the forces of nominalism, voluntarism, and atomism, subsequently by the methodological revolutions of mature modern thought—as the scholarly backstory of Heidegger's metaphysics of subjectivity. There is one more thing. As Schmitz contextualizes the crisis of representational thinking in the well-established wider narratives of the West, he invites us to understand what he calls the "bleaching out" of the thing explicitly in terms of an earlier metaphysical robustness—a "thickness" or "density."[7] This invitation—which takes us, in the pivotal chapter of *The Recovery of Wonder,* back to Aquinas and the high Middle Ages—constitutes a third and most thought-provoking saturation of Heidegger's logic. Responding to it we both confirm what I stake above as his fundamental claim—that thinghood is essentially liturgical—and give ourselves a language for articulating the shortfall of what seems to me his later excessive pessimism regarding the philosophical tradition. At bottom, on Schmitz's argument, the thickness or density of the thing comprises a kind of ontological generosity, the adequate conception of which inspires in us not only a "companionate love" of the external world but a more hopeful, more forgiving reading of our own overstepping subjectivity.[8] How so? Let us turn first to "The Thing."

The Thing as Invocation: Heidegger and the Phenomenology of Accommodation

Heidegger is a phenomenologist. Truth, for him, must emerge from the matters of philosophical inquiry as a self-showing—an attestation of and from either Being as such or determinate modes of being *about* that Being/being. In this respect, the phenomenology of the thing is complicated from the outset by the fact that its reduction to *Bestand* suppresses its testimony. Denatured, it appears to have lost the voice it requires to speak for itself—if only to protest its ruin. And yet if that were wholly true, the oblivion of our condition looming in the crisis of representational thinking would overwhelm us entirely. The possibility of phe-

6. Ibid., 85.

7. Ibid.; cf., for example, 80.

8. Ibid., 119.

nomenology requires that things retain, at a minimum, the capacity to express some kind of outrage in the face of their devastation.

As early as *Being and Time,* Heidegger displays an ear for that outrage. His analysis of anxiety, for example, is a portrait of things refusing their inauthentic significance. This refusal registers initially—and significantly—as a feeling of "uncanniness" or "not-being-at-home," subsequently as the occasion for *Dasein*'s encounter of the nullity of its own Being-in-the-world, and finally as the condition for the possibility of its choosing itself, of its invoking the entirety of its past in the resolute projection of a possibility it claims as its own.[9] In existential analysis, to put it perhaps more starkly, the manifest outrage of things presages the self-gathering call that culminates in authenticity. The thematized devastation of the everyday is a prelude to the recognition and embrace of what we might call our own ontoliturgical foundations.

These moments recur, writ large, in most if not all of the documents that comprise Heidegger's assessment of technology. Surveying postwar Europe, he saw the manifest outrage of things (quite presciently) in the increasingly stubborn refusal of our natural and social environments to accommodate us. This refusal registers initially—and significantly—as a kind of collective experience of "uncanniness"—at one point in the *Letter on Humanism* "homelessness" is described as the fast-approaching "destiny of the world"[10]—subsequently as an occasion for wonder at the deep contradiction of a metaphysics that begins as an attempt to secure the thinking subject's belonging in the world and ends with the paradoxical destruction of intimacy, and finally as a prod to recover from the outraged thing itself, a sense of its ontoliturgical kinship with *Dasein.*

Our text—"The Thing"—is a case in point. As we saw above, it begins in "uncanniness" and wonder. (How, Heidegger asks, could "the abolition of great distances" fail to promote "nearness"?) The prod follows directly in a single dense paragraph of transition that sets the agenda for the remainder of the piece. It is worth citing in full:

> What about nearness? How can we come to know its nature? Nearness, it seems, cannot be encountered directly. We succeed in reaching it rather by attending to what is near. Near to us are what we usually call things. But what is a thing? Man has so far given no more thought to the thing as a thing than he has to nearness. The jug is a thing. What is the jug? We say: a

9. Cf. Heidegger, *Being and Time,* trans. John Macquarrie and Edward Robinson (New York: Harper and Row, 1962), 233.

10. Heidegger, *Basic Writings,* 219.

vessel, something of the kind that holds something else within it. The jug's holding is done by its base and sides. This container itself can again be held by the handle. As a vessel the jug is something self-sustained, something that stands on its own. This standing on its own characterizes the jug as something that is self-supporting, or independent. As the self-supporting independence of something independent, the jug differs from an object. An independent, self-supporting thing may become an object if we place it before us, whether in immediate perception or by bringing it to mind in a recollective re-presentation. However, the thingly character of the thing does not consist in its being a represented object, nor can it be defined in any way in terms of the objectness, or over-againstness, of the object.[11]

This passage contains three important general claims: (1) A propos of what we recognize now as a repeated gesture, the key to the mystery of nearness lies in understanding the thing. (2) The hallmark of the thing—its thinghood—consists in a kind of independence or self-support, a distinctive mode of being, hitherto unthought by metaphysics. (3) As a consequence, the thing is not reducible to an object of representation. In the play of these generalities Heidegger also introduces us to what he takes to be an exemplary thing: the jug. It bears the weight of subsequent phenomenological analysis. That is to say, the concept of the thing's thinghood emerges in its careful description. As regards this description, two points above all merit our attention: (1) The jug is independent and self-supporting, thanks, first and foremost, to the very power of accommodation the reduction of things to *Bestand* threatens to withdraw. (2) The power of accommodation flows, at bottom, from the invocation of what Heidegger calls the fourfold of earth, sky, mortals, and divinities.

In what sense is the jug *qua* jug thanks to the power of accommodation? In the sense that its vessel-being is constituted not by its sides, bottom, handles, and so forth, but by a sheltering nullity. It is, in effect, defined by its capacity to receive and hold—water and wine, for instance:

From start to finish the potter takes hold of the impalpable void and brings it forth as a container in the shape of a containing vessel. The jug's void determines all the handling in the process of making the vessel. The vessel's thingness does not lie at all in the material of which it consists, but in the void that holds.[12]

The sheltering nullity of the jug's void is not the mere nothing of science and/or metaphysics. On the contrary, it makes room as a host might for

11. Heidegger, *Poetry, Language, Thought*, 166–67.
12. Ibid., 169.

a guest. It takes and keeps what is poured into it. Taking, it welcomes the bounty of what it holds. Keeping, it safeguards that bounty until the time comes to pour it out—at a meal with family or friends, as a sacramental offering at a service of worship, or for a meeting of workers charged with the care of an institution. In its pouring out, the jug's taking and keeping—the capacity of its void to hold—is attested and justified, as when education is justified in the sharing of wisdom, or years of patient labor in bestowing on the world a work of art. Indeed, the act of outpouring is the truth of the jug's sheltering nullity in the Hegelian sense—the becoming explicit of a process of being. Gift is the culminating reality of accommodation. Heidegger writes:

In the outpouring, the holding is authentically how it is. To pour from the jug is to give. The holding of the vessel occurs in the giving of the outpouring. Holding needs the void as that which holds. The nature of the holding void is gathered in the giving. But giving is richer than a mere pouring out. The giving, whereby the jug is a jug, gathers in the twofold holding—in the outpouring. We call the gathering of the twofold holding into the outpouring, which, as a being together, first constitutes the full presence of giving: the poured gift. The jug's jug-character consists in the poured gift of the pouring out.[13]

In what sense does the power of accommodation flow from the invocation of the fourfold of earth, sky, mortals, and divinities? The answer, in the case at issue, is nested in a more penetrating phenomenological account of the jug's outpouring. Its gift is not exhausted in the simple voiding of its contents ("giving is richer than a mere pouring out"). On the contrary, it is, as the passage just cited attests, a gathering. The water harbors the spring and the rock, themselves outcomes—configurations—of the play of the earth and the sky. It slakes the thirst of mortals at mealtime and appeases the gods in the offering of a libation. This does not happen in sequence. Indeed, we oughtn't to separate earth from sky or mortals from divinities even conceptually. The harboring of the gathering gift *is* in the form of a reciprocal calling near—a mutual invocation. Like T. S. Eliot's mermaids, the constituents of Heidegger's fourfold sing "each to each." That is, at bottom, what the outpouring—which is to say what the jug-thing itself—*means*:

The gift of the outpouring is a gift because it stays (i.e., harbors) earth and sky, divinities and mortals. Yet staying is now no longer the mere persisting

13. Ibid., 172.

of something that is here. Staying appropriates. It brings the four into the light of their mutual belonging. From out of staying's simple onefoldedness they are betrothed, entrusted to one another. At one in thus being entrusted to one another, they are unconcealed. The gift of the outpouring stays the onefold of the fourfold of the four. And in the poured gift the jug presences as jug. The gift gathers what belongs to giving: the twofold containing, the container, the void, and the outpouring as donation. What is gathered in the gift gathers itself in appropriatively staying the fourfold. This manifold-simple gathering is the jug's presencing. Our language denotes what a gathering *is* by an ancient word. That word is: thing. The jug's presencing is the pure, giving gathering of the one-fold fourfold into a single time-space, a single stay.[14]

Walk once more through this unorthodox equation. The "abolition of great distances" in the advance of technology fails to promote "nearness." The key to the mystery of nearness lies in understanding the thing. The hallmark of the thing is a kind of independence or self-support hitherto unthought by metaphysics (and so beyond objective representation). In the case of the jug, the self-support in question—its distinctive mode of being—consists in the power of accommodation. The truth of that power is the gift of its outpouring. The gift itself is a gathering, the constitution of which reveals itself to the phenomenological observer as the mutual invocation of earth, sky, mortals, and divinities. But that means—joining the end to the beginning—that things are liturgical.

The Thing as Commission: Schmitz and the Metaphysics of Generosity

Imagine this insight now as the foundation of philosophy's future. Unpacking it accessibly would be more difficult, no doubt, than finding productive work for Plato, Aristotle, and company in the contemporary knowledge economy or cataloguing the traps and illusions of capitalist hegemony. Our students would almost certainly need a less idiosyncratic language in order to find themselves and their own meaningful experiences in the invocation of the earth, sky, mortals, and divinities. Nevertheless, a patient development of something like Heidegger's ontology of accommodation and gift could not but revolutionize completely our notions of perception and understanding, language and plastic art, religious devotion—indeed, an entire range of things the academy has been

14. Ibid., 173–74.

trying for decades to compress into the object-driven representational thinking of evolutionary psychology, critical Marxism, and their disciplinary correlates. Philosophy itself would consist in restoring the dignity of things, uncovering in each the force of Proust's madeleine, rekindling the possibility of intimacy—"nearness"—in the habitation of those environments that stand presently on the verge of disowning us.

And yet the pessimistic presupposition of the later Heidegger's phenomenology of accommodation—the notion that metaphysics has *never* given thought to the self-supporting or independent nature of the thing—threatens to circumvent engagement of the very world it proposes to heal. The power of his liturgy notwithstanding, he gives us little or nothing in the way of guidance on the stewardship of institutions—including those of professional discipline and scholarship—or the formation of wider political culture. These activities are, for him, hopelessly contaminated by the Cartesian/Kantian/Nietzschean quest for self-security. The problem for most philosophers, however, is that they also dominate professional life. Having rescued the thing from the devastation of the overstepping subject, what does Heidegger tell me about the nature of everyday service to my department, its program, and its students? About how I might negotiate a contract for my faculty association or interface with the government and its funding organizations? In short, what devolves on me from "The Thing," "The Question Concerning Technology," and works of a similar spirit as a commission?

I can imagine this last question turned back on me as follows: if the liturgical method is supposed to constitute an alternative to the notion of philosophy as a response to economic, technological, and ideological forces external to it, why would we ask it to send us back into that maelstrom? The hypothesis was that teaching follows being; that the method Heidegger adopts in instructing others is liturgical because *thinghood* is liturgical. What if the deepest lesson in things—a lesson, remember, that begins in thingly outrage with the experience of "uncanniness" or homelessness—is that the world of the overstepping subject is simply an unsalvageable assault on the real? It is time to pursue the argument of Schmitz I broached above in commenting on his saturation of Heidegger's logic. For *The Recovery of Wonder* is, as a whole, an answer to this question. In it, we discover a liturgy of the thing that culminates in commission, and so the possibility of engaging the institutions of the overstepping subject without being contaminated by them, of transfiguring them without destroying them.

In what sense does Schmitz's liturgy of the thing culminate in commission? In the sense that it presents every thing *qua* thing as called out beyond itself—marked by a kind of transcendence that models for us the ecstatic nature of all existence. The explicit grasp of this transcendence in the metaphysics of the high Middle Ages constitutes the truth of the Greco-Christian tradition in the same way that, for Heidegger, the gift of outpouring constitutes the truth of accommodation. Among other things, that means: the tradition itself shelters and nurtures in its development an authentic understanding of the real. What the early Greeks experience in terms of utility as *pragmata* and *chremata,* their mature philosophical tradition encompasses, in relation to the governing principle of the *cosmos* or justly ordered whole, as being *simpliciter.* With the advent of Christianity, the pagan *cosmos* is reread as *creatio,* the things that populate it *creaturae.* When, exercising his genius for synthesis, Aquinas sets about reconciling the Aristotelian tradition with the doctrines of Catholicism, the thing as formed matter is framed self-consciously and systematically by the aspiration of transcendence:

> In its expansiveness, each thing "escapes" *in a certain way* from the confinement of the isolated individual which it is. Such immateriality is distinctive of form ... [F]orm is by its very nature an expansive principle moving towards community, for it is unable to be contained within the confinement of material particularity. [15]

In form itself, to come back to our liturgical theme, the thing is commissioned. To apprehend its nature is to see both an unmistakable trace of the divine origin that captivated the ancients and at least an outline of the self-surpassing freedom (what Schmitz calls "the new freedom," in contrast to the more superficial freedom of choice) that was to be the leitmotif of philosophy after Descartes; to make transparent the wager underlying the entire sojourn of the thing in Western thinking:

> If the universe is the gift of the Creator, then it must reflect in its depths the freedom that is native to its origins. Here the new and deeper sense of freedom is convergent with the freedom of things, not as objects given, but as gifted creatures. And so, if the created universe has a spiritual origin, it is not surprising that the immateriality of form holds within itself a generosity that presages freedom. For the elevation of freedom beyond choice points to the original freedom that underlies a world created freely by an act of divine generosity. It is the creation as gift. All things are situated within this

15. Schmitz, *The Recovery of Wonder,* 101.

deeper spiritual medium, a medium pervaded by freedom, by the spirit of creative generosity.[16]

The linchpin here is the notion of generosity. If the outcome of Heidegger's liturgical phenomenology is that things are essentially or primordially hospitable—capable of gathering and bringing near *qua* things the fourfold of earth, sky, mortals, and divinities—the outcome of Schmitz's liturgical orchestration of the metaphysical tradition that culminates in Aquinas is that things are essentially or primordially generous—capable, as formed matter, of transcending *qua* things their own individuality. This is no casual metaphor. On the contrary, the generosity of form is the being of things, the concrete manner in which they exist in community with each other and the environment.

In what sense does the metaphysics of generosity give us the possibility of engaging the institutions of the overstepping subject without being contaminated by them, of transfiguring them without destroying them? First, we avoid in it what we might call the Heideggerian incommensurability of discourses. Thinking needn't break or withdraw from the philosophical tradition nor, accordingly, ponder the problem of how to return to the institutions yoked to it. If things are to be resurrected, they will be resurrected by the recovering of its riches, not by abandoning them. More concretely, perhaps: Kant's "bleached out" phenomenon and Aquinas's thick or textured synthesis of form and matter belong to a single Western conversation linking existence and transcendence. Our place, expressing concern about the thing, is ultimately in the midst of that conversation.

For Schmitz, this means two things at a minimum: (1) While a thoroughgoing critique of "the new freedom" may be harmonious with Heidegger's indictment of the metaphysics of subjectivity—especially in accounting for the ruined thing, it must at the same time acknowledge the fundamental insight of modern thought. The freedom of the self-securing subject retains the trace of "the original freedom that underlies a world created freely by an act of divine generosity." That is to say, the freedom of the overstepping subject shows us a strand of transcendence insufficiently emphasized in the premodern tradition. Grasping it helps us appreciate more fully the thickness or density of the thing. (2) But more to the point, full appreciation of this thickness or density makes possible a rereading of "the new freedom" itself, which at once recog-

16. Ibid., 104–5

nizes the cost of "bleaching out" the thing and establishes metaphysical generosity as the truth of self-securing subjectivity. And this, in turn, produces a new principle of engagement. What if we were to transfigure the understanding of self-securing subjectivity as *power* or *domination* everywhere at work in our economies, technologies, and ideologies, in our institutions and our wider political culture, in terms of *generosity?* What if our task as philosophers, as students and teachers, as citizens, were to recuperate from the appearance of coercion that dominates modern life the truth of commission?

The best teachers always give us our labor. Any such project would be a work of many generations. But *The Recovery of Wonder* gives us our point of departure. It says with all the force and reserve of mature scholarship, and with the authority of a life dedicated to the teaching of philosophy, "Praise the world to the angel!" "Tell him of things":

> Even today, [the] properties of the reality of things invite us to look beyond their familiar presence to the mystery of things themselves: and in *seeing them anew* we are invited to recover the wondrous splendor that gives rise to *theoria*. It is in recognition of our solidarity with things that we find a fuller freedom.[17]

17. Ibid., 126

PART 2

READING THE HISTORY OF PHILOSOPHY IN THE SPIRIT OF KENNETH L. SCHMITZ

Michael Baur

4. COMING-TO-KNOW AS A WAY OF COMING-TO-BE

Aristotle's De Anima III.5

The Object of Human Knowledge

In book III, chapter 5 of the *De Anima,* Aristotle introduces the distinction between *poetikos nous* and *pathetikos nous.* The former term was not used by Aristotle himself, but gained currency later among his Greek commentators.[1] In my own treatment of book III, chapter 5, I shall employ the conventional English terms for the two forms of *nous*—active intellect and passive intellect, respectively. I believe that it is possible to make use of such terminology without adopting as a result any distorting views concerning the nature of the two forms of *nous.* While Aristotle does not consider *nous* to be limited to the human being alone (414^b18), it is quite clear that book III, chapter 5 refers to a distinction that must be made with respect to human *nous.* Finally, it should be noted that Aristotle's distinction between the active and passive intellect appears in no other part of his entire *corpus;* nowhere else in his known writings does he even allude to such a distinction. Yet as I hope shall become clear as I proceed, it would be rash to conclude on account of this that the distinction is therefore unimportant.

Any treatment of book III, chapter 5 might well begin with some ac-

1. Sir David Ross, "Introduction," *Aristotle, De Anima*, edited with an Introduction and Commentary by Sir David Ross (Oxford: Clarendon Press, 1961), 41–44.

count of the reason for the distinction that Aristotle draws therein. Aristotle begins the chapter by saying:

> Since in every class of things, as in nature as a whole, we find two factors involved, a matter which is potentially all the particulars included in the class, a cause which is productive in the sense that it makes them all (the latter standing to the former, as e.g. an art to its material), these distinct elements must likewise be found within the soul (430^{a}10–14).[2]

It seems that Aristotle introduces the distinction in *nous* by reference to the notion of production, or generation, since the mind, like sense, becomes (cognitionally) the objects it apprehends (429^{a}15–18).[3] But in order to grasp the need for Aristotle's distinction, more must be said about these objects. While the objects of sense are the sensibles (proper, common, or incidental; see II.6), the objects of the mind or intellect are what might be called the intelligibles. In book III, chapter 4 of the *De Anima,* Aristotle identifies the proper object of thought as the *ti en einai* of a thing (429^{b}11–23; the phrase as it is used here governs the possessive dative of the terms "magnitude" and "water"). As Hicks notes, the phrase *to ti en einai* is a technical designation of the specific form or formal cause. Like the phrase *to ti esti,* this phrase denotes specific or generic form, the rational description of which may answer the question of "*ti esti?*" It should be noted, however, that while the phrase *to ti esti* may designate matter and composite as well as form, the phrase *to ti en einai* denotes only the form, as opposed to the matter and the composite. Thus the objects of thought are the immaterial forms of things, or what might be called the intelligible forms of things.[4]

There remains the need for some further clarification if we are to say that the mind becomes its objects, and that its objects are the intelligible forms of things. Properly speaking, the mind does not become the intelligible form alone. For the human mind as actually knowing is

2. All direct quotations from Aristotle are taken from *The Complete Works of Aristotle: The Revised Oxford Translation,* ed. Jonathan Barnes (Princeton, N.J.: Princeton University Press, 1984).

3. On the identity of sense and its object, see also Aristotle, *De Anima,* 418^{a}2 and 425^{b}26; on the identity of the mind and its object, see 429^{b}6, 430^{a}2, 430^{a}19, 431^{a}1, and 431^{b}18. On the identity of each with its respective object, see 431^{b}24.

4. This is corroborated in other passages throughout the *De Anima:* at 429^{a}15, Aristotle writes that the mind is, in a sense, the "place of forms"; at 431^{b}2, he tells us that the mind "thinks the forms"; and at 432^{a}2, he tells us that the mind is in a sense the "form of forms." It is clear, then, that the mind apprehends forms; but the phrase *to ti en einai* (as well as several other passages; e.g., 432^{a}2) tells us further that these are not the sensible, but the intelligible forms of things.

something that has come to be, and as such, it must contain within it an element of potentiality as well as actuality (see Aristotle's *Metaphysics,* 1032^{a}21 ff. and 1033^{a}24 ff.). Of course, it is equally improper to say that the mind becomes the intelligible object itself (432^{a}1). Rather, it is more accurate to say that the mind receives into itself the intelligible forms of things, and in so doing, becomes (cognitionally) the intelligibles.

Thus the mind, like sense, becomes in actual thinking the object it apprehends. But anything that is moved or comes to be must be moved or produced by something that is already in act (417^{a}15–18).[5] Mind and sense, therefore, while potentially their respective objects, become their respective objects actually only in virtue of something that is already actual. In sensation, this productive actuality is external to the sensing subject; it is the sensible object itself (417^{b}20).

While thinking differs from sensing with respect to its objects (429^{b}11–23) and its passivity (429^{a}30–^{b}6), it is analogous to sensing insofar as the faculty of thinking—while potentially its objects—becomes its objects actually in the exercise of actual thinking. Since thinking is analogous to sensing in this respect, thinking must be either a process in which the mind is made to be its object by the object itself, or else a process in which some similar actuation takes place (429^{a}13). But the mind is not acted upon by any external object; this is because knowledge is of universals, and these exist, in a sense, in the mind itself (417^{b}20).[6]

This requires some further clarification. In book M, chapter 10 of the *Metaphysics,* Aristotle specifies what he means when he says that knowledge is of universals:

> For knowledge, like knowing, is spoken of in two ways—as potential and as actual. The potentiality, being, as matter, universal and indefinite, deals with the universal and indefinite; but the actuality, being definite, deals with a definite object,—being a "this." it deals with a "this." But *per accidens* sight sees universal color, because the individual color which it sees is color; and this individual α which the grammarian investigates is an α. (1087^{a}15–21)

Knowledge of anything is knowledge of a "this" (*tode ti*); it is not actually universal, but only potentially so. For knowledge of a thing is according

5. See also 430^{a}21 and 431^{a}4. This principle is summarized, among other places, in Aristotle's *Metaphysics* at 1049^{b}24.

6. It is clear from 429^{a}15 that the sensible object cannot act upon, and therefore cannot actualize, the mind's thinking of the intelligible object. But in what follows, I hope to show why even the intelligible object outside the mind cannot in itself actualize the mind's thinking or knowing of it.

to its intelligible form (*to ti en einai*), or the source of its "thisness." As a result, knowledge of this "this" may be applied to any other "this" whatsoever. In a similar manner, sensation in its apprehension of a "this" may attain the universal *per accidens*.

The above account suggests a complete isomorphism between thinking and sensation concerning grasp of the universal (for both, such grasp is only potential). But at 417^b20 in the *De Anima*, it is clear that Aristotle wants to affirm a basic dissimilarity. Aristotle is not simply attempting to contrast here potential knowledge (which is of the universal) with actual sensation (which is of the particular). Rather, Aristotle wants to assert that actual sensation is limited in a way that actual intellectual knowing is not.

While actual sensation and actual intellectual knowledge are both of a "this," actual intellectual knowledge is accompanied by knowledge of its own potentially universal application; actual sensation is not. In book II, chapter 2 of the *Posterior Analytics*, Aristotle writes that the question, "What is X?" is equivalent to the question, "Why is X a Y?" The answer to the first question is, similarly, equivalent to the answer to the second. Thus to know what something is (*to ti en einai*) is to know also its cause for being so. Thus if one knows what an X is, he will also know why X is Y. And if one knows this, he knows by implication that in every case, if this is an X, it must be accompanied by certain other properties. Thus if any X is an eclipse, there will have to be a privation of the moon's light by the interposition of the earth. Knowledge of the cause is the knowledge of the universally applicable *as* universally applicable. To put it differently, the answer to the question *ti esti* gives one the cause as well; and knowledge of the cause entails knowledge of necessity and therefore of the possibility of the universal application. Thus to know the cause of an eclipse is to know that whenever a certain set of conditions is met, an eclipse *must* take place. And to know this is to know what may apply at any time, in any place, as long as the conditions are met.

On Aristotle's account, then, it is not plausible to hold that knowledge of what something is, and therefore of its cause, may be knowledge of the universally applicable, but not knowledge of it *as such*. As Aristotle writes, if one were on the moon and saw the earth shutting out the sun's light, one would not know the cause of the eclipse (*Post. An.* 87^b40). Nor would one know the cause if he simply perceived sensorily that a triangle has its angles equal to two right angles (*Post. An.* 87^b36). Now this is certainly knowledge of the universally applicable, but what is lacking is the concomitant knowledge of it *as* universally applicable; and this lack, Aristotle writes, entails that there is no knowledge of the cause. The reason one would not know the cause is that one would not know anything about the phenomenon *as* universally applicable (*Post. An.* 87^b38–88^a2). So if one does not know the universally applicable *as* universally applicable, then one does not know the cause. Conversely, if one does know the cause, then one knows the universally applicable *as* universally applicable. Thus "man" and "horse" may be terms applied to individuals, though "treated" as universals (*Metap.* 1035^b30), and the same definition can be known to apply to many things (*Metap.* 1074^a35).

Thus while actual intellectual knowledge is always of a "this," it entails knowledge of its potentially universal application. The situation is different in the case of actual sensation. While actual sensation may attain the universal *per accidens,* it does not and cannot entail knowledge of this universality. For the content of sensation must always be that which is sensible at a definite place and time (*Post. An.* 87^b30). Of course, intellectual knowledge, also, is always of a "this"; but it is not knowledge merely of a "this." It is also knowledge of the cause of the "thisness" of the "this" (it is knowledge of the *ti en einai* or the intelligible form), and so it is knowledge of the "this" *as* universally applicable. The content of actual sensation, by contrast, is limited to the sensible at a definite place and time. Thus there is no knowledge in actual sensation of its potentially universal application. Even if one is speaking of actual sensation as *per accidens* universal, one is doing so, not by sensing, but by thinking.[7]

The Object of Human Knowledge and the Ground of the Distinction

For Aristotle, while actual intellectual knowledge entails knowledge of its own potentially universal application, actual sensation or sensory knowledge does not. But this shows why thinking cannot be a process in which the mind is made to be its object simply by the object itself (see 429^a13). To know by means of *nous* is to become the intelligible object cognitionally. But intellectual knowledge of an object (knowledge of the intelligible form or cause) entails knowledge of the potentially universal application of this knowledge. While the object outside the mind may be actually intelligible as a single "this," it is not some-

7. The so-called "philosophic" imperfect tense of *to ti en einai* is used to express timeless being, and therefore being exempt from the contingency of matter and change. See G. R. G. Mure, *Aristotle* (London: Ernest Benn, 1932), 13n1.

thing that, in itself, stands for others of its kind; it does so only potentially. But if actual knowledge entails knowledge of its own potentially universal application, then any object outside the mind (which is always a single "this") cannot, in itself, be the cause of actual intellectual knowledge. Any object outside the mind is only potentially intelligible in the sense required. Of course, actual intellectual knowledge is also always of a "this," and so, too, is universal only in potency; but actual intellectual knowledge (as knowledge of intelligible form or cause) must also entail knowledge of this potential for universal application. Such knowledge of potential universal applicability can never be derived from any single object alone. As a result, there is needed some other actuality by virtue of which the mind actually comes to be its proper object.

The object outside the mind—while it may be actually intelligible as a single "this"—does not on its own imply anything about potential universal applicability. But since actual intellectual knowledge must entail knowledge of such potential universal applicability, no object that stands outside the mind—even if it is intelligible as a single "this" independent of the mind—can be the cause of actual intellectual knowledge. Thus knowledge, in a sense, exists in the soul itself (417^b23). Of course, it is not because we think truly about a state of affairs that a state of affairs is actually so; rather, it is because a state of affairs is actually so that we think truly about it (*Metap.* 1051^b7–9). Thus the object outside the mind may be actually intelligible in one sense, that is, as a single "this." But since actual intellectual knowledge (as knowledge of the intelligible form or cause) entails knowledge of the potential for universal application, the object outside the mind (which is actually intelligible only as a single "this") is not actually intelligible in the sense required for actual intellectual knowledge.

Since Aristotle affirms the complete cognitional identity of the sensible object and the sensitive subject, the object that the human being has become on the sensitive level may also be actually intelligible as a single "this" (still independent of the mind). For example, the angles in the triangle that a human being now perceives (which the human being *is* sensorily, but not yet intellectually) may, in fact, be equivalent in measure to the sum of two right angles (see *Post. An.* 87^b36). But for a human being to become the object intellectually is for him to know the cause, and therefore to know of the potentially universal application of this knowledge.[8] Since the object that the human being has become

8. To see the fact, yet to fail to apprehend its cause, is to fail to know the intelligible form (*to ti en einai*), and therefore is to fail to know the object intellectually.

sensorily can be actually intelligible (like any object independent of the mind) only as a single "this," it cannot be the cause of actual knowledge in the human being. For actual intellectual knowledge entails knowledge of the cause, and therefore knowledge of its universal applicability; such knowledge cannot be brought about by any single "this" alone. The sensible object that the human being is (just like the sensible object outside the mind) may be actually intelligible as a single "this." But it is knowledge of possible universal application, as we have seen, that must be included in actual knowledge of the intelligible form or cause. As a result, there is needed some further actuality that causes actual intellectual knowledge in the human being.

Actual intellectual knowledge is identical with its object ($430^{a}21$), with the difference that while the intelligible object outside the mind (as a single "this") stands potentially for all others of its kind or in its class, actual intellectual knowledge entails knowledge of such universal applicability. Such knowledge of potential universal applicability cannot be conveyed by the single object itself. This, of course, is not to deny the identity of intelligible object and intelligent subject in actual cognition. Let us call the intellectual knowledge of a thing—which entails knowledge of its potential for universal application—the knowledge of a "this" *as* universal (i.e., of a "this" that is "treated" as universal; *Metap.* $1035^{b}30$). Of course, no one has actual knowledge of a universal as such. The object outside the mind, however, while actually an intelligible "this," is a "this" *as* universal only potentially. On its own, it cannot convey or bring about knowledge of its own potential for universal application. Thus the object itself cannot actuate intellectual knowledge in the human being. In short, because intellectual knowledge of a thing (knowledge of the *ti en einai,* which is equivalent to knowledge of the cause) entails also knowledge of the potential for universal application, it cannot be caused by the object outside the mind (which is always a single "this"). As Aristotle writes, it is because the objects of the mind are universals that external objects cannot be the cause of actual intellectual knowledge; and for this reason, intellectual knowledge, in a sense, exists in the soul ($417^{b}20$–25).[9]

9. To know the intelligible form (*to ti en einai*) of a thing is to know its cause; and as we have seen, knowledge of this type entails knowledge of its own potentially universal application. Therefore, to say that the singular object cannot, on its own, actuate knowledge of potential universal applicability is to say that the singular object on its own cannot actuate knowledge of the cause, or knowledge of intelligible form. There must be some-

I believe that this is the sense in which one should understand the Aristotelian doctrine that the object outside the mind is only potentially intelligible (for in one sense, it is actually intelligible—as a single "this"); and the doctrine that knowledge is of universals (more accurately, one does not actually know universals, but one may know a singular "this" *as* universal). Finally, with this understanding, I believe that it is possible to see why there must be some prior actuality besides the object itself that "moves" the mind or intellect from a state of potentiality to a state of actuality with respect to its proper object. As we shall soon see, this prior actuality is what has been called the active intellect.[10]

Coming to Know as a Kind of Coming to Be

In the preceding section, I hoped to elucidate the reasoning behind Aristotle's distinction between active and passive intellect. The question to be answered in book III, chapter 5 of *De Anima* is the following: "In virtue of what prior actuality does the mind become (cognitionally) the intelligible objects it knows?" For this reason, it seems reasonable to hold that, of the two questions Aristotle raised at the beginning of book III, chapter 4 (namely, "what is the distinguishing characteristic of the thinking faculty?" and "how does thinking come about?"), only the first is addressed in that chapter; the second question is left for book III, chapter 5. As we have already seen, the cause or agency that makes the mind its object actually cannot be the external intelligible object itself. This cause or agency, rather, is the active intellect. At this stage, I would like to examine more carefully the nature of the distinction between active intellect and passive intellect, and, in particular, how the active intellect functions in relation to the passive intellect.

As we have already seen, the distinction between the active intellect and the passive intellect is made by reference to the notion of generation

---

thing already actual, besides the object outside the mind, that actuates knowledge of cause (and thus of intelligible form).

10. Aristotle writes further that, since knowledge is of the universal, one may use one's mind at will (417^b24). The reasoning, it appears, would be as follows: Since intellectual knowledge entails knowledge of its potentially universal application, once one has attained a certain kind of knowledge, it is in principle possible for him to make use of this knowledge or make an application of it in any relevant situation whatsoever. In other words, it seems that one can think at will precisely on the grounds that one can know of the potentially universal application of one's own knowledge. Of course, this is a corollary to the assertion that, since the external object does not (and cannot) actuate knowledge, one may think at will. For the object (which is singular) does not actuate knowledge precisely *because* knowledge is of the universal (i.e., it is of the singular, but *as* universal in application).

(430^{a}10–14). This is because knowing is a process by which the mind becomes cognitionally identical with the object it knows. It would seem reasonable, then, to pursue further discussion of the active and passive intellect also by reference to the notion of generation. Aristotle's primary treatment of generation (or, as it is also called, coming to be, or "production" in the case of artificial processes) occurs in book *Z*, chapters 7–9 of the *Metaphysics,* to which we now turn.

Aristotle writes that, of all things that come to be, some come to be artificially, some naturally, and some spontaneously. The type of coming to be that Aristotle is concerned with in book III, chapter 5 of *De Anima* is the mind's coming to be (cognitionally) the object it knows. This type of coming to be cannot be considered artificial (except in the most tenuous sense).[11] Artificial production takes place only if there is some kind of intellectual knowledge in the soul (*Metap.* 1032^{b}2, 1032^{b}27). But the kind of coming to be that Aristotle is investigating in book III, chapter 5 is the mind's becoming its objects cognitionally; this is the coming to be of intellectual knowledge itself. So the coming to be of actual intellectual knowledge as such cannot be explained on the basis of artificial production. For any artificial production already presupposes that actual intellectual knowledge has come to be. Nor can the coming to be of actual intellectual knowledge be explained as a type of spontaneous coming to be, for spontaneous generation occurs when nature has failed in some way, as in the case of a monstrosity (*Physics* 195^{b}31–198^{a}13). Aristotle is not concerned with the anomalous in his treatment of the active and passive intellects.

The mind's coming to be its objects cognitionally is neither artificial nor spontaneous, but must be considered, it seems, natural in some sense. Thus Aristotle begins book III, chapter 5 of *De Anima* by speaking of a distinction that is to be found in every class of things, but particularly in nature (*physis*) as a whole (430^{a}10). Nevertheless, since natural coming to be is analogous to artificial production (*Metap.* 1034^{a}34), reference to the latter may help in understanding the former. It is no coincidence, then, that Aristotle draws an analogy to art at 430^{a}13.

Aristotle explains that everything that comes to be or is generated

11. The coming to be of intellectual knowledge may be considered an artificial process insofar as teaching, for example, is an art by which knowledge is said to be generated. But again, in the process of teaching, knowledge is generated in the student and not in the teacher; the art of teaching, like the other arts, presupposes that knowledge has already come to be in the practitioner. And this more fundamental kind of coming to be is what Aristotle is concerned with in book III, chapter 5 of *De Anima.*

(either naturally or artificially) is generated by something, from something, and becomes something (*Metap.* 1032^{a}13). When he says "becomes something," Aristotle means "becoming" in any of the categories: in other words, an X may come to be a particular thing or of some quantity or quality or in some place (*Metap.* 1032^{a}17). It is clear, then, that Aristotle's account here may also apply to the process in which the human being becomes cognitionally the intelligible object he knows. In natural generation, that *from which* things are generated is called the matter, and that *by which* they are generated must be something that already exists (*Metap.* 1032^{a}18). As Ross notes in his commentary on the *Metaphysics,* that *by which* things are generated is not, strictly speaking, an actual thing as a composite of form and matter, but is rather the thing's nature in the sense of form. Thus, as Aristotle writes later, that *by which* a thing is produced is the form of the thing produced—that is, the "substance without matter" or essence (*to ti en einai*) (*Metap.* 1032^{b}11–15).

That which is generated or comes to be, Aristotle writes, "is a man or plant or one of the things of this kind, which we say are substances if anything is" (*Metap.* 1032^{a}20). Despite ambiguities in Aristotle's doctrine of substance,[12] it is clear that he is referring to substance as a composite of matter and form. He wrote earlier in the *De Anima* that it is the concrete body, a composite of matter and form, that is most properly called a "substance" (412^{a}12). Later in his account of generation, Aristotle writes that that which is generated must be a composite of matter and form (*Metap.* 1033^{b}13–20). His examples of "man" and "plant" at 1032^{a}20 serve to confirm such meaning in the present context.

That which is generated, then, is a composite of matter and form. Furthermore, the form of that which is generated is the same as that *by which* it is generated (*Metap.* 1032^{a}25, 1033^{b}30, 1034^{a}21). More precisely, the form of that which is generated *is* that *by which* it is generated. Again, I am referring to that *by which* generation takes place, not as a composite of matter and form, but as a "substance without matter," or essence (*Metap.* 1032^{b}11–15). Thus, that *by which* generation occurs is the efficient cause of generation, not *qua* composite, but *qua* its essence or form. For this reason, Aristotle writes that the agency *by which* generation takes place is in a sense a part of that which is generated (*Metap.* 1033^{a}1, 1034^{a}26). This is not the material part of the composite generated, but rather its formal component. Accordingly, the art of medicine *is*

12. See Mure, 101n1, and 179; see also Sir David Ross, *Aristotle* (London: Methuen, 1930), 165–67.

the form of health (*Metap.* 1032b14). Furthermore, natural generation is analogous to artificial generation in this respect (*Metap.* 1034^{a}35). Just as *health* is said to come from "health," and "house" from "house" (*Metap.* 1032^{b}12), "man" may be said to come from "man" (*Metap.* 1034^{b}3). The efficient and formal causes of a thing in nature may coincide with one another (*Metap.* 1075^{b}25; *Physics* 198^{a}25). And so the agency *by which* a thing is generated (*qua* essence and not as a composite thing) *is* also the form of the thing generated.

Aristotle argues that that *by which* a thing is generated (the form) and that *from which* it is generated (the matter) cannot themselves be generated, and must preexist the act of generation itself (*Metap.* 1033^{a}1 ff., 1033^{a}28 ff., 1034^{b}7 ff.). Of course, both the matter and the form (as efficient cause) may be generated in the absolute sense. But both must preexist the particular instance of generation in which they play their respective roles. Were this not the case, the processes of generation would "regress to infinity" (*Metap.* 1033^{b}5). Furthermore, since both the form and the matter must preexist the act of generation, generation is really a process in which *this* form (which already exists in some sense) is induced in *this* matter (also preexistent) (*Metap.* 1033^{b}9; see also 1033^{a}35). The efficient cause (as the form of the thing to be generated) acts on the matter, thereby enforming it and causing it to be what it is. That *by which* generation takes place acts upon and enforms that *from which* generation takes place, and thereby produces that which is generated: the composite product.

I believe it is possible to identify, in the coming to be of knowledge, those three elements that Aristotle says are involved in any type of coming to be whatsoever. That *from which* actual knowledge comes to be (that which plays the role of matter) is what has traditionally been called the passive intellect (*pathetikos nous*). As Aristotle writes in book III, chapter 5 of *De Anima,* in all coming to be, there is something that plays the role of matter insofar as it is potentially all of the things in a particular class (430^{a}11). In the class of knowledge, or beings as known, the element must be passive intellect, which has the potential to become (cognitionally) all things (430^{a}12). The agency *by which* actual knowledge comes to be is to be identified with what has traditionally been called the active intellect (*poetikos nous*). As the agency in generation, this must be something that is already in act, and that can act upon the passive intellect (the matter *from which* the thing is generated), enforming it and causing it to "become" the composite product.

That which is generated, or comes to be, in the process of knowing, must be the mind as actually knowing, as identical (cognitionally) with its object. As in any type of generation, this must be a composite of matter and form. The matter in this case would correspond to the passive intellect, or to the capacity for becoming all things (cognitionally). The formal element in this composite must be the same in form as the active intellect that has caused it to be.

Since the passive intellect is potentially all beings (cognitionally), it is necessary that it should have no positive quality of its own. For if it did, it could not be, potentially, all things whatsoever. For just as a bitter residue on the tongue prevents one from tasting certain flavors, so too any positive quality in the passive intellect would prevent it from becoming all things whatsoever. Since, then, the mind (as potentially all things) can have no characteristic except its capacity to receive; it can have no actual existence until it thinks (429^a20–24). Until it is actually identical with the object or objects of thought, the mind (as potentially all things) is nothing (430^a1).

The foregoing, however, is in need of some clarification, for the active intellect acts on the passive intellect to make it actually identical with the object or objects of knowledge. Of course, the passive intellect upon which the active intellect acts is not yet identical with the objects of knowledge. For if it already were, there would be no need for the active intellect to act upon it. But until it is actually identical with its object, the passive intellect is nothing. The implication is that the active intellect acts upon nothing at all. One is forced into this strange conclusion, however, only if one forgets a significant distinction that Aristotle had drawn earlier in the *De Anima*. Properly speaking, it is not the soul that pities or learns or thinks, but it is the human being, by means of his soul, that does these things (408^b12–14). Accordingly, it is not the active intellect that knows or the passive intellect that knows, or even a composite of these two. Rather, it is the human being by means of these that knows. The passive intellect therefore designates a potency in the human being, and the active intellect some type of actuality. That *from which* actual knowledge is generated in the human being is the passive intellect. That *by which* actual knowledge is generated in the human being is the active intellect.

As we have already seen, both that *from which* and that *by which* generation takes place must preexist the act of generation itself. Now the type of generation we are presently concerned with is the generation of actual knowledge, the human being's coming to be (cognitionally) the intelligible object that he knows. But how can that *from which* generation takes place (the passive intellect, which is, as of yet, nothing) preexist actual knowing? Again, it is the human being, by means of his soul, that does the knowing. The capacity for knowledge must somehow preexist *in* the human being. Now as we have already seen, knowing entails grasping the intelligible form *in* what is presented through sensation. The objects of knowledge reside potentially in the sensible forms (432^{a}7). Thus one cannot know anything, except through what one has experienced (see *Post. An.* 81^{a}38–^{b}10; *Metap.* 981^{a}4). One cannot become (cognitionally) on the level of intelligibility what one has not already become on the level of sense. Thus, to be more specific, the passive intellect refers to a potency in the human being as *sensitively qualified*—that is, it refers to a potency in the human being who has already become the object on the level of sense. Of course, this is not to say that the passive intellect is in a human being *only insofar* as the human being is sensitively qualified: presumably there is a passive intellect (a capacity for intellectual knowing) even in the hypothetical case of a human being who has never experienced anything at all. But since there cannot be any intellectual knowing without some relevant sense experience, the passive intellect refers most properly to a potency in the human being as sensitively qualified in some way or another. Only in a remote and hypothetical sense does it refer to a potency in the human being who has not had any sense experience. The active intellect, then, does not act on nothing whatsoever, but on a potency in the human being as sensitively qualified. In the next section, I hope to shed some light on what the nature of the active intellect must be—that is, shed some light on what is meant by the preexistent actuality *by which* knowledge is generated in the human being.

The Active Intellect As Actual Knowledge About All Being

As we have already seen, the active intellect and that which it actuates (the actually knowing *nous,* or the human being as actually knowing by the means of his *nous*) must be the same in form. The general form of the active intellect must then be in the class of *nous;* and more specifically, it must be *nous* as actual, for that which actuates must itself be in act. Now *nous* as actual is *nous* as actually knowing, and so the active intellect must be some form of *nous* as actually knowing.[13] Since

13. This is corroborated by at least two significant passages in the Aristotelian *corpus* (see *Posterior Analytics* 71^{a}1 ff. and *Metaphysics* 1049^{b}30 ff.) Aristotle was aware that all knowledge must come from some prior form of knowledge.

nous in act is identical with its object, it would not be inappropriate to identify the active intellect, in shorthand, as a type of knowledge. In addition, it would seem that this type of knowledge must always be actual;[14] for if it were not already actual, it would itself have to be actualized by something else, and this further actuality would have to be the same in form as that which is to be actualized. Thus there would be the need to postulate the existence of another active intellect to actuate this one, and so on *ad infinitum*.[15] Finally, the active intellect must be knowledge about all things whatsoever. For the active intellect is that *by which* the human being becomes (cognitionally) all things (430^{a}15). And if the active intellect were not actual knowledge about all things, then it could not make the human being (cognitionally) all things whatsoever.

This gives rise to two questions. First of all, why would a human being need to come to know about anything at all, if he already knows actually about all things through his active intellect? And secondly, if, in fact, a human being does know actually about all things in virtue of his active intellect, how is this knowledge manifested in him? I believe it is possible to suggest answers to both of these questions by reference, again, to the notion of generation.

The passive intellect, as that *from which* things are made (the matter) (430^{a}11), is potentially all the different members of a given class, but actually none of them. Since the class in this case refers to the class of all beings whatsoever, the passive intellect can be in actuality nothing at all. The passive intellect refers to a potency in the human being, as sensitively qualified, to become on the level of intelligence those things he has already become on the level of sense. The active intellect, as that *by which* all things of a certain class are made (430^{a}12), must in some sense be the general form of those things that it makes. For health comes from health, house from house, and man from man (*Metap.* 1032^{b}12, 1034^{b}3). Since the class in this case refers to the class of all beings whatsoever, the active intellect must in some way be the general form of all beings whatsoever. Since the active intellect is a type of *nous,* it is *cognitionally* the general form of all beings; in other words, it is actual knowledge of this general form. Just as that which causes the production of any sphere

14. Aristotle makes this point explicitly at 430^{a}18.

15. On this matter, I am following Aristotle's own way of proceeding, suggested at 425^{b}12–18. There may be some operation or process that requires actuation by another, or else that in some sense must be actual in itself. If the former alternative suggests the possibility of a problematic infinite regress, then one may well assume that the operation or process in question does contain within itself the principle of its own actuation.

(whether bronze or iron or wood) must be the general form of "sphere" in the mind of the artist, so too that which makes or produces all beings (cognitionally, in the mind of the knower) must be the general form of all being as cognitional, as a type of actual knowledge.

But if the active intellect is to be identified as the actual knowledge of the general form of all beings, what, then, is this general form? What can be said of all beings whatsoever? Roughly stated, the general form of all beings is *that* they have a form. All that is, has a form. Following Aristotle, we can say that the form of something is to be identified with its intelligibility. Thus to know the general form of all beings is to know *that* they all have intelligibility. What the human being knows by means of his active intellect is that all being is intelligible.

This may help explain how a human being may already know about all things in virtue of his active intellect, but still need to come to know particular things.[16] For Aristotle, the principle of individuation is matter (*Metap.* 1034^{a}5–8)[17]; so that if we have the general form of "man" and *this* flesh and *these* bones, we have Socrates and not Callias. By implication, matter is also a principle of limitation. So we may, in fact, have the general form of "man"—a form that must inhere in all men whatsoever—but if we have only *this* flesh and *these* bones, then we have only Socrates and not all men whatsoever. The same applies in the case of coming to know. In this case, the matter—and therefore the principle of individuation and limitation—is a capacity to know that resides in the human being as sensitively qualified. While the human being may know by means of his active intellect that all being is intelligible, he is sensitively qualified only in a certain way. As so qualified, the human being can come to know *this,* but not *that.* Thus one comes to know only through what one has sensed (*Post. An.* 81^{a}38 ff., *Metap.* 981^{a}4).

This general point may be illustrated by means of an analogy with artistic production. In order to make any sphere whatsoever, the artist must have in his mind (or must be intellectually informed by) the form of "sphere" in general (a form that applies to all spheres whatsoever). Still, even if the artist does know this form (or have this form in his mind), the only type of matter available to him may be *this* wood. As a result, the artist makes, not all spheres, but *this* wooden sphere.

16. If, in fact, Aristotle's doctrine of the active intellect did eliminate the need to come to know, then it would be a self-defeating doctrine. For the doctrine of the active intellect is meant (at least in part) to explain how one comes to know when he does not know already.

17. See also Aristotle, *Metaphysics* 1016^{b}32, 1035^{b}27–31, 1054^{a}34, 1074^{a}31–34, and Aristotle, *On the Heavens,* 278^{a}6–^{b}3.

Similarly, the man must know the form of all beings (he must know their intrinsic intelligibility) in order to "make himself" (cognitionally and intelligently) any being whatsoever. Still, even if one does already know (by means of his active intellect) about all his beings whatsoever, he does not thereby know the particular forms of all beings; he must *come to know* with respect to any particular being. The matter that the man is (cognitionally, on the level of sense), is a limiting factor. One cannot become on the intellectual level what one has not already become on the level of sense. To know the form of all spheres whatsoever is not to make all spheres whatsoever; there must also be the requisite matter, and matter is a limiting factor. Similarly, to know the form of all being whatsoever (its intrinsic intelligibility) is not to know the particular forms of all beings whatsoever.

Because it depends on sense data, actual human knowing is limited. As a result, one may know about all being whatsoever, yet still need to come to know particular beings. Still, as we shall later see, even once one has become an object on the level of sense, the mere presence of the active intellect does not guarantee that he will become the object on the intellectual level. The presence of the active intellect and sense data are necessary, but not sufficient, conditions for actual knowing.

I have identified the active intellect as the actual knowledge of the intrinsic intelligibility of all being. Yet to know the intrinsic intelligibility of all being is not to know automatically of the particular intelligibilities of all beings. This interpretation receives some indirect support from other parts of the Aristotelian *corpus*. My account has already revealed a metaphysical principle that underlies Aristotle's doctrine of the active intellect:

> For from the potential the actual is always produced by an actual thing, for example, man by man, musician by musician; there is always a first mover, and the mover already exists actually. We have said in our account of substance that everything that is produced is something produced from something and by something, and is the same in species as it. (*Metap.* 1049^{b}24–29)

But, Aristotle notes directly afterward, this principle has given rise to a certain philosophical difficulty:

> And thence arose the sophistical quibble, that one who does not know a science will be doing that which is the object of science; for he who is learning it does not know it. But since, of that which is coming to be, and, of that which, in general, is changing, some part must have changed (this is shown

in the treatise on movement), he who is learning must, it would seem, know some part of the science. It is surely clear, then, in this way, that the actuality is in this sense also, viz. in order of becoming and of time, prior to the potentiality. (*Metap.* 1049^{b}32–1050a3)

Just as in all becoming, there must also be in the becoming of knowledge some prior actuality, and this the same in form as that which becomes. Thus in order to learn a science, a person must in some sense already know some part of that science itself.

A more complete response to the "sophistical quibble" appears in book I, chapter 1 of the *Posterior Analytics.* Aristotle first presents the problem: "All teaching and all intellectual learning come about from already existing knowledge." (*Post. An.* 71^{a}1) Since all things must come from things that are already in act, and these the same in kind, one must in some sense already know what he comes to know. Before learning something, one does not already know it *simpliciter,* for then one would not really be learning it. Rather, one must know it "universally" (*Post. An.* 71^{a}28). Take, for example, the mathematical proposition that all pairs are even. In virtue of this proposition, one knows about all individual pairs universally, and it is this knowledge that enables him to come to know about certain pairs *simpliciter.* So even if one does not know of the existence of certain pairs, it does not follow that he does not know that all pairs are even. For what is known in the mathematical premise pertains not merely to every number and triangle that is known, but to "every number and triangle *simpliciter*" (*Post. An.* 70^{b}3). Thus one may know the general properties of all members of a certain class, though remain ignorant even about the very existence of certain members within that class. Aristotle concludes:

But nothing, I think, prevents one from in a sense understanding and in a sense being ignorant of what one is learning; for what is absurd is not that you should know in some sense what you are learning, but that you should know it in *this* sense, i.e., in the way and sense in which you are learning it. (*Post. An.* 70^{b}6–9)

If what Aristotle writes here is generalized to refer not merely to knowledge of a particular science, but to knowledge of anything whatsoever, the result will be—very roughly—what I have argued is Aristotle's doctrine of the active intellect. As I have tried to show, one may know (in virtue of one's active intellect) the general form (the intrinsic intelligibility) of all members in the class of being, yet still not know of the particular forms or even the existence of several members within that class. Thus one already knows about all beings "universally," but not *simpliciter.* While this generalization from knowledge of a particular science to knowledge of any being whatsoever is not explicit in Aristotle, I do not believe it is out of line with his thought. Again, as Aristotle writes, "All teaching and all intellectual learning come about from already existing knowledge." (*Post. An.* 71ᵃ1). Thus even the general principles that ground the particular forms of knowledge in a certain science must themselves be derived from some other type of knowledge. And this other type of knowledge—if it is knowledge—must also be derived from some other type. This process will continue *ad infinitum* until one finally hits upon some final type of knowledge that is not itself derived from any other.

But what kind of knowledge must this final type be? This kind of knowledge, I suggest, is what one knows by means of his active intellect. It must be about all being whatsoever, if it is the kind of knowledge that all other knowledge presupposes. Furthermore, insofar as this final type of knowledge must not be derived or demonstrable from any other, it must in some sense be always actual;[18] otherwise, the infinite regress would continue. Finally, while my generalization from a particular science to knowledge of any being whatsoever is not explicit in Aristotle, I do believe it is in line with the general tendency of his thought, for, as Aristotle writes, it is the distinction between knowledge of a thing universally (which must preexist) and knowledge of a thing *simpliciter* (which comes to be) that is crucial in surmounting the *aporia* in Plato: "Otherwise the puzzle in the *Meno* will result; for you will learn either nothing or what you know" (*Post. An.* 71ᵃ30; see also 67ᵃ21). And the problem in the *Meno* is not about the coming to be of knowledge in just any one science, but of the coming to be of any knowledge whatsoever.

Just as knowledge of any particular mathematical entity presupposes the prior and universal knowledge about all mathematical entities of that type, so too, it seems, knowledge of any particular being presupposes some knowledge of all beings whatsoever. To know the general form, or intrinsic intelligibility, of all being, however, is not to know the *forms* of all beings. It seems to follow from what has been said so far that knowledge of the intrinsic intelligibility of all being must be preconceptual and prelinguistic. For the intelligent grasp and meaningful use of concepts and words are themselves functions of one's knowledge of particular things. If knowledge of the intrinsic intelligibility of all being (by

18. Aristotle writes that the essence of active intellect is *energeia* (430ᵃ18).

means of one's active intellect) is itself the prior condition of all such particular knowledge, then evidently it cannot itself be conceptual or linguistic. This brings us to the second crucial question posed at the beginning of this section: if, in fact, a man does know actually about all things in virtue of his active intellect, how is this knowledge manifested in him? It may be manifested linguistically or conceptually only in a derivative sense. For example, I may now express such knowledge in the direct philosophical proposition: "All being is intelligible." But presumably, one knows of the intrinsic intelligibility of all being, even before he acquires the specific ability to use such words and concepts.[19] In fact, such knowledge is requisite to the acquisition and meaningful use of such words and concepts. If not through words or concepts, how is the primordial knowledge of the intrinsic intelligibility of being expressed? To this topic we turn in the next section.

Actual Knowledge About All Being and Its Expression

I would like to suggest that the knowledge of the intrinsic intelligibility of being that one has in virtue of his active intellect is expressed, not directly by means of words or concepts, but indirectly through the wonder (*thauma*) that Aristotle says is the beginning of all science and philosophy (*Metap.* 982[b]12), and indeed of all intellectual knowledge whatsoever. Aristotle writes:

> For all men begin, as we said, by wondering that the matter is so (as in the case of automatic marionettes or the solstices or the incommensurability of the diagonal of a square with its side; for it seems wonderful to all men who have not yet perceived the explanation that there is a thing which cannot be measured even by the smallest unit). (*Metap.* 983[a]14–18)

One wonders about that for which an explanation is not yet known (in this case, for example, of automatic marionettes, the solstices, or the incommensurable diagonal). But what is presupposed in this and all wonder is that there is an explanation to be known; in other words, that all things are intelligible. Thus knowledge of the intrinsic intelligibility of all being (which one has by means of his active intellect) finds indirect expression in wonder. Since one comes to know things (even concepts and words) only by first wondering, this wonder may be both preconceptual and prelinguistic.

19. Furthermore, even if all human beings know of the intrinsic intelligibility of being in virtue of their active intellects, it is clear that not all express it in such philosophical propositions. How, then, is it expressed even in the nonphilosopher?

This is corroborated in a further passage, where Aristotle writes that wonder does, in fact, presuppose a type of knowledge: "A man who is puzzled and wonders thinks himself ignorant" (*Metap.* $982^{b}18$). Now there can be no ignorance unless there is something to be known. And what is to be known must be knowable and therefore intelligible. Naturally, what is to be known cannot be known already *simpliciter,* for then there would be no ignorance concerning it, and therefore no need to wonder and find out. Yet while the thing to be known cannot be known *simpliciter,* there is something about it that must be known, and this is, roughly stated, that there is something *to be* known (and therefore something knowable and intelligible). Were this not known, then one would not think himself ignorant, and there would be no reason for wonder. Thus no matter how unintelligible something appears *to us* (take, for example, the case of the automatic marionettes), our wonder about it always betrays our primordial knowledge that it must in some way be intelligible *in itself* (see the *Physics* $184^{a}16$ for this distinction). Thus when one wonders, one already knows in a way, but in another not (see, again, *Post. An.* $71^{a}25$f.). One does not know the thing *simpliciter;* if one did, there would be no need to wonder. But one does know the thing "universally" (*Post. An.* $71^{a}28$), as something *to be* known (as knowable or intelligible); for if this were not presupposed, there would be no wonder about it, and therefore no coming to know about it in itself.

Were it not for our knowledge of the intrinsic intelligibility of all being, we would not wonder and seek a reason for the yet unknown (for how does one know that the unknown is intelligible, if it is yet unknown?); and thus no other knowledge would come to be.[20] Yet while one must know of the intrinsic intelligibility of all being, it does not follow that he must know of the intelligibilities of all beings. Aristotle draws an analogy between the active intellect (what I have identified as our knowledge of the intelligibility of all being) and light at $430^{a}17$. Light is a kind of color ($418^{b}12$) by which all other colors are mediated, but that does not contain within itself the determinations of any of the colors in the spectrum.[21] Similarly, knowledge of the intrinsic intelligibility of all being (the active intellect) is a type of knowledge by which all other knowledge is mediated, but that does not contain within itself the deter-

20. This is confirmed by the last line of *De Anima* III.5 ($430^{a}25$), if one accepts the last of the four possible renderings that Sir David Ross suggests: "and without the active reason nothing knows"; see his Ross, *Aristotle,* 152.

21. This, of course, is according to Aristotelian physics.

minations of any particular knowledge. Thus one may know the general form of all being without knowing the forms of all beings. Furthermore, just as the presence of light is the necessary but not sufficient condition for the actualization of color, so too the presence of the active intellect (actual knowledge of the intelligibility of all being) seems to be necessary but not sufficient for the actualization of particular forms of knowledge. Finally, we do not see the light directly, but see it only indirectly by seeing other colors mediated through it. Similarly, we do not know directly of the intelligibility of all being; we do not begin with the formally expressed premise that all being is intelligible, then deduce other knowledge from it. Rather, we come to know several particular things first (by means of the active intellect), then discover only later that this particular knowledge presupposes the more fundamental knowledge of the intelligibility of all being.

As we have seen, the fundamental expression of one's knowledge of the intrinsic intelligibility of being is not conceptual or linguistic. For knowledge of the intrinsic intelligibility of being is the prior condition of the coming to be of all particular forms of knowledge, and the proper use of words and concepts is possible only if some particular knowledge has already come to be. Thus, knowledge of the intrinsic intelligibility of all being precedes all words and concepts. I have therefore suggested that one's knowledge of the intrinsic intelligibility of being is expressed only indirectly through one's wonder. One does not wonder and seek reasons unless he knows already that there is something to be known. Furthermore, while knowledge of the intrinsic intelligibility of being is not expressed fundamentally in words or concepts, one may, with time, acquire the words and concepts necessary for giving direct expression to such knowledge. Finally, while wonder (as the indirect expression of the knowledge of the intrinsic intelligibility of all being) may itself be caused (*Mechanics* 847^{a}11), such knowledge itself is neither derived nor demonstrable nor caused. A person's wonder is compelled by those things that seem unintelligible to him; but one would never be so compelled to understand unless he first knew that—no matter how unintelligible things seemed to him—they are intelligible in themselves.

Two Possible Objections

I shall dedicate the final section of this chapter to anticipating what I consider might be two very reasonable objections to my account thus far. I argued in the last section that our wonder about things presupposes and thereby gives indirect expression to our knowledge of the intrinsic intelligibility of being. Of course, one may argue that, in wondering, one does not *know* of, but one merely expresses some sort of *faith* in, the intrinsic intelligibility of being. Of course, I have not tried to suggest that our wondering alone is sufficient to demonstrate our knowledge of the intrinsic intelligibility of being; such knowledge is only expressed (indirectly) in such wonder. Nevertheless, I believe that there are sufficient passages in the Aristotelian *corpus* to support the claim that, in wondering, one not only anticipates, but actually *knows* (in a primordial and underived way) of the intrinsic intelligibility of being.

The principle that all being is intelligible seems for Aristotle to entail, and to be entailed by, the principle of noncontradiction. Now all being is intelligible if and only if all beings have a form; for Aristotle identifies the form of a thing with its intelligibility. Furthermore, there is form if and only if there is definiteness; for Aristotle, the "definite" is the formal cause. Now for Aristotle, the principle of noncontradiction applies once there is something "defined" or "definite" (where there is form) (*Metap.* 1006^{b}1, 1006^{b}4, 1008^{a}34). Conversely, where there is only indefiniteness (i.e., only matter and therefore no form), the principle of noncontradiction does not apply, and there can be no possibility of meaningful dialogue (*Metap.* 1006^{b}6–7). By the logical operation of transportation, this latter assertion is convertible to the proposition that, if the principle of noncontradiction applies, then there is definiteness and therefore form. Thus if the principle of noncontradiction applies, there is form (intelligibility); and if there is form (intelligibility), the principle of noncontradiction applies. Thus the principle of noncontradiction applies if and only if the things under discussion are intelligible. By implication, the principle of noncontradiction applies universally if and only if all beings are intelligible.[22]

For Aristotle, it is clear that the principle of noncontradiction is not demonstrable nor—strictly speaking—need it be so (*Metap.* 1006^{a}8–12). For anyone who attempts to deny it must implicitly affirm it, even in his denying; as soon as the skeptic says anything he takes to be meaningful, he has already confirmed the principle (*Metap.* 1006^{a}13). Since the principle of noncontradiction cannot be denied with self-referential consistency, it is self-evident (*Metap.* 1006^{a}12). There can be no demonstration of this principle, nor need there be. In fact, any demonstration of any

22. On form as the basis of the principle of noncontradiction, see Joseph Owens, *The Doctrine of Being in the Aristotelian Metaphysics* (Toronto: Pontifical Institute of Medieval Studies, 1951), 166–67.

truth whatsoever already presupposes the truth of this principle (*Metap.* $1006^{a}22$). By implication, to know that the principle of noncontradiction applies in some case, is to know of some definiteness, form, or intelligibility. Furthermore, since one knows primordially that the principle of noncontradiction applies universally, one knows primordially that all being is intelligible. Since this is a type of knowledge that can have no demonstration and that needs no demonstration, it is a type of knowledge that is in some sense always actual; furthermore, it is presupposed by all other forms of knowledge.

Thus when one wonders, one not only assumes, but one also knows of the intrinsic intelligibility of all being. In one's questions, one not only anticipates intelligibility, but one knows that there is some intelligibility to be grasped. This is not to say, of course, that a *particular* intelligibility anticipated by a certain question will necessarily be discovered. Questions, and indeed entire research projects, may be misguided, wrongheaded, ill-informed. But even if a particular anticipated intelligibility is not discovered, it does not mean that there is no intelligibility to be discovered at all. While certain anticipated intelligibilities may be doubted, what is not doubted is the intrinsic intelligibility of being itself. (Such cannot be doubted with self-referential consistency, since for Aristotle, to doubt this is to doubt also the principle of noncontradiction). One might say that the principle of noncontradiction and the intrinsic intelligibility of being are known self-evidently.

I believe that this is Aristotle's meaning when he writes that the active intellect "is in its essential nature activity" ($430^{a}18$). It is clear that he does not mean that one must always cogitate or think (see $430^{a}7$ and *Metap.* $1072^{b}24$). Rather, he seems to mean that the knowledge we have of the intrinsic intelligibility of being (which is to be identified with the active intellect) cannot and need not be demonstrated. Insofar as such knowledge cannot be caused or induced, it is always actual. Any other rational demonstration presupposes such knowledge. This, of course, does not mean that one must always think, but rather that one cannot think without presupposing this kind of knowledge. So as long as one is in a position to know anything (i.e., as long as one is conscious and intellectually aware), he must know—however inexplicitly—that all being is intelligible. Without this underived type of knowledge, no other knowledge would come to be.[23]

23. Again, this is corroborated if one accepts the last of Ross's four possible renderings of $430^{a}25$: "and without the active reason nothing knows"; see note 20, above.

A second possible objection to my account concerns whether the active intellect should be identified as the efficient cause of the coming to be of knowledge. In my account, I have consciously resisted such an identification.[24] I have noted in several places that the presence of the active intellect seems to be a necessary but not sufficient condition for the actualization of knowledge. I have shown that the presence of an appropriate sense content is also a necessary condition in the coming to be of knowledge. But even when the requisite sense content or image is present, along with the active intellect, still no actual knowledge is guaranteed. Thus one may know already that all being is intelligible, and in virtue of this knowledge wonder and ask questions about the image or sense data before him, yet still fail to achieve the desired increment in knowing. One may have already become an object on the level of sense, and may already know (by means of active intellect) that all being is intelligible; but one may still be unable to have the relevant insight or become the object on the intellectual level. Thus even the simultaneous presence of the active intellect and the relevant image is only a necessary, but not quite sufficient condition for the occurrence of actual understanding (or specific intellectual knowing). Just as the presence of light is a necessary but not sufficient condition for the actualization of a particular color, so too, it seems, the presence of the active intellect is a necessary but not sufficient condition for the occurrence of actual understanding.

In spite of my refusal to identify the active intellect explicitly with the necessary and sufficient condition of one's coming to know, one might object that my heavy reliance on the notion of generation may betray this basic intention. For in Aristotle's writing on generation (*Metap.* Z.7–9, esp. 1034^{a}22–1034^{b}8; also the *Physics* 198^{a}25), the efficient cause (in both natural and artistic production) is identified with the final and formal cause. It would appear, then, that the necessary and sufficient condition for the coming to be of knowledge would be the presence of the active intellect (the formal, final, and efficient cause) in the man as sensitively qualified and possessed of a passive intellect (the matter, or material cause). Of course, this conclusion stands in direct contradiction with the conclusion suggested by the light analogy.

I believe there is no real contradiction here if a crucial distinction is kept in mind. As John Rist writes:

24. Joseph Owens offers some good reasons for resisting such an identification. See "Aristotelian Soul as Cognitive of Sensibles, Intelligibles, and Self," in *Aristotle: The Collected Papers of Joseph Owens*, edited by John R. Catan (Albany: State University of New York Press, 1981), 96.

As we know from the *Metaphysics* (1071ª20–22), Man is the father of man, but there is no such existent as Man. Rather we should say that Peleus is the father of Achilles. Similarly Art is not the efficient cause of the sculpturing of a block of marble into the form of a statue. The cause is rather the particular form of the statue in the mind of the sculptor who is the efficient cause of the product.[25]

Thus the efficient cause and sufficient condition of the production of the artwork are not merely an idea in the mind of the artist, but rather this idea in the mind of this particular artist. With this sort of qualification, it becomes possible to include further determinations that would make the idea in the artist's mind both the necessary and sufficient condition for artistic production. For example, presupposed in such artistic production is an appetitive element. As Aristotle writes in the *De Anima* III. 9, knowledge itself is not a sufficient condition for motion in the individual; and disease can be produced by the medical art no less than health can. (Metap. 1032b2–4) So it is not merely the idea per se in the mind of the artist that is the efficient cause of the artistic production, but this idea in the mind of this artist, as so predisposed appetitively. Such will guarantee the appropriate action. Thus a valid practical syllogism will "force" the relevant action (see Mov. An., ch. 7). It is not, then, merely the idea in the mind of the artist that is the efficient cause of the artistic production; rather it is this idea in the mind of this artist who is predisposed appetitively in this way. In the artist in whom such appetitive conditions already exist, an idea may become the efficient cause of artistic production; in itself, the idea (like light) remains a necessary but not sufficient condition.

In a similar way, the active intellect alone is not the efficient cause of the occurrence of knowing in the man. Rather, the efficient cause is the active intellect in *this* man, who is already predisposed sensitively and intellectually in a certain way. With this sort of qualification, it becomes possible to include other factors that would then make the active intellect not only the necessary but also the sufficient condition for the actualization of knowledge in the individual. As we have already seen, the idea in the mind of the artist is not automatically the efficient cause of the artwork. So, too, the active intellect is not automatically the efficient cause of knowing in the thinker who is already (cognitionally) the object

25. John M. Rist, "Notes on Aristotle's *De Anima* 3.5," *Classical Philology* 61 (January 1966): 8. While I believe Rist is correct about this, I am not convinced that he can be so certain with regard to his conclusions about the immanence of the active intellect. Of course, a rigorous treatment of this issue is well beyond the scope of the present effort.

on the level of sense. Certain other conditions must be fulfilled in the man if the active intellect is to become the efficient cause of his knowing. But once those conditions are fulfilled, the active intellect does become the sufficient condition for his knowing. Like light, the active intellect is not automatically a necessary and sufficient condition. But in a man predisposed properly, it *can* be such. As a result, when light does, in fact, actualize certain colors, it may be called the efficient cause of such actualization. But it is not called so *qua* light alone; it is the efficient cause as light in *this* circumstance.

A final question then remains: what is the prior condition in the man that must be fulfilled if the active intellect is to be the efficient cause of knowledge in him? In other words, how must *this* man be qualified if the active intellect is to be the efficient cause of knowledge in him? As already noted, being sensitively qualified alone cannot suffice; for one may be perceiving the requisite image, yet still fail to understand it on the intellectual level. I believe that an answer is suggested in the *Metaphysics*, book IX, chapter 9. There Aristotle writes that the proper alignment of the image in the man as sensitively qualified will guarantee that understanding will take place: "If, then, the line parallel to the side had been already drawn, the theorem would have been evident to anyone as soon as he saw the figure." (*Metap.* 1051^{a}26) In practical action, one's desires must be aligned properly; and so too in knowing, the image must be aligned properly. Once the relevant elements in an image are arranged in a suitable constellation, the act of understanding cannot but take place.

Of course, what constitutes a properly aligned image will vary with each individual and will depend—in part—on how much the individual already knows. Thus one cannot prescribe in any universal fashion what the necessary and sufficient conditions will be for the occurrence of acts of understanding in human beings. Furthermore, what an individual already knows will determine to some extent how successful he will be in aligning an image in his mind's eye, so that the image is most conducive to new acts of understating. Accordingly, one's previous acts of knowing make possible still further development in one's knowing, and there arises the possibility of geometric (and not merely arithmetic) progress in one's knowing. As Aristotle illuminatingly writes: "For it is owing to their wonder that men now begin and at first began to philosophize; they wondered originally at obvious difficulties, then advanced little by little and stated difficulties about the greater matters" (*Metap.* 982^{b}12).

John W. Burbidge

5. REVISITING ANSELM'S ONTOLOGICAL ARGUMENT

There is something beguiling about Anselm's argument for the existence of God. By combining a negation with a comparison, it creates a definition that is both subtle and ambiguous. By telling us more about what God is not than about what he is, it bears a whiff of Eastern negative theology. And the delicate relationship between thought and existence, between concept and reality, carries within it the ongoing puzzle about how our (very human) reflections and theoretical constructions could possibly lead us to conclusions about what the world is really like, beyond all appearances.

Intrigued by these considerations, it is tempting to attempt a rethinking of the argument to see whether it can bear the weight that Anselm puts upon it: can we in fact be driven to conclude that God exists simply on the basis of a definition? One such attempt will be the focus of this paper. We shall start from the crucial definition of the deity, upon which every step of the reasoning hangs, and explore possible meanings that might unfold its full potential.

"We believe," writes Anselm, "that thou art a being than which none greater can be thought."[1] The original does not have that question-begging term "being," but rather a much more innocuous "something":

1. I am using Anselm, *Proslogion*, tr. Eugene Fairweather, in *The Library of Christian Classics*, vol. 10, *A Scholastic Miscellany: Anselm to Ockham* (Philadelphia: Westminster Press, 1956), 73.

"aliquid qua nihil maius cogitari possit." But even so we have a—puzzle. What does it mean to think; what is involved in "cogitation"? Gaunilon, in attempting a refutation, thinks of a perfect island; Kant of a hundred thalers. For Gaunilon and Kant, as for John Locke and David Hume, thoughts are pale copies of experiences that have impressed themselves on our mind—images that can be manipulated to eradicate all imperfection. But their examples, used in refutation, only highlight a fundamental ambiguity in that term "cogitari." For some translations have rendered it with "conceive," a stronger term that somehow seems to escape such imaginative constructions. "Thinking" can well be used for both. But are conceiving and imagining identical? And can results drawn from one type of cogitation justify conclusions that apply to all sorts? What, indeed, does it mean to think?

It is Gottlob Frege who makes this ambiguity explicit. Taking his stand against the introspective psychology of the late nineteenth century, Frege distinguishes "between image and concept, between imagination and thought."[2] For the former, which includes "sensations" and "mental pictures, formed from the amalgamated traces of earlier sense impressions,"[3] Frege adopts the term *Vorstellung,* which his English translators, drawing on Locke and Hume, render as "idea," but which is also translated by "representation" in texts from Kant and Hegel. For the latter, he uses *Begriff* and *Denken,* regularly translated as "concept" and "thought."

For Frege, the problem with *Vorstellungen* or ideas is that they are subjective. "A man never has somebody else's mental image, but only his own; and nobody even knows how far his image (say) of red agrees with somebody else's."[4] Ideas are frequently saturated with feeling; they are internal images, "arising from memories of sense impressions which I have had and acts, both internal and external, which I have performed." As a result it is highly unlikely that two people will have the same idea or *Vorstellung* for any term that they happen to use in conversation. "A painter, a horseman, and a zoologist will probably connect different ideas with the name 'Bucephalus.'"[5] Because "an idea in the subjective

2. Gottlob Frege, "Review of Husserl's *Philosophie der Arithmetik,*" reprinted in *Translations from the Philosophical Writings of Gottlob Frege,* edited by Peter Geach and Max Black, 79 (Oxford: Blackwell, 1966).

3. Frege, *The Foundations of Arithmetic,* trans. J. L. Austin (New York: Harper, 1960), xvii.

4. Frege, "Review of Husserl," 79.

5. Frege, "On Sense and Reference," in *The Frege Reader,* edited by Michael Beaney, 154 (Oxford: Blackwell, 1997).

sense is what is governed by the laws of association, it is of a sensible, pictorial character"; and so ideas may well be demonstrably different in different people.[6]

Frege distinguishes this subjectivity of *Vorstellungen* or ideas from the objectivity of concepts and thought. Thus, in "On Sense and Reference," he refers to the sense of a sign, "which may be the common property of many people, and so is not a part or a mode of the individual mind."[7] Because "one and the same thought can be grasped by many men[, . . .] the constituents of the thought, and *a fortiori* things themselves, must be distinguished from the images that accompany in some minds the act of grasping the thought—images that each man forms of things."[8]

A similar contrast between *Vorstellungen* and *Begriffe*—representations and concepts—is drawn by Hegel, who claims that "philosophy does nothing but transform representations into thoughts—although, of course, it does go on to transform the mere thought into the concept."[9] But he does not draw the sharp distinction that Frege does. To be sure, "*representation* has sensible material . . . as its content; but it is posited in the determination of its being *mine*—that the represented content is in *me*—and of its *universality,* of its self-relation, or of its *simplicity.* Apart from the sensible, however, representation also has material that has sprung from self-conscious thinking as its content, such as the notion of what is right, of what is ethical or religious, and also of thinking itself."[10] So representations have some features that relate to the basic meaning or sense of a term. For Hegel, then, the task is to draw the right separation between the isolation and subjectivity of representations or ideas and the objectivity of pure thought—the sense of concepts. They are not thoughts that stem from two quite different sources.

So it is worth our while to reflect on the difference between ideas and concepts—between representations and pure thoughts. For that may well have a bearing on the reliability of Anselm's reasoning.

While the British empiricists have made the philosophical world familiar with the way representations develop from the immediate im-

6. Frege, *The Foundations of Arithmetic,* 37.

7. In *Frege Reader,* 154.

8. Frege, "Review of Husserl," in *Writings,* 79.

9. G. W. F. Hegel, *The Encyclopaedia Logic,* trans. T. F. Geraets, W. A. Suchting and H. S. Harris (Indianapolis: Hackett, 1991), 50, §20. I have deliberately used lowercase for "concept" to remove its mysterious quality.

10. Ibid., 49.

pressions of sensation and reflection so that they retain something of the specificity of their origins, less attention has been paid to the formation of concepts. For Frege, they are simply abstract entities, there to be discovered: "Thoughts are not mental entities, and thinking is not the mental generation of such entities but the grasping of thoughts which are already present objectively."[11] Yet, for all that these concepts appear to exist in the eternity of a Platonic heaven, we can think them; our minds are able to "grasp" their sense. Indeed, Frege goes to great lengths to clarify for us the concepts he wants to use in establishing the foundations of arithmetic. So there may be some merit in following Hegel, in his Psychology, when he traces the way different intellectual functions develop—a path that leads us from the most basic intuitions we have of the world through representations to the objectivity of pure thought. As language becomes so familiar that we can talk without thinking, he suggests, our thoughts lose their focus on retained images and memories, and can center on the sense that enables a word to apply in many different contexts. For Hegel realized that representations are not just the faded images of imagination. The images are conjoined with a sense that enables them to be applied to cases other than those directly remembered. And that sense is not a direct result of our experiences, but involves intellectual mediation.

Consider what happens when we want to define a term. We first set it within a general context, and then draw distinctions, isolating it from those elements of the context that are inappropriate or are to be excluded from our consideration. Critical here is the ability to notice differences and highlight contrasts. Our minds do not passively experience differences; we compare, pay attention to contrasting features, and recognize that some are more significant than others.[12] Despite the theoretical assumptions of Locke and Hume, there are no impressions for the particle "not."

Concepts result from this kind of mental initiative. By drawing distinctions within general contexts, they isolate a distinctive and particular sense. That nucleus of meaning retains, however, tentacles that reach out toward other terms and other concepts. Implicit is its being embed-

11. Frege, "Letter to Husserl (1906)," in *Frege Reader,* 302.

12. In the midst of one of his *Metalogues,* "What Is An Instinct?" Gregory Bateson has a delightful episode in which the conclusion is reached that "the 'not' is absent in animal behavior because 'not' is part of verbal language, and there cannot be any action signal for 'not'"; see Bateson, *Steps to an Ecology of Mind: Collected Essays in Anthropology, Psychiatry, Evolution, and Epistemology* (Northvale, N.J., and London: Jason Aronson, 1987), 55.

ded within the more general framework of meaning; and essential to its significance are the contrasts with other elements of that "genus"—elements through which its specific limits are crystallized and established. Indeed the network of meanings extends further. For a particular term can contain within its own meaning a number of elements and moments brought together in a specific way to generate its singular import. Those elements are not simply collected into a haphazard assembly, but bonded together by means of other tentacles of meaning, so that they can be integrated into a compact unity.[13] Once again, the tentacles of meaning that bind this complex together are not the result of our immediate sensations and associations, but the work of thought, applied to the conceptual resources of our minds.

It has long been understood that thought and reasoning involve analysis and synthesis. The process of grasping or developing concepts involves variations of these two functions: drawing discriminations and integrating a diversity of subordinate thoughts into a unity. This pattern of conceiving, then, can in its pure form be distinguished from the representations that have emerged from our experiences, and that follow each other in streams of consciousness according to associations remembered from the past, emotions affecting us in the present, and desires projecting us into the future. For all that these ideas retain elements of sense and meaning, only pure concepts manage to free themselves from the temporal flow of our subjective lives and, through language, become the coins of intellectual commerce with our fellows.

There is, however, one further aspect of concepts that is often overlooked. Locke and Hume turned to ideas and representations because discourse on ethics and religion too readily moved into the realm of abstraction, theoretical confusion, and disagreement. They wanted to ensure that our thoughts had some purchase on reality. If our representations are the copies of our sensations and impressions, they assumed, they can provide a solid basis for drawing conclusions about the way the world is. However, as Frege has argued, that goal is frustrated by the very processes they describe; the resulting ideas are conditioned by the particularity of the original experiences and the feelings that accompanied their occurrence; they easily reflect subjective and idiosyncratic interests. Nonetheless, the initial concern that triggered the empiricists' quest retains its legitimacy. If ideas and representations cannot do justice to this concern for

13. It is Kant, in the *Critique of Pure Reason*, who contrasts the integrated unity of a concept with the simple synthesis of imagination; see B 102–4.

adequate knowledge about the world, is there any way by which concepts can be more successful?

Indeed there may be. When Descartes sets out the rules for his method, he first insists that we should only trust what our minds confirm as reliable. The process of confirmation then involves three steps: drawing distinctions ("divide each of the difficulties"); generating complex unities ("beginning with the simplest and ascending little by little to knowledge of the most complex"); and taking as comprehensive a perspective as possible ("reviews so comprehensive, that I could be sure of leaving nothing out").[14] While the first two steps remind us of the analytical and synthetic functions in concept formation already discussed, the last step introduces considerations that can take us beyond the thinking mind to its interaction with the environment.[15]

To be sure, Descartes does not make that move. But, as Charles Sanders Peirce and other pragmatists realized, when one considers what it would mean for a concept to be comprehensive, one realizes that it needs in some way to capture the way the world actually is.[16] This is clearest in the area of biology. The way a definition takes a general framework and introduces distinctions has turned out to be fairly effective in capturing the relationship among various birds or flowers. We start with a genus, and then introduce a difference that will adequately isolate the species. Over the years we have learned from experience that some definitions (like "featherless biped") do not capture what is essential about a species, and have adjusted our concepts until they do match. And matches become the stronger when we find, within the internal workings of a species, the interconnections that have led it to become distinct from related animals of the same genus—the genetic roots and the environmental challenges to survival. Through our experience of the world we discover what links and conceptual patterns are inappropriate to the nature of things, and gradually replace them with better and more effective thoughts that enable us better to understand why

14. *Discourse on Method,* in *The Philosophical Writings of Descartes,* trans. John Cottingham, Robert Stoothoff, and Dugald Murdoch (Cambridge: Cambridge University Press, 1985), I, 120.

15. Though Descartes did not draw that implication.

16. Consider Peirce's pragmatic maxim: "Consider what effects, that might conceivably have practical bearings, we conceive the object of our conception to have. Then our conception of these effects is the whole of our conception of the object," in "How to Make Our Ideas Clear," in *Collected Papers of Charles Sanders Peirce,* edited by Charles Hartshorne and Paul Weiss, vol. 5, 258 (Cambridge, Mass.: Harvard University Press, 1934).

things are the way they are. Only by taking account of our experiences and learning from them do our concepts begin to be comprehensive.

That pattern by which, over time, our concepts are refined so they begin to capture reality works well in areas such as biology and the other natural sciences where we want a kind of thinking that enables us to predict, fairly accurately, what is likely to happen in the future. But the relationship between concepts and reality becomes murkier when we apply our thoughts to the human and social realm. For here the concepts we form do not simply describe, but structure and organize, the way we act in the world. And those actions construct a reality that was not there before. To be sure, concepts become refined as we put them into practice. The "liberty" that was the goal of the French Revolution started out as a freedom from the oppression of the feudal state, but the term became much modified as we learned through the extremes of the Reign of Terror and the events of the nineteenth century that freedom is achieved most effectively within a framework of law, where individual discretion, particularly on the part of those who govern, is restricted. It may take a long time, indeed millennia, before our human experience learns that something like absolute monarchy (or dictatorship) does not produce a vibrant and productive society. And when we come to economic concepts like "recession" and "depression," we find that the fluctuating dynamic that characterizes how markets function does not easily provide distinct dividing lines that will facilitate clear predictions. If the construction of theories (which are really complex concepts) can take place in physics and chemistry within a fairly rigorous framework of experimental testing, the more amorphous process of human history makes it more difficult to achieve a fully comprehensive conceptual understanding.

Indeed, there may be a more structural reason for such inconclusive results. It may be the case that time introduces genuine novelties—realities that did not previously exist—that can only be grasped once they have occurred. Such a possibility is at least suggested in the natural world as we have come to understand the processes of evolution. It is certainly characteristic of history, where it is our very ability to look back to the past that enables us to react to events in radically new ways. And new capacities produce new possibilities. Without the development of instant communication around the world, for example, we could not begin to entertain the thought of a global society, with a fabric of institutions that begin to approximate a world government.

Be that as it may, it is clear that our concepts become more comprehensive as they show themselves to be successful in describing the world and in predicting what is likely to happen. The features that distinguish concepts from representations and ideas—the discriminations among distinct elements, and the tentacles that link aspects and components together—are to capture as best they may natural and historical types and those networks of reciprocal causes that make things function the way they do. Any thought that fails in some way or other is less satisfactory than a comparable one that, to the present, has not. Essential to the process of grasping concepts is this progressive adaptation of our thoughts to the way the world is organized.

By introducing the test of comprehensiveness to our understanding of concepts we have come to the conclusion that clear concepts are the result of human experience. Over the ages we have refined the reliability of our thoughts by matching the distinctions they draw to the significant types discovered in the world, and discovering the links by which things differentiate themselves from each other and integrate their internal diversity into a unity. There is no need, then, to appeal to Frege's Platonic heaven to ensure that concepts escape the subjectivity and unreliability of ideas and representations. Human interaction with the world and among ourselves has refined our thoughts to the point where they achieve a permanence that extends well beyond the idiosyncratic interests of particular individuals.

But it does something else. For the test of comprehensiveness enables us to compare concepts and to decide that some are better than others. In particular, it means that whenever a concept fails in its description of the way things are, we are confronted with the challenge of finding some concept that will be better and more successful.

With this final observation we are ready to return to Anselm's definition of God: "something than which none greater can be thought" "*aliquid quo nihil maius cogitari possit.*" For we now have a standard by which we can measure how one thought may be greater than another. That thought will have to be more comprehensive in successfully describing the world, with all its complexity.

Such thoughts cannot be ideas or representations. Retained images and memories by themselves cannot fill this role. Even though our normal representations function because they carry with them elements of conceptual meaning that enable us to communicate effectively with our fellows, that significance is not understood through clear discrimination and conceptual integration, but remains a sense learned and retained from our early education, and carries with it irrelevant emotional baggage. One needs to move into the refined air of pure concepts, where we struggle to keep our thoughts rigorously defined and are familiar with how effectively they apply in our historical life, before we can begin to compare concepts and decide which are genuinely greater and which need to be rejected. The only adequate translation for Anselm's *cogitari,* then, is "to be conceived." Because "to be thought" can include not only rigorous thought but also imagination and the flow of representations, it is much too ambiguous, allowing the facile refutations put forward by Gaunilon and Kant with their appeals to perfect islands and one hundred thalers. Perfection is not what fits with the ideal creations of our imagination, but rather what adequately understands all that there is to know.

So what are we looking for, when we start out with Anselm's definition? We are looking for an understanding of the way the world is, such that, once we grasp it fully, we shall never again find ourselves discovering its comprehensive inadequacy. Or more precisely, the definition tells us that, whenever we learn from experience that a conceptual explanation is flawed, we know it cannot be describing God—that being than which no greater can be conceived. The goal of our quest is to find the ultimate rationale that explains why everything in nature and human affairs is the way it is.

In an interesting way, this definition of God was captured by Kant, despite his rejection of the ontological argument. In his introduction to the section of the *Critique of Pure Reason* on "The Idea of Pure Reason," he suggests that, in our effort to understand the world, we need to understand why things are the way they are. Each entity is determined to be what it is by deriving the predicates that describe it from the sum total of all possibilities—in German, *der Inbegriff aller Möglichkeiten.* Ultimately this means fitting things into the framework of a disjunctive syllogism: in the major premise we have the conception of all real possibilities; in the minor premise we show why many of these cannot apply; in the conclusion we show that the entity can only be what it in fact is. In other words we have a framework of explanation, through which the connections and interrelationships that determine why things are the way they are can be fully understood. Kant goes on to say that, in our rational quest for completeness, this sum total of all real possibilities, together with the fact that these function in such a way as to determine the specific determination of individual things, should be integrated into something singular and comprehensive, a unity that integrates universal reality. This, he says, would be the concept of God.[17] God is not simply equated with nature in the manner of Spinoza; but he is the reason why, given the sum total of all possibilities, things are the way they are.

Kant concludes, however, by pointing out that the rational necessity of such an ideal does not entail its actual existence. It is possible that the universe, and reality generally, do not have a single integrated explanation. There may not be an answer to the question: why is there anything at all; why not nothing? In which case our revision of Anselm's argument fails.

Nonetheless, the incremental successes of scientific investigation and our improved ability to maintain complex and intricate social structures suggest that our efforts to improve our concepts—to make them greater by dismissing those that are less successful—are in some sense matched by the world. We continue to learn more about how and why things function the way they do, and these discoveries integrate our thoughts into more intricate and complex concepts. In the process we are learning that the theories that we previously held are not true—that they do not capture the nature of God. And by pursuing that process we are affirming our conviction that there is, at the end of the road, an ultimate explanation that will make sense of things. There is a reality that our conceptual resources can hope to grasp. For the ultimate goal is an explanation that cannot be bettered—that is so comprehensive that we will never be surprised. That explanation, whatever it turns out to be, will tell us the nature of God.

But there is a second possibility to which we have already alluded. The world itself may not be something complete in itself. Contingencies may continually erupt, not simply as incidental byproducts, but also as significantly new structures and processes, interconnections and integrations. As they emerge, the ultimate principles that would explain why things are the way they are may also need to be transformed. In other words, an explanation that may, for the time being, capture reality may, as events unfold, fail to do justice to reality. It becomes something than which a greater *can* be conceived. Were this to be the case, the reality to be grasped by our understanding would be continually changing and amending its character, incorporating what went before into a new

17. Kant, *Critique of Pure Reason,* Transcendental Dialectic, book II, chap. 3, sect. 2: "The Transcendental Ideal," A571–83/B599–611.

kind of integrated being. God, so to speak, would be continually changing his mind, learning from the past. And since he is nothing else but the ultimate principle that undergirds reality—the sum total of all real possibilities—he would be, at the same time, changing his nature.

Surprisingly enough, it is Hegel who provides the philosophical perspective that can do justice to this metaphysics of contingency. Absolute knowing, he claims, is a process where, using all the accumulated knowledge acquired through generations of human experience, we act, only to discover that things turn out differently from what we had expected. What we had intended as the good emerges as evil; what we had dismissed as unworthy becomes significant. And we respond by incorporating these new, contingent discoveries into a more comprehensive understanding of the ways of the world.[18] This dynamic incorporation of novelty is, he says, not just a result of our limited perspective as humans. For the absolute idea, which marks the culmination of the logic, is nothing else but the method of conceptual logic: of starting with something simple and immediate, finding that it involves complexity and mediation that were not there in the beginning; and then learning how the new and the old are reciprocally interconnected.

More importantly for our initial interest in Anselm is the way Hegel integrates this philosophical comprehension into the traditions of Christian religion. For he finds in the basic structure of Christian doctrine the same pattern of integrated beginnings that act to produce novel complexity that needs to be reintegrated into comprehensive community: a trinitarian God who, before creation, integrates a comprehensive universality with determinate particularity through the dynamic of spirit, acts to create a world, only to discover that the result is the emergence of evil. This deity acts again to allow this evil to work its utmost by abandoning itself to a life in the world subject to destruction, so that finite beings in the world may, in their turn, abandon themselves to a share in the divine dynamic that results. In other words, the tradition that talks of trinity, creation, fall, incarnation, atonement, Pentecost, justification, and sanctification attributes to the ultimate ground of all things the very dynamic by which contingencies emerge even within the most comprehensive structures—contingencies that, in their turn, are to be incorporated into a new integrated reality.

18. To be sure, this is not the conventional wisdom concerning Hegel's absolute knowing; but I have shown how it is based in his texts in *Hegel's Systematic Contingency* (Basingstoke, UK: Palgrave Macmillan, 2007), especially 70–80.

For Hegel, then, God is nothing else but the process by which a greater is always being conceived. Whereas Anselm's definition results, when successful, simply in the conviction that the universe ultimately is conceivable, even if we never in fact achieve that goal, Hegel transforms this general schema into a specifically Christian pattern that names God, not simply as the sum total of all reality, but as the ultimate dynamic by which the world continues to expand, develop novelty, and remain comprehensible. When looked at in this way, there is still life in Anselm's ontological argument.

†*Ralph McInerny*

6. ARISTOTLE AND AQUINAS

There are some men who seem venerable even in their youth, and Ken Schmitz was one of them. When I was young and he was already venerable, a function of wisdom, not of age, we met mainly at meetings. He moved often on the academic checkerboard, although many will perhaps imagine that he was in Toronto throughout his career. Not so. He taught in California, he taught in Indiana, but when he was called to Toronto it must have seemed a homecoming. There was something deeply fitting about it. Surely Ken is one of the finest flowers of the Pontifical Institute of Mediaeval Studies, a worthy student of his master Etienne Gilson. In these last years he seems, like Bede, to wear "venerable" as a title; of course the beard helps. In recent years, we have met in Argentina, in Taiwan, even in Chicago, a wonderful town; to hear Ken lecture, to dine and talk with him and with others of those strong survivors for whom seventy years did not suffice, is one of the deep pleasures of the twilight years. It seems to me that Schmitz has published more in his age than in his youth. His glosses on the teaching of John Paul II—doubtless the fruit of his long association with the Institute on Marriage and Family—are mandatory reading. I wish I had something more fitting with which to honor him. I am afraid my essay may seem sweepings from a depleted mental warehouse. Would that it were straw in the Thomistic sense. Nonetheless, I offer it as my poor tribute to Ken Schmitz. *Ad multos annos!*

"I was that narrowest of specialists, the well-rounded man."

Thus does Nick Carraway, the narrator of *The Great Gatsby,* describe himself at the outset of the novel. But then, suggesting the effect the events about to be narrated have had on him, he adds: "Life is much better looked at from a single window after all."

That is my text. There is much talk nowadays about a dialogue of cultures. Nick Carraway might be taken as describing the contrast between, on the one hand, occupying a plurality of points of view, embracing diversity, one might say, and on the other, having a single unifying point of view. But the object of each is presumably the same.

I wonder if those engaged in present dialogues of culture might not learn a thing of two from an earlier. The dialogue I shall speak of is between the culture of the Greeks, as represented by Aristotle, and that of the Christian, represented by St. Thomas Aquinas.

The Aristotelian Corpus

We must first consider the vagaries of the transmission of texts. Aristotle lived in the fourth century B.C., Thomas in the thirteenth century of the Christian era. It might perhaps be thought, mistakenly, that since the thirteenth century was appreciably closer to the Golden Age of Greek culture, when Socrates, Plato, and Aristotle brought philosophy to a peak it has never since exceeded, that Aristotle, being chronologically closer to the medievals, was thereby more known and familiar to them than he is to us. Perhaps this would have been true if they had been able to read him.

The tale of the fate of the writings of Aristotle seems almost fanciful.[1] In the first century B.C., Cicero, Horace, and others went to Athens, and when later in their writings they refer to Aristotle, we find no mention, certainly no analysis, of any of the treatises of Aristotle. Rather, the Stagyrite is thought of as the author of dialogues similar to those of Plato. Students of the treatises are startled to find Cicero lauding Aristotle's literary style. The treatises of Aristotle seem to have dropped out of the picture. We are told of their being hidden away, somewhat like the Dead Sea Scrolls, to be found after centuries, during which no one knew of their existence. Andronicus of Rhodes, in Cicero's century, edited the recently discovered treatises. Of course, none of this would have affected Thomas's access to Aristotle, except for one thing: Aristotle wrote in Greek, and knowledge of that language was a rare thing throughout the early Middle Ages. Thomas himself did not read Greek.

1. See Enrico Berti, *Struttura e significato della Metafisica di Aristotle* (Rome: EDUSC, 2006).

In one of those surprising asymmetries of history, it was the dialogues of Aristotle that then dropped out of the picture, only to be reconstructed in the manner of the writings of the pre-Socratics over the last century and a half.

Boethius, in the fifth century of our era, knew Greek. He may have studied in Alexandria, whither the school of Athens had fled, and there he would have listened to Hellenistic Aristotelians—most of them neo-Platonists—and have read the treatises. In the previous century, St. Augustine had lamented the dying of the light of learning as the barbarians—our forebears, perhaps—continued to sweep down on the hapless Roman Empire. In book VIII of *The City of God,* Augustine gives a sketch of Greek philosophy.[2] Aristotle is notable by his absence from the account. Socrates is there, mention is made of some of the pre-Socratics, but Plato occupies pride of place. Platonism is presented as the pagan philosophy most akin to Christianity. It is in this account that Augustine rejects one possible explanation of this kinship, an explanation he had previously held: namely, that Plato had access, direct or indirect, to the Bible. Now he realizes that this could not have been. All the more amazing, then, the affinity of Platonism with Christianity. Augustine tells us he had little Greek. His knowledge even of Plato seems filtered through intermediaries. Augustine's account is largely a borrowed one—high-level hearsay. My main point is that he seems not to have heard of the Aristotelian treatises.

In the next century, Boethius (480–524), linguistically equipped for the task, conceived a great project. He would translate into Latin the whole of Plato and the whole of Aristotle, and he would add commentaries on them, of the kind that Ammonius had written on Aristotle. All this was undertaken with an eye to showing the fundamental agreement of Plato and Aristotle.[3] Boethius was of an ancient Roman family; many of the traditional imperial offices were retained by Theodoric, the Ostrogoth king of Italy, an Arian reigning from Ravenna. Boethius and his sons served their terms as consul. His was a busy, active life, but for all that, he remained a student, a scholar. Even if he had lived to a biblical longevity, it is difficult to see how he could have completed the task he had set himself. In any event, it was only begun when Boethius was suspected of

2. Augustine, *City of God,* trans. Henry Bettenson (London: Penguin Books, 1981), 299–342.

3. See Ralph McInerny, *Boethius and Aquinas* (Washington, D.C.: The Catholic University of America Press, 1990), 1–6.

treason, of plotting with the Emperor, in Constantinople, against Theodoric. He was condemned to death. To this we owe that classic of prison literature, *The Consolation of Philosophy,* in which Boethius, in verse and prose, considers his plight over the course of five books. Why do the innocent suffer; why do the wicked prosper? Under the tutelage of Dame Philosophy, the whining Boethius of the outset of the work becomes the resigned philosopher who accepts his fate. Boethius was a Christian; he was also the author of theological tractates of enormous pith and profundity. But there is no appeal in the *Consolation* to Christ, the innocent victim par excellence.[4] Taking note of this, Dr. Johnson, dropping into Latin, marveled that in such a plight Boethius proved himself to be *magis philosophus quam Christianus.*[5] I will return to this.

Because Boethius' project was brought to so untimely an end, Aristotle throughout the early Middle Ages is represented in the liberal arts curriculum by the few logical works of his that Boethius had put into Latin. It is not until the twelfth century that the treatises begin to find their way into Latin, beginning with the *Nicomachean Ethics,* to be followed at the beginning of the thirteenth century with more and more until, after Thomas's death in 1274, it became complete. Thomas did not know *The Poetics* of Aristotle, for example.

This belated arrival of Aristotle in Latin divides into two streams: the Arabo-Latin and the Greco-Latin. The first stream consists of translations made from Arabic translations of the Greek, perhaps through intermediary translations. These Latin versions were often accompanied into the university system with Muslim commentaries attached, sometimes literally surrounding the text of Aristotle on the page. Averroes, Avicenna, and others were thus introduced to the West along with Aristotle. This is a fact fraught with significance.

The Greco-Latin stream, as the term suggests, consists of translations made directly from the Greek, in Venice, in Sicily, elsewhere. As is well known, William of Moerbeke, contemporary with and fellow Dominican of Thomas, provided translations of Aristotle directly from the Greek, whose faithfulness to the original has led some modern editors to consult them as an alternate Greek text. He ended, fittingly, as bishop of Corinth.

4. Ibid., 14–17.

5. James Boswell, *Life of Johnson,* ed. R. W. Chapman (Oxford: Oxford University Press, 1980), 444; "Speaking of Boethius, who was the favorite writer of the middle ages, he said it was very surprizing, that upon such a subject, and in such a situation, he should be *magis philosophus quam Christianus.*"

Thomas Aquinas, as a student, first in Naples, then in Cologne, then in Paris, and later as a master, had the benefit of the now fairly complete Aristotelian corpus.

With these familiar matters recalled, I turn now to the dialogue between Thomas and Aristotle.

The Errors of Aristotle

There are a number of ways to consider the consequences of this influx of Latin translations of the Aristotelian treatises. First, it made mincemeat out of the liberal arts curriculum that had been developed over the centuries since Cassiodorus Senator, a contemporary of Boethius.[6]

The seven liberal arts had been taken to sum up secular learning, but where in the trivium or quadrivium was there room for treatises on ethics, politics, physics, psychology, metaphysics? That this curricular conundrum should have happened precisely at the time universities were being founded had a profound effect on these institutions, explaining their difference from the arts schools out of which universities arose.

The problem of course, was far more than curricular. Once the seven liberal arts had been thought an adequate summation of secular learning and their compatibility with and complementarity to the faith a matter of received opinion. So a second and far more important consideration was this: How do the contents of these Aristotelian treatises square with Christianity? This question did not loom all that large during Thomas's—and Bonaventure's—student days in Paris. When Thomas and Aristotle became *magistri sacrae paginae,* after a delay because of the opposition of the faculty to these mendicants, Bonaventure was elected to be Master General of the Franciscans and never occupied a professorial chair, whereas Thomas taught for three years in Paris before returning to Italy. If one consults their respective commentaries on the *Sentences* of Peter Lombard, one of the set tasks for an aspiring master, he will not find much anguish over the compatibility of the philosopher and the faith. There were problems, of course, but they did not loom large. This is particularly striking in the case of Bonaventure, given later developments; he begins his commentary by giving the four causes of the *Sentences.* It is true that the Aristotelian treatises could not be read at Paris—that is, be the subject of public lectures, before their compatibility with the faith had been established—by committee, of course.

6. See Cassiodorus, *Cassiodori Senatoris Institutiones,* ed. R. A. B. Mynors (Oxford: Oxford University Press, 1937).

But this ban came to be more honored in the breach than in the observance. Early on in Thomas's writings there is criticism of Avicenna's and Averroes' readings of Aristotle. It was a decade later, when Thomas was summoned back to Paris in 1268 to occupy one of the chairs allotted to Dominicans, that serious controversy over the matter had broken out. The controversy was prompted by what has been called, variously, Latin Averroism and heterodox Aristotelianism.[7]

Lists of the errors of Aristotle were drawn up, three of which were of greatest moment. Aristotle taught—did he not?—that God did not know what was going on in the created world, since that would be demeaning; that there is a single soul for all men; that the world is eternal. In what sense would these be errors? Well, they conflicted with Christianity, with belief in God's providence, in the destiny of each soul to be united with God, as well as with the clear statement of Genesis that in the beginning God created heaven and earth. In short, they were in contradictory opposition to truths of the faith.

This seemed not to bother certain feisty masters in the Faculty of Arts, now, effectively, the Faculty of Philosophy. There is controversy about the so-called two-truth theory attributed to the Latin Averroists, but neither Thomas nor Bonaventure had any doubt that it was being maintained that one need not worry that a position attributed to Aristotle was in conflict with the faith. One simply did philosophy and let theologians worry about its relation to the faith. This was taken to mean that something could be true in philosophy and false in theology.[8]

Unsurprisingly, Bonaventure became a foe of Aristotelianism, so understood, and in sermons preached in Paris went after such philosophers. Thomas's reaction was more complicated, and it is his reaction that provides my theme.[9]

7. This is the suggestion of Fernand van Steenberghen; see chapter 8 of *La philosophie au xiiie siècle* (Louvain: Publications universitaires, 1966).

8. The Latin text of the *De unitate intellectus,* with an English translation, can be found in Ralph McInerny, *Aquinas Against the Averroists: On There Being Only One Intellect* (West Lafayette, Ind.: Purdue University Press, 1993).

9. The question of whether or not there is a *philosophy* of St. Bonaventure supplied the basis for a most interesting exchange between Etienne Gilson and van Steenberghen. Gilson thought it impossible to extract philosophical nuggets from the theological writings of Bonaventure and string them together as his philosophy; van Steenbergen thought this possible and desirable. Here is a case where one can agree with both sides. Surely van Steenberghen is right in finding in the theological writings of Bonaventure passages that are philosophical rather than theological: that is, they do not depend for their force on revelation. Nor does Gilson deny this. But Gilson is right in insisting that these passages play a

The Eternity of the World

Bonaventure and Thomas would have been as one in saying that if indeed a philosophical doctrine contradicted the faith, then it was false. Obscurantism? Hardly. It is simply an application of the principle of non-contradiction. Of contradictories, if one is true the other is false. *P* vs. –*P*. Let *p* stand for "the world and time had a beginning," then its contradictory was false, since the faith is true. This was simply sweet reason. Of course, such a swift settlement of the matter did not establish why the conflicting philosophical tenet was false, so there was work to be done. It is that work that characterizes Thomas's approach.

Let us concentrate on the "error" concerning the eternity of the world. Already, in his commentary on the *Sentences,* Bonaventure regarded this teaching of Aristotle as false, not simply because it contradicted Genesis, but also because he thought it was an incoherent claim. The eternity of the world, when analyzed, simply does not make sense. And Bonaventure gave reasons why this is so. For instance, given an eternal world, there would be an infinite number of souls, and infinity would be continually added to. The upshot was that an eternal world is impossible. That is, one had reason for rejecting it other than an appeal to scripture.

Thomas's treatment of the eternity of the world is most subtle. On the one hand, as in his commentary on book XII of the *Metaphysics,* he shows that Aristotle's argument for the eternity of the world is probable at best, and certainly not conclusive. He had even toyed for a time with holding that this was how Aristotle himself advanced the claim. On the other hand, as in his opusculum, written in 1271 during his second Parisian professoriate, Thomas held that the arguments that the world *could not have been* eternal are flawed.

Of course, if one meant that an eternal world did not exist in dependence on the First Cause, that would be nonsense; but could God have created an eternal world?[10]

If it were impossible, this would be either because it was something

theological role in the text. Of course, the fundamental problem is: into what wider whole would the abstracted philosophical nuggets fit?

10. It must not be forgotten that it was on the assumption of an eternal world that Aristotle argued that there must be a Prime Mover. The next few paragraphs of the text paraphrase passages from the *De aeternitate mundi contra murmurantes.* An English translation may be found in McInerny, *Thomas Aquinas: Selected Writings* (London: Penguin Classics, 1998), 710–17.

God could not do or because such a world is impossible in itself. If the latter, this would be based on the nature of becoming and the role of passive potency in it, or because an eternal world is conceptually incoherent.

In the first sense, for something to come into being, it might be thought that there must always have been something that could become that thing. But before an angel was created there was not some prior thing that could become an angel. Thus, to hold that there was always something that could become the world is to be rejected. What is being adumbrated here is the distinction between creation and the becoming that presupposes a passive potency that is actualized when a thing comes to be.

It is no limitation on God's omnipotence that he cannot cause what makes no sense—for example, create something that does not depend on him, or that what happened didn't happen. Is an eternal world like that? It is this that Bonaventure affirmed and Thomas denied. Why did Thomas deny it? Well, an eternal world could be said to be impossible, either because the efficient cause must precede its effect in duration, or because nonexistence must precede existence. Thomas proceeds to show that neither of these alone or both together establish the impossibility of an eternal world.

The second sense may surprise. Isn't creation precisely bringing something into being out of nothing? Indeed it is. So how does Thomas escape the seeming result that an eternal world is possible if nothing did not precede? First he says that we must not be governed by our imagination, and think that nothing is some previous state of affairs, as it were, prior in duration to the created thing. On the supposition of an eternal world, which of course is created by God, and thus from nothing, the *ex nihilo* here can be understood as what you have if God's causality were removed.

Let this suffice as a taste of this polemical opusculum on the eternity of the world directed *contra murmurantes*. Doubtless among these murmurers are those seeking to discredit Aristotle by means of the arguments Thomas rejects. There is not, however, any overt mention or defense of Aristotle in the opusculum.

It is easy to see that such subtle argumentation in favor of an unrealized possibility—the world was after all created in time—seemed to some to align Thomas with those pesky masters in the Faculty of Arts. Shortly after his death, teachings of Thomas would be among those condemned by his fellow masters.

An unstressed aspect of the discussion of the eternity of the world is this: if the contradictory of a truth of faith could be definitively proved false, would one thereby have established the truth of an article of faith? If one of contradictories is false, the other is true. But that would seem to be a claim to *know* that a mystery of the faith is true.

How to Read a Pagan Author

This discussion of one defense of an Aristotelian tenet (namely, the defense that consists in holding that it is factually false that the world is eternal but that an eternal world is not an incoherent notion) could be multiplied again and again in the writings of Thomas, though the defenses take other forms. Aristotle did after all hold that the world is eternal, but that does not make him the village idiot. In the case of the other two "errors" mentioned above, Thomas did what Bonaventure never did. He asked if the text supports the interpretation involved in those errors. In short, he uses textual analysis to show, first, that Aristotle never held that God is ignorant of the world and, second, that he taught that each individual soul is immortal. Another polemical opusculum of the period—*De unitate intellectus contra averroistas*—is a remarkable exegetical performance that establishes that the Averroist reading of book III of the *De anima* simply won't wash. It is ironic that the Averroist interpretation is favored to this day by many, perhaps most, Aristotelians. I recommend this opusculum to them.

This defense of Aristotle by means of exegesis may be thought to lie behind one of the great projects of Thomas's last years. Beginning in 1268 and continuing to 1273, the year before he died, Thomas composed line-by-line commentaries on twelve treatises of Aristotle, not all of which were completed, though the more important were. These are sometimes dismissed, even by Thomists, as a twisting of the texts in such a way that they do not collide with Christian doctrine. Quite apart from the suggestion that one's chosen master is a master of deception, I find it difficult to believe that anyone saying this has immersed himself in those commentaries. Bonaventure, of course, wrote no commentaries on Aristotle.

If a Christian thinker like Thomas finds Aristotle congenial, comes to his defense, reads him with painstaking closeness, this is not because Aristotle taught truths specific to revelation. Rather it draws our attention to something shared and basic between believer and nonbeliever alike: reason, natural reason, arguments that appeal for their cogency, not to mysteries of the faith, which can only be believed, never in this life fully comprehended, but to truths that are in the public domain, available to believer and nonbeliever. Philosophy thus provides a kind of *lingua franca* for Christian and pagan. As one can see, this presupposes that philosophy and theology are distinct because their starting points or principles are distinct.

Forgive me for dwelling so long on matters both familiar and obvious. I recall them because they can be seen as providing some guidance to dialogue between cultures. If the believer's attitude toward pagan philosophy were simply to juxtapose it to Christian doctrine, with the suggestion that they are simply different outlooks, adding that the pagan must cede to the Christian, that would not be much of a dialogue. Perhaps it exemplifies Nick Carraway's notion of the well-rounded man.

Thomas, by contrast, when doing philosophy, looks out the same window that Aristotle did. This is not to be borne back ceaselessly into the past. It is not the study of Aristotle without concern for where the truth lies. Rather, it is to occupy the same window, appeal to principles common to believer and nonbeliever, and come to see how much one has in common with the pagan or the nonbeliever. Dialogue is no longer stopping at the surprising surface differences, but seeking truths that can be recognized as such by believer and nonbeliever alike.

I mentioned Dr. Johnson's expression of surprise, in Latin, that Boethius did not invoke his Christian belief in seeking consolation. This is a vexed question. One answer to it, one that justifies calling Boethius the first of the Scholastics, is that the work thereby exhibits the distinction between philosophy and theology.

To say that Thomas baptized Aristotle is as silly, at least as it is often understood, as to say that in the *Commedia* what Dante did was to put Thomas into verse. Thomas's defense of Aristotle, even when an Aristotelian tenet is ruled out by one's faith, makes clear how the dialogue can continue. It also is conducive to modesty in what one thinks can be established philosophically. Sometimes the only thing the believer can say about something that contradicts his faith is that it is at most probable, or not impossible. Most philosophical arguments establish opinion, not knowledge in the strong sense. Grounded opinion, no doubt, more or less firm opinion, but for all that short of apodictic truth. Aristotle wrote that the adverb of old, perhaps wise, men is "perhaps." I think that is true—perhaps.

John Russon

7. SUBJECTIVITY AND OBJECTIVITY IN HEGEL'S *SCIENCE OF LOGIC*

When I undertook graduate studies in the 1980s, the University of Toronto was internationally recognized as a center for study in the history of philosophy. The presence of Kenneth L. Schmitz in the department made it especially strong as a center for the study of Hegel's philosophy, and I had the great privilege and pleasure of attending many courses that he taught on Hegel, Kant, and German idealism. The jewel in this crown was his graduate seminar on Hegel's *Science of Logic,* in which I was able to participate in three different years. Hegel's *Science of Logic* is much maligned, typically because it is much misunderstood.[1]

1. Misunderstandings typically take the form of claiming that "absolute knowing" marks a (supposed) kind of knowledge that is discontinuous with the rest of the dialectic of experience in the *Phenomenology of Spirit* and that this absolute knowledge—in which everything is comprehended, and all opposition overcome—is presupposed by the *Science of Logic* (and, indeed, even by the *Phenomenology* itself). This form of knowledge, it is then asserted, does not exist, and so the very project of the *Logic* is vitiated (along with the conclusion of the *Phenomenology*). A classic statement of this view is found in the (generally subtle and sympathetic) interpretation of Jean Hyppolite, *Logic and Existence,* trans. Leonard Lawlor and Amit Sen (Albany: State University of New York Press, 1997), 3, 34: "Absolute knowledge means the in principle elimination of ... non-knowledge, that is, the elimination of a transcendence essentially irreducible to our knowledge.... If we just stayed with the *Phenomenology,* by separating it from its conclusion as well as from its preface, we would remain at a humanism, at a philosophical anthropology, and the Logic, the Logos of Being, which is of such importance to Hegel, would be incomprehensible." Though it is true that the standpoint of absolute knowledge is the scientific standpoint from which the *Phenomenology* and the *Logic* are written, this common view fundamentally misunderstands the nature of absolute knowledge or the nature of the project of the *Logic.* For a corrective view

For this reason, it was a matter of great good fortune for me that I had the opportunity to study with one of the few who have mastered this book, and a teacher, furthermore, who could communicate to students both its meaning and its majesty.

It was characteristic of Schmitz's seminars on the *Science of Logic* that they always ran out of time: we would get through the "Doctrine of Being" and the dialectic of "Reflection" that begins the "Doctrine of Essence," but there would only be time for what Schmitz called a "Cook's Tour" of the remainder of the book. These "Cook's Tours" were provocative and infuriating, for they allowed one a glimpse of the riches that remained in the book—indeed, the riches that remained in Schmitz's own understanding—but gave one no opportunity to explore them further, except on one's own. It is this situation that left me for about twenty years struggling to determine on my own what Schmitz would have told us, had we had the time to read to the end of the book.

This paper is the fruit of my effort. It will clarify the basic tripartite division that organizes Hegel's *Science of Logic,* and, in particular, what Hegel is talking about under the third heading, "Doctrine of the Concept." To accomplish this, I am going to show how Hegel is responding to central arguments from the transcendental analytic of Kant's *Critique of Pure Reason,* particularly in the section on the "System of All Principles of Pure Understanding" (anticipations of perception, axioms of intuition, analogies of experience, postulates of empirical thought), and with the transcendental deduction in general. The first half of the chapter will focus mostly on a general discussion of some Kantian themes from the *Critique of Pure Reason,* and I will be trying to show how the basic tripartite division of Hegel's text is visible in Kant's work and its development in Fichte.[2] Roughly, I will here be telling the story of the logical buildup

---

of absolute knowledge, see John W. Burbidge, "Hegel's Absolutes," *Owl of Minerva* 29, no. 1 (1997): 23–37, and John Russon, "Absolute Knowing: The Structure and Project of Hegel's System of Science,"in *Reading Hegel's Phenomenology* (Bloomington, Ind.: Indiana University Press, 2004). For the project of Hegel's *Logic* in general, see chapter 3 of John W. Burbidge, *The Logic of Hegel's Logic: An Introduction* (Peterborough, Ont.: Broadview Press, 2006), and chapters 1, 2, and 6 of Stephen Houlgate, *The Opening of Hegel's Logic: From Being to Infinity* (West Lafayette, Ind.: Purdue University Press, 2005).

2. Burbidge, in chap. 3 of *The Logic of Hegel's Logic* (23–24), has a helpful discussion of ways in which Hegel's *Logic* emerges from the themes at work in Immanuel Kant's *Critique of Pure Reason,* translated by Werner S. Pluhar, introduction by Patricia W. Kitcher (Indianapolis and Cambridge Mass.: Hackett 1996), and makes a similar link to the work of Fichte that I make in this chapter. A helpful explanation of Hegel's project in the *Logic* in terms of Kant's agenda in the *Critique of Pure Reason* is given by Houlgate, *The Opening of Hegel's Logic*, 9–28.

of an object. I will then turn to some reflections on Hegel's own text, in an effort to understand what the nature of a "conceptual" determination is. Specifically, I will argue that a conceptual determination is realized only in and as a structure of opposition. Throughout we will be attending to the inherent demands of the objectivity and intersubjectivity that characterize our experience.

Kant and the Logic of the Object

Kant draws a basic distinction within the table of categories. The categories of quantity and quality he calls "mathematical," those of relation and modality "dynamical."[3] The mathematical, he says, pertain to intuition, the dynamical to the existence of an appearance in general. What this means, essentially, is that the categories of quantity and quality are the basis of the very *constitution* of an "is." They are what Hegel would call categories of "immediacy." The dynamical categories of relation and modality are about the relations that pertain *to* or hold *between* such immediacies; these categories are regulative—they are the rules that govern their relation—not constitutive, and they pertain, he says, to what admits of discursive, rather than intuitive, certainty.[4] These are what Hegel would call categories of reflection. In the analyses of the categorical syntheses that follow this discussion, Kant effectively builds up an object by showing what the necessary parameters are for anything to be an object.[5]

3. Kant, *Critique of Pure Reason,* A160/B199.

4. Ibid., A161–2/B201.

5. Ibid., A162–235/B202–94. Compare Hyppolite, *Logic and Existence,* 170–71, who argues that the doctrine of being corresponds to the transcendental aesthetic, the doctrine of essence to the transcendental analytic, and the doctrine of the concept to the transcendental dialectic. This association of the doctrine of the concept with Kant's transcendental dialectic is hasty, for the correlation is not as direct as is the case with the former two parts of each philosopher's work; my argument in this chapter would suggest that the closer correlation is between the doctrine of the concept and the "paralogisms" section of the transcendental dialectic (see next note). For the language of immediacy (*Unmittelbarkeit*), see G. W. F. Hegel, *Wissenschaft der Logik,* in *Werke in Zwanzig Bande,* vols. 5 and 6, ed. Eva Moldenhauer and Karl Markus Michel (Frankfurt: Suhrkamp Verlag, 1986), translated into English by A. V. Miller as the *Science of Logic* (New York: Humanities Press, 1976), vol.1, book 1, sect. 1, chap. 1, part A, "Being"; for the language of "reflexion," (*Reflexion*), and vol.1, book 2, sect. 1, chap. 1, part C, "Reflection." (Further references to this work will give the English pagination first, followed by the volume number and pagination for the German text.) For the logic of immediacy as it first emerges in Hegel's *Logic,* see Dieter Henrich, "Anfang und Methode der Logik," in *Hegel im Kontext,* edited by Dieter Henrich, 73–94 (Frankfurt am Main: Suhrkamp Verlag, 1971); for the logic of reflexion as it first emerges in Hegel's *Logic,* see Henrich, "Hegels Logik der Reflexion: Neue Fassung," in *Die*

In the "Axioms of Intuition," Kant argues that for anything to have, so to speak, a purchase on reality, it must have some *extent*—it must be situated in space and time: it must be a quantitative magnitude. In the "Anticipations of Perception," he argues that whatever is to be must have some intrinsicality, a qualitative or intensive magnitude. This is just what we mean by calling something "something." It is by virtue of being thus constituted that something has *immediacy,* that it can be *intuited*. These are the characteristics by virtue of which something can enter into relation with something else—specifically, can enter into relation with sensibility.

In the "Analogies of Experience," Kant argues about the relations that must hold among these immediacies for them to be able to be objects of a coherent experience. Basically, they must one and all be modifications of a single, enduring, coherent field of the real as such—substance. They must have their own integrity that explains their order, such that our experience can be said to be of a real object, and not just of a figment of fantasy—they must be involved in relations of cause and effect. And, finally, the multiple, individual causal histories that hold among things must fit coherently together—they must form a system. In short, for something to assume the status of real object, it must be the coherent world of independent nature. These are the necessary parameters that define relations internal to the immediacies that constitute the world of experience; as they are themselves not immediacies but relations of immediacies, they are the dimensions of the real that demand to be apprehended by understanding.

Through these analyses, Kant is able to show both what the logic must be of anything that can bear the title of reality, and also why reality itself can only be comprehended by the coordinated efforts of both sensibility and understanding: reality itself is both immediate and reflected (in Hegel's terms) and therefore can only be apprehended by a cognition that is both intuitive and discursive.

Hegel's analysis of the categories of immediacy and reflection is more complex, more thorough, and more dialectical than Kant's (though it should be noted that, despite Hegel's generally insulting tone toward Kant here, Kant does not arbitrarily grab a bunch of categories that he thoughtlessly takes over from the tradition, but, on the contrary, has quite a rigorous argument in these sections to show why these catego-

---

Wissenschaft der Logik und die Logik der Reflexion, edited by Dieter Henrich, 203–24, Hegel-Studien 18 (Bonn: Bouvier Verlag, 1978).

ries are the necessary ones, and Kant's mode of argumentation is explicitly dialectical in the sense of showing that the categories work as triads in which the third unites the opposed first two while offering a qualitative advance that is not reducible to those first two; and, further, the argument he makes about substance, cause, and reciprocity is very much the archetype for all the German idealist arguments that centrally use these notions, including Hegel's own)—Hegel's analysis is more complex, but its basic orientation is the same, in its distinguishing or immediacy and reflection.

Kant and the Transcendental Logic of the Subject

Let us now turn to our central question: what is "concept"? I want to approach this by drawing on the idea above that in his analyses of the mathematical and dynamical categories, Kant effectively establishes why cognition must be both intuitive and discursive—he establishes, in other words, why knowing takes the dual form of sensation and understanding. To establish what concept is as the third missing triplet to being and essence, we can ask, "what mode of cognition is necessary but not recognized in the dyad of sensibility and understanding?" As I said above, I think for our answer to this question, we can again turn to Kant. Quite simply, what is missing is the cognition accomplished in transcendental analysis.

In his transcendental argumentation, Kant takes up subjectivity on its own terms. My contention is that this comprehension is not adequately characterized by the terms laid out in his bipartite table of categories and its corresponding duality of sensation and understanding. The categories, recall, were explicitly the categories of *objectivity:* they are derived in the course of answering the question "how can subjectivity be objective?" His analysis of these categories in the section we have just been referring to precisely shows how they are necessary to explain the constitution of the object. But Kant's transcendental argument itself is a study of *subjectivity.* His categories have given us, as Hegel says of the first two books of the *Logic,* an objective logic. What Kant's table is missing is the logic of subjectivity, the "subjective logic," as Hegel refers to the doctrine of the concept.[6] Let us turn, now, to Kant's discussion of

6. Compare Kant's own remark at the beginning of the discussion of the "Paralogisms of Pure Reason": "We have now come to a concept that was not entered in the above general list of the transcendental concepts, and that must yet be classed with them, but without in the least changing the table and declaring it deficient. This is the concept, or, if one

transcendental subjectivity, to see why this presents a field of "the real" that is not comprehended by his table of objective categories.

If we think of what Kant is discerning in his transcendental analysis, we can see that the dimensions of experience that he uncovers do not strictly belong either to the side of the empirical subject or the side of the empirical object. The transcendental dimensions are both structures of subjectivity and structures of objectivity. They do not, for example, belong in the world of nature—the proper object of experience on Kant's conception[7]—for nature contains only the system of sensible bodies subject to the laws of physical causality. The transcendental unity of apperception—the "I think" that is the necessary context and structure of any experience[8]—for example, is not an immediate object of sense, and it is

---

prefers, the judgment: *I think*.... [T]his concept is the vehicle of all concepts as such and hence also of transcendental concepts.... [H]owever pure of the empirical (the impressions of the senses) this concept may be, it still serves to distinguish two kinds of objects taken from the nature of our power of representation. *I*, as thinking, am an object of inner sense and am called soul; what is an object of the outer senses is called body," (*Critique of Pure Reason*, A341–42/B399–400, trans. Werner S. Pluhar, emphasis in original). Kant is concerned to show that we cannot have knowledge of the "I" as a worldly substance; what he effectively establishes is that the logic of the "I" is not defined according to the terms of the opposition of subject and object that characterizes empirical life, but is, instead, what makes that opposition possible. As we will see, this is remarkably close to Hegel's logic of the concept.

7. In Hegel's view, nature is not the proper object. We need an object that adequately reflects back to us our own nature. For that reason, our ultimate object is spirit. Nature does demonstrate a logic of the concept, but in too immediate a form. I have discussed this point in Russon, *The Self and Its Body in Hegel's Phenomenology of Spirit* (Toronto: University of Toronto Press, 1997), 39–41. Compare also Giambattista Vico's argument that, whereas historical acts are acts by self-conscious agents like ourselves with whom we can identify, natural processes are the result of a non-self-conscious agency with which in principle we can never identify; therefore, it is only history, and not nature, that can offer to us a proper object for knowledge: "Whoever reflects on this cannot but marvel that the philosophers should have bent all their energies to the study of the world of nature, which, since God made it, He alone knows; and that they should have neglected the study of the world of nations, or civil world, which, since men had made it, men could come to know"; Vico, *The New Science of Giambattista Vico,* trans. Thomas Goddard Bergin and Max Harold Fisch (Ithaca, N.Y.: Cornell University Press, 1984).

8. Transcendental apperception is introduced at *Critique of Pure* Reason A106–7. It is the central subject of the transcendental deduction; see especially B131–32: "The *I think* must be *capable* of accompanying all my presentations. For otherwise something would be presented to me that could not be thought at all—which is equivalent to saying that the presentation either would be impossible, or at least would be nothing to me.... I call it *pure apperception,* in order to distinguish it from *empirical* apperception. Or, again, I call it *original apperception;* for it is the self-consciousness which, because it produces the presentation *I think* that must be capable of accompanying all other presentation[s], and [because it] is one and the same in all consciousness, cannot be accompanied by any further presentation. I also call the *unity* of this apperception the *transcendental* unity of self-consciousness, in order to indicate that a priori cognition can be obtained from it," (Pluhar, trans., emphasis

not a regulative structure for the participation of such a sensible object in nature. The transcendental unity of apperception, rather, and, indeed, the whole of the transcendental, is the articulation of the very field of appearing, the articulation of the medium within which all sensing and all understanding happens. This dimension is not an alien other to the world of experience: it is realized only as that world. Rather as understanding discovers the "inner" of sense—*what* it is—transcendental analysis reveals something like the "inner" of all objects. In so doing, it does not just take a given immediacy (sense) and identify its identity (as understanding does), but, in finding this new inner, transcendental analysis also recognizes a different immediacy from that of sense: whereas sense recognizes spatial bodies as the immediate, transcendental analysis reveals experience itself—the identity of subject and object—as the immediate.

This brief reflection on the transcendental identifies a variety of dimensions in which the logic of the transcendental does not fit within the logic of sensible immediacy or of the reflectivity of understanding. It explains and redefines them both, while being explicable in terms of neither. Let us now think further about the "categories," so to speak, of the transcendental. What I mean is, I want to consider the characteristics of a determination of the transcendental, and how these differ from the characteristics of a sensible object or an object of understanding.

The most important characteristic of a determination of the transcendental is that it is a relation. Not, however, a relation of cause and effect, which is more or less the exemplary relation within understanding. In cause and effect, the two related elements are outside each other, and *both are objects:* we look on at two things within the world that produce a change in each other. The relation within the transcendental, on the contrary, is a relation of *subject* and object, rather than a relation of two objects. The transcendental structure is a structure of *appearing,* a "for" structure or an intentionality. In such a structure, the one term is realized only as the other term: the appearing does not happen to some separate entity called a subject, for the subject is just the "being aware" that pervades the experience; equally, what appears is not something other than the fact of appearing. At the same time, however, the subject and object are not conflated. Subject and object are "the same" in relation to itself, but relating to itself as differing from itself: this is, at

---

in original). Hegel introduces his own discussion of the concept through discussion of the transcendental unity of apperception (Hegel, *Science of Logic*, 584–85/2:254–56); note especially, "Thus we are justified by a cardinal principle of the Kantian philosophy in referring to the nature of the *I* in order to learn what the *Concept* is" (585/2:255).

a minimum, what Hegel calls a negative self-relation, or a determination of reflection. But beyond the relations of reflection that populate the doctrine of essence, the relation that is a transcendental determination is not "blind": this is what it means to say that the appearing is "for." In other words, the starting, definitive dimension of a transcendental structure is that it is "for." Indeed, we could say that this is not just a structure of reflection in itself, but it is reflective for itself, or, it is self-reflective.

What we can already see in Kant, then, is that the very transcendental analysis in which Kant works out the "objective" logic of immediacy and reflection enacts a "subjective" logic that exceeds and grounds these two; that is, the logics of immediacy and reflection depend on the logic of subjectivity, but it is not itself reducible to their terms. Behind the logic of sense and understanding, we need a logic of the transcendental ego. Most simply, this is the logic of concept, which grounds the logics of being and essence in Hegel's *Science of Logic*. Let me turn, now, to a further consideration of the transcendental ego before turning, finally, to Hegel's the *Logic* itself.

Fichte and the Transcendental Ego

Fichte's "Fundamental Principles for the Entire Science of Knowledge" is a helpful place to turn to allow us to make the transition from Kant's *Critique of Pure Reason* to Hegel's "Doctrine of the Concept." Fichte begins from Kant's transcendental unity of apperception—the transcendental "I"—which means he takes up the logic of the transcendental on its own terms, rather than approaching it through the logic of sense and understanding. Let us look briefly at Fichte's version of this "logic of the concept."

Experience always has as its object some identity: A = A. The recognition of that identity requires an act of experience that holds on to the sense of the first A throughout the experience of asserting its identity with the second A. In other words, to assert that "A = A" is not the same as simply saying A: we acknowledge something about it, integral to it. That means the one doing the recognizing must know what she was saying at the beginning in order to meaningfully assert what it claims at the end. To recognize that A = A, then, requires that I who do the recognizing hold on to the coherence of my experience throughout this assertion: I must still retain my initial recognition, and I must recognize it as my own. To assert that A = A, then, always tacitly involves recognizing that I am I, that I who assert the first A am also the I that completes the recognition of self-identity. Since the recognition of A = A is the logical form implicit in the recognition of any self-identical object, it follows that "I am I" is the logical form of any recognition of an object. At the most general level, then, in all experience I am recognizing myself. This self-recognition is the *universal* form of all experience. Fichte's first principle, the ego positing itself, is the absolute or ultimate context, the presupposed field within which the notion of "object" makes sense at all.[9]

But, there would be no experience, no "I am I" happening, if there were no recognition of an object. In the absence of the recognition of an object, an "other" to me, there would be no asserting, and therefore no self-experience. For there to be experience, for there to be an "I am I," there must be a determinate positing, which means an op-positing, an opposing of myself as recognizer to something I recognize. This is Fichte's second principle: the ego op-poses to itself a not-self. This opposing, though, is still a positing; it is, that is to stay, still a recognition. The I must say "it," but that is still a saying. This means that the opposition of self to not-self itself occurs within the form of the ego's self-positing. The op-posing of self to not-self is the *determinate* form that self-positing takes, and there is no self-positing—the *universal* form of all experience—except insofar as it is *determinate*.[10]

There are thus two opposed demands that experience takes: experience is founded in the demand that I only ever experience myself, and on the demand that I always experience what is not myself. The ultimate form, then, the absolute, is both universal and determinate, and this, its own immanent nature, is a self-opposition; that is, these two demands, inherent to its very character, contradict each other. And thus, experience is inherently characterized by a third demand, namely, that this contradiction be reconciled, and that this unresolved duality be a coherent singularity. It is this demand that is realized as the dynamism of experience.[11]

9. Johann Gottlieb Fichte, *Science of Knowledge*, ed. and trans. Peter Heath and John Lachs (Cambridge: Cambridge University Press, 1982), part 1, "Fundamental Principles of the Entire Science of Knowledge," sect. 1, "First, Absolutely Unconditioned Principle," 94–102, especially 99.

10. Fichte, "Second Principle, Conditioned as to Content," in *Science of Knowledge*, 102–5. I am taking the language of "universal" and "determinate" from Hegel's discussion of the logic of the concept in Hegel, *Science of Logic*, vol. 2, sect. 1, chap. 1, "The Concept": the relation of universality and determinateness is the central issue in the dialectic of the first two moments of the concept, "the universal concept" (*der allgemeine Begriff*) and "the particular concept" (*der besondere Begriff*).

11. Fichte, "Third Principle, Conditioned as to Form," in *Science of Knowledge*, 105–19. Compare Hegel's discussion of the "I," *Science of Logic*, 583/2:253.

In place, then, of Kant's transcendental unity of apperception, Fichte has developed what we might call the transcendental trinity. This trinity is the logic of subjectivity; not, however, the subjectivity of empirical life that is only one side of the domain of worldly objects; this, rather, is the transcendental subjectivity that precedes and makes possible the very opposition of subject and object. Here, then, we see Fichte's version of the logic of the concept, and its logical dynamism is precisely the ground for ultimately explaining why the world of objects takes the form of a logic of immediacy and a logic of reflection.

The concept is the universal that is self-sundering: its determinacy is an opposition that calls for reconciliation. A concept, then, has its determinacy as the appearance of an other, where that other is to-be-oneself, or equally, oneself is to-be-that-other. What is distinctive of conceptual relations, as contrasted with relations of being and essence, is that they take the form of a self-consciousness realized as an opposition. In this last section, I showed how this is so by considering the most general logic of the ego, and this analysis parallels Hegel's discussion of the concept as such, the concept of the concept. Now I want to turn more broadly to thinking about Hegel's *Logic* in general, and about the doctrine of the concept in particular.

Concept and Absolute Idea: Being Through Another

Now, finally, I want to talk about Hegel. I want first simply to identify the distinctive character of each of the three moments of the logic—being, essence, and concept—and to focus on the nature of concept with the goal of saying a little bit about the ultimate implication of this for how we should think about reality.

Though the dialectic of the *Logic* develops to ever more sophisticated categories, none of the earlier categories of the *Logic* is lost in the later.[12] We will, for example, always think in terms of things. Said otherwise, reality will always be articulated in terms of things. Things are not the absolute, though; that is, they do not exhaustively realize the nature of the real, and they are not the ultimate concepts needed to understand the real. Things will always be situated in a larger context of a reality that has its own autonomous principles. Things, therefore, are not metaphysically absolute, but metaphysically relative: they always exist relative to a larger whole, and must be understood in terms of that. The

12. Again, I here take myself to be in agreement with Burbidge's analysis.

same is true of forces, of chemical relations, of finitude, of the distinction between quality and quantity, and of identity and difference. All of these determinations are necessary dimensions of reality and necessary dimensions of thought, but none is the absolute.[13]

At the broadest level, there are three basic dimensions of reality or characteristics of thought that must be distinguished. These irreducibly necessary determinations are being, essence, and concept. First, reality as a whole and anything real within it will always necessarily be immediate; that is, it will be the first: that before which there could be no other, that is, most basically, what it means to "be" at all. This immediacy takes a variety of forms—catalogued in the doctrine of being—and these forms are all the forms of single-term concepts that identify something like the simplicity of the fact of being. Second, reality will always be mediated (reflected) in itself, which means it will have an identity, a meaningful "itself-ness" that pervades and permeates the entire range of its determinacy. This is essence, the realm of two-term relations of, basically, a self and its appearance (such as thing and property, force and expression, substance and accident) or generally essence and show. Third, reality will ultimately always be realized only through intrinsic relations to an opposed other. This is reality as concept, reality as intrinsically having the form of being-through-another, a three-term relation of an identity accomplished through a self-opposition. I want to say a few words about this last sort of determination.

The doctrine of the concept is the study of the forms of reality that can only be insofar as they are self-identities realized only as a relation of opposition, that is, identities that are only through another. In relations of reflection, it might look like we have this, inasmuch as essence and show stand in negative relation; that is, the thinghood and the property are *not* the same. This *not*, however, is insufficiently strong for the concept. At an obvious level, the properties, inasmuch as they are *of* the thing, are the same as the thing: thinghood and properties are two ways of talking about the same thing, and the relationship of dependency between them is significantly asymmetrical, in that the properties do not have an autonomous identity apart from the thing. The being-through-another of conceptual determinations is characterized, on the contrary,

13. The dialectic of things, forces and substance is at the heart of the "doctrine of essence," book 2 of the *Science of Logic*. It also provides the central structure to the dialectic of "Consciousness" in Hegel's *Phenomenology of Spirit*, tr. Arnold V. Miller (Oxford, New York, Toronto and Melbourne: Oxford University Press, 1977).

by a relation of *opposition* between the two elements; that is, the other for the self must be inherently expelled from the self, and must itself inherently expel the self from itself.[14]

A good example, I think, of a concept is the relation of an organism and its environment. In *Biology as Ideology,* Richard Charles Lewontin argues that there is no organism without *its* environment, and equally no environment without *its* organism, that is, each is defined in terms of the other, (what James Jerome Gibson calls a relation of "complementarity").[15] But the "otherness" of environment and organism is not like that of property and thing. The relationship of organism and environment is a relationship of *opposed things:* the thrush, for example, eats the snail, which snail itself opposes this ingression and hides from the thrush. To get the snail, the thrush will have to smash the snail against a rock, and oppose the snail's self-seclusion behind its protective wall of shell. That same rock on which the thrush does the smashing could also hurt or kill the thrush if the thrush were to smash its beak or wing against it too sharply, or if the thrush were to be under it when someone stepped upon it. Or again, the same sun that supplies life-sustaining warmth to the healthy gazelle will kill it when the gazelle with broken legs lies exposed on the plain. And of course the mosquito that takes my blood will die when I express my opposition to it with my hand. In each situation, the organism is able to be itself only by virtue of active relations of dependence upon the other determinations of its environment, but these other determinations are oppositional, which means they inherently resist the organism's assimilation of them, and equally must be resisted by the organism, or their own oppositional natural activity will destroy the organism. In the being-for-other of conceptual relations, the relation to other must be one of opposition.

What I have been describing here under the heading of "organism and environment" roughly falls within the category of "life" from the *Science of Logic,* or of "desire" from the *Phenomenology of Spirit.* In my earlier discussion of Fichte, I discussed this conceptual logic of being-through-another inherent to the self-positing of the ego, or to the con-

14. *Science of Logic,* 600–/2:273–79. On the developing nature of "the negative" throughout the *Logic,* see Dieter Henrich, "Formen der Negation in Hegels Logik," in *Seminar: Dialektik in der Philosophie Hegels,* edited by Rolf-Peter Horstmann, 213–29 (Frankfurt am Main: Suhrkamp Verlag, 1978).

15. Richard Charles Lewontin, *Biology as Ideology: The Doctrine of DNA* (San Francisco: HarperPerennial, 1993), chap. 5; James J. Gibson, *The Ecological Approach to Visual Perception* (New York: Houghton Mifflin, 1979).

cept as such. I want to conclude simply by identifying three other essential realizations of the concept, namely spirit—the central concept of the *Phenomenology of Spirit*—the absolute—the central concept of the *Science of Logic*—and philosophy itself as dialectical phenomenology. These, like the logic of the ego or the ecosystem, are again examples of aspects of reality that could not be conceptualized simply with a logic of immediacy or a logic of reflection. They are realities that can only be self-identities as relations to an opposed other.

After the ego or ecosystem, the next-most-obvious conceptual reality is what Hegel calls spirit, that is, the reality of a "we." Whether in the unity formed by a romantic couple or in a historically continuous political community, there is an intersubjective reality established that exceeds and redefines the individuals who enter into it. The identity each and all have is a shared one, but it is one that, far from effacing, is essentially premised on the opposed autonomous identities of the members. This is perhaps clearest in the spiritual (therefore conceptual) reality of language.

Communication requires something to communicate; that is, there must be something emanating from me that you cannot have on your own without the mediation of language, hence the existence of opposed, alienated realities; but, equally, I can communicate it to you only because the language is neither mine exclusively, nor yours, but inherently ours. Language is premised on both the essentiality of subjective alienation and the essentiality of intersubjective union. This also means, incidentally, that the reality of spirit is not settled in advance: it is real, but inasmuch as it is realized through autonomous individuals, it is uniquely realized through what we do. The universal is given as an inherent imperative, but not as an already accomplished fact.[16] It is, however, mostly the task of the *Phenomenology of Spirit* to articulate the reality of spirit, and it is not explicitly present in the *Logic,* so I will not dwell on it further. I mention it, rather, only to help make clear how we must think in the sphere of the concept.[17]

16. See my discussion of morality in "Spirit and Scepticism," in Russon, *Reading Hegel's Phenomenology (Bloomington: Indiana University Press, 2004).*

17. On the relation of spirit and logic, see Kenneth L. Schmitz, "Hegel's Attempt to Forge a Logic for Spirit," *Dialogue* 10 (1971): 653–72. On the general theme of the relationship between Hegel's *Logic* and language, see James Vernon, *Hegel's Philosophy of Language* (New York: Continuum, 2007), and Houlgate, *The Opening of Hegel's Logic*, chap. 4, especially 75–79; see also Wolfgang Wieland, "Bemerkungen zum Anfang von Hegels Logik," in *Seminar: Dialektik in der Philosophie Hegels*, edited by Rolf-Peter Horstmann, 194–212 (Frankfurt am Main: Suhrkamp Verlag, 1978).

A closely analogous conceptual logic is required to understand reality itself, or the nature of being as such—the absolute. I mentioned above that the logic of thinghood is ineffaceable, meaning that things are real. At the same time, the participation of things in a single self-same reality—substance—is also real. In the logic of the absolute relation—which is the absolute understood as a relation between itself *qua* substance and itself *qua* things, or itself *qua* universal and itself *qua* determinate, this relation that maintains the reality and autonomy of both the universal and the particular, both things and substance, is called, in Hegel as in Kant, "reciprocity," or the recognition of reality as a system. But what is the inner logic of this system?

For each thing *both* to retain its autonomy *and* to be a member of a system that itself is real and autonomous, and not just an epiphenomenon, the reality *of the system* must be the reality *of the member,* which means the whole must be internal to the member. Each member must then be unique, but a reflection of the whole; it must be, in Leibniz's language, a monad. But this monad, *qua* unique thing, must be intrinsically opposed to the other things, which means it can live up to the demand to embody the system only inasmuch as it is a unique individual that carries in itself the intrinsic imperative to reconcile with its others. This means the ultimate terms in which the reality of things (and of the whole) is to be understood are expressive terms: the reality of the thing is how it articulates the nature of other things, and the reality of the system is how a common reality is spoken—accomplished—through the reciprocal action of things. Reality itself, then, as reciprocity, is really in Hegel's sense a concept—or, rather, *the* concept—in that it exists only as a being-through-another, an identity accomplished as a communication between intrinsically opposed members.

Reality, then, the absolute, is no separate entity over and above the actual things, but is the immanent demand within things themselves that they reconcile. Things, then, are not effaced or surpassed, but they are also not metaphysically self-sufficient, for their very nature can only be understood out of the cooperative and self-definitive reality they interactively constitute. This again means that *what it is to be* cannot be settled in advance, but must be accomplished uniquely on the basis of the life of things. This is the idea of dialectic, or the absolute idea, namely, that reality is what is worked out immanently through the life of things, of the determinateness of reality.

Note finally that these notions of spirit and the absolute are not indifferent to each other. If the absolute is the universality realized internally to the real individuals, then it is only as spirit that the absolute can be, inasmuch as those individuals include us, and, indeed, include us preeminently: it is only in the context of the communication of the we that the unity of reality is accomplished. The need for spirit is thus internal to the absolute. And equally the immanent demand *to reconcile* that we saw must be internal to things is precisely the lived demand of the I as a self-consciousness: we precisely saw above that the nature of self-consciousness is to experience itself as realizing itself only through the comprehension of its other; that is, the need to accomplish the realization of the absolute is internal to the logic of self-consciousness. Indeed self-consciousness and being, subject and substance, name the ultimate opposition, the very opposition of mind and body, consciousness and reality that plagues the history of philosophy.

If our analysis of reality as concept, as absolute idea, announces that the reconciliation of subject and object is thus inherent to reality as such, then this means that reality is *significance*—it is *meaning*, "for."[18] What this means in the end is that reality itself is not, as philosophers inspired by William James like to say, a "brick" universe: reality is not some immediate stuff. The accomplishment of reality is not given—it is not "a" given in the sense of an immediacy, and it is not given "how" it will be realized. The accomplishment of reality is the task that defines us—that is what it means to be spirit.

Conclusion

Finally, what is the name for the reality that is accomplished precisely through this opposition, that is, the conceptual reality whose being-through-another is this reconciliation of subject and substance? This is philosophy. Philosophy is precisely self-consciousness living as the need to allow reality to show itself. And, inasmuch as this dynamic of being is integral to one's own self, it is the stance of resolute openness to a kind a bearing witness, a facilitation or shepherding of being, where that revelation of being is as much a redefinition of oneself. Hegel's *Logic,* then, concludes with something like Heidegger's ontology of *Dasein* as care, and this philosophy is, as Hegel says in the *Phenomenology,* a pathway of despair in which all one's fixed certainties are lost.[19]

18. Hyppolite's construal of the concept as "sens" and "love" (*Logic and Existence,* 4–5, 19) is thus quite accurate; See Hegel, *Science of Logic,* 603/2:277.

19. Hegel, *Phenomenology of Spirit,* paragraph 78 of Miller's translation.

Jay Lampert

8. VIOLENT AND NONVIOLENT TELEOLOGY IN HEGEL'S *SCIENCE OF LOGIC*

Some modern and postmodern philosophers favor violence as a means of outflanking authoritarian forms of peace and philosophy, and find promising concepts of violence in the great philosophers, above all in Hegel. This motivation is not altogether incorrect, but perhaps there are other ways besides violence to slip out of classical constraints. Kenneth Schmitz's philosophy of freedom is, among other things, a move away from modern violence philosophies. Yet with all his classical philosophical commitments, Schmitz is as modern a philosopher as there is, particularly regarding the modern proof of unconditioned freedom. For these reasons, his work is not only crucial for the advancement of philosophy in our day, but also for our interpretations of Hegel.

One thing I learned from having the great fortune to have studied Hegel's *Science of Logic* with Professor Schmitz is that close critical studies of that text can illuminate a vast range of philosophical concepts, whose power and importance go far beyond the historical study of German idealism. The present paper has this form, explicating a few points that Hegel makes concerning violence in teleology, with an eye to opening some possibilities for nonviolent ontology.

Schmitz himself develops an important account of teleology in *The Recovery of Wonder*.[1] He is not focused on Hegel in this book, and his tra-

1. Kenneth L. Schmitz, *The Recovery of Wonder: The New Freedom and the Ascetism of Power* (Montreal and Kingston: McGill-Queen's University Press, 2005); I draw especially on 68–101.

jectory of thought is different from mine, but his ideas there give valuable context to my own narrow focus. Schmitz is concerned that the history of modern philosophy has separated teleology from the Good, thereby separating the how from the why, and separating subjective freedom from the thickness of things. (Depending on one's choice of vocabulary, one could describe this modern view as teleology without the Good, or as freedom without teleology).[2] In fact, it seems to me that Hegel falls under this modernist sphere, as there is very little about ultimate purposes in Hegel's chapter on teleology that deals almost exclusively with what happens to means on the way to becoming ends (an ontology of desire-fulfillment that would fall under Schmitz's heading of conatus). Hegel is concerned with the mutually dialectical collapse of means in the face of subjective will, and the collapse of ends in the face of pragmatic activity. This would seem to put Hegel into the two-headed modernist camp: the technicians on the one side, and the voluntarists on the other, who are paradoxically united in their unwillingness to synthesize theory and practice. But the lineup of freedom with modernism, and the opposition of means-end teleology to ethics teleology, are made more complex by Schmitz's proposal for a "new freedom," namely the proposal to insert the very independence of freedom back into teleology oriented toward the Good. Subjective freedom has the virtue of expressing autonomy and self-renewal (its negative values), as well as creative imagination (its positive value). Subjective values would, considered by themselves, separate the form of freedom from the content of principles with inherent objective value. But reoriented toward objective value (or natural law), these features of freedom rather enhance the process, and indeed the content, of value. Combining "teleological dynamism" with "nonteleological conatus" has the ultimate benefit of expanding individual ends toward universal community and simultaneously bestowing the gift of community on each individual (Schmitz 2005, 101).

Schmitz calls for an "asceticism of power" (119)—humanism with humility. The idea is that natural law implies acting on behalf of the natural world instead of categorizing nature as means and ourselves as ends. I do not want to presume that the flow of ideas in my paper lives up to this call. But I think that a certain interpretation of Hegel's transition from

2. In fact, Hegel's discussion of teleology is part of this modernity, emphasizing the how over the why. Hegel does have room for the why, but more under the category of "right" than of purpose. Hegel obviously affirms the universal that gives meaning and value to the particular, but he does not associate that level of universality with teleology.

the moment of violence in means-ends relations to the moment of nonviolence can contribute to Schmitz's model of noncoercive teleology.

Determining the precise location of violence in a system of causes—efficient or final—turns out to be extremely difficult. In the sections of the *Science of Logic* on cause and effect, Hegel says: "Violence (*Gewalt*) is the *appearance (Erscheinung* [Miller: 'manifestation']) *of power,* or power as *external*" (Hegel 1969, sect. 567/200).[3] Ultimately, a cause will suffer as much violence when it is manifested in some other thing as the caused thing does when it manifests another thing's power. We might say that violence occurs whenever an object is made to suffer power passively. (Hegel almost always pairs violence with suffering, *Gewalt* with *leiden.*) Indeed, whenever an object is affected, it is "broken within itself" (567/200). A part of it internalizes the intruder, and this treasonous part of the object makes the other parts of the same object passive to it. Now, this could be considered a standard definition of internalized violence, and even a standard definition of dialectic. On this definition, a late modern reader would expect (and I did expect) to find violence all over Hegel's *Science of Logic,* particularly when the internalization of externality is at issue near the end of the book. So it is not surprising to find this statement at the heart of the "Teleology" chapter: "That the end relates itself immediately to an object and makes it a means ... may be regarded as *violence*" (746/397). This is again a common attitude toward teleology: the teleological structure does violence to the objects that were previously happily going about their business. To the extent that Hegel's philosophy of history may be regarded as teleological, it would be normal to speak of history as a slaughter-bench. But of course, teleology is not the last word in Hegel's logic, and his philosophy of history is not ultimately teleological;[4] so the thesis that teleology is violent may not, after all, imply that dialectic in general is violent. In fact, Hegel is cautious with the term "violence," attributing it to just one specific moment in the teleology chapter: the moment at which an activity directed toward an end manipulates the objective means in order to realize a subjective goal. But while there is this moment of violence in teleology, by the end of the chapter Hegel will conclude the opposite, namely that there is "no

3. Textual references to Hegel are given both according to the A. V. Miller translation, *Hegel's Science of Logic* (Atlantic Highlands, N.J.: Humanities Press, 1969), and according to G. W. F. Hegel, *Wissenschaft der Logik, Zweiter Teil* (Leipzig: Felix Meiner, 1948); I use Miller's translation as a foundation, but occasionally the translations are my own.

4. For my brief argument to this effect, see Jay Lampert, *Deleuze and Guattari's Philosophy of History* (London: Continuum, 2006), 87–92.

violence" even in teleology. Indeed, by the end of the book, Hegel will say that the Absolute Idea releases itself through inner peace. In a broad sense, this has made me question the conflictual model of Hegel, which most of us left-wingers have adopted against the right-wing structural model of Hegel. I have started to wonder whether dialectical contradiction might not be a kind of repose more than it is a kind of conflict.

I will discuss three passages in the objectivity section of Hegel's *Logic,* where the issue of violence and nonviolence arises: one from the pre-teleological chapter on mechanism; one from the teleology chapter on realized ends; and one from the post-teleological chapter on the idea of the Good. To schematize the flow of ideas: there is a kind of protoviolence in mechanism, but true violence exists only in teleology; yet even within the contours of teleology, violence starts to be overcome; the Good ultimately realizes ends in a postviolent order. To preview the definitions in these passages: violence is the internalization of negation; violence is the wearing-down of objects; and violence is delay.

I begin with a brief point and an important definition from the mechanism chapter. The essence of a mechanical system is that it has a structural center (sect. 721/371). (In one passage, Hegel simply refers to "centrality" when he means mechanism [sect. 745/396]). To say that its center is structural means that it has a point of ignition. Spatially, the engine could be anywhere, but functionally, the engine is the center. And because the center is functional, the material parts that perform various functions are replaceable. A system with a formal center is indifferent to the particular parts that occupy that center. For that matter, the center is indifferent to the periphery, and the energy of the engine is indifferent to the results it produces elsewhere (sect. 740/391). In short, the parts of a mechanical system are functional, and have no intrinsic value or indispensability. The various parts put up mutual resistance, but also succumb to the power of the others. In truth, they are overpowered by their *own* fragility. Nevertheless, in a mechanism, power appears to be extraneous to the parts affected, and this generates the first definition of violence: "What turns power into *violence* is this, that though power is *identical* with the *nature* of the object, its determinateness or negativity is not its own *negative reflection* into itself by which it is an individual" (sect. 720/370). The important element of this definition is that power is not violent in itself, nor is negation, nor is destruction. Obviously, everything undergoes change or negation at some level; but there is no violence in that, as long as (a) the thing does not care, or (b) the thing is the source of, or at least freely appropriates and internalizes, that negation. A thing only suffers violence if it tries, but fails, to take itself to be the source of its own negation. Even if a thing contains the spirit of its own changes, it still suffers violence to the extent that it does not recognize that fact, that is, if it sees its own internality as a foreigner.[5] If I am reading this correctly, it means that mechanism never exhibits violence per se, since mechanical parts are incapable of suffering the *lack* of negative reflection. Only free purposive beings, for whom power *could* have meant internal negativity, can experience mechanical power as violence and suffer by it.

For Hegel, the main difference between a mechanical system and a chemical one is that the latter does not require a center. In a chemical solution, the center falls asunder (sect. 726/376), and the system becomes fluid. It is still determined by causal relations, but each chemical cause saturates the region of its effects. Love (sect. 727/377), communication (sect. 729/379), and tension (sect. 735/385), for example, are causal systems that are closer to chemical than mechanical. At the extreme end of saturation is the freedom to be determined by "another nature" (sect. 746/398), a decentering whose telos is to let the future in. Of course, a machine can be used and even designed purposefully, but since its pieces are mutually indifferent, it cannot be a purposive whole in and for itself. But a whole that is saturated throughout by its own elements, and thereby unable to resist infection, is both purposive and corruptible.[6] Self-saturation for the first time makes function *inherent* in a causal system, and so is the first and simplest version of natural teleology. The possibility of true violence is now just a few steps away.

In teleology, "content becomes important" (sect. 736/386). In mechanism, any result of water might be important. Its capacity to crush can be as salient as its capacity to moisten. But once we are concerned with inherent function, or telos, only certain results of water, namely when wet substance wets something that can be wet, are interesting. This, Hegel says, is why an end often seems only trivially different from functionality. Important results are inherently tautological. So since teleology will be the site of violence, we will have to ask why trivial causes are especially violent. Why are mechanical results (lead makes you dead) less violent than teleological results (water makes you watery)?

5. "Spirit is in this individual as his universal and as the power over him from which he suffers violence, as his pathos, by giving himself over to which his self-consciousness loses its freedom"; *Phenomenology of Spirit*, trans. A. V. Miller (Oxford: Oxford University Press, 1977), sect. 704, 427/515; *Phänomenologie des Geistes* (Frankfurt: Suhrkamp Verlag, 1973).

6. See Jennifer Bates's article in this volume.

Hegel's teleology chapter is divided into sections on the subjective end or aim, the means, and the realized end.[7] I should say that since I am focusing here on the topic of violence in teleology, there are some issues of textual explication that I am not going to develop. If I were concerned primarily with the continuous argument of the text of Hegel's *Logic,* I would need to ground the distinction between subjective will and objective fact. It is not too difficult to see the dialectical progression from mechanism to chemism as the direct consequence of the infusion of attributes across portions of a system. It is also not too difficult to see the dialectical progression from chemism to natural teleology, that is, to proper organic functions, as the holistic consequence of saturated attributes. But organicism is only one of three common paradigms of teleology, alongside instrumentality and ethical and social value. When Hegel structures his account of teleology around the distinction between subjective aim and objective results (and all the dialectical reversals and mediations that follow), he effectively begins with an instrumentalist paradigm and moves toward a paradigm of the social good. But even in this general flow of paradigms, Hegel sometimes places an example of organic teleology where we do not expect it, and in fact he does not draw examples from social teleology nearly as often as we expect. I think there might be a satisfactory argument for Hegel's mixed paradigms under the heading of teleology. We might be able to show how the dialectical progression from organicism to instrumentalism to sociality is a consequence of a functional system absorbing, transforming, and expelling elements from its environment. But for my purposes here, I want to enter more quickly into Hegel's discussions of violence in teleology, so I will adopt without critique Hegel's terms of subjective aim, objective ends, and mediation through means.

Where does violence enter into a teleological system?

In Hegel's discussion, violence does not come up at the stage of subjective ends. In Hegel's account, there is no violence in desiring things to change, no violence when the intellect introduces interpretations, values, or projects into objects, no violence in the "urge to posit the self externally" (sect. 740/391).[8] For one thing, as we will see later, ideas are violence-free.[9] For another thing, while purposive intelligence confronts objects

7. The German term for both ends of the end is *Zweck,* but Miller sometimes translates subjective end as "aim" and realized end as "end," which I find helpful.

8. Not even when it is "directed against external objectivity" (sect. 741/392).

9. We commonly think of universalizing concepts as doing violence to the individual reality of things, but sometimes it is the real phenomenon that does violence to a con-

and is repulsed by them, it "presupposes" the power of the already existing world. Intellect never questions, let alone abolishes, the object's mechanical power. If anything, the concept needs objects in order to become objective, which is just why teleology is so important to the concept. Indeed, when a subject expresses its goals over against the world, it is these goals that seem weak and "other-worldly" (sect. 742/393), powerless, and subject to interminable delays.[10] Of course, the intent of subjective aims is to overcome both the independent strength of the object and the detached weakness of the subject through their middle term, namely, through the means. The subjective aim aims to make a tautology out of subject and object, aim and end, to make the object's function exhibit nothing other than the subject's purpose. So if the subjective aim is not the source of violence, is it the means that exercises violence against things in the world?

The means, or purposive process, treats the object as a mere stage toward an end. We could call this the mean's first negation of the object. But the mean's second negation of the object sublates the very difference between subject and object, and between aim and end, absorbing both, treating both as intermediaries in a world that is always carrying something out,[11] whether instrumentally or vitally. Everything is already "identical with the end" (sect. 745/396). On the one hand, every event succeeds in bringing about some end or other. On the other hand, no object "has the force (*Kraft*) of resistance against the end"; every object is "penetrable and receptive of this communication (*Mitteilung*)" (sect. 745/396). Mechanical and chemical entities had at least limited ways of distinguishing themselves from the ends they arrive at. But once an object is a being-for-self, it cannot separate itself from its fulfillment, and so "the object has the character of being powerless (*machtlos*) against the end and of serving it" (sect. 745/396). Now, the inability to resist communication sounds like an expansion of the definition of violence proposed

---

cept. For example, "the status of the slave injures (*verletzt*) the concept [of a human being]"; G. W. F. Hegel, *Hegel's Philosophy of Right,* trans. Allen W. Wood (Cambridge: Cambridge University Press, 1991), 2 and 27; Hegel, *Grundlinien der Philosophie des Rechts* (Hamburg: Verlag von Felix Meiner, 1955), 20.

For an example of the more common picture: "As *actual universality,* [the ethical power of the state] is a violence (*Gewalt*) against individual being-for-self" (Hegel, *Phenomenology of Spirit,* 449, 268/330).

10. The twist is that the objective world, the source of power, prevents the real world, as it ought to be, from arising.

11. But the second negation remains in the *form* of the first negation, since it posits the means-end process within objectivity.

earlier, namely that an object suffers violence when it incorporates negative externality. One might have used the term "violence" to refer to any occasion when a finite thing is caught up in a larger whole. But Hegel is saving the term "violence" for something more. Being forced into servitude is not sufficient to suffer violence; for Hegel, one suffers violence only when one's *own* ends are realized. In a sense, this means that one has the right to violence only over oneself, and even when it is justified, it is still a kind of falsehood.[12] Hegel saves the term "violence" for the situation where purposive activity negates the object for the third time, namely the situation where the confrontation with a hostile object is the obliquely desired result of the subject's own goals, that is, where realizing one's own ends leads to the downfall of something in the subject, in addition to the downfall of something in the object, not to mention the downfall of something in the very process. So it is in a sense not the aim or the means, but the realized end, that must be the source of violence in teleology, if anything is.

Hegel discusses the realized end under the moments of activity, product, and return.

Hegel finds violence not in the transitory world of mutual absorption, transformation, or even generalized destruction, but only when an object is destroyed by something that recognizably deserves to destroy the object (and in so doing destroys itself). Yet Hegel's argument cannot be that the end is greater than the sum of the means. The end is after all just another activity or potency. In a real sense, ends are completely accounted for as soon as we regard the whole world as a network of means. As we noted before, the relation between means and ends is a trivial tautology. If ends nevertheless have superior value to means, it has to be something immanent to the web of means that accounts for this.

The first implication for the world of means is that it is indifferent to what counts as its provisional ends. The end will not be a final cause or force, but the contingent result that substitutes one situation for another (sect. 746/397). The end is the *next* objectivity after the means, some "other" object. But this implies a second point, namely that the end consists

12. One concrete example where Hegel makes this point concerns reason's right to violence; but the only things over which reason *can* exercise its violence are things that are already in principle rational. "Herein lies the absolute *right* [Miller: "authority"] of violence which insight exercises over faith; but the *reality* on which it exercises this violence lies just in the fact that the faithful consciousness is itself the concept, and therefore itself acknowledges the opposite which insight puts before it" (Hegel, *Phenomenology of Spirit,* sect. 565, 345/419).

not in the particular new object, but in the form of total objective effectiveness. Paradoxically, it is precisely because the end does not appear as some special result, but can in turn become a means, that it has a value superior to that of any particular means. The end is the purposive character of objectivity, which makes every object unable to remain itself.

This relation between end and object, finally, is the point where Hegel articulates the source of violence.

> That the end relates itself immediately to an object and makes it a means, as also that through this means it determines another object, may be regarded as *violence,* in so far as the end appears to be of quite another nature than the object, and both objects similarly are mutually independent totalities. But that the end posits itself in a *mediate* relation with the object and *interposes* another object *between* itself and it, may be seen as the *cunning* of reason (sect. 746/397–98).

Now, one could read Hegel's "may be regarded as" clauses as asserting that in fact there is no real violence at all in teleology, only the cunning of reason that uses apparent violence to bring about legitimate ends. But I think the text is asserting a real violence and a specific kind of cunning that shields the end from the violence it perpetrates.

The end is present primarily as a subjective goal and as an ideal result, but both of these forms of presence are ideal. In actual fact, the end is present only to the extent that the means are producing it in some particular object. The end thus turns an object into the end's secondary presence. This secondary presence of the end, that is, the object, wears itself out and perishes, but shields the primary presence of the end while doing so, so that the end is not worn out along with the object. The end is protected by the object-shield while it is metamorphosing. So when the object is remade in the form of the end, the standpoint of the end can claim that nothing of importance suffered during the process. "The end puts forward an object as means, allows it to wear itself out in its stead, exposes it to attrition and shields itself behind it from mechanical violence" (sect. 747/398).

The first moment of violence is thus that the object *qua* means wears out (sect. 745/396). Insofar as the end comes into existence through reason, reason takes the concrete form of a tool, so that it is the tool and not reason itself that is worn down in producing an effect. Destroying something that is not a tool—for example, breaking a tree into pieces to make a house—would not count as violence (sect. 750/402). Only when an object has already been shaped as a tool, for example, a plow, does the fact that it wears out in doing its job count as violence. Similarly, smashing up a plow for no reason is not violent in this sense. Violence occurs when the object is worn down by the success of its own purpose. Hegel's examples do not touch on treating people as means to an end, but perhaps they should. Obviously, violence is suffered less by the plow than by the laborer whose wages are too low to keep up repairs to his plow. The homeowner suffers violence when her means to finish building the house are exhausted, when the finished house turns out to be too expensive for her to keep. The point is that when we think of a human being treated violently as a means, we are not usually thinking of a tool being worn down; we are thinking of the person's aims being worn down *with* the tool.

The second moment of violence is that the object *qua* "product" (sect. 748/400) also wears out. An end, after all, is always just a provisional phase in a world of means. The end co-opts the means, so that the means can claim the honor of bringing about a superior result. But this is precisely how the end cunningly reestablishes its superiority: not by futilely attempting to subordinate the means to some hypothetically higher nature, but by co-opting the means, guaranteeing that the means are always fulfilled, so that it is the means that claim to be bringing about a superior result. The cunning of the end is to bring the means onside, to make the means into its own other-nature, so that violence is suffered only by the bare physical object, and not by any part of the logic of means and ends. In transferring its value to the means, the end cunningly continues to rule the causal system, precisely by conceding that the means are ontologically superior to the "finite ends of external purpose" (sect. 747/398). To use Hegel's example, the value of the plow is superior to that of the daily pleasures of food, "which pass away and are forgotten" (sect. 747/398). The glory, the concept, and the long-range success of the plow outlast both the mechanism of the instrument and the empirical ends it achieves. In other words, the end does violence to objects *as ends,* as well as to objects as means. If we can still speak of an end that does the violence, then that kind of end is not in any way or at any time an actual result. Actual results are not the sorts of ends that do violence. The end that does violence is nothing but the "totality," or the "truth of the process," or the "freedom" of the negative (747/399). Freedom is violent here not because it demands perfection; on the contrary, freedom enjoys every object and moves happily on to the next, treating every one as the "translation" of its concept into practice, "meeting itself through itself" as the "becoming of what has become" (748/399).

To summarize, the means wear out, the ends pass away, and violence is done to every object *qua* aim, *qua* means, and *qua* end as well. Hegel's examples of the erosion of stones in a house do not quite make this point, but it is not hard to imagine cases where decay in the stones is identical with urban decay (violence to the means and violence to the ends being inseparable), and ultimately destroys the purpose of communal living.[13] The whole package of value hierarchy has to be sent back to the intellect for rethinking. Ultimately, it is not just purposes that do violence to objects; teleology does violence to purposes. And yet, this picture of all-pervasive violence and the return to thought will be the premise for Hegel's conclusion that there is no violence in teleology, after all.

The last points in Hegel's teleology chapter are designed to show that teleology is not ultimately about finite ends, and indeed that it is ultimately not even about ends at all, finite or infinite, but about a "return" (*zurückkehren,* sect. 751/403).

That ends and means wear each other out implies that the means already presuppose their conclusions, and yet never quite arrive at them. It is as though purposiveness is supposed to be a syllogism, but remains only an "infinite progress of mediation" (sect. 749/401).[14] The means perish on the way to the end; the end never arrives through the means, anyway; yet since the end can arrive in no other way but through the means, the very idea of the end is undermined as well. On the one hand, the end *is fully realized* when it is distributed across time and does not have to wait for the end. But on the other hand, teleology at all levels is the "destiny to be destroyed" (sect. 750/401). Yet it is at this moment that Hegel affirms nonviolence.

Hegel's idea is that once the conceptual status of an end is communicated into objectivity by its means, and once the end is defined as whatever the means happen to produce—not constricting the means into some special result but merely a relay station in the network of pro-

13. To give some more examples, the scrapping of plows by high-tech agriculture ultimately destroys the purpose of providing nutrition. The destruction of the finite enjoyment of love destroys the whole teleology of love. The assent to false propositions destroys the whole purpose of thought.

14. Hegel makes several word plays in this section around *Schluss* (syllogism): *Entschluss* (resolve), *Ausschluss* (exclusion), and *Aufschluss* (explication) (sect. 742/393, 751/403). It seems to me that the motif of the syllogism is oversaturated by these word plays. At some point in Hegel's system, after all, the syllogism form is sublated (by sect. 837/498, this is clear). To my mind, the sublation of syllogism happens here in teleology. The moment when syllogism is sublated is also the moment when nonviolence can be affirmed.

visions—we find that the end is less a form of command than a form of reinforcement.

In order to make the object a means, the subjective end needs to use *no violence* against the object, and no reinforcement against it, other than the reinforcing of itself (sect. 751/403).

In almost exactly the same words that Hegel earlier used to assert the violence of turning an object into a means for the sake of an end, he now denies that there is any violence involved. Now the object just needs reinforcement (*Bekräftigung*).

Why does the identity of aim, means, and end imply practical nonviolence? Perhaps, to generate an example, Hegel's idea is that if we take farming as a large-scale system, a well-distributed teleology, then the depreciation of plows can be taken into account and need not harm the enterprise. Of course, plows and peasants and professors surely do get destroyed. It is not as though Hegel is saying that there is no such thing as violence, let alone destruction or death. He is only saying that teleology is not the reason individuals suffer violence. He is only saying that dialectical logic does not entail that there is violence in the practical world, or in the theoretical world, or in any necessary relation between intellect and mechanism.

We can construe three reasons for saying there is no violence once an end is realized distributively. Of course, we cannot use as a reason the idea that the end transcends the suffering of finite objects. That idea of the end has been long since refuted. The *first* argument for nonviolence is precisely the opposite of this. That is, teleology shows that there is no end still to come, no end we are waiting for—in short (these are my words, not Hegel's), teleology shows that there is no point. And where there is no point, there is no violence. Hegel is quite clear that "the end is not merely an *ought-to-be* and a *striving* to realize itself, but as a concrete totality is identical with the immediate objectivity" (753/405). Even when Hegel said earlier that "the object ... fulfils its end not by a peaceful (*ruhig*) existence in which it preserves itself, but only in so far as it is worn away" (sect. 750/401–02), he never suggested that some more real end survives the demise of the finite end.

The subjective aim seemed earlier to be naive in assuming that its ideals could be enacted nonviolently. Violence seemed to appear the instant any end overhauled some object. But once ends perish, too, the whole process appears less as a purposive series and more as a single, if complex, thought experiment. The subjective aim is, in a way, confirmed in its claim to nonviolence. It sees in advance the nonviolence that will define it after it has finished being subjected to violence. Indeed, this sort of definition, which revises itself in advance, is the paradigm of teleology. Violent teleology is just what suffers violence at the hands of nonviolent teleology.

This sounds like sophistry, but it has content. Hegel's term for what I am calling the post-teleological telos of teleology—in other words, the structure that includes negative self-reflection without an end product; the subjectivity that does not presuppose objectivity as the basis for improvement but pervades objectivity as its inner reflection; the standpoint from which, to cite Hegel's phrase again, "the subjective end needs to use no violence against the object" (sect. 751/403)—is the idea. The *second* reason teleology ends without violence is, then, that ideas are contemplative rather than insistent. In fact, we meet the realized end *as* an idea, as the "Idea of the Good," sixty pages later. Hegel says there that the realized end and the Idea of the Good are "altogether the same" (sect. 819/478), except for the latter's relation to the True. In the Good, as in teleology, the end is expressed in the means, subject to "external contingency" and internal "conflict" (sect. 820/479–80).[15] The difference that explains why Hegel does not use the vocabulary of violence to describe the path toward the good is that the end of the Idea of the Good "does not first have to have its truth received through its realization, but already, for itself, has the true" (sect. 819/479). In Miller's translation, the end of the good "does not have to wait" (sect. 819) to be realized before it distributes the theory and practice of freedom. "The Good, the absolutely Good, is eternally accomplishing itself in the world; and the result is that it needs *not wait* upon us, but is already by implication, as well as in full actuality, accomplished" (*Encyclopedia,* sect. 212Z).[16]

This is the *third* reason teleology converts to nonviolence. To the extent that teleology does have a stage of violence toward objects, it is because the object's self-satisfaction is delayed, sometimes permanently. The other elements in violence—namely becoming passive, reflecting the negative, becoming unshielded, perishing, wearing out before perishing—are all functions of delay.

15. As in teleology, "the finite end in its *realization* gets no further than a *means*"; again, "[the Idea of the Good] is not only subject to destruction by external contingency and by evil, but also by the collision and conflict of the good itself"; again, the good "remains an *ought*" (sect. 820/479–80).

16. G. W. F. Hegel, *The Logic of Hegel,* trans. William Wallace (London: Oxford University Press, 1965), 352.

Hegel's section on the realized end concludes with a similar point. Accomplishing an end means closing the circle (*eingeschlossenen*) of its own negative moments (sect. 752/404), so that *all* the means get fulfilled. In the *ausgeführte Zweck,* Hegel's general term for "realized end," a process is accomplished in such a way that the means are no longer needed; but in the *realisierte Zweck*, a process wraps itself up so that the object is the "return (*Rückkehr*) of the end into itself" (sect. 751/403). Hence, the final reason teleology ends nonviolently is that what had suffered violence returns. The object's own goals are not simply delayed by an end that jumps the queue and takes its place; rather, the end gives the object its turn in return. Of course, when Hegel speaks of getting the good out of a process without having to wait, the image is not a *totum simul,* eternity visible in an instant. In some respects, after all, even the Good "stands in its own way" (sect. 822/482). The image is rather a "moment immediately doubled, and a first that is always also a second" (sect. 752/404). A teleological process is in effect two processes running simultaneously on two different temporal structures: in one of the two, objects do get destroyed and their ends do arrive too late to do them any good; but in the other process, which runs contemporaneously with it, the object's future alter ego is its idea, the mark of the object's truth. The second is still the first; "the end is *reached* (*erreicht*) in the means" (sect. 753/405).

It is important that Hegel solves the problems of teleological violence not with a transition to the inner substance of things expressed in external effects, that is, not in categories of ontological fulfillment, but with a transition to the sphere of cognition, or ideas. Hegel's *Philosophy of Mind* ends with the affirmation that "the idea engenders and enjoys itself" (sect. 577, 315/463).[17] In the *Phenomenology of Spirit,* for example, speaking of the teleology of knowledge that drives consciousness, Hegel says that "The goal (*Ziel*), however, is as necessarily fixed for knowledge as is the serial progression; it is the point where knowledge no longer needs to go beyond itself. . . . Whatever is confined within the limits of a natural life cannot by its own efforts go beyond its immediate existence; it is driven beyond it by something else, and this uprooting entails its death. Consciousness, however, is explicitly the *concept* of itself. . . . Thus consciousness suffers this violence at its own hands" (sect. 80, 51/74). In other words, the goal of self-conceptualization drives consciousness beyond its actuality to death, but also drives it beyond the beyond, back to

17. G. W. F. Hegel, *Philosophy of Mind*, trans. William Wallace (Oxford: Oxford University Press, 1978); Hegel, *Enzyklopädie* (Hamburg: Felix Meiner, 1975).

its idea of itself. Consciousness suffers violence in metamorphosing into a concept, but thereby successfully moves beyond violence.

Now, perhaps ideas have nothing to wait for just because they arrive too late in the day to prevent the violence they comprehend. Of course, when Hegel speaks of ideas, he is not speaking of mental representations, so he is not merely saying that acts are violent if carried out but nonviolent when only thought about. And an idea, for Hegel, is not simply a holism, so he is not merely taking the apologist position that acts are violent when seen in isolation but nonviolent when taken in context (though it is fair to say that false and one-sided divisions, between nations or between individual interests, are the source of much unnecessary violence).[18] In order to read the ideational logic of processes, we have to focus on just what it is in their teleological structure that is superseded by ideas. In the flow of Hegel's argument, what is superseded in the transition from the violent to the nonviolent is specifically the shield. In reality, even when conceived under the category of ideas, there are still means and ends, processes and decay, destruction and success. But if, under the category of ideas, there is no shield—no shield at the level of visibility, and no shield at the level of temporality—no deception and no waiting—then there is no violence. To be sure, it would be unpalatable if we had to say that for Hegel, a quick death in the light of day was by definition less violent than death awaited under cover of darkness. But again, it is not the death that Hegel says is ultimately nonviolent (death itself is both violent and inevitable), it is the way in which the negation of death can or cannot be incorporated into the self-determination of the thing, with or without the concealment of agency and ecstatic temporality. Without introducing any theological content to the categories, we might say that the violence of death (but not death itself) is cancelled under the categories of revelation and eternity. Or in categories more suitable for action theory, we might say that deshielding toward nonviolence means not just that the facts of means-ends relations become known, but that ends are returned to those whose labor produced them.

Now, if it were possible to act in ethical life according to one category of Hegelian logic rather than another, it might seem that the con-

18. Schmitz has a brilliant discussion of Hegel's fraught attempt to balance the inevitability of war between individual nations with the universalizing conditions that might ground a kind of peace; Kenneth L. Schmitz, "Hegel on War and Peace," in *Conceptions de la paix dans l'histoire de la philosophie*, ed. Venant Cauchy (Montreal: Éditions Montmorency, 1987), 127–40.

clusion to Hegel's story is that we ought to act from ideas and not from goals. But the nature of logical categories is that each one applies to every possible object. Because of this, we should expect to see both violence and its eventual conversion to nonviolence within the becoming of every object and every process, whatever the subjective motivation. What, finally, is the space of this conversion? Hegel's answer is space.

The very end of the *Science of Logic,* which announces the transition from logic to nature, contains Hegel's last word about logical peace: "the Idea *freely releases* itself in its absolute self-assurance and inner peace (*in sich ruhend*)" (sect. 843/505), into all-inclusive natural space. In the final analysis, means and ends are laid out side-by-side as a series of events on the horizon, simply occupying diverse places in space and time. The inner repose in logic's last word is that there is nothing that cognition is supposed to struggle to actualize, other than to "freely release itself" into "the externality of space and time" (sect. 843/505). Not the time of anxiety and suffering, but the material time of whatever happens.

Martin Donougho

9. PERFORMING HEGEL

Theodor W. Adorno remarks of Hegel that "for a contemporary of Humboldt it is striking how little he is concerned with language."[1] The same could hardly be said of Adorno, who in stark contrast presents himself as the self-conscious stylist, ever alert to the subtleties of form and attitude. Yet his own practice was often to set language *against* itself, to push the envelope of intelligibility, the opposite of transparent communication. And this, oddly enough, was the trait he admired above all in Hegel. For example, a few pages after the above we read: "The dialectic's protest against language cannot be voiced directly except in language" (121)—language that resists any congealing into determinate concepts. Hegel's texts, Adorno contends, are in fact "antitexts" (119). There follows another observation about Hegelian language, even more subversive than the previous one. Citing Horkheimer's squib that only someone who knows Swabian can really understand Hegel, he adduces Hotho's well-known description of Hegel's lecturing manner: a rebarbative stuttering, metallic in tone, relayed in the thickest of accents.[2] Hegel is seen—heard, rather—as in revolt against high-flown academese, even in his most elab-

1. Theodor W. Adorno, "Skoteinos, or How to Read Hegel," in his *Hegel: Three Studies* (1963, 1971; repr., Cambridge, Mass.: MIT Press, 1993), 89–148, 155–57, at 118. Page references in this chapter are to this edition.

2. Alexander Koyré also cites the passage, in his still-worth-reading "Note sur la langue et la terminologie hégéliennes" (1931), in *Études d'histoire de la pensée philosophique* (Paris: Gallimard, 1971), 191–224, at 211n. Koyré considers Hegel one of the greatest *writers* in Germany. Adorno's point would be that he is a great writer precisely *because* his writing is so awkward.

orate texts staying closer to speech than to writing proper. Adorno concludes: "his books are not actually books but rather annotated lectures (*Vortrag*); often a mere reverberation (*Nachhall*), deliberately inconclusive (*unverbindlich*) even in published form" (119). To expand on Adorno's observation, you could say that Hegel's books are more like instructions for musical performance—as if we could sing (or at least hum) along.

Now I don't want to be taken to imply that Professor Schmitz ever offered his students music lessons—let alone in some metallic Swabian accent (his own voice is engagingly melodious)—when over several years he was regularly teaching his course on Hegel's *Science of Logic* at the University of Toronto. (It is incidentally a matter for regret that Schmitz came to publish little from this enormous and thoroughgoing effort, which remains, if you will, a book that was not actually a book.) Yet among the many insights offered in his classes I well remember the suggestion that the reader can and should identify several distinct levels of "warranted speech" in this most intricate of texts. The *Science of Logic* was something that stuck in my mind and which I have tried to make use of in referring to the "*performative*" element in Hegel's writing: what is assumed or implicit in what is said, and the context, mode of address, rhetorical strategies, or conventions in use (e.g., exemplification). While the scholarly literature has paid due attention to various aspects of Hegelian language—to the logical format of his dialectic on the one hand, or to his semantics and syntactics on the other—thus far its *pragmatics* (what it may be taken as presupposing, what normative commitments it implicates) has been little heeded, it strikes me.

I'd like, in tentative spirit, to advance some ideas as to how different levels or modes of operation might be discerned in Hegel's texts (scripts, scores), including those "texts" not even conceived for publication—specifically his *Lectures on Aesthetics*. A secondary aim would be drawing a comparison between Hegel and a more contemporary figure—who isn't even a philosopher, strictly speaking, though a good dose of philosophy went into his grand project—namely the late German sociologist Niklas Luhmann. He too envisaged theory (even meta-theory) as a form of communicative praxis: an intellectual operation as much as settled doctrine or system, for which the subject of "*énonciation*" is as salient as the subject of the "*énoncé*" (to use Benveniste's distinction, itself inspired by Kojève's lectures on *Phenomenology*).[3] First comes a brief sortie into

3. In Benveniste's view, the use of the deictic "I" serves to project subjectivity into discourse, but equally to instantiate the linguistic system, and confer on it a real context. "I"

Hegel's *Science of Logic,* then a section briefly introducing Luhmann as Hegelian manqué (or at least ironized), followed by a conclusion on a Luhmannian (or Luhmanntic) approach to art, from a Hegelian point of view.

Pragmatics in Hegel's Science of Logic

What is Hegel's own preferred mode of address, or at least, the address found in various instances of text published under his name? Does the mode of presentation (*Darstellung*) change as we go along? How many presentational "levels" or "registers" can we plausibly identify? Sometimes an "official" text is followed by a remark (*Anmerkung*); let us ignore here problems raised by "additions" (*Zusätze*) due to various auditors. Is this akin to Spinoza's "double-aspect" procedure: pure (if finite) thought followed by a proliferation of "how to do it" scholia? Does it lead to paradox—the remarks are also marked, at once part of and outside the body of the text—and if so, does that render any reading "undecidable"? Freud tells the joke (relayed in turn by Lacan and Žižek) about the Jew from Krakow who complains to another, "Why do you tell me you are going to Lemberg, when you'd say that only if you wanted me to think you were *not* going to Lemberg?"[4] The point? Simply to ask how we are to settle questions of textual intention. What are we to suppose Hegel means us to take him as meaning when he writes something? What is he (what are his texts) trying to get us to *do* when we read him (them)?

These are big (if not undecidable) questions, of a sort Hegel scholars and exegetes have hardly begun to explore, it strikes me. In the remainder of this section I propose a brief foray into Hegelian texts (or should I say, typical Hegelian "utterances"?). In turning to Hegel's *Logic,* I might preface what I say by noting that it culminates in *judgment* (*Urteil*) rather than the *proposition* or *principle* (*Satz*), and that the act of judging is taken, by Hegel, as essentially a practical involvement, not something neutral or disinterested. In that respect it takes Kant's reflective judgment

signifies "the person who utters the present instance of discourse containing *I*"; Emile Benveniste, *Problèmes de linguistique générale,* vol. 1 (Paris: Gallimard, 1966), 252. For Benveniste, the utterance (or enunciation) is the act by which the speaker sets the entire "*langue*" in motion; it is an all-or-nothing matter. The Hegelian question, reiterated at each stage of his system, concerns the squaring of subjective act (or performative) with the substance of what is claimed (its meaning).

4. Savoj Žižek, *The Sublime Object of Ideology* (New York: Verso, 1989), 195; Jacques Lacan, *Four Fundamental Concepts of Psychoanalysis* (New York: W. W. Norton, 1979), 112.

to its extreme: not merely the grammatical but equally the enunciating subject is implicated in the matters adjudged.[5] Or again, a judgment supposes a context, in which the language (as Wittgenstein says) does work; it answers a question, resolves a problem or a doubt. Judgments are on a par with what the movie *Finding Forrester* calls "soup questions," ones that *involve* the speaker, propose or set the stakes, request or convey information beyond the "literal" meaning of the sentence as such (if there is ever an "as such"). The further question—not an academic but a "soup" question, incidentally—concerns what Hegel's judgments, as tacitly performed by the text the reader brings to life, are *doing,* that is to say, in the context of the book as a whole as well as the particular sentence or paragraph.

Again, that is a huge question, so I'll narrow my focus to look first of all at the role of remarks (*Anmerkungen*), which appear in other texts (e.g., Hegel's *Encyclopedia*), as Jean-Luc Nancy points out in his *La Remarque spéculative.*[6] In Hegel an "economy of remarks" shadows the field of a properly logical discourse; the surface text is constantly "thrown into relief" (or *relève*) by appendices or marginal comments, which both are and are not part of the text proper, while in turn the mark is always already remarked. Note, we don't at this point have to freeze (here and now) in the headlights of some looming Derridean gaze: all we do is read on.... We might (as observed) compare Hegel's procedure with Spinoza's *Ethics,* which alternates theorem and corollary with scholia intended to make the proofs and their deductive structure more comprehensible by the finite mind, and—no less important—to ward off errors caused by metaphor and representation. But given Hegel's *critique* of Spinoza—namely, that he ultimately fails to integrate thematic content with methodological presentation—any division of pure thought and ancillary, finite procedure is inadmissible here, at least in principle (though Hegel admits to many defects in the actual construction of his masterpiece).

Let me take up one particular section in the *Science of Logic,* indeed the crucial one labeled "Contradiction," and ask exactly how that is presented for us to read (or conversely, how we are to read it *as* presentation, *Darstellung*). In the text it figures as one of the "determinations of reflexion," (*Reflexionsbestimmungen*) which come on stage after "Posit-

5. See Michael Theunissen, *Sein und Schein: Die kritische Funktion der Hegelschen Logik* (Frankfurt am Main: Suhrkamp, 1980).

6. Jean-Luc Nancy, *The Speculative Remark (One of Hegel's Bons Mots),* trans. Celine Surprenant (Stanford: Stanford University Press, 2001), here 47ff.

ing," "Presupposing," and then "Determining Reflexion" (already we should mark the line between determining and determination, "*Bestimmung*"). Other such determinations are "Identity," "Difference," "Variety" or "Diversity" (*Verschiedenheit*), and "Opposition" (*Gegensatz*). Hegel devotes several remarks to these several determinations: first a general remark on the whole section, then a remark on "Abstract Identity," another on the "Principle" of Identity, one on "Diversity," another on "Opposite Magnitudes" in arithmetic, followed by three remarks on "Contradiction," including one on the "Law of the Excluded Middle" and another on the "Law of Contradiction." (I capitalize all these to bring out their logical status as opposed to their existence or reality.) Yet the burden of many of the remarks, oddly enough, is that these are not *laws of thought* at all; neither are they to be conceived as *ontological categories,* of the sort proper to book 1 (the *Logic of Being*). Béatrice Longuenesse is right, I think, to adduce Hegel's critique of Kant here, that is, the critique of Kant's critique of rationalist metaphysics (Leibniz, Wolff).[7] In his "Amphiboly" Kant attacked the confusion characteristic of (e.g.) Leibniz's Principle of Indiscernibles: it confounds pure concepts of understanding with relations between empirical objects, or again, logical and real contradiction. By transcendentally remarking the antinomies that result from such confusion, Kant sought to avoid contradiction.[8] While Hegel could not go along with Kant's division between thought and existence, of course, neither did he wish to fall back into pre-Kantian metaphysics. The problem, then, is how to think *identity* (the "Principle" of Identity) as more than a projection of thought, and yet also more than a universal feature of being or reality. In Hegel's late revision of the text of book 1 we see him taking greater account of the role of reflexion in conceiving in thought what are properly *ontological* determinations; "*Insichsein*" ("inward being") is thus the epitome of what is (to be conceived as) self-same, purely internal, determined as not determined relative to other beings or indeed to thought. The challenge in book 2 is similar, but the inverse: to articulate reflective determinations as self-related

7. Béatrice Longuenesse, *Hegel's Critique of Metaphysics,* trans. Nicole J. Simek (Cambridge: Cambridge University Press, 2007).

8. Paul Davies, "This Contradiction," in *Futures: Of Jacques Derrida* (Stanford: Stanford University Press, 2001), 18–64, at 28; Davies provides a clear overview of the field, which he divides into pre- and post-Hegel. Oddly enough, however, Davies neglects to discuss Hegel himself, supposing that he must be committed to a "principle" of some sort. As I argue, that is too simple a view. In any event, despite his neglect, Davies helpfully compares the tradition with later thinkers always trying to escape Hegelian dialectic, notably Blanchot and Derrida.

principles, not determinate over against an other, and yet at the same time as distinct.[9] To cut a long story short—it simply can't be done! Yet we *speak* of such principles, even write of them, just as Hegel's text articulates how we are to think them.

Nevertheless, when one examines sentences dealing with the individual distinctions, they actually say very little: rather we are told how to *treat* of them, and even more how *not* to approach them (as Kantian principles). It is quite unlike the procedure of book 1: thus, "Being, pure being, without any other determination" presents us with a frame within which we are to arrange certain distinctions, only to dissolve the frame once more, as if there were something definite "out there," which we are attempting to capture. (At the same time we might note that Hegel's language makes no claim; it is not propositional, more like an injunction—"Think pure being!"—or a Wittgensteinian paragraph, holding up a more or less familiar practice for our inspection.) By contrast, book 2 lacks even that provisional frame, and with the text we are considering all we have (in a remark) is a proscription on the Leibnizian "principle" of identity. Thus we read that "identity" in fact/deed—*in der Tat*—expressly or self-reflexively *presupposes* difference (unlike the "self-sameness"—*Sichselbstgleichheit*—of book 1); something is identical with itself if it reflects what differs from it, and this is not a tautological process. We have to *perform* the text, in effect, rather than simply "read off" its fixed and complacent meaning; we have to observe how it *works* or *operates*. Let us then—Hegel suggests, in pragmatic mode—come up with an *example,* a Wittgensteinian *criterion,* perhaps, of the "principle" in action.

Let me recall for a moment the best-known (indeed "exemplary") instance of Hegel's discussions of "example," of exemplarity: the beginning of the *Phenomenology* and the section on "Sense-Certainty." Several commentators have wondered whether Hegel's presentation (in the "dialectic of experience") doesn't put words in consciousness' mouth, or at least force it to speak. I don't think it does, but to save time I want to take up a different criticism leveled by Andrjz Warminski in his sharply worded piece "Pre-positional By-play."[10] Since Warminski is a disciple of Paul de Man's, one might expect him to do such things as comparing Hegel on

9. G. W. F. Hegel, *Science of Logic,* trans. A. V. Miller (London: Allen and Unwin, 1969), 409–10.

10. Collected in Andrzej Warminski, *Readings in Interpretation: Hölderlin, Hegel, Heidegger* (Minneapolis: University of Minnesota Press, 1987), 83.

signs (parable, simile, example), or fastening on to disparities between representation and trope—here (for example) the trope of exemplification, the act of providing an instance of a rule or universal. And indeed he brings out Hegel's word play with *"Bei-spiel"* and *"beiher-spielen"*—playing alongside the text—seeking to turn the tables on the master by uncovering an implicit hierarchy of thought over sense, such that it unfairly predetermines the dialectical result. Now, it is a commonplace that Hegel's dialectic is close kin to Derridean deconstruction. Both thinkers will reverse the value placed on the terms of any binary opposition: the marked term is shown to be parasitic on the unmarked, while in turn the "unessential" tail turns out to wag the dog. "Exemplification" is a particular target of Derrida's satire. How *are* we supposed to adduce a good example of exemplarity? In practice we are thrown *"en abyme,"* unable to get outside the supplemental process so as to frame it once and for all, or even to ask whether we get the point (if you get my point). Warminski likewise draws attention to what Hegel (or the text) is doing: how it enjoins us readers to mimic the figure of consciousness, the only difference being that "we" can see the implications of what it is trying to do, that is, in all innocence to provide an example of exemplarity.

Warminski pushes hard: how is it possible to present (as *Darstellung*) an example (as *Vorstellung*), which is itself a presentation (as exemplification) of how one provides a representation? and what is the relation between *reading* a text and *writing* it (say, on a slip of paper)? He turns to Hegel's *Philosophy of Religion* (on scriptural parable) and the *History of Philosophy* (Aristotle's discussion of examples) to make the point about repetition even more damning. Ultimately, he concludes, Hegel does not *repeat* Aristotle's lesson, namely that the impress of the signet ring leaves not so much gold matter as the shape of the boss: rather he *rewrites* it, declaring that the soul, unlike wax passively imprinted by experience, actively takes up form. Passivity is sublated, with the result that the soul now holds sway over the material, repels it, relates only to the form, so transforming it. Hegel substitutes a *digestive* for Aristotle's *mimetic* model, in short (105). Hence it is little wonder that Aristotle's *De anima* in Hegel's view gets so close to the truth: Hegel reads his own bias into the text. But Warminski's point is not simply that Hegel's reading is circular—perhaps that is unavoidable, after all (don't you agree with me?). Rather it is that the example—in the very excess of sensuous determinacy—is what thought *needs* to posit in order to presuppose itself. What is really presupposed—the *"un-thought"*—is that the passive example itself produces its distinction from active thought, while active thought assimilates the alien example: "the two sides contaminate one another by means of a (chiasmic [*sic*]) exchange of properties" (110). And—if I might repeat and extend the lesson—Hegel is guilty of co-opting *us* into providing just such exemplification of exemplification, in a complicit (chiasmatic) exchange.

Yet—of course you could see it coming—this is all mother's milk to the dialectician, since Warminski himself needs to presuppose Hegel's need to rewrite the example; he needs, in other words, the binary of thought/unthought, or blindness/insight, so as to effect his own deconstructive mastery, or at least to run the deconstructive machinery one more time, co-opting us readers into the required lesson.[11] This is politely pointed out by Slavoj Žižek—one of the very few to attend to Hegelian pragmatics—who nevertheless adopts the phrase "a "chiasmic exchange of properties" for his own use.[12] It illustrates (exemplifies, if you will) "a basic feature of Hegel's thought," he declares: how a universal lever operates at the same time as a subordinate *moment* (to use Hegel's metaphor). Deconstruction or "demarcation" (John McCumber's term) signals that "there is work left to be done, that everything is not settled, that there is a future."[13] Yet that does not mean that it is "always already" deferred, that meaning can never be construed, that "the letter never arrives" (in Poe's story, as franked by Lacan the postmaster). The letter *always* arrives at its destination—and will *continue* to do so.... And the same goes for our—readerly—enunciation of textual meaning (which is not to foreclose *mis*readings, just as there will always be poor examples). We may discern a constituent "blind-spot" in any operation or enunciation: but that is a necessary contingency, not something we can expunge, and certainly not by denouncing it in others. "They know

11. For de Man's analogous need of Hegel's rhetorical slipperiness, see Martin Donougho, "On the Hegelian Sublime: Paul de Man's Judgment Call," in *Philosophy and Rhetoric* 34, no. 1 (2001): 1–20.-

12. Slavoj Žižek, *For They Know Not What They Do: Enjoyment as a Political Factor* (New York and London: Verso, 1991), 39–41; he also points out (62) that Hegel's critics seem always to need a straw man. Žižek has been unjustly neglected by Hegel scholars, it seems to me. He is one of the most astute of Hegel interpreters, combining close attention to contextual pragmatics in general with an enthusiasm for unexpected or witty illustration and anecdote. It is paradoxical that his analyses (e.g., of films, for example) are often *thematic* rather than formal, and fixated on *narrative* rather than structure. When it comes to Hegel, though, he performs the score (*pace* Adorno) as well as any virtuoso.

13. John McCumber, *Poetic Interaction: Language, Freedom, Reason* (Chicago: University of Chicago Press, 1989), 13.

not what they do," to cite Žižek's title. But neither do we, save in retrospect (which is—to anticipate—a typically Luhmannian point).

Returning now to the *Science of Logic:* Hegel's examples are neither innocently self-serving nor haplessly self-contradictory. His example of *Identity* is: "a plant is a plant." Such a statement seems of no interest; it says nothing, makes no difference (in context). Yet, as Hegel presents it, identity—so far as it has meaning—does indeed make a difference; and a difference that more and more makes a difference.[14] Hegel's exposition moves progressively through variety, then opposition, eventually to a difference that may be understood as (at least tacitly) specifying the very respects in which it differs, just as *Beispiel*—a *good* example, anyway—was seen to do. The result is—"Contradiction." "Opposites ... contain contradiction in so far as they are, in the same respect, negatively related to each other or *sublate each other* and are *indifferent* to each other."[15] And yet we have no principle or theorem to consider, except in the remarks *forbidding* such principles! Or else we have statements showing how other moments entail contradiction, and ultimately a posited (or articulated) contradiction. What is enunciated here is an end to all *aspectual* thinking, the ruse of the "*insofar*" that sustains Spinoza's dual-aspect monism (which may stand in for many determinations in book 2). Nevertheless, in the enunciative act itself the aspects or moments remain to haunt us: in one and the same respect each moment differentiates and yet is indifferent to the other.

Hegel even suggests that this amounts to "speculative" thinking, "holding fast to contradiction, and in it, its own self" (*daß das Denken*

14. Niklas Luhmann borrows Gregory Bateson's formula of "the difference that makes a difference" to define information. The point here is that we need not be able to specify in advance which differences make a difference, that is, reduce difference to a formula or principle, an identity statement. Consider the Zen koan Arthur Danto likes to tell (from Ch'ing Yuan): it speaks of the neophyte's seeking of wisdom from the master, and being asked what he sees. "Nothing but mountains, and rivers flowing past forests," he replies. "Fool!" says the master, "come back when you have learned something." Ten years later he returns: "What do you see?"—"Nothing but illusion."—"Fool! etc." Ten years later: "What do you see?"—"Nothing but mountains, and rivers flowing past forests." "*Now* you are getting some wisdom!" he is told. The answer is identical—but is different; it conveys information. Of course, for the Zen master it makes no difference in the end; history itself is illusion. For Hegel it makes *all* the difference.

15. Hegel, *Science of Logic,* 441; this occurs in the third remark, on the "law of contradiction"; cf. Žižek's remarks on the passage in "Hegel's "Logic of Essence" as a Theory of Ideology," of his *Tarrying with the Negative: Kant, Hegel and the Critique of Ideology,* 130–31 (Durham, N.C.: Duke University Press, 1993). His remarks apply more to the void or "*Insichsein,*" which the subject is taken to be.

der Widerspruch und in ihm sich selbst festhält).[16] Yet this "holding fast" cannot be *expressed* as such, even though we have a word for it, in German, anyway (*festhalten:* to hold fast, retain, capture, write down). What Žižek calls a "retroactive positing" is always (already) provisional. The "operational closure" performed in the text—or which we readers perform *on* the text—cannot be *grasped* as such. This constitutes what Graham Priest calls a "*dialethic*" perspective, though "perspective" is not the word: the view that there *are* indeed "true" contradictions. In his book *Beyond the Limits of Thought* he suggests that Hegel was the first to profess such a heresy, even if modern logicians (from Frege on) have developed better tools for doing so.[17] He refers mainly to Hegel's "True Infinite"—though the thought process is much the same as with "Contradiction," Priest's main concern. He speaks of what he calls "*inclosure*": a grasp *in* thought, which at the same time posits the inability *of* thought to grasp what is beyond the limits of/to thinking. In his account, the ways of paradox and contradiction are relatively peaceful, a set of problems with which we can come to terms, even write books about. What I would emphasize in Hegel is more the practical difficulty of expressing our hold on the speculative moment of "inclosure," and the equal difficulty of grasping it as we read the text, that is, in rehearsing the movement of thought beyond itself. It constitutes perhaps a variation on the famous ending to Samuel Beckett's *The Unnamable:* we can't go on—but what is *going on with us?*

Luhmann and Hegel

Niklas Luhmann (1927–1998) is hardly a familiar name in Hegelian circles. He was a jurist-turned-sociologist whose thinking was shaped initially by Talcott Parsons and then by cybernetics and systems theory, while always pursuing its own eccentric path. He became somewhat better known when he collaborated—only to disagree publicly—with Jürgen Habermas; I am not alone in thinking he won that particular debate. His influence was and is as much on literary theorists as in social theory. Disdainful of philosophy, he owes debts all the same to Husserl and Kant, and, as we'll see, to Hegel. It is worth pointing out that Luhmann received the 1988 Hegel Prize—to his own evident surprise. The speech he gave on that occasion—"Paradigm Lost: On the Ethical Re-

16. Hegel, *Science of Logic,* 440.

17. Graham Priest, *Beyond the Limits of Thought* (Cambridge: Cambridge University Press, 1995): 4, 186; Priest has a chapter on Derrida as well.

flection of Morality"[18]—must have puzzled its audience, for it deliberately adopts a distanced, sociological stance in making various observations about morality (*Moral*) and ethics (*Ethik*) considered as social practices situated in history, then leaves it up to others to see whether or not a "fruitful dialogue" with Hegel ensues. (How a dialogue between philosophy and sociology could take shape is an intriguing question, when each seeks to frame the other's stance.) Let me briefly outline the attitude Luhmann strikes here.

Ethics is taken to be a theoretical description of *morality,* which is then defined (in almost Hobbesian or Humean fashion) with respect to approving or disapproving of someone (or presumably his actions)—*not,* however, according to given norms or rules. Several consequences are noted: that morality always verges on conflict, since it promises to trump all political, legal, or religious communication; that in modern times it can't therefore be integrated into a social system, which, since the late eighteenth century, comprises specialized and autonomous spheres (of law, love, society itself); most important, that ethics is most vulnerable to the paradox by which all binary codings—something any subsystem applies in defining its purview (e.g., legal/illegal)—may be applied to themselves. Thus one may ask: what is *good* about the binary *good/evil*? In an eighteenth-century system based on the sentiment of self-love, congeniality or humor was always there to oil the wheels of moral practice. But with the advent of Kant (or Bentham or Sade) ethics becomes fully self-reflexive, hence "toxic"—for theory now begins to infuse practice (Luhmann doesn't go into the details of, say, Kant's attempt to define "morality" in formal terms in such a way as to avoid appeal to heteronomous justification even for its own stance, but one might do so).[19] The "paradigm lost" of his title comprises the innocent, unproblematic observation of stratified normative practices; our "fall" into self-observation was perhaps contingent but then became irreversible. "And paradigm regained?" Luhmann wonders (88). Perhaps the new model of *language* hinted at in Herder and Humboldt, although (Luhmann immediately adds) it too would have to be reformatted as a model of communication—his own preferred approach. Luhmann hints that instead of looking for an *ethical grounding* of moral judgment-*cum*-practice, we—the sociologist anyway—should substitute a study of *social communication* about how moral dis-

18. Niklas Luhmann, "Paradigm Lost: On the Ethical Reflection of Morality"; I cite the translation found in Luhmann, *Thesis Eleven* 29 (1991): 82–94.

19. Cf. Bernard Williams, *Ethics and the Limits of Philosophy* (London: Fontana, 1985).

tinctions are drawn. He doesn't attempt here to map his own distinctions onto Hegel's: the complex relations between formal "morality" and communitarian "*Sittlichkeit*," for example. Yet Hegel's conception of freedom is not too far from Luhmann's framing of it as a "by-product" of social communication, which avoids the whole debate about freedom vs. determinism: Hegel sees formal or individual freedom embedded in communal structures—including civil society—and these too could be seen less as ontological givens, more as contingent products of reflecting on seeming givens. Hegel uses the word "mediation" for Luhmann's "distinction" and its "communication" to others: each usage points nevertheless to possible reflection on any supposed given.

But rather than tracking such complexities right away, let me focus instead on Luhmann's important shift to generalize the *paradoxes* he sees besetting ethical talk in modern times. That is where he glimpses his own proximity to Hegel's project. He would phrase it differently, it's true, appealing to Gotthard Günther's discussion of self-referential logic, to second-order cybernetics, to systems theory and its constructivist epistemology—or more generally to the *sociological* stance, which does no more than make observations (still an operation, a drawing of distinctions, yet laying no metaphysical claim to what "really" is, beyond what is observed or distinguished). But the grand model for such a general "distinguishing of distinctions"—as opposed to determining the nature and quality of *objects*—is to be found in Hegel's *Logic,* Luhmann proposes, even if in the end its air becomes too rarefied for him, while his own interest in society will lead him to declare "if only it could be done" (92). We may detect an ironic tone here, perhaps, not to mention a certain disdain for all airy speculation. Yet I think Luhmann also indulges in wishful thinking: he really *wants* a "super-theory," to replace Hegel's, and Geoffrey Winthrop-Young was therefore not wholly tongue-in-cheek when he speaks of Luhmann's aiming at "Hegel's throne."[20] Moreover, Luhmann's focus on the operation of distinguishing—drawing distinctions—maps onto Hegel's dialectic in fascinating ways, as I shall now try briefly to show.

Let me proceed by listing some of the chief characteristics of Luhmann's general approach (in an admittedly stripped-down version, and with a view to understanding art and artworks):

20. Geoffrey Winthrop-Young, "Silicon Sociology, or, Two Kings on Hegel's Throne? Kittler, Luhmann, and the Posthuman Merger of German Media Theory," *Yale Journal of Criticism* 13, no. 2 (2000): 391–420.

1. He looks not to *production,* but rather to *reception,* or more precisely, to what he calls *"observation"* (or "description"). The approach looks also to *discourse*—or rather *"communication"*—*about* a given social practice, which in turn conditions the systematic, intentional production of, say, art and artworks. Unlike the semiotic model of sender/receiver, a systems-theoretical take on communication requires no agent or psychic subject. If communication is not understood it simply won't continue. So, as with beauty, art exists only in the eye (or ear) of the observer (an observer that doesn't imply consciousness, merely a perspective).[21] More to the point—

2. Art (or it could be some other phenomenon) exists in the eye/ear of the *observer* of such observers: observation requires a distinction from what is observed. But to observe *that* process requires yet another distinction, a "second-order" observation, which, far from leading to an infinite regress, achieves a provisional closure as a unified system. To put it another way, the *theory* of the system lies *within the system itself.* The system is characterized by *self*-observation—observation that distinguishes self-reference from external (or hetero-) reference. Another paradox: a system's environment is defined—distinguished—by the system itself (it is like the sign on the hiking trail that warns us that we are now entering Nature). A third paradox: observation always supposes a vantage from which it is made, one that cannot be observed (except in a further observation, which has its own blind spot); to observe reality requires a blind spot. Self-reflexivity cannot be completely transparent—a view Luhmann shares with Derrida, among others (and arguably with Hegel—a suggestion to which I'll return).

3. More important still, this "second-order" observation is what gives institutional weight to the practice itself, providing stability, legitimation, and hence confidence or trust. This whole process is what Luhmann calls *"autopoiesis"*—that is to say, recursive self-constitution, where structure is defined by itself—a term he borrows from the biologists Maturana and Varela, for whom it captures how organisms monitor, and in that sense reproduce, themselves in their environment.[22] Au-

21. Cf. the typically Hegelian approach to production and work found in the section on "The Spiritual Animal Kingdom," in chap. 5 of the *Phenomenology of Spirit.* Subjectivity is created in the very reception of its work, and doesn't precede what it produces. Luhmann is more radical still: "subjectivity" and "spirit" are mere flags of convenience.

22. The system both produces and comprises its own elements, in an essentially recursive process; see Luhmann, "The Work of Art and the Self-Reproduction of Art," in *Essays on Self-Reference* (New York: Columbia University Press, 1990), 191–214, at 191; and cf. "The Autopoiesis of Social Systems," ibid., 1–20.

topoietic, self-referential systems monitor their own relation to their environment—but a system never communicates directly *with* the environment it defines and so constitutes.

4. Luhmann distinguishes *medium* from *form,* while noting that such distinction is itself formal. His point is that any medium of communication allows possibilities of formal discernment, while form in turn constitutes the medium in which form is discerned: the medium doesn't preexist the form that actualizes—and reveals—its potentialities. (To that extent the distinction is dialectical, each side defining the other, though the other side to form is not ontologically derived—say, as matter or content—but rather differentially defined as that with respect to which form may be discerned. I should note that Hegel's ideas about *artistic* media seem in contrast more tied to substantive features of sight, hearing, and linguistic representation, measured by which the medium is more or less "ideal." Even so his strictly dialectical stance is never just beholden to given "facts" but also open to interpretation by theory or practice: mediation is all.) A medium is characterized by "loose coupling" of elements, where form is more "rigid," imposing itself on the medium. There is no guarantee that form will in fact communicate—that is, be recognized. Moreover, if formal differentiation becomes too stylized, it will cease to communicate, "make a difference." Taking the art-system as illustration once again, works will then be shunted off to museums, showing how they used to do it in the old days, and will communicate only *as* museal specimens rather than "living" art.[23]

5. At this point a short excursus: I need to draw a distinction—make an observation—about Luhmann's theorizing, and about how autopoietic systems have evolved to be what they are. (In my example, how and when did art become the art-*system,* or the fine arts become Art?) Since any "outside" to system or "meaning" is defined *by* that system, Luhmann tends to resort to evolutionary accounts to tell of the emergence of systematicity.[24] Historical thinking itself results from a systemic move *viz.* the wholesale "temporalization" of the past and indeed of

23. See Luhmann, "The Medium of Art," *Thesis Eleven* 18, no. 19 (1987): 101–13; also see Jonathan Hay's review of Lothar Ledderose, *Ten Thousand Things,* in *Art Bulletin* 86 (2004): 381–84, and the latest in the series of *Interventions* in *Art Bulletin* 89 (2007): "Interventions: The mediating work of art," again by Jonathan Hay, with various responses and his own reply (435–59).

24. The other side to this historicizing tendency is a naturalizing one: constructive epistemology is naturalized; see Luhmann, *Political Theory in the Welfare State* (New York: de Gruyter, 1990), 43.

the future—a move we now label "historicism" (*Historismus*).[25] "History" is an invention of the late eighteenth century, as Reinhart Koselleck has shown. Luhmann supposes that this period witnessed a number of decisive shifts from *stratified differentiation* (everyone in his or her place, ontologically anchored, as parts to whole, whether in a divine or natural order) toward *functional differentiation*. All manner of social systems came to define themselves in this way: law, morality, society itself (not merely "civil society," so far as that remains a component of the whole), the state, history, love[26]—and not least, Art (most clearly as "Literature," an invention of the 1790s).

How far may Hegel be taken as heir to this putative shift, and how far does he retain a foot (or more) in the older stratified and ontological thinking? *Social Systems,* Luhmann's attempted overview of his systems-theoretical approach, urges two paradigm shifts in sociological theory: first to "open" systems, that is, system/environment thinking, and second, a shift defined by the "difference between identity and difference."[27] In case readers don't get his allusion, he spells it out in a footnote:

> we are discussing the difference between identity and difference, and not their identity. This is where the following reflections diverge from the dialectical tradition—despite similarities that may be noted from time to time.

Luhmann will not countenance an overall or essential unity or self-identity to systemic thinking. There are always blind spots, and they are constitutive of observation; or—in another idiom—there is no "God's-eye" view or "skyhook." So far as Hegel's system—the *Science of Logic*—claims ultimate closure, it violates this stricture. Hans Georg Moeller cites Luhmann's late *Die Gesellschaft der Gesellschaft* (1997) on Hegel's attempt to see the whole picture, as it were, from outside:

25. See Luhmann, *The Differentiation of Society* (New York: Columbia University Press, 1982), 305. Reinhart Koselleck was the first to point out the peculiar formation of a singular "History"; see his *Futures Past: On the Semantics of Historical Time,* trans., foreword by Keith Tribe (Cambridge, Mass.: MIT Press, 1990).

26. Yes, *love*—how unromantic! See Luhmann, *Love as Passion: The Codification of Intimacy,* trans. Jeremy Gaines and Doris Jones (Cambridge, Mass.: Harvard University Press, 1986; reprinted by Stanford University Press in 1998)—that is, a systematic thinking of love that elicits "pure" love, along with the risk of unrequited desire and contingent "falling out" of love.

27. Luhmann, *Social Systems (Writing Science)* (Stanford, Calif.: Stanford University Press, 1996); this is the translation of *Soziale Systeme: Grundriss einer allgemeinen Theorie* (Frankfurt am Main: Suhrkamp), 1984, 10. The footnote is at 498.

The novel, the romance, but also Hegel's novel of the love between world-history and philosophy localizes the observer who can also see what he previously could not see at the end of the story. This makes it necessary to exclude the narrator who has known everything already from the beginning, and thus also Hegel himself, from the story.[28]

Hegel, in other words, forgot to include himself (or the perspective of a theory of subjectivity) within the system, which in excluding itself is no genuinely "autological" theory of observation. Sociology "is not a science of spirit (*Geisteswissenschaft*)," Luhmann concludes.[29] His own supertheory expressly includes itself within itself, but neither as some final closure, nor yet in a pragmatist projection as forever for the nonce. Only God (if he exists) has no need to differentiate—though even he required creation, damnation, and the devil so as to observe himself, Luhmann is fond of suggesting (in allusion to Cusa's remarkable theology).[30] Luhmann's own view is no "God's-eye view" and would instead qualify as diabolical or divisive—he is proudly of the devil's party. Hegel accommodates reflective division and mediation, but ultimately supposes a unified and mystical "sym-bol," as movement of forming if not as static form.

Even so, as Luhmann allows, there are "similarities to be noted from time to time." What might they be? Writing about his constructivist epistemology, Luhmann insists that constructivism remains an *empirical* theory, revisable by experience, and adds, surprisingly: "No traditional epistemology (Hegel's logic would have to be further examined) could dare go this far."[31] Although Hegel is speaking of thought determinations rather than actual situations, Luhmann's point might be that the logic presents successive observation of positions taken (i.e., blind spots enabling such positions). Distinctions—or what Hegel terms "mediation"—can always in principle be drawn and redrawn; as Hegel would say, there is no unmediated immediacy. In an important article, "The Cognitive Program of Constructivism," Luhmann remarks that

28. Luhmann, *Die Gesellschaft der Gesellschaft* (Frankfurt am Main: Suhrkamp, 1997), 1081, as translated by Hans-Georg Moeller in his excellent *Luhmann Explained: From Souls to Systems* (Chicago: Open Court, 2006), 175.

29. *Die Gesellschaft der Gesellschaft,* 1122, as quoted by Moeller. The section is entitled *"Invisibilisierung."*

30. See "Cognition as Construction," Appendix B in Moeller, *Luhmann Explained,* at 251; Luhmann, "Identity—What or How?"in *Theories of Distinction: Redescribing the Descriptions of Modernity,* translated by Joseph O'Neill and Elliott Schreiber (Stanford: Stanford University Press, 2002), 113–27, 205–7, at 117.

31. Moeller, "Cognition as Construction," 250.

constructivism does not question the existence and reality of the world—but only constructs.... If a philosopher were to ask this question [why world-construction is of value], he would be faced with the deeper problem of a deeper analysis of Hegelian logic, which is the most profound scheme so far developed for the processing of distinctions and of what is implied in them with regard to the identical and its contrary.[32]

As Hans Georg Moeller puts it, "Cognition produces reality by producing system/environment distinctions."[33] At the same time no ultimate claim is here made beyond what is or might be observed: the "unity of the difference between the actual and the possible" (a unity that defines *Sinn* or meaning, in the Husserlian sense) is always provisional, never final. My argument here is that Hegel too may be viewed in such a light (or twilight, at the falling of dusk). Not only does the arbitrariness of the beginning lose its arbitrariness as the system proceeds,[34] in addition the narrative or focalizing perspective in practice won't exclude itself from the account being given. Indeed, much of the dialectic in book 2 of *Logic* devolves upon the inability to observe (distinguish) the whole, as it were from the outside, in "external reflexion." Spinoza's insight, that Being (or nature) cannot be thematized, encapsulated, delimited, is betrayed by his own procedure in talking about it aspectually—"aspect-thinking" or the ruse of "the insofar" being the last resort of the old-style ontology of books 1 and 2.

Let me further mark the parallels by commenting on Luhmann's "Identity—What or How?" which considers the shift from old-style metaphysics to post-Kantian procedural approaches.[35] He understands ontology as a form of observing and describing, that is, "the form that consists of the distinction between being and nonbeing" (115). Nothing metaphysical is implied here; rather it concerns how formal distinctions can be drawn, in reality or the world. Hence "form is the marking of a difference (*Differenz*) with the help of a distinction that compels one to designate one or the other side, in our case, either the being of the nonbeing of something" (116). Luhmann prefers the idiom of the logi-

32. Luhmann, "The Cognitive Program of Constructivism and the Reality that Remains Unknown," in *Theories of Distinction*, 128–52, at 150-51. Luhmann adds, "For a sociologist the matter is simpler"—he can appeal to an evolutionary theory by which constructivism turns out to be suited to modern scientific society (though appeal to evolution is hardly simple, in my view).

33. Moeller, *Luhmann Explained*, 70.

34. Luhmann, *Social Systems*, xlix, again noted by Moeller.

35. See note 31, above; citations refer to this translation.

cian George Spencer Brown (a personal discovery of his, you might almost say), which doesn't presuppose negation in the process of drawing distinctions. Spencer Brown begins with the injunction "Draw a distinction!"—*not* "Distinguish a distinction," which would be circular; compare that with Hegel's beginning with "Being, pure being," a similar nonpropositional speech act (injunction, recommendation, or what?). After the initial operation—act of distinguishing—we may observe that the form has an inside and an outside, the latter being "that which is left over from the 'unmarked state' when the caesura of form is posited. The inside of the form, that is, being or the positive value, designates the possibility of attaching further observation and description" (116). So the "unmarked state" is labeled "non-being," and the distinction "being/non-being" then becomes specifiable; "being" is applicable as a concept. Important to note is the result that "no operation of distinction can completely eliminate what is affected by the distinctions as the remainder of the world, as an 'unmarked state'" (116).

This seems astonishingly close to Hegel's own operating procedure at the beginning of book 1 of *Logic* (again I emphasize that a pragmatics of address always complements the semantics). There too we (readers?) are encouraged to distinguish, demarcate, then reflect on what follows from our entertaining of such a distinction. It must be conceded, however, that *distinction* is a more primitive operation than *negation,* which Hegel applies in a subtle manner so as to generate a powerful dialectic (I'll just cite Dieter Henrich's work on "doubled negation," whereby what is negated is both excluded from and included in the negating term: cf. Graham Priest on "inclosure").[36] In short, rather than accepting the invitation to remember or internalize the negated past, Luhmann politely returns the entry ticket, emphasizing only the provisional stability that results from second-order (or self) observation; or more subtly, he won't speak a meta-language of the "for us" overseeing what goes on "in itself" at the level of dialectical observation and self-observation. But, even if we grant that, the procedures remain much the same: a continual observing (or distinction) of the blind spot, which had rendered the previous distinction (or reality) improbably possible. Two

36. Hegel's revisions to book 1 are much exercized with the problem of subtracting—in reflexion—the effect of reflexion upon thought determinations. In thinking of difference, Hegel cites Spinoza's "Omnis determinatio est negatio." In a letter to Jellis (1674) Spinoza wrote, with reference to distinction as "figura," "determinatio est negatio" without the "all."

consequences drawn by Luhmann apply with equal force to Hegel's dialectic. First, an operation (namely, of distinction) takes time, which entails the paradox of what Luhmann describes as "the simultaneity of the before and after in a time that anticipates further befores and afters," since a crossing of the border is built into the border itself. Hegel's dialectic of the limit (*die Schranke*)—better, self-delimitation—fits this description exactly.[37] Second, form applies to both sides, that is, to the form "being/non-being"; "it does not vanish when one crosses the border (for one can always return)" (117)—in what Spencer Brown dubs "the reentry of the form into the form." Again, Hegel's discussion of finitude and delimitation fits here, and even the tenor of inside/outside parallels his thematizing of the true infinite as, so to speak, playing both sides of "being-for-self" (or later, "for-one") and "being-for-(an)other." And if Hegel seems by contrast to favor the positive (he calls it "reality") over negation, that is only provisional, never final, justified in the way that formal distinction is made always from one side and not the other (but only for a moment). *Identity* or *non*identity of identity and nonidentity? That depends on how you look at it.

To generalize: Luhmann's appeal to Spencer Brown's calculus allows him to render self-contradiction manageable in the form of paradox, the paradox of the reentry of form into the form, and that strategic move resembles quite closely the way Hegel himself "presents" *identity* and *contradiction* in book 2 of the *Logic*. To thematize such thought determinations in the first place is to observe them from the side of form, as if the other side were unmarked, without form and void. Yet "determining reflexion" both posits and reflects, *ab extra*, form or determinacy; has its cake and eats it.

Coda: On Hegel's Conception of Art, Considered in a Systems-Theoretical Light

A plausible objection to Luhmann's approach to art is that, in his magisterial *Art as a Social System*, he simply *presupposes* such a perspective.[38] In fact, as I've suggested, he always *begins* from a current or at least modern meaning of a term ("society," "law") and will then offer an evolutionary account of how such a self-differential or autopoietic usage

37. One commentator who has seen the parallel is Drucilla Cornell, in *The Philosophy of the Limit* (New York: Routledge, 1992).

38. Luhmann, *Art as a Social System* (Stanford, Calif.: Stanford University Press, 2000; translation of *Die Kunst der Gesellschaft* (Frankfurt am Main: Suhrkamp, 1995).

emerged. As long as one remains aware of the dangers of anachronism, there seems little problem or indeed choice. Elsewhere I have proposed that Hegel proceeds in much the same way.[39] Hegel's understanding of art is complex, in part because he sees it as historically reflexive and reflective in nature, or rather, because he acknowledges the fact that it *has* no given nature or essence. His approach to art reflects both on various cultural *phenomena* in the past and on a contemporary *classification* of such "data"—a classification we might call post-Kantian or "Romantic" (in our sense rather than the sense of "romantic" current in Hegel's day), or even "autopoietic," as Luhmann would put it. Seen thus, in a kind of "stereoscopic" vision, art or the work of art may be said to have multiple beginnings (and, as we'll see, multiple endings):

1. In Egypt, with the production of architectural signs, which then reflect on their failure to signify;
2. In ancient Greece, with the production of sculptural signs, which at least *seem* (but turn out not to *be*) a perfect fusion of intellectual meaning and sensuous embodiment;
3. With postclassical art, as cultic image differentiating itself from the divine it is also meant to serve;
4. In what we now call "Romantic" art, ironically reflecting on its own semiotic and cultural status *as* art. Doubtless such Hegelian storytelling could have been continued after his untimely death;
5. To late nineteenth-century symbolism and a nascent modernism/avant-gardism (what Peter Bürger calls the "institution" of art); and further,
6. To late modernism and even postmodernism, reflecting in turn on the conditions of possibility for autonomous art, for a properly artistic meaning (or import—Adorno's "*Gehalt*").

All of these narratives of origin (and declension) are brought together thanks to the "medium" of philosophical "*Vermittlung*" (mediation, conveyance, communication). But it should be noted at the outset that the classical "norm," in both form and content, is not to be taken as normative for Hegel: the "Ideal" is not his ideal. Hegel was no (neo-)classicist, in other words, even though the fusion and confusion of shape (*Gestalt*)

39. Donougho, "Art and History: Hegel on the End, the Beginning, and the Future of Art," in *Hegel and the Arts,* edited by Stephen Houlgate, 179–215 (Evanston, Ill.: Northwestern University Press, 2007); I argue that Hegel supplies an emergent account of artistic distinctions, and draw on that for the summary following.

and meaning (*Bedeutung*) acts as a paradigm of what he terms "art-religion." Philosophical mediation functions also as a distancing critique of the norm and its "cold pastoral."

Pivotal to my argument is a paradox:[40] How is it that Hegel was able to pronounce an end to art at the very moment when art—Art "proper," as Collingwood courteously dubs it—was just emerging?[41] (By a capitalized "Art" I mean both the Romantic aesthetic of expressivism—a self-consciously singular concept-*cum*-practice, different in kind from the preceding loose colligation of "fine arts"—and an emergent culture of collection and performance, in museums and concert-halls built to display masterpieces taken from the past.) Luhmann's account is not invested in transcendental subjectivity or expressivism as ultimate value; nevertheless, autopoiesis marks the shift to self-reflexion, system thinking defined by self-delimitation—so to say, a minimalist redescription of the Romantic revolution.

Hegel's dialectical procedure consists of a demarcating of meaning or sense, beginning with what he dubs (following his friend Creuzer) "symbolic" art—though perhaps we should simply reserve the description "symbolics" or "symbolic worldview," for calling it "art" is to jump the gun. Art emerges when something is discerned as no longer determined by or in a natural context— indexical meaning or utility, where, let us suppose, a house is perceived as serving various needs (actual or virtual), a flight of stairs as "meaning" a possible climb to another level or access. Architecture (as opposed to building) comes about when its shapes self-reflexively signify a meaning, typically a human meaning (Oedipus' answer to the Egyptian sphinx), including the *failure* to mean (the empty pyramid means meaninglessness). In formal terms, what we observe is a process of self-discerning, self-observation, or in short, "second-order" observation. Luhmann too fastens on processes of self-reflexive observation, that is, of what it is to observe (or find meaning in) the world of perception and sense. Although very different, there are once again formal similarities with Hegel's *Aesthetics*. Let me propose a few such parallels between the two theorists of art, putting Hegel's view in parenthesis.

- Luhmann posits that art originates in ornament (216)—the point here being to emphasize its independence from other distinctions (of con-

40. Martin Donougho, "Hegel's Art of Memory," in *Endings: Questions of Memory in Hegel and Heidegger*, edited by Rebecca Comay and John McCumber, 139–59, 229–36, at 155 (Evanston, Ill.: Northwestern University Press, 1999).

41. Robin George Collingwood, *The Principles of Art* (Oxford: Clarendon Press, 1938).

tent or matter or function), and a continuity via design, arabesque, up to what might be taken as its successor, irony. (Hegel too takes symbolics to devolve upon ornament and figure, ultimately, it might seem, to its own disadvantage, so far as an "essential" content—the anthropomorphic "Ideal"—is missed. The third part of the section on Symbolics discusses such "mere" formalism, yet "figure" is at least the semblance of artistic meaning, even with abstract art).

- Art adopts a playful relation to questions of rational agreement/disagreement (75–76). That is to say, second-order observation of artworks operates in perceptual terms, without conceptual or rule-generated distinctions coming first. *Any* object or performance with perceivable form can count as art—if people agree to it (in contrast Hegel does observe certain thematic—anthropomorphic—constraints even on formalist irony and humor).
- "What is at stake in art is not a problem to be solved once and for all but a provocation—the provocation of a search for meaning that is constrained by the work of art without necessarily being determined in its results" (24). Art explores the difference between utterance (*Mitteilung* or "imparting" as self-reference) and information (as hetero-reference), so far as it is understood. (Hegel takes art to be an "address" to the communing soul, and as such implicitly self-reflexive).
- Art allows observers to observe themselves as observers and to experience themselves as individuals (93). They become individuals by observing themselves *ab extra*, and art allows them to experience that process. As observers of art, we catch ourselves in the act of second-order observation. (Hegel's complex account of the "classical Ideal" is predicated upon a normative "individuality" [*Individualität*], which comprises a self-observation of what it means to be and act in the sensuous world, as demeanor, as gesture, as "plastic" and self-sufficient *deed* above all, Tragedy is the self-aware presentation of the logical problems inherent in living with such a figurative mode of existence, where justice must be *seen* to be done but cannot be so *thought* or *conceptualized*.)[42]

42. For some preliminary thoughts about "*Individualität*" and normativity, see Donougho, "Hegel's Pragmatics of Tragedy," *Idealistic Studies* 36 (2006): 153–68. I'll add that Luhmann likewise sees the possible end of art in the inability to construe such "*individual*" meaning; his later thoughts on mass media represent an attempt to understand their own—often false—projections of individual meaning in a globalized world-system; see Niklas Luhmann, *The Reality of the Mass Media*, trans. Kathleen Cross (Stanford, Calif.: Stanford University Press, 2000), esp. chap. 15,"Schema Formation."

Besides descriptions of the *emergence* of art/"art," we find in Hegel accounts of its eclipse: the symbolic art form dissolves into abstract figure or rhetoric; the classical unity of demeanor and deed splits into abstract personality and tragedy; "romantic" art devolves into the extremes of subjective feeling and external nature (e.g., realism in painting or novel). We might further discern parallels between Hegelian ideas on the *"end"* (not death) of art and Luhmann's descriptions of the toxicity of modernist experiment. Hegel supposes that late "romantic" (our "Romantic") art verges on formalism: irony or "subjective" and "objective" humor risk emptying out any content for artistic form to present, and the new "saint" of *Humanus* becomes a quasi-parodic "religion" of art, human-all-too-human.[43] Briefly, Luhmann too looks at the problematic status of modern/postmodern art:

- Art can accept multiple descriptions of reality (306); it represents to society the "emancipation of contingency" (David Roberts).[44] This is postmodernism, we might say—but with a difference. For while the epistemology is constructivist, the tone is not at all skeptical. The fictions of art are ones we live by, its reality that in which we move and have our being; yet, conversely, the new continues to emerge. (We might recall Hegel's "objective humor," for which the artist freely surveys previous models and peoples her stage with figures from the past.) Last, in every sense.
- Art is unlike all other systems in dissolving, in the forms of art itself, the boundary between self-reflexion (or theory) and the system's productive operations (306). Elsewhere, legal theory is kept apart from juridical deliberation and decision; theology is not preached; pedagogy is not used to train teachers. But art calls its own bluff, and especially in modernist practice, trades upon the dissolution of the boundary. Not that art ever becomes theory or philosophy—here Luhmann criticizes Danto's ironic claim to that effect (note 236, at 401). Yet there are dangers here, falling under the topos of "the end of art" (a topos for art itself); and Luhmann does speculate on what might happen if there is "too much" identity between operations and self-descriptions—namely, no future (308). (For Hegel, too, if form and

43. See Donougho, "Art and History."

44. Luhmann, *Art as a Social System,* 309; cf. 313: "one could then pursue the suggestion that art tests arrangements that are at once fictional and real in order to show society, from a position within society, that things could be done differently, which does not mean that anything goes."

meaning can no longer be distinguished, there is no more task for the artist to perform, no more "work" left to do; yet even in his own day Hegel continues making distinctions.)

Admittedly what Luhmann proffers with one hand he takes away with the other. There is no denying that from his perspective we should translate all talk of subjectivity into talk of systems (psychic, social, or natural). Moreover, while he starts from historical semantics ("*Sinn*"), his sociological stance observes empirical *effects* that follow from drawing distinctions as much as *implicatures* or *presuppositions* (though it does that, too, and the distinction is sometimes fine). Last though not least, there is no ultimate worldview, no absolute Idea (even if we factor in Hegel's procedural understanding of this moment in book 3 of *Logic,* rather than as some metaphysical state or Platonic form).

Whether the dialogue I have been conducting is a "fruitful" one, as Luhmann has it, would not be for me to say. My main point, however, was less to put the two thinkers on the same page than to bring into relief the performative element in Hegel's thinking. Hegel was no neoclassicist, or so far as he admitted the normative force of the classical "Ideal," it was in Romantic and even ironic spirit. Speaking in the strange half-light of a nascent Berlin rapidly becoming one of the great sites of a new modernity, Hegel reflected upon the paradoxical legacy of a practice—Art—that was at once coming to its end and yet in process of being founded (both conceptually and institutionally) *as* Art. He resisted its wholesale secularization or reduction to "sensuous taste" or "material" (polemicizing against Rumohr's skepticism with regard to Winckelmannian allegory) and continued to focus on the "Ideal" of art. But equally he was no Romantic believer in the new cult of "Art-religion," that is, a wholesale reenchantment of the world. Art no longer served such a transcendent purpose, no longer has the task of discerning a meaning or content for artistic form to embody, while in turn we no longer bend the knee. Works were now collected in the museum, performed in concert hall or theater (often in historicizing or high-cultural spirit). Hegel's own involvement with the arts was very much practical and bourgeois in that sense, as he habitually attended opera or exhibitions of paintings. Annemarie Gethmann-Siefert has underlined this new finite, secular, middle-class function that art served, the disillusioned obverse of its new definition as *Art,* capitalized and idealized. What he may be observed as enjoying was that modern phenomenon, the "art firm"—"a place where art is made to work, where aesthetics is the operative management theory for the enterprise,"[45] and both practitioners and consumers are encouraged to perform an aesthetic "*Schwung*" (Schiller) or dance between matter and form, body and mind, pleasure and intellect. It amounts to the aesthetic education of "management."

A tension remains then between art *qua* figuration (allegory) and art as the shimmer or *Schein* of semblance—Plato's scandalous or magical "image." The aesthetic landscape Hegel envisaged in his last lectures on the philosophy of art—after the "end of art," we might say—hardly appears in a brightly heroic, classical light, nor did Hegel take it as a normative given. Hegel wrote, if not the epitaph of art, perhaps an extended series of *epigrams* on it—and we should always recall that he saw "epigram" as a transitional figure, which in its sheer amalgamation of external shape (drawn from nature or history) and subjective "*Einfall*" or inspiration holds open a future of sorts.[46] Even in his disenchanted gaze, the landscape of art can speak to us, momentarily enlivened by a Romantic gesture, a subjective act. Epigram is the drawing of a distinction, an act of conferring distinction, and that goes for Hegelian philosophy and modern poetry (Goethean lyric, for example). One measure of Hegel's continuing achievement is that he took the body of Western art as he knew it and sought to bring it to life through discerning a series of distinctions he then could observe as having been drawn, with at least an emergent self-awareness. By the same measure we today must draw distinctions about Hegel's systemic project, revealing new horizons of meaning. His *Aesthetics* no less than his *Logic* still needs performing, and I think that Luhmann helps us out in the attempt.

45. Pierre Guillet de Montheux, *The Art Firm: Aesthetic Management and Metaphysical Marketing* (Stanford, Calif.: Stanford Business Books, 2004), xi. Montheux takes the notion of "*Schwung*" from Friedrich Schiller's *On the Aesthetic Education of Man, in a Series of Letters,* trans. Elizabeth M. Wilkinson and L. A. Willoughby (Oxford: Clarendon Press, 1968). *The Art Firm* is a serious (if playful) book, marred however by an obtuseness with regard to Hegel's own thinking on art. The author seems to believe what Schopenhauer said about his rival. But if we factor in what we know about Hegel, the book provides an unusual sidelight on the social development of art from 1750 to the present.

46. See *Lectures on Aesthetics,* trans. T. M. Knox (Oxford: Oxford University Press, 1975), 425–26, and Donougho, "Hegel, Philosopher of the Secular [*irdischen*] World: On the Dialectics of Narrative," in *Hegel and the Tradition: Essays in Honour of H. S. Harris,* edited by Michael Baur and John Russon, 111–39 (Toronto: University of Toronto Press, 1998). Adorno uses "*Einfall*" in just that way, as a fugitive mark upon nature.

Daniel E. Shannon

10. BEAUTY AND THE GOOD IN HEGEL'S *AESTHETICS*

Kenneth Schmitz has written on a great number of philosophical subjects, often dealing with questions of humanity and its relation to the transcendentals: being, truth, unity, beauty, and goodness. In some of his writings he has focused not just on the metaphysics, but also on the aesthetics of this relationship. For instance, in a recent essay, "The Lustrous Power of Beauty," he holds that "To claim that being is itself beautiful is a statement about the fundamental character of reality. It is an affirmation of the positive character of existence" ("Lustrous," 237).[1] Later in the same lecture, he ties the concept of beauty to the concept of goodness: "the attractive power of beauty presents itself as a kind of good. Indeed, genuine beauty and true good are twinned; they are conceptual twins in the same one reality" ("Lustrous," 243). In this context, Schmitz addresses three features of beauty: clarity or radiance, proportion or harmony, integrity or wholeness ("Lustrous," 237–41). It is this last feature that I wish to focus on in this chapter. What is the meaning of integrity in the ideal of art as it relates to a conception of the good? I submit that this feature addressed the fine arts through the concept of the good and how we have knowledge of it.

While Schmitz is well-known for his writings on metaphysics and his study of St. Thomas Aquinas, his long association with interpreting

1. Kenneth L. Schmitz, "The Lustrous Power of Beauty," in *To the Mountain*, edited by William Sweet, 233–45 (Xinzhuang, Taipei: Fu Jen Catholic University Press, 2004). Hereafter this essay will be cited as "Lustrous," followed by the page number.

the works of G. W. F. Hegel must be noted as well. It is on the basis of this association that I intend to explore in the first two sections of this chapter how Hegel deals with the question of aesthetical integrity in his *Lectures on Aesthetics,* which he treats under the subject of *ideal beauty.* While endorsing the view that ideal beauty requires integrity, Hegel's analysis is proscriptive; that is, it shows how the arts can be conceived as integral to the good by showing what they *ought not to do.* Aesthetical failure presents a hindrance to our understanding of the good and also a limit, or boundary, that art should not cross. The proscriptive nature of Hegel's argument informs us how beauty, in its ideal composition, relates to an objective understanding of humanity and the divine.

At the heart of Hegel's analysis is his treatment of the German playwright Heinrich von Kleist (1777–1811) and his best-known play, *Prince Frederick of Homburg* (first performance, 1821). Hegel's interpretation of Kleist's plays is severe. He comments, for example: "the higher splendors of the mind are hypostatized in a perverse way and interpreted as independent [dark] powers" (*Ästhetik* 13:314; *Lectures* 1:242).[2] His judgment is even starker:

> These dark powers are to be banned from the realm of art immediately, for in art nothing is dark; everything is clear and transparent. With these supersensibles nothing is spoken other than a sickness of spirit; poetry runs jumping into nebulousness, conceit, and emptiness, of which examples are provided in ... Kleist's *Prince of Homburg* (*Ästhetik* 13:315; *Lectures* 1:243).

The proscription is clear; since art is clear and transparent, those artistic creations that oppose this quality are to be rejected.

Part of what "wholeness or integrity" must mean is something negative for those creations that fail the ideal, just as it must also mean something positive for those works that fulfill it. Hegel is, of course, attempting to show through a consideration of artistic norms how objectively knowledge of art proceeds toward absolute knowledge: that is, toward the highest level of philosophical science. He is not principally concerned with subjective experience: that is, how you or I might have satisfaction in a particular judgment of taste. His sights are set on Objec-

2. G. W. F. Hegel, *Vorlesungen über die Ästhetik, vols. 1–3,* in *Hegels Werke,* Bände 13–15, edited by Eva Moldenhauer and Karl Markus Michel (Frankfurt am Main: Suhrkamp Verlag, 1970). Hereafter this work will be abbreviated as *Ästhetik,* followed by the volume and page number. Translations from the German are my own, but I will follow the conventions found in the Knox translation. Citations will be also given to T. M. Knox's *Hegel's Aesthetics: Lectures on Fine Art,* vols. 1 and 2 (Oxford: Clarendon Press, 1975). Hereafter this work will be abbreviated as *Lectures,* followed by the volume and page number.

tive Spirit, the world community, as it strives toward knowledge of the absolute. Thus, for him integrity is set objectively according to the purpose of his science.

Schmitz, unlike Hegel, is concerned primarily, or so it seems, with the fulfillment of a personal subject in his or her experience of beauty.[3] Integrity is part of the human's experience of goodness on an individual level. But, like Hegel, Schmitz recognizes that there are aesthetic conditions that set a limit or boundary to art and that relate directly to our understanding of good and evil. In the final section of this chapter, I will return to this understanding and address it from Hegel's perspective. I will attempt to show there, briefly, why Schmitz does not follow Hegel's path; nonetheless, it is just that pathway that presents a challenge to Schmitz's approach.

The Ideal of Artistic Beauty: Hegel in Relation to Kant and Schelling

In the aftermath of the Enlightenment and throughout the Romantic period, German thinkers held that the ideal of art is beauty—that is, beauty that is pure according to its form. Pure here indicates the kind of aesthetical appreciation we employ in a judgment of taste. The beauty of Mozart's *Requiem* (1791), for instance, would be pure simply on the basis of form and execution. If it is well-composed and performed skillfully, we should expect any intelligent listener to find it beautiful. The reason for this is that the moving tonalities of the *Requiem* harmonize our imagination with our intellect.[4] To judge something to be beautiful appeals to certain norms of what should be appreciated, even if there is variation among individuals' tastes. The norms are, however, *objective* in the sense that they should apply not simply to an individual composi-

3. "The radiance of beauty attracts us, its goodness empowers us, and its integrity perfects us. Integrity is the capstone of the fullness of beauty; for if we let the radiance alone cast a spell over us, we fall into a superficial pursuit of pleasure; and if we separate the good from its attractiveness we reduce the good to a joyless moralism of rules and imposed duties"; "Lustrous," 240f.

4. This formulation comes from Eduard Hanslick: "By this [musical kind of beauty] we understand a beauty that is self-contained and in no need of content from outside itself, that consists simply and solely of tones and their artistic combination.... The content of music is tonally moving forms.... [T]he tones readily absorb every idea of the composer. Since tonal connections ... are achieved ... by spontaneous activity of the imagination, the spiritual energy and distinctiveness of each composer's imagination make their mark upon the product as character"; *On the Musically Beautiful,* trans. Geoffrey Payzant (Indianapolis, Ind.: Hackett, 1986), 28–31, *et passim.*

tion, but also to a wide variety of artworks within a particular genre. In general terms Hegel, belonging to this tradition, considers the ideal of art to be beauty, not because we have subjective interests in any given art form, but because the form and execution of the artwork harmonize with our higher cognitive powers.[5] With this understanding of beauty in art Hegel agrees with Kant, who treated judgments of taste as employing the concept of *purposefulness without any purpose.*[6] The pure aesthetical judgments are materially disinterested; they are judgments that agree with our intellectual capacities simply on the basis of the *form* of the presentation (cf. *KU,* §2, 40–41).

Hegel also follows Kant on what we contemplate and esteem in the beautiful object. Kant speaks of the ideal of beauty as involving an intellectual judgment in which we esteem in a human being the perfection of the species.[7] Such an intellectual judgment would involve moral interest, because the form and arrangement of physical shapes lead the intellect to judge and appreciate the regularity (*Regelmäßigkeit*) of the overall effect.[8] This regularity is in the area of practical judgments—that is, value judgments, or what pure practical reason considers intrinsically right in morality. Thus, the concept of beauty, as it relates to the ideal in art, is associated with our moral interests because we are practitioners in practical reason.

5. Hegel speaks approvingly of Kant's aesthetical principle in the introduction to the lectures; see *Ästhetik* 13:86–89; *Lectures* 1:57–60.

6. Immanuel Kant, *Kritik der Urteilungskraft,* ed. Karl Vörlander (1924; repr., Hamburg: Felix Meiner Verlag, 1974): "Whereas this relation in the determination of an object as something beautiful is bound to a feeling of desire which is, at once, explained through the judgment of taste as valid for everyone ... it, therefore, can be nothing other than subjective purposefulness in the representation which is without any purpose"; § 11, 60; hereinafter *Kritik der Urteilskraft,* or *Critique of Judgment,* will be abbreviated as *KU,* followed by the section and page number. Translations from the German are my own.

7. Cf., Kant, "First, it would do well to note that the beautiful which should be sought as an ideal is not something *vague* but is *fixed* through the concept of objective purposefulness; it follows that the object is not entirely pure but in part must belong to an intellectual judgment of taste. [...] Only that which has purpose inherently in its existence, namely, a *human being,* which has determined its purpose through reason ... is also capable of such an aesthetical estimation; this *human being* is, therefore, an ideal of the *beautiful,* just as humanity alone is capable in its person, *qua* intelligence, to be the ideal of perfection"; *KU,* §17, 73–74, *et passim.*

8. Kant, "Taste, indeed, achieves something by virtue of this connection between aesthetical and intellectual satisfaction, namely, that it becomes fixed, and although it does not become universal, rules can become ascribed to it in respect to certain objects which are determined to be purposive. These rules, however, are not also rules of taste but simply belong to the unification of taste with reason, that is, of beauty with the good"; *KU,* §16, 71. Cf. Kant, "Satisfaction is Bound with Interest in the Good," in *KU,* §4, 43–46.

The ideal of art is not simply a form that, when presented in the imagination, agrees with the intellect; it has also a determinate content in which moral purpose is presented. In the Kantian scheme the ideal of art is an *echtype,* or silhouette, of reason itself, and as such the artistic forms, created according to this silhouette, will themselves embody the directives of reason.[9] In Kant's argument the ideal of beauty expresses moral interests; thus all art forms that present the moral in light of beauty are to be aesthetically appreciated. His own example is a poem by Frederick the Great; while it is not the best example of good poetry, it still is good art, because the imagination's depiction comes under an idea of reason, which at the same time enlivens the concept through an intuition.[10]

Hegel's position is both more erudite and in-depth than Kant's, since Hegel recognizes that the ideal of beauty does not lie in the reflective pattern of reason over imagination and sentiment, but subsists through the entire relationship between form and content. The ideal of beauty is *heroic* for him, because the hero embodies conflict and struggle—that is, a pathos—and because a depiction of his life shows that reason achieves insight into the moral sphere and has identity with it.[11] Hegel refers to Achilles' character in Homer's *Iliad* as a case in point.[12] Achilles' weak-

9. The ideal of reason comes to act as an archetype in the minds of artists from which imaginary forms are created as echtypes or silhouettes (*Schattenbilde*) of this ideal; cf. Kant, *Kritik der reinen Vernunft,* ed. Raymond Schmidt (1956; Hamburg: Felix Meiner, 1976): A570–78; B598–606; Hereinafter the *Critique of Pure Reason* will be cited in the traditional fashion of A for the first and B for the second edition, followed by the respective page numbers. All translations are my own. In Kant's *Critique of Judgment* the echtypes of pure reason are called symbols: "All intuitions under which lie *a priori* concepts are, therefore, either schemata or symbols; the first contains the direct and the second the indirect presentation of concepts. I can now say that beauty is the symbol of the ethically good"; *KU,* §59, 212–14, *et passim.*

10. Kant, "The great king thus expresses himself in his poem: 'Let us depart life without raising grumblings as we leave the world with mainly good acts....' In this way, he animates his rational idea of a cosmopolitan sentiment at the end of life with an attribute which his imagination sets ... by this representation and which makes regular the myriad of feelings and associative images for which no expression can be found"; *KU,* §49, 170.

11. Hegel, "The main thing [in order to have a genuine, ideal character] is to have an inwardly determinate, essential pathos within a rich, full breast, in which the pathos of the inner individual world penetrates in such a way that this penetration, and not just the pathos itself, comes to be presented as such. But, equally, the pathos must not destroy itself inwardly within the human breast, thereby showing itself to be something unessential and nugatory"; *Ästhetik* 13:316; *Lectures* 1:244.

12. Hegel describes Homer's Achilles as the ideal character at *Ästhetik* 13:308–9; *Lectures* 1:237f. He also uses Achilles as the model against which he faults the characters in Kleist's works; cf. "Achilles, for instance, in his noble heroic character, whose fundamental

ness—his petulance at the loss of his booty—is only one aspect of his character that stands in contrast to his divine nature. This divine quality appears in his destiny as the warrior who is the true representative of the gods' vengeance for Paris' theft of Helen.

Hegel sees in such a character art at its best precisely because Achilles is not a shadow of any moral idea; instead he is the artistic embodiment of the divine idea working through a weakness in human life. Achilles' own death (by Paris acting as an assassin in the night) shows the greater drama unfolding in the conflict between the Greek and Trojan ethical lives; namely, what qualities of soul shall be victorious? There are two possible answers to this question: the Greek ideal, where courage and justice act in the daylight, or that aspect represented by the Trojan stratagem, where thievery and seduction cloak themselves under the cover of darkness. The collision between these two qualities is what drives the drama and, for Hegel, shows its perfection. Even though the resolution to the question is ironic, since the Greek side wins only by following Trojan cunning, there is the fullness of human interest and character. Fullness of human interest and character is what makes a drama great (Cf. *Ästhetik* 13:308; *Lectures* 1:237). A failure to develop the story line in terms of human aspirations and real characters would be a failure in art.

Hegel would say that, in this Homeric epic, reason is also being shown with all of its dialectical tensions, collisions, and misunderstandings. He would agree with Kant that the best art depicts a rational content, and because of it morality enters into the action, but the ideal of art is also filled with conflicts, mistaken sensibilities, and confused purposes, all of which are resolved in the artwork and its determinate heroic content (Cf. *Ästhetik* 13:311–16; *Lectures* 1:234–47). Hegel would not agree completely with the reflective character of Kant's position, however, which results simply in an intellectual agreement between the imaginative and rational faculties and is, on the whole, indifferent to the production of art. This is why, for instance, Hegel considers Kant's "ought" in the aesthetical judgment—namely, that all people ought to appreciate the beautiful in the same object—to be an empty expression, since it determines

trait is his youthful force of beauty, has a tender heart in respect to father and friend; how is it possible then ... [to have a] cruel thirst for revenge? [It is illogical to the understanding.] But in light of *what is rational,* what is inherently total and thus alive, this illogical character is exactly what is right and logical. For a human being is not only the bearer of the contradiction within his diverse nature but the sustainer of it, remaining therein equal and true to himself"; *Ästhetik* 13:311; *Lectures* 1:240 The point is that inconsistency in character has to make logical sense. It does in Homer's account, but not in Kleist's presentation.

neither the appreciation of the beautiful nor the production of art. It has only a distant regulative function over reflection on the beautiful.[13]

Hegel goes far beyond Kant and his aesthetics of taste by contending that the ideal of beauty as heroism is the appearance of the divine in sensible form. In the ancient drama either the gods actually appear or someone speaks for them. In modern drama the will of God, or his designated representative, is conveyed either through some natural sign or in a dream. For Hegel this connection between art and divinity is crucial to his philosophical system. He considers art to be one of the absolute sciences, and as such the artwork must be appropriate to Providence. It would be profane to have the gods send false messages or for the signs of nature not to represent divine forewarnings. Even while Hegel adheres to this convention, the form that Providence takes is quite varied. He is willing to see creation, even in the shape of the profane, as presenting the divine in some determinate content. The command of a just ruler or the uprising of righteous citizens against oppression is for him just as much a sign of the divine presence working in humanity as a thunderbolt or a prophetic vision.

In general and at first glance Hegel looks to consider the aesthetical judgments on form as a kind of subset of moral judgments, where goodness and heartfelt virtue are confronted with the actuality of worldly limits. Unlike Kant, who presents a model of correspondence, where a particular artistic content either agrees or disagrees with a moral imperative, Hegel sees that aesthetics is built upon the conflict between a moral vision and the actualities of the world; these two in opposition present a necessary condition for great art. To cite some of Hegel's favorite examples, the tragedy of *Antigone* is *not* the conflict between a man and woman with differing social interests, but is the opposition between the divine ideal law of family obligation and the human positive law of civic duty (Cf. *Ästhetik* 13:287; *Lectures* 1:221). What makes Schiller's *Don Carlos* (1787), in Hegel's mind, one of the finest plays of the Roman-

13. Hegel contends that the universal beauty, arising from reflection, has validity for everyone, including both audience and creators, but this point does not actually occur in Kant, because the judgment of reflection is in his account nondetermining: "In this sense the beautiful should also be recognized universally, although simple intellectual concepts are not capable of judging it"; *Ästhetik* 13:86; *Lectures* 1:58. While the criticism seems unfair to Kant because of his commitment to the ideal of beauty as the symbol of morality, Hegel is right that Kant emphasizes that what makes beauty universal is common *pleasure*. Hegel believes that the concept of beauty—understood according to its characteristics—is universally valid irrespective of its effect.

tic movement is the moral conflict between the Marquis d'Posa, who espouses virtue and political liberty, and King Philip of Spain, who seeks only power and state control. Here, the form of the aesthetical judgment is how the conflict is resolved, not in terms of who prevails, which is a tragedy for the heroic protagonists, but how it affects our moral sensibilities. We are to see the tragedy as an indictment against worldly power, a corrupt use of religion, a warning on how dangerous the endeavor for political liberty truly is. The divine calls us to morality and liberty, but only through heroic self-sacrifice.

If art is in part a subset of morality, then we might ask, does morality alone include art, or is there a higher sphere of inclusion? We might think the former were it not for the fact that, in Hegel's system, morality itself seems to be subservient to divine comprehension. It was initially Schelling who made the point that art is the presentation of the divine, as the infinite, in a sensible, finite form. As well, it is probably Schelling who is responsible for Hegel's idea that the ideal of beauty has its best exemplification in the *poetical arts*.[14] In fact, if we take Schelling's *Philosophy of Art* (1805) as the entry point to Hegel's system, then we can say that the ideal of art belongs to the absolute itself as it has been incarnated in the world as beauty in nature and art.[15]

Hegel, who shared with Schelling the understanding that art is one of the three absolute sciences, seems to agree with him on the point that art and morality are subservient to the perfect comprehension of the divine.[16] Thus, the fine arts, no matter their medium, are all parts of what

14. "This established order which we have presented is based in the factual evidence itself [*die Sache selbst*] and we will encounter a similar relationship also, once again, on the ideal side in poetry in which even more so the highest potency rests upon that transformation of the ideal into the whole being, into a reality that is exhibited as something *actual*"; F. W. J. Schelling, *Philosophie der Kunst* (1859; repr. Darmstadt: Wissenschaftliche Buchgesellschaft, 1980): §133, 274. Hereinafter all citations to this work are to this edition, abbreviated as *Kunst*, followed by the page number. Translations from the German are my own. I am also providing page number to Douglas W. Stott's translation of Schelling's *Philosophy of Art* (Minneapolis: University of Minnesota Press, 1989), which hereinafter will be abbreviated as *Art;* see *Art*, 201.

15. Schelling, "*To the three powers of the real and ideal world corresponds three ideals: truth, goodness, and beauty.* (The idea of the divine belongs neither to the real nor the idea world but what lies between them.) The first power of the ideal and real world expresses truth; the second expresses the good; the third expresses beauty in both the organism and art. . . .Thus beauty is posited where the particular (the real) is attuned to its concept; that is where the concept itself, as the infinite, enters into the finite and becomes intuited *in concreto*": *Kunst*, §16, 26; *Art*, 29.

16. Hegel says, "With Schelling the science [of aesthetics] entered into its absolute standpoint. Although art had already been asserted to prepare its particular nature and val-

is generally called religious art, even as it takes upon itself the shape of the world. Schelling's own examples of the best of the fine arts demonstrate this point. The greatest works of art he cites are Dante's *Divine Comedy* (c. 1310–14), Shakespeare's tragedies, especially *Macbeth* and *Lear* (both first performed 1605–6), Calderón's comedies, especially *Alcalde of Zalamea* (c. 1640), and the best of them all, Goethe's *Faust* (org. version, *Urfaust*, 1795–96; Part 1, 1808).[17] Each of these works develops a religious theme in terms of the world and its ways: the road to redemption; divine retribution; the failings of pride; the need to defend justice and honor; divine forgiveness. What we are to understand in the artwork is how the divine should be comprehended through principles of justice, mercy, and retribution.

Hegel shares with Schelling the sense that the divine is to be comprehended through art. In fact Hegel shows the continual development of how the divine comes to be shown and comprehended in everything from the curve in the Gothic arch,[18] to Correggio's and Titian's paintings,[19] up to the portrayal of the romantic hero. But the ideal of art is beauty for Hegel, and, as with Kant, it is the beauty of humanity both in body and soul. Schelling took beauty to produce a feeling resulting from an awareness of where the divine has been conceived through art. But for him beauty is not paradigmatically a concept concerning the depiction of human character or action; rather he equates it with the sublime feeling—what transports us beyond the ideas of humanity and natural beauty. The sublime is itself the ideal, not rooted in external reality, but belonging to a greatness of power that is beyond human comprehension. This is where Hegel parts company with Schelling's aesthetics.

Hegel contends, in contrast to Schelling, that in modern drama the subject matter is not the divine will as such, but the choices of a subjective will and the personality of individuals who follow their hearts. He uses many of Schelling's own examples to make the contrasting point. He notes that in Goethe's *Faust*, Shakespeare's and Calderón's tragedies, and Schiller's histories, human choices and the desire for personal accomplishment appear as the underlying motif for the characters' pathos

ue in connection to the highest interests of humanity, now [with Schelling] its concept and scientific place came to be established as well"; *Ästhetik* 13:91; *Lectures* 1:63. The more telling connection to Schelling's philosophy of art appears when Hegel connects the concept of art to religion; see *Ästhetik* 13:142–44; *Lectures* 1:103–5.

17. Schelling, "On Modern Dramatic Poetry," in *Kunst*, 362–79; *Art*, 267–80.

18. *Ästhetik* 14:347–48; cf. *Lectures* 2:689.

19. *Ästhetik* 15:123; *Lectures* 2:882.

(cf. *Ästhetik* 15:557f.; *Lectures* 2:1225). Hegel, unlike Schelling, never confuses the sublime with the beautiful; he does not transcend the limits of human understanding, but looks to art that conveys insights into the human will and its consequent action. Thus, for Hegel the ideal of beauty is a human character performing worldly actions; these combined *should* further our understanding of the divine, but they need not present the divine in an earthly form.

The ideal of fine art is for Hegel a complex notion. It is the ideal of beauty in art, but it is not a concept that is static. In drama, in particular, the ideal requires a heroic character, but one who must face his or her own limitations and struggle with the actualities of the world. The ideal represents Providence, but this does not mean that any end is preordained; it means only that in the heroic action the appearance of the divine takes shape in questions concerning moral qualities and/or honorific intentions. The characters themselves need not be pure, but they must not be self-contradictory; that is, they should be not both good and wicked or both strong and weak. Contradictions in character would only confuse the audience and hinder moral reflection.

When Art Fails the Ideal: Kleist

If the ideal of art is beauty as seen in depictions of heroic representatives of humanity in the fine arts, then we may begin to see the reason why Hegel objects to Kleist. For Hegel the greatest accomplishment of humanity is the ethical actions of persons who are being directed by their own rational powers. This implies, of course, both that people are rational and that they can follow their own choices. Kleist, while an accomplished playwright, is noted for his disturbing psychological portraits of presumed rational agents. For instance, to use a parallel to Hegel's paradigm of the ideal character, in Kleist's play *Penthesilea* (1808) Achilles is the bravest and most self-controlled of all warriors except when he encounters Penthesilea, queen of the Amazons, where all at once he loses all desire for honor and would prefer love making and collecting flowers.[20] These acts in themselves do not undermine the ideal of beauty, but when Penthesilea believes she is spurned by Achilles and attacks, kills, and then cannibalizes him, we find that all rational sense is abandoned and, what is equally important, there is no moral insight into the characters' actions. Madness rules. Kleist's Achilles is totally devoid

20. *Penthesilea* can be found in Kleist's *Werke in einem Band,* ed. Helmut Sembdner (Munich: Carl Hanser, 1966), 249–342.

of the divine character found in Homer's poem. There is no sense that higher powers are at work or even that rational agency influences the characters' actions. Kleist's play presents an opposing view of how characters should be formed and understood, since for him strength of body and soul is abandoned in light of animal passion.

According to Kant, Schelling, and Hegel, the ideal of beauty presents a prescription for the actions and intentions of the protagonist. The model of ideal beauty is supposed to be that of a heroic Achilles whose sense of duty resides in honor and obedience to country and divine authority. What this model does not permit is any confusion in the character's qualities. For instance, the hero could not be honorable one moment and then dishonorable in the next. This would not be fitting with the unity between a noble principle and honorific intentions. Beauty in the human form is in the nobility of character. One lesson in great drama is that pathos teaches, and the characters develop qualities based on their suffering. Nobility appears in the characters' actions as they are tried by the realities of the world. For Kleist, however, we are left without such a lesson. After Penthesilea kills Achilles she shows grief and remorse, but she does not learn anything from her actions. She simply dies of sorrow. Her death is still another sign that her passions are destructive and overwhelm all good intentions.

When we turn to Kleist's other plays we see that there is both the presumption of nobility of soul and its opposite in the same character. This is clearly demonstrated in his play *Prince of Homburg*.[21] This work illustrates how the purpose of art, as Hegel sees it, is undermined. Of course, even Hegel admits there could be artistic purpose in contradicting an aesthetical norm: for instance, to extend our imagination beyond the limits of beauty and its conformity to the ideal. In this way we may be induced to consider the sublime as the collision with the ideal of beauty. For instance, Victor Hugo's *Hunchback of Notre Dame* (1830) develops a contradiction in the story between moral purpose and savage will, and contrasts the beauty of Esmeralda, as naive and shallow, to the ugliness of Quasimodo, as spirited and having a depth of goodness. This contradiction does not defeat moral reflection, since the characters are not themselves self-contradictory, but instead the contradiction between

21. *Prinz Friedrich von Homburg* can be found in Kleist's *Werke in einem Band*, 515–84. For the *Prince of Homburg* I will rely on Peggy Sherry's translation in Kleist's *Plays*, ed. Walter Hinderer (New York: Continuum, 1982), 269–341; hereinafter this work will be abbreviated as *PH*, followed by the act and scene number.

them serves to heighten our moral insights. It agrees with the principle that human interests must be served by the drama and that the fullest of human character should be developed. In *Homburg* we receive an opposite impression, since there seems to be no purpose to any contradiction, and the depictions of the characters only show antithetical tendencies in themselves. The characters are self-contradictory, and there is very little sense that anything done in the play serves human interests.

There are three elements in this play that Hegel would decidedly condemn as violations of artistic norms. First is the *inconsistency within a unified character.*[22] Homburg is a hero; he shows no signs of fear or trepidation on the battlefield. Quite the contrary; he is Harry Hotspur and shows by his actions that he has courage and stamina above all of his peers. The inconsistency occurs in the aftermath of the battle, when he is condemned to death because he led a charge before the order was given. His condemnation is also irrational, but we will come to that point shortly. Once he is condemned all of his bravery leaves him, but what is worse in terms of art is that he denounces honor as he cowers beneath the wife of his liege, the Elector of Brandenburg. He speaks to her that he would implore the lowest stable boy who tends a horse, The meanest servant, begging him to save me! (*PH*, 3:v).

The words of the Prince contradict everything that has previously been presented to us about him. He pleads to the Elector's wife,

> Oh let me not, before the hour strikes, Descend to those black shadows, I implore you! If he must punish me for doing wrong, . . . Demote me. . . . Discharge me from the army: God in heaven! I ask for nothing honorable anymore! (*PH*, 3:v).

This failure to act consistently in character in itself might not be damaging to the artwork and could even be used as a catalyst for us to grasp the weakness of the human heart, even in one who has valor, if it were not for the fact that when the Prince is initially pardoned, he refuses it on the grounds that he has been wronged by the Elector. As the letter of pardon is presented to him, shortly after he had been pleading for his life, he changes his attitude, and when asked why, he says,

22. "To such wryness, which opposes the unity and firmness of character, we can also attach the principle of 'new irony.' This false theory has misled poets to place in their characters a diversity which can never pass as unity, thus every character *qua* character destroys itself"; *Ästhetik* 13: 315; *Lectures* 1:243.

You've not reflected on the letter's contents! I cannot write him under these conditions That he has wronged me. And if, in this mood, You force me now to send an answer to him, By God, I'll put, You've dealt with me correctly (*PH,* 5:iv).

The shift in mood is bewildering, even to such an extent that another character in the scene, his fiancée, Princess Natalie, comments that "he must be mad" (PH, 5:iv).

The last twist in character is that even when he is later given another pardon, and this time without conditions attached and with full restitution of all of his glory, he still refuses it. In a peak of bravado he gives what appears to be his final soliloquy:

Now, o immortality, you're mine! Your light, intenser than a thousand suns, Pierces the bindings of these earthly eyes. Mightly pinions grow on both my shoulders, My spirit soars into silent aether. (*PH,* 5:x).

The shifts and contortions in the hero are not supposedly indicative of anything other than his hotheadedness. But Hegel appears to reject this line of interpretation. He sees only confusion of motif in the play. There is a corollary to this violation of an artistic norm, which one can see in the inconsistency of the hero's character. There is *no moral lesson* one could possibly glean from Homburg's actions, and thus it is difficult to see why he is admired by every soldier in Brandenburg's forces. Hegel, I suspect, saw in Homburg an immoral message. Under storm and stress the human character loses its dignity and falls into ignobility; the words "honor" and "noble" indicate nothing acquired in the human soul. When there is an immoral message human interests are not being served. Thus the play, here again, fails to correspond to the ideal of beauty.

The second element that Hegel would condemn is *the removal of justice and reason from the characters' motives.*[23] For instance, the Elector's condemnation of Homburg appears so gratuitous and unreasonable that even his own troops plot to thwart his will (*PH,* 2:iii). The reasons for the Elector's displeasure are explained by two different set of premis-

23. Hegel makes this point indirectly when he notes that the formal understanding might not recognize either justice or rationality in the character, but it should nonetheless be there and acknowledged to be present by the power of reason. Hegel contends, "The understanding . . . will itself abstract and select only *one* side of the character and stamp upon it a single rule of humanity. [. . .] But for what is rational *en toto* and thereby alive, what lacks consequence is equally right and consequential. . . . In this way [in pathos] the human being is not one within himself, and thus the various sides of his senseless and thoughtless character fall apart. Equally, having unity within itself belongs in art to what constitutes the infinite and divine of individuality"; *Ästhetik* 13:311–12; *Lectures* 1:240, *et passim.*

es, only one of which is ever developed consistently. The first premise, the one developed, is that Homburg violated the Elector's orders. Such a transgression must be punished, even though Homburg's violation of the orders resulted in such a thorough defeat of the Swedish enemy that they immediately sued for peace. (In point of fact Homburg did not disobey the orders, because he never actually heard them, but by his actions he did violate them.) The second premise, which Homburg himself gives, is that he is being condemned because his fiancée, the niece of the Elector, has been pledged to the king of Sweden. The Elector plans to have Homburg killed to expedite this marriage of convenience (*PH,* 3:i).

Neither premise makes any sense, but together they demonstrate an irrational content to the explanations given. The Elector's reasons are opaque enough that even his aides-de-camp, Count Hohenzollern and Field Marshall Döfling, find them impossible to understand. The Elector's actions and words not only show a lack of comprehension of the situation—his mortal enemies have been utterly routed by the man he now condemns to death—but he places his own position as the liege lord into jeopardy by foolishly adhering to an obstinate impulse that is opposed by every general, knight, and soldier in his command. A heroic and noble leader, which the Elector supposedly is, would not act in such a way.

To make the contrast more apparent, let us consider the actions of a character in a play that Hegel admired. In Schiller's *Wallenstein* (1799) the general also operates in an enigmatic and capricious manner, but Schelling gives reasons for Wallenstein's actions—he is superstitious—and in the end Wallenstein is destroyed in part by his lack of foresight and general insensitivity. In *Homburg,* however, the motivation for the Elector's actions remains a mystery, and, in fact, Kleist appears to emphasize the point that they are inscrutable to everyone, even to his closest associates.

Homburg's own reasons for why he is being treated this way also makes no rational sense, not because such intrigue is impossible, but because he knows that it is not necessary for the Elector to kill him to make peace with the Swedish king. The king has already been defeated. And even if the marriage were necessary, Homburg makes it quite clear that he is willing to give up the girl if his life depended on it. I should note that as soon as Homburg thinks that this is the Elector's motive, he immediately renounces his love for Natalie and insists that she be taken directly to the Swedish camp (*PH,* 3:i). This is just another sign of his cowardice and fecklessness. The more important point, however, is that these assumptions reinforce in the audience's mind the injustice of the

Elector and, since Homburg's reasons are easily recognized to be flawed, the irrationality of the hero's beliefs.

From the first two sets of violations of the artistic norms we can see why Hegel might have thought that this play was poor art and even inconsistent with the ideal of beauty, but we do not see why he thinks it is sick and perverse. The inconsistencies in character and the irrational, unjust motives notwithstanding, we should hardly call Kleist's play a perversion of art as Hegel does.

I submit that it is only in the third contradiction to an aesthetical norm that we see the wickedness that Hegel contends occurs in the play and that he opposes vehemently. Kleist contradicts the norm *that the divine should be comprehended through principles of justice, mercy, and retribution or, at least, that the signs of the divine should not be confounded.* In contrast, to undermine divine authority or trust in the divine authority would be perverse. In *Homburg* the lack of moral purpose in the protagonist's character and the role of the dream sequence in the play appear to undermine trust in Providence; thus Hegel finds the play to be wicked. In the final scene, where we are expecting to see the death of Homburg, we find instead that he has been having a dream; that the entire play has been a creation of his imagination (*PH,* 5:xi). The complete cast is present to awaken him and urge him on to the battle that is just then underway. The play ends at this point.

What is significant about the play as a dream story is that it reveals that nothing that has happened in the drama is significant in terms of aiding our moral insight or self-conscious reflection, and that the dream itself is a warning that the irrational, unjust, feckless, and chaotic are powers that govern us.[24] It is these two elements that undermine divine authority. The former may not need justification, since it is fairly obvious that moral insight and self-conscious reflection presume a waking mind and coherent world, which is not the way of the dream. But the second might surprise some.

Traditionally, in art and literature dreams were the vehicle of warning that either the dreamer or the soothsayer could use to prophesize coming events. For instance, the Pharaoh's dreams in the forty-first

24. The living and socially obligated individual has become transfixed according to these dark powers.... To them belongs the magical, magnetic, demonic, the rumored specters of mediums, and the sickness of sleep walkers, etc. [...] The genuine, ideal character has nothing to do with the Beyond and ghost filled realms but is filled with real interests which he retains in himself, that is, with his character and pathos"; *Ästhetik* 13:314–15; *Lectures* 1:243, *et passim.*

book of Genesis foretells of the coming droughts and plagues, or the dream of the chief baker to the Pharaoh is interpreted by Joseph as a prediction of the baker's death. Normally these dreams are divine warnings—messages from a higher and nobler spirit that convey a moral certainty to those who receive the dream or hear its contents. The dreams of Lady Macbeth, Caesar's wife, and Attinghausern (in Schiller's *William Tell* [1804]) are divine warnings, judgments, or predictions. With Kleist's play, however, there is no sense that we are receiving a message from a divine or nobler authority; quite the contrary, the message is that the natural and moral order is lacking in authority. The underlying pathos of the hero is without purpose, and the command of the person over his or her own actions and desires is a ruse. This is the perversion that Hegel is condemning. When Hegel says that such pretense to art should be banned, he is thinking principally of this dream motif as a channel to the irrational that undermines moral authority.[25] In a more general way, Kleist's play violates all the norms associated with the ideal of fine art. It is not just that the dreams convey uncertainty or that the commands of the Elector are obtuse; it is rather that everything that the ideal of beauty stands for is contradicted. There is inconsistency of character; there is a lack of justice or reason in the characters' motives; there is no comprehension of the divine at work, but instead a sense that the signs of the divine (the dreams, the commands of the just ruler, and the moral uprising of the people) are themselves signs of irrational powers or purposelessness. Kleist's play presents a complete contradiction to what Hegel holds to be normative qualities of fine art.

Hegel's opposition to Kleist's plays is now understandable. Within the plays there are specific violations of artistic norms. Also, these violations cannot be sanctioned by appeal to some higher principle, since the plays neither convey to us the fullness of humanity nor serve our ends as rational agents. Without just and rational motivations within the play, there cannot be moral reflection on our part; thus without moral reflection the audience will not be able to see any clear and transparent moral conclusion to the work. While Hegel is willing to admit that

25. Hegel might well be thinking of such a dreamscape when he ways, "In another way this deficiency with the inner substantial solidity of the character occurs when what is formed is also the distinctive higher splendors of mood [*Gemüt*] that become hypostatized by inversion and grasped as independent powers. The living and socially obligated individual ... is placed into a relationship with what, on the one hand, is within himself but, on the other hand, is wholly beyond and alien to his inner being but which determines and rules him"; *Ästhetik* 13:314; *Lectures* 1:243, *et passim*.

these norms are not absolute, they cannot, however, be dismissed unless the playwright, by violating these norms, is seeking to fulfill the general purpose of drama—namely, to place art in the service of humanity. This general purpose, however, must be served rationally and is to be itself transparent. This is a condition for art itself to fulfill its function within the system of knowledge that Hegel has devised; it is a condition rooted in the conception that the arts in general develop knowledge of humanity and are one stage in absolute knowledge. In this sense the norms are objective, and a violation of them hinders knowledge of humanity and our relation to the divine.

Conclusion

My original question was, what is the meaning of integrity in the ideal of art as it relates to human goodness? We have seen that for Hegel the meaning lies in art's agreement with aesthetical norms that allow us to understand the heroic character clearly and furthers our knowledge of the divine. In his account beauty and goodness are objectively intertwined; they are part of the conceptual unified way of approaching the absolute. They are present together in the ideal of beauty. Earlier, I mentioned that the objective nature of Hegel's account is due to his consideration of art as being on the pathway to absolute knowledge. He is not particularly concerned in his *Aesthetics* with subjective experience—that is, with the fulfillment of the subject in his or her own judgments of taste. He is concerned, instead, with what the artwork communicates to us through the logic of motives. In contrast to Hegel's emphasis, Kenneth Schmitz relates goodness and beauty to each other aesthetically in terms of an individual's fulfillment. The experience of beauty, like the experience of the good, is in part how individuals understand a happy life, one of meaning and completion. But in terms of conceptual unity, it is safe to say that Schmitz is in agreement with Hegel, since he acknowledges that norms are essential to grasping the boundaries of art. He does not, however, address the proscriptive nature of aesthetic norms. Schmitz simply accepts that they are a feature of the concept. Let us consider his position more precisely.

For Schmitz, goodness and beauty are twinned not in the art object *per se,* but in the subject's relation to them through his or her experience of aesthetical satisfaction. He also recognizes that the art object itself presents an objective presence of aesthetic norms. His account implicitly agrees with Hegel's claims. I say "implicitly" because Schmitz addresses this issue obliquely through an analysis of what he calls the "non-consideration" or "bypass" of what should be considered in a work of art. As he is addressing the issue of the boundaries to a work of art, he makes the following statements:

> The evil act can emerge initially only insofar as it is grounded in the possibility of an indifference to the relevant norm, an indifference that can eventually be transformed into defiance of the norm. The root of evil, then, takes shape as non-consideration that ... nonetheless lets something noticed slip by. This bypass is a curious form of absent-mindedness, a *distraction* or distractedness brought about by the inclination of the agent under the attractive power of the object toward the immediate end sought through the action ("Bounds," 147).[26]

Schmitz, then, relates this non-consideration back to the subject's own experience, acknowledging, almost in Hegel's footsteps, that this artistic form of non-consideration provides a key to the outline of the being of an artwork as an entity ("Bounds," 148). How this particular sort of non-consideration occurs, relating to good and evil in respect to art, is neither addressed again nor elaborated on any further by him. Nonetheless, the essential point is conceded to Hegel because, as the latter has shown in Kleist's works, the defiance of the norms is aesthetically the corruption of art. I should clarify, however, that we are not speaking in this context of the art produced by a Camusian artist revolting against totalitarianism or nihilism. Kleist is not George Grosz and *Homburg* is not a *Grey Day* (1921), which in its ugliness caricatures a corrupt, decadent social-political life. In contrast, we are speaking of works that undermine unity, rationality, and good sense by distracting us from the normative role art plays in knowledge. The evil that Hegel finds in Kleist's works is due, in Schmitz's terminology, to a distraction, namely, a self-conscious slipping-away from the good that we should be anticipating in the arts.

It seems that Schmitz shares a similar insight with Hegel into the relationship between the substantive form of art as ideal and the morally good. But, whereas Hegel follows through on his philosophical insight in order to develop aesthetic norms and their relation to the ideal of beauty, Schmitz pulls back from any such development. For him the objective disclosure of norms is to be contextualized, first, in terms of the subject's own satisfaction, but also in terms of a particular art-

26. Kenneth L. Schmitz, "The Bounds of Art," in *Philosophy and Art*, edited by Daniel O. Dahlstrom, 143–59 (Washington, D.C.: The Catholic University of America Press, 1991), 143–59. Hereinafter this work will be abbreviated as "Bounds."

work's other relationships. He notes, for instance, that "Art dances to its own tune, being neither simply physical nor simply imaginary. The distinctively artistic boundary lies *between* the artwork and the other entities, distinguishing and uniting artworks and art lovers, and coexisting with other artworks" ("Bounds," 151). This concession—that art belongs to its own sphere of interrelationships— places a restraint on any claim to the validity of proscriptive artistic norms when it comes to knowledge and morality. On such a basis, the artist could always say that in art nothing is proscribed. Thus, when art is excluded from the wider sphere of knowledge and value, we are left with the difficult question: can artworks fail norms if their creators and critics neither recognize nor accept them? Hegel, at least, sees the arts as a piece of the entire cloth of knowledge, and they cannot claim against the whole their own independence and uniqueness. Art succeeds or fails in light of the complete adventure in knowledge. Hegel can be proscriptive because he sees clearly that art either assists or hinders us in the approach to the absolute. In terms of Objective Spirit knowing itself and its vocation to the absolute, art can fail when it violates its norms; that is, when it bypasses reason.

Schmitz does not have Hegel's idea of how to approach the absolute, even though he too sees art as involved in our endeavors to reach knowledge of divine things. He emphasizes the accomplishment of the arts when they uphold norms. They are joyous and uplifting vessels for the fulfilled man or woman. The problem for him is that, given his acceptance that the fullness of experience is necessarily related to beauty and the good, and given his acceptance that the consideration of norms in terms of artistic experience is also necessarily part of defining objectively the artwork, he cannot *bypass* aesthetic proscriptions. Beauty is not simply an important way toward self-fulfillment; it also calls us to consider what *ought not to be.* It is no doubt true, however, that there is a temptation fostered by artists and critics not to prohibit anything in the art world, because art ought to be free creation. But this temptation—to restrain from a presentation of norms and to remain reticent on how arts may fail us in the pursuit of knowledge—is not to do service to the *philosophy* of art when it considers norms or values. Schmitz clearly sees the temptation and even attempts to avoid it by acknowledging the root of wickedness in non-consideration, but he does not pursue further his own line of thought. In this way, I suggest, Hegel's philosophy of art presents a logical and coherent challenge to Schmitz's treatment. Indeed, it is friendly challenge, but one that nonetheless calls for attention.

Jennifer Bates

11. THE PROBLEM OF GENIUS IN *KING LEAR*

Hegel on the Feeling Soul and the Tragedy of Wonder

Hegel on the Feeling Soul and Its Genius

Hegel's discussion of the genius of the "feeling soul" (*Die fühlende Seele*) is found in his *Anthropology* (under "Mind Subjective" in Hegel's *Encyclopedia Philosophy of Mind*).[1] The feeling soul is a singular inwardness of feeling. It embraces the corporeal in itself as its substance. It does not experience the multiple parts of the external body as divisions of the soul. Rather (like Aristotle's *sensus communis*), it gathers them up into

This chapter was originally written for inclusion in this volume in honor of Kenneth L. Schmitz. An expanded version appears as chapter 4 in Jennifer Bates, *Hegel and Shakespeare on Moral Imagination* (Albany: State University of New York Press, 2010).

1. The term "genius" (in German, *Genius*) comes up in two very different ways in Hegel's works. In Hegel's critique of the Romantic theory of genius, the term denotes roughly what we normally associate with the word—an unusually brilliant individual. Hegel rejected the Romantic celebration of the creative genius: he criticized Romantic philosophers for raising genius above philosophy and thus for assigning to it the highest role in the individual; see *Hegel's Phenomenology of Spirit,* trans. A. V. Miller (Oxford: Oxford University Press, 1977): 6, para. 10, and Jennifer Bates, *Hegel's Theory of Imagination* (Albany: State University of New York Press, 2004), 139–49. The other meaning of the word "genius" is Hegel's word for a particular, subconscious level of the soul. It is with this subconscious kind of genius that we are concerned here. "Feeling soul" can also be translated as "sentient soul." Hegel's "Anthropology" in the *Encyclopedia Philosophy of Mind,* trans. W. Wallace, with Zusätze in Boumann's Text (1845), trans. A. V. Miller (Oxford: Clarendon Press, 1971), 92, para. 403. "Anthropology" is followed by two other subsections: "Phenomenology of Mind" and "Psychology."

one experience. "[T]he 'real' outness of parts in the body has no truth for the sentient soul."[2] The feeling soul in the body is "one simple, omnipresent unity."[3]

While Hegel's feeling soul is not Kant's self-conscious synthetic unity of apperception (the "I" that accompanies all my representations),[4] it is nonetheless a synthetic unity. It gathers the multiplicity of corporeal experience together into "an intelligible unity" that Hegel calls "the existent speculative principle."[5]

To add to the mix, Hegel explicitly invites us to think of Leibniz: the "soul is a monad."[6] For "The soul is the totality of nature ... it is itself the explicitly put totality of its particular world—that world being included in it and filling it up; and to that world it stands but as to itself."[7] The feeling soul reduces the multiplicity of outward parts of the body to "ideality (the truth of the natural simplicity)."[8]

Finally, Hegel is careful to distinguish this unity from consciousness: the feeling soul is "not yet mind."[9] It is individual, but it is not aware of the separateness of its object in the way that consciousness is: "[the soul's] object is its substance."[10] As such, "this stage of mind is the stage of its darkness."[11] (Indeed, if a fully developed *consciousness* falls back into this stage, it is diseased, or insane.)[12] The soul's efforts are precisely to develop a dialectical complexity with itself as substance so that it rises out of its *sensus-communis*-like, monadic existence, enough to become a conscious "I":

> What we have therefore to consider [with the feeling soul] ... is the struggle for the liberation which the soul has to wage against the immediacy of its substantial content in order to become completely master of itself and adequate to its Notion, or to make itself into what it is *in itself* or in its *Notion,* namely, into that self-related, *simple* subjectivity which exists in the "I."[13]

The Feeling Soul goes through three *moments* in this struggle. These are (α) The feeling soul in its immediacy; (β) Self-feeling; and (γ) Habit. Hegel summarizes the development:

2. *Hegel, Encyclopedia Philosophy of Mind,* 93, para. 403.
3. Ibid.
4. Immanuel Kant, *Critique of Pure Reason,* trans. Werner S. Pluhar (Indianapolis, Ind., and Cambridge, Mass.: Hackett, 1996), B132: 177.
5. *Hegel, Encyclopedia Philosophy of Mind,* 93, para. 403.
6. Ibid.
7. Ibid.
8. Ibid.
9. Ibid., 29, para. 388.
10. Ibid., 94, para. 404.
11. Ibid.
12. Ibid.
13. Ibid., 91, Zusatz to para. 402.

> In the first stage we see the soul entangled in the dreaming away and dim presaging of its concrete and natural life. In order to comprehend the miraculous element in this form of the soul ... we must bear in mind that here the soul is still in immediate, undifferentiated unity with its objectivity.
>
> The second stage is the standpoint of *insanity,* which means the soul divided against itself, on the one hand already master of itself, and on the other hand not yet master of itself, but held fast in an isolated particularity in which it has its actuality.
>
> Lastly, in the third stage, the soul becomes master of its natural individuality, of its bodily nature, reduces this to a subservient means, and projects from itself as an objective world that content of its substantial totality that does *not* belong to its bodily nature. Reaching this goal, the soul appears in the abstract freedom of the "I" and thus becomes *consciousness.*[14]

Thus the moments of the feeling soul are the last shapes of subconscious experience prior to consciousness. According to Hegel, genius is a function of the first moment in this subconscious triad—that is, of the feeling soul in its immediacy. Our genius is thus subconscious.

Let us look now in more detail at how genius fits into this overarching development.

Hegel explains that as yet, the feeling soul is itself but "not yet as its self."[15] The soul is not reflected into itself. It is *passive.*[16] The interesting thing about this condition of doubleness and passivity is that, even though the feeling is one of unified individuality, the organizing principle of the unity can be *but does not have to be* the same as that which is unified.

Thus, on the one hand, the feeling soul can be a predicate of *its own* dreams. Indeed, this is the first "state" of the feeling soul in its immediacy. In dreaming, "the individual who has attained to a feeling of himself is gripped in a simple, immediate self-relation, and this, his being-for self, has at least the *form* of subjectivity."[17] On the other hand, the soul can equally have its guiding principle in another. The example Hegel gives is that of the "child in the mother's womb:—a condition neither merely bodily nor merely mental, but psychical—a correlation of soul to soul. Here are two individuals, yet in undivided psychic unity."[18]

In either case, the unified substance (the self in dreams or the child in the womb) is "set in vibration and controlled without the least resistance on its part."[19]

14. Ibid., 92, Zusatz to para. 402.
15. Ibid., 94, para. 405.
16. Ibid.
17. Ibid., 99, Zusatz to para. 405.
18. Ibid., 94–95, para. 405.
19. Ibid., 94.

Here we get a definition of genius: "[t]his other subject by which it [the soul] is so controlled may be called its *genius*."[20]

Now, the formal subjectivity of the self in dreaming is not quite a genius, whereas the mother is the genius of the child in her womb.[21] But this notion of genius, this state of passive influence is not limited to the mother-child link. First, Hegel writes that

> [s]poradic examples and traces of this *magic* tie appear elsewhere in the range of self-possessed conscious life, say between friends, especially female friends with delicate nerves (a tie which may go so far as to show "magnetic" phenomena), between husband and wife and between members of the same family.[22]

Second, as the soul develops, it ceases to be controlled by a genius that is other to it and becomes a genius to itself. In that third moment of the feeling soul, the soul unifies the first two moments in a higher stage. That is, the self that, in the dream, was merely the form of subjectivity, becomes that which replaces the genius from outside. The outer influence is replaced by an "inner oracle."[23] This is genius proper:

> Th[is] third mode in which the human soul achieves the feeling of its totality is the relation of the individual to his *genius*. By *genius,* we are to understand the particular nature of a man which, in every situation and circumstance, decides his action and destiny.[24]

The self is not dreaming, nor is it directed by something outside it: the self is self-directed, but nonetheless not conscious. As we mature, this must change.

Ideally, we eventually become the "dominant genius" to ourselves, when we are "self-possessed and healthy" subjects.[25]

So the overall struggle of the feeling soul is first to develop its genius as *its own*. Then, it develops its relationship to its genius into a *conscious* relationship between subjectivity and external world. At that point, the

20. Ibid., 94.

21. Ibid.; in the Zusatz to paragraph 405, Hegel also says a number of ridiculous things about the "corporealization of the mother's inner feelings" into the child (e.g., birthmarks or even limb breakages derived from maternal anxieties). We cannot take these examples seriously, but we can ponder the general point.

22. Ibid., 95.

23. Ibid., 100, Zusatz to para. 405.

24. Ibid.

25. Ibid., par 408: 123; Hegel's theory therefore prefigures Freud's theory of the ego in its relation to both the unconscious Id and the unconscious Superego(s); see Sigmund Freud, *The Ego and the Id,* standard ed., ed. James Strachey, introduction by Peter Gay (1962; New York: W. W. Norton, 1994).

person is no longer subservient to the work of her genius upon her. However, Hegel points out that, even at this later stage (that of conscious life) we often have the feeling of being led by fate, providence, or magic. That is nothing other than a sensibility toward our soul's genius.

Wonder

Hegel[26] agrees with Aristotle that philosophy begins with wonder.[27] But he adds that wonder is only a beginning: it must be replaced with the labor of coming-to-*know* that in the face of which we first wonder; that labor must produce comprehensive, scientific knowledge.[28] This is true with regard to self-knowledge as much as any other science.

Wonder is not discussed in Hegel's *Philosophy of Mind*. I cannot speculate here as to why this is so. But we can hypothesize its place. Consistency demands that it would be a *beginning* of something. *Philosophy of Mind* concerns the science of mind. Wonder must therefore come at the beginning of the mind's *knowledge* of mind.

The soul is not sufficiently self-differentiated to have an experience of wonder. The child in the womb is not in a condition of wonder toward its mother: the child merely "vibrates" with her genius. By contrast, the hallmark of consciousness is that it is aware of the distinction between self and other and therefore aware of influences upon itself.[29] Wonder arises, therefore, in the transition from the soul to consciousness.

Let us be more specific about what is entailed in this transition. Hegel writes of consciousness that "along with the abstract certainty of being at home with itself, mind has the directly opposite certainty of being related to something essentially other to it. This contradiction must be resolved."[30] According to Hegel, the entire project of consciousness is

26. Hegel uses the word *die Verwunderung*.

27. Aristotle, *Metaphysics*, trans. Hippocrates G. Apostle (Grinnell, Iowa: Peripatetic Press, 1979), 16; and Hegel, "Introduction to the Philosophy of Nature," in his *Philosophy of Nature*, trans. Michael John Petry (London and New York: Humanities Press, 1970), 194.

28. See again Hegel's "Introduction to the Philosophy of Nature," in his *Philosophy of Nature*, 194–95. Similarly, in the preface to his *Phenomenology of Spirit*, Hegel rejects *love* of knowing in favor of *actual* knowing (*Phenomenology of Spirit* 3, para. 5).

29. It is true that, in the soul, the self is other to itself (as genius). But that contradiction is subconscious. In consciousness, the contradiction is something of which the self is aware.

30. Hegel, "Phenomenology of Mind," in *Encyclopaedia Philosophy of Mind*, trans. W. Wallace, with Zusätze in Boumann's Text (1845), trans. A. V. Miller (Oxford: Clarendon Press, 1971), 157, Zusatz to para. 416.

to raise contradiction *to* self-certainty and truth by comprehending the contradiction as the dialectical relationship between self and other.

Hegel asserts next that *"the urge to resolve it [the contradiction] lies in the contradiction itself."*[31] The urge to overcome the contradiction is always already a part of the contradiction and is what drives the development from the soul to consciousness. In other words, that contradiction is actively present in the *soul,* but not something of which the soul was aware (we saw that the soul is passive to its genius). It is only as consciousness that the urge is a dislocation of the soul from its genius.

In Hegel's *Lectures on Aesthetics,* Hegel asserts that "the sense of this contradiction along with the urge to remove it is precisely what generates wonder [*die Verwunderung*]."[32]

The *soul* is passive to its genius. It is only as *consciousness* that the urge is a dislocation of the soul from its genius. The dislocation is the moment when otherness ceases to be subconscious influence and opens up as possibility. It is the transition from oracle to the possibility of proper speech, from predestination to the beginning of philosophical self-determination.

Wonder is traumatic. It dislocates the soul's dreamscape, derailing genius's destiny. Wonder is also related to dreams because it is pure teleology, a feeling, an urge, a being-toward. To avoid being captive of repetition or awe, the urge to overcome contradiction must produce knowledge about its contradictions. Wonder, as the urge of consciousness to overcome contradiction, is the beginning of speculative wisdom and therefore of Spirit's development.

Schmitz on the Recovery of Wonder

In *The Recovery of Wonder,*[33] Schmitz traces the history of thought from the Greeks to the present in terms of how we think "things" and their causes. He claims that from the high metaphysics of Aristotle and Plato, through to the medieval Schoolmen's Christianization of that, there is some consistency with regard to viewing things and their causes as external to the subject. He explains that as the modern Enlighten-

31. Ibid., 157, Zusatz para. 416; my italics.

32. Hegel, *Lectures on Aesthetics,* 315; for the German, see Hegel, *Vorlesungen über die Ästhetik,* Band I, in *Hegels Werke in Zwanzig Bande,* edited by Eva Moldenhauer and Karl Markus Michel, 408 (Frankfurt am Main: Suhrkamp Verlag, 1970).

33. Kenneth L. Schmitz, *The Recovery of Wonder: The New Freedom and the Asceticism of Power* (Montreal and Kingston: McGill-Queen's University Press, 2005).

ment era developed, truth and causation lost their external character, becoming qualities of the human subject. The Enlightenment declared knowledge to be determined by human judgment and viewed the human will as a free, autonomous source of causation. As modernity progressed, that complete freedom of the subject was faced by a world of discrete objects that were to be understood through empirical scientific observation and used for the subject's ends.

Schmitz traces the modern changes to Descartes' *Cogito* and finds its completion in the Kantian Copernican revolution. Schmitz claims that even though some post-Kantians do open up the subject to larger notions (such as Hegel's Absolute Spirit, which encompasses the single individual within the historically developed community), these post-Kantians do not return us to a metaphysics of *res* (things).

Schmitz claims that, while this new view of things and of our own freedom has led to marvelous advances in our control of and insight into nature, something important has been lost. What has been lost is the ancient and medieval view of a thing and of a human subject, each existing in a community of other things and other subjects, whose interdependence and interrelatedness are beyond the scope of a single human subject or even community of knowers. What has been lost is a sense of the givenness of things, of their cause lying not in our own judgment about them, but as having been created. He advocates rediscovering the wonder of looking at something as a gift.

Schmitz does not want us to go backwards in time and take up an antiquated metaphysics that rejects the developments of the modern world. He calls for a new look based on the developed history of metaphysics, one that puts modernity in its place within our history (rather than agreeing with postmodernity that history has ended).

Schmitz points us beyond our view of things as merely or primarily useful. He reengages the Schoolmen's association of "certain transcendental and omnipresent characteristics with being."[34] These are, first, the truth or intelligibility of things, that "capacity in things to respond to the questions with which we approach them and even to draw those questions out of us";[35] second, the transcendental good in things that is "worthy of respect in itself, as when we admire the gait of a tiger but prefer the gate to be closed."[36] Schmitz asserts that "it is this power or actuality in things that engenders wonder in us."[37]

34. Ibid., 125.

35. Ibid.

36. Ibid.

37. Ibid.

According to Schmitz, this is not limited to the Kantian experience of the sublime, since "we do not simply experience the superiority of our freedom through the independence and resistance of things; we recognize instead a kind of secret mutual bond, and we also sense the thickness of that bond."[38] Finally, according to Schmitz, the Schoolmen recognized the beauty in things: "things quicken with a *luminosity* and *effulgence* that expresses a distinctive configuration ... a characteristic which escapes the confines of species and transgresses the formal limits of the thing even as it heightens their formal quality." For Schmitz, this "is the grace that invites us to celebrate the rhythm of things, the call to music, poetry, and art. It is the very 'dance' of things."[39]

Schmitz concludes:

> Even today, these properties of the reality of things invite us to look beyond their familiar presence to the mystery of things themselves: and in *seeing them anew* we are invited to recover the wondrous splendour that gives rise to *theôria*. It is in the recognition of our solidarity with things (*aliquid*) that we find a fuller freedom.[40]

Schmitz is a Catholic philosopher, and his argument exhibits that conviction. His view is challenging and inviting and right in important ways, even for non-Catholic and nonmonotheistic philosophers. As Schmitz rightly points out, our current environmental situation calls for us to stop viewing the world in an anthropocentrically utility-based way. I would add that, even if we do not go so far as to see the natural world as the creation of God, we need to regain a sense of wonder at nature if we are to counter current trends leading us into a human-made world that is out of touch with its own survival.

Nonetheless, I think that engaging in a metaphysics of being and returning to *theôria* is a one-sided solution. And Schmitz is wrong to claim that Hegel's commitment to subjectivity does not allow him to develop a metaphysics of things.

First, according to Hegel, "everything turns on grasping and expressing the True, not only as *Substance,* but equally as *Subject.*"[41] This statement must be read both ways—as affirming substance as well as subject, and not just subject as well as substance. The urge of consciousness to overcome the contradiction that it itself is must be understood in

38. Ibid.

39. Ibid., 125–26.

40. Ibid., 126.

41. Hegel, *Phenomenology of Spirit* 10, para. 17.

terms of a metaphysics of substance as well as a metaphysics of subjectivity. Let me explain.

I agree with Schmitz that we do not want to be blind at the moment we think we see most clearly. In other words, we do not want the certainty and freedom of the modernized *Cogito* to blind us to the given. I agree that we must make sure that theory is not oracle, that our encounter with otherness is not the kind of trauma that leads us to seek mastery over the other through violence. But, as we will see shortly, a *Hegelian* account of *Lear* that draws on the dialectical nature of subject and object shows the logic involved in such violence (that of fate), and how to avoid it by means of a different logic (that of wonder as the beginning of self-knowledge).

Second, let us address Schmitz's call for *theôria*. According to Schmitz, wonder is a kind of admiration: it is a theoretical attitude toward the given. By contrast, in Hegel, theory is inseparable from praxis.[42] This does not mean that, according to Hegel, the will dominates *theôria*. It means that there is a balanced dialectic between subject and object. If this were not the case, wonder could not arise. For wonder arises as an *aporetic* encounter with the other, an encounter in which the other is separate from ourselves (and from our desire to vibrate with or consume it). That encounter marks out for us the *urge* within us to overcome contradiction, the urge that drives the dialectical development in any coming-to-know.

The inseparability of theory and praxis has its origins in the fact that consciousness is a contradiction with itself and an *urge* to overcome that contradiction. We do not rest in knowledge; knowledge is our practice.

Finally, for Hegel, wonder is just the beginning: we need to develop that *aporia* into actual knowledge. This is not a return to a subjective condition, for, just as the actual soul is being, reason (at a much more developed level) is also being.

Thus to conclude here, insofar as we consider the beginning of the philosophy of *mind* and therefore the beginning of *self*-knowledge, we place wonder at the inception of consciousness. Wonder is the initial trauma of realizing that being one is a contradiction to oneself. For Hegel as much as for Schmitz, the *Cogito* is not a solution, for it ignores the substantial side of the contradiction: it ignores the objectivity, the givenness at which we wonder. The urge to overcome the contradiction has both a content side and an active side, a spatial and a temporal side

42. See Allen Wood's *Hegel's Ethical Thought* (Cambridge and New York: Cambridge University Press, 1990), 31–32.

(a *bestehende* and *vergehende* side).[43] Wonder is not just a theoretical attitude toward a given. It is a dislocation, an *aporia,* a breach in the flow of dreams that wakes us (from our merely theoretical or merely practical attitude). It is that which makes us step out of the comfort of our genius into the alienation of difference. Wonder is the trauma that wakes us up to otherness, thereby initiating the possibility of empathy as well as self-certainty. But wonder would remain traumatic if it did not develop into something more than the breach of dreams.

Schmitz is right to assert that wonder is always of something, toward something. Whether we call this the "given" or the "substantial actuality of being that is both substance and subject" is irrelevant here. Hegel's philosophy offers us the insight that whatever we might wonder at, we cannot separate that wonder from the primordial urge of consciousness to know (itself/being) more completely.

One challenge nonetheless remains for us in our defense of Hegel's wonder as the beginning of philosophy: we need to show that this urge is not violent, and that it does not ultimately privilege either the theoretical or the practical. For this we need to turn to *Lear.*

Lear's Genius and the Tragedy of Wonder

The play *The Tragedy of King Lear* is a dreamscape of geniuses. The dream in general is fate: it is the destinies of the geniuses. Within this dreamscape, wonder, the beginning of wisdom, grows. These two logics—that of fate and that of wonder—work their way through the play.

The Problem of Geniuses and their Logic of Fate in The Tragedy of King Lear

Quality and Quantity Since a genius is both one and two without knowing it, it fails to properly relate quality and quantity. It does so either by equating them, or keeping them absolutely distinct. In the first case, it fixates on measures of power; in the second, it merges empathically. Let us take each in turn.

According to the dictates of Lear's "inner oracle," his kingdom is to be parceled out in proportion to the quality of his daughters' adorational speeches. Lear invites his daughters to verbally quantify their love and in return, Lear, god-like, will give them parts of the earth to rule. Regan and Goneril comply. They provide a chorus for his oracular self.[44] They

43. See Bates, *Hegel's Theory of Imagination,* 42–43.

44. See Hegel's discussion of the Chorus in tragedy in *Aesthetik,* 1210–11.

chime in—vibrate—with his genius. Lear's soul feels no dissonance, since their incantations are properly tuned to it. Indeed they know that they will get more land if they make their love inestimably large: Goneril: "Sir, I love you more than words can wield the matter; Dearer than eyesight, space, and liberty.... Beyond all manner of so much."[45] Similarly, Regan says of her sister "I find she names my very deed of love— / Only she comes too short."[46] Regan rejects all pleasures "which the most precious square of sense possesses" and she finds herself "alone felicitate in your dear Highness' love."

But his third daughter, Cordelia, does not chime in:

LEAR: Speak.
CORDELIA: Nothing, my lord.
LEAR: Nothing?
CORDELIA: Nothing.
LEAR: Nothing will come of nothing. Speak again.
CORDELIA: Unhappy that I am, I cannot heave
  My heart into my mouth. I love your majesty
  According to my bond; no more nor less.[47]

Cordelia's silent and strange language affronts Lear's genius. He is threatened because it dislocates his sense of destiny. She has rejected the logic of his oracle. He is forced out of his complacent self-adoration (with its vibrating chorus). He is forced to wonder.

Initially, Lear suppresses his wonder.[48] He rejects Cordelia because he thinks that Cordelia has rejected him. He is partially right, for she has rejected his genius. But he is wrong that she has rejected her *father.* She loves him.

In one respect, Lear is right to chastise her. The kind of love she bears him is related to *her* failure to separate herself from *her* particular kind of genius. She also, like Lear, has not achieved a proper consciousness of her political surroundings.

45. William Shakespeare, *The Tragedy of King Lear* (The Conflated Text), in *The Norton Shakespeare,* based on the Oxford edition, ed. Stephen Greenblatt, Walter Cohen, Jean E. Howard, and Katharine Eisaman Maus, 2479–2553; 1.1.53–59, 2480 (New York and London: W. W. Norton, 1997; hereafter *Lear,* followed by act/scene/line nos. and page nos.

46. Ibid., 1.1.70–71, 2481.

47. Ibid. 1.1.85–92, 2481.

48. Note his oracular, god-like language as he rejects her: "Let it be so. Thy truth, then, be thy dower; / For, by the sacred radiance of the sun, / The mysteries of Hecate, and the night; / By all the operation of the orbs / From whom we do exist and cease to be, / Here I disclaim all my paternal care" (*Lear,* 1.1.108–13, 2481–82).

Her soul is more like the child in the womb than a man caught in the dreamscape of his own genius. She loves and does not speak. Her inner oracle is the opposite of Lear's relating of quality to quantity: hers is the unspoken belief that quality (feeling) cannot become quantity (word). Ironically, her soul cannot even declare this, for that would be to put the quality of her feeling into words. Instead, she meekly asserts that she "cannot heave her heart into her mouth." For Cordelia, quality cannot be located. She expects to vibrate with her father. Her word "Nothing" is the closest she can come to expressing that vibration.

Lear and Cordelia are feeling souls, each related to their geniuses in a way that is not salutary in human affairs. Neither is more articulate than the other. Though Cordelia's silence makes her appear more admirable (indeed closer to the wonder needed for philosophy), in fact, her language, like Lear's, is that of a soul's genius, not the language of consciousness. Her raw empathy is not ethical sensitivity.

The Dislocating Effect of Trauma and of Wonder Their encounter is dislocation. When Cordelia encounters Lear, her soul does not have a fixed location. This lack is itself dislocated as a result of the encounter. For this lack is what her father turns on her as a fate: she will not have any land, and this lack of dower is offered as grounds for rejection by suitors; if Lear has his way, she will have no place in the social order. The comfortable vibrations of her silent genius have loud political consequences.[49] She cannot but wonder at this.

Her original lack of location also dislocates her father. His soul becomes dislocated from its genius: his words and the destiny they invoke become something other. Lear feels his purposiveness, but the purpose is now unclear. He is in a condition of wonder. This interruption dislocates Lear's speech more and more as the play develops.

There therefore emerge two kinds of dislocation, one within the other. Within the bad dislocations there is the good check of wonder. Wonder sets up an alternative to the destiny of genius. It sets up the possibility of conscious self-knowledge.

Banishing and Hypocrisy vs. Uniting Theory and Practice The response of genius to difference is not just to retaliate, but to banish from sight or to engage in hypocrisy. Let us take each in turn.

Lear banishes Cordelia and Kent (who pleads on Cordelia's behalf).

49. It is for this reason that nonaction is rejected by Sartre: it is existentially unviable.

To Cordelia, Lear says, "Hence, and avoid my sight";[50] to Kent, "Out of my sight!"[51] Kent protests: "See better, Lear; and let me still remain / The true blank of thine eye."[52] While Regan and Goneril chime in Lear's chorus, those who contradict his judgment offend his eyes.

By contrast, Regan's and Goneril's genius deal with difference by severing theory and practice. Their loving words are never acted upon.

Cordelia, however, recognizes in what is going on a distinction and interconnection of theory and practice. In this, she is closer (than Lear and her sisters) to the urge to overcome contradiction. She attempts to correct Lear's impression that she merely presents a theory that contradicts his. In her reply, she makes clear that a true assessment of her must take theory *and* practice, sight *and* action into account. She rejects her sisters' hypocrisy, "that glib and oily art, / To speak and purpose not."[53] She insists that her intentions will be borne out in action.

Kent likewise rejects hypocrisy. He challenges Goneril and Regan: "your large speeches may your deeds approve / That good effects may spring from words of love."[54]

But at this point in the play, Cordelia cannot convince. Lear and her sisters are busy responding to her earlier naïve empathy. Her argument gets lost in the dreamscape of words and images. Later in the play, she develops her insight into action and becomes properly political. This change in her will in part has resulted from her initial encounter with Lear. It is that encounter that interrupts her genius's empathy and causes her to wonder. It generates in her the urge to overcome the contradictions into which her genius, and Lear's, have plunged her. But we can see from her reply that her initial step in this process has been to argue first against her father's theory about her (and her entrapment as a kind of theory that must be banished) and second against her sisters' hypocrisy in keeping theory and practice apart.

The Logic of Fate vs. the Logic of Wonder

The Logic of Fate In his response to Cordelia, Lear chooses his genius—his soul's dream—over his paternal feelings and responsibilities. In that moment, he chooses his particularity over the universal, a choice that for Hegel defines evil.[55] (In this, we have something of an expla-

50. *Lear,* 1.1.124, 2482.
51. Ibid., 1.1.157, 2483.
52. Ibid., l.1.158–59, 2483.
53. Ibid., 1.1.225–26, 2484.
54. Ibid., 1.1.185–86, 2483.
55. Hegel, *Hegel's Philosophy of Right,* trans. T. M. Knox (London, Oxford, and New York:

nation of Hegel's off-the-cuff remark that "Shakespeare . . . in *Lear* . . . brings evil before us in its entire dreadfulness.")[56] Lear blocks his wonder at her words. His genius condemns her and therein sets a troubled course for his future.

Cordelia also chooses her particular genius over the universal. We might think her genius closer to the universal good, since its shape is empathy. But it is equally one-sided, and therefore her choice is as evil as Lear's. She exemplifies the evil of the "beautiful soul."[57] Her empathy cannot express a rational real any more than Lear's oracular selfishness can. The logic of her evil genius also works its way through the plot.

So far, the logic of their fates is as follows. Cordelia, the genius whose oracle is only qualitatively *felt*, is banished by the genius who hears only its own quantifying, hegemonic oracle. The latter, narcissistic genius attacks because it cannot tolerate otherness. Lear is then attacked in the same manner by other geniuses who cannot tolerate *his* otherness.

The other characters aid the fateful logic of geniuses. Most do so by being exaggerations of Learian or Cordelian genius: they are either oracular power-mongers (Goneril, Regan, Edmund), or empathic souls without power (Edgar).[58] The first kind of character is passive to their genius and to its spell of power.[59] The second kind is captive of their innocence. They become captives of a world illegitimately determined by others. They turn inward upon themselves, becoming captives of their own inner worlds, worlds dislocated from what others see.

These characters' naïve empathy-turned-imaginary is closer to the wonder that is the basis of open-ended relationship to otherness. From their dislocation, they are able to judge differently. Such characters need to externalize their judgment before they can begin to mature. But when they first do so, they use mad symbolic language. They transition through Hegel's second level of the feeling soul: self-feeling or the

---

Oxford University Press, 1967), 92, par. 139; see chap. 8 of Bates, *Hegel and Shakespeare on Moral Imagination* (Albany: State University of New York Press, 2010).

56. Hegel, *Aesthetik*, 222.

57. For a discussion of the Beautiful Soul, see *Phenomenology of Spirit*, 383, para. 632; basically, it is the Kantian pure will that cannot act, because to act is to become determined in the heteronomy of nature, and therefore to become impure.

58. Edmund says of Edgar that he is "a brother noble, / Whose nature is so far from doing harms/ That he suspects none; on whose foolish honesty / My practices ride easy!" (*Lear*, 1.2.163–66, 2490).

59. *Hegel, Aesthetik*, 585: Hegel holds Macbeth responsible rather than the witches, precisely because the witches merely represent Macbeth's desires. We can say that the witches represent Macbeth's genius (which is hell-bent on power).

madness of contradiction. (In a moment, we will discuss how Lear joins these characters when he appears to go mad.) Edgar's development is a case in point: he traces the process from naïve empathy through madness (as Poor Tom) to ethical certainty. But he is the only one in the play to develop from genius to consciousness and *survive* the process.[60]

So, to summarize, at the start of the play, we have those who want power (quantity) on the one side, and those who want love (quality) on the other. These geniuses constitute the thick, dreamlike world of the plot. The logic of fate in this play is this dreaming logic of geniuses. Geniuses seek to annihilate what contradicts them. It is a zero-sum game, a view of contradiction in which only one side can win.

In this logic of fate, conflict is cruel. We have already seen how Lear's genius attacks Cordelia's. Let us look at how Lear fares.

Lear's genius sees itself as the great quantifier, counting and dispensing worth (of words and of people). Goneril and Regan make him suffer for this. In act 2, scene 2, these sisters cruelly play with him by progressively reducing the number of men they will allow to attend him:

> REGAN [TO LEAR]: I entreat you
> To bring but five and twenty. To no more
> Will I give place or notice.
> LEAR: I gave you all—
> REGAN: In good time you gave it.
> LEAR: What, must I come to you
> With five and twenty, Regan? Said you so?
> REGAN: And speak't again, my lord; no more with me.
> LEAR [TO GONERIL]: I'll go with thee.
> Thy fifty yet doth double five-and-twenty,
> And thou art twice her love.
> GONERIL: Hear me, my lord.
> What need you five and twenty, ten, or five,
> To following in a house where twice so many
> Have a command to tend you.
> REGAN: What need one?[61]

This is painful to Lear because his genius's worth is measured in the number of his adoring and subservient subjects. The sisters are cutting back his chorus.

60. I have discussed him elsewhere (see my "Moral Luck in Hegel and Shakespeare," in *Hegel and Shakespeare on Moral Imagination*.)

61. *Lear*, 2.4.242–58, 2512.

On one side, then, we have the logic of fate acting on Cordelia and Lear: the cruel designing of geniuses who torment by intentionally hitting the other where they know it will hurt most. But there is another logic at work.

The Logic of Wonder In the encounter between Lear and Cordelia, the logic of wonder is initiated into the plot. Lear and Cordelia wonder at the violence that the other does to their feeling soul. Each wonders at the dislocation of their soul from their genius. Lear and Cordelia are each checked by the other into consciousness of a larger ethical sphere. Lear's oracular power is gradually shot through with Cordelian empathy, and Cordelia's empathy becomes articulated by strategy (of war).

Let me briefly trace Lear's development, then Cordelia's.

Just as fate causes him to suffer his genius, Lear's wonder puts into question the established story of his genius. In wonder, the link between quality and quantity is opened up. Wonder is purposiveness whose purpose has yet to be revealed. It is a being-toward.

Lear's struggle to understand eventually drives him to be-toward the most elemental and existential of things: the storm on the heath. There, Lear enters into a relationship with the elements. He gives up his genius' efforts to control exchange. Lear cries out:

> LEAR: Rumble thy bellyful! Spit, fire! spout, rain!
> Nor rain, wind, thunder, fire, are my daughters:
> I tax not you, you elements, with unkindness;
> I never gave you kingdom, called you children,
> You owe me no subscription. Then let fall
> Your horrible pleasure. Here I stand, your slave,
> A poor, infirm, weak, and despised old man.[62]

Lear also discovers Poor Tom on the heath. For Lear, Poor Tom (dispossessed Edgar) represents the sheer nakedness of the human condition. Poor Tom is nothing but being-toward (by Edgar's own words, he is "poor Tom! / That's something yet! Edgar I nothing am.")[63] Lear says:

> Is man no more than this? Consider him well. Thou owest the worm no silk, the beast no hide, the sheep no wool, the cat no perfume. Ha, here's three on's are sophisticated! Thou are the thing itself; unaccommodated man is no more but such a poor, bare, forked animal as thou art. Off, off, you lendings! come unbutton here. [*Lear takes his own clothes off*].[64]

62. Ibid., 3.2.13–19, 2515.

63. Ibid., 2.3.20–21, 2506.

64. Ibid., 3.4.95–101, 2519.

Lear also recognizes for the first time the otherness of other people, and he senses their suffering:

> Poor naked wretches, wheresoe'er you are,
> That bide the pelting of this pitiless storm,
> How shall your houseless heads and unfed sides,
> Your looped and windowed raggedness, defend you
> From seasons such as these? O, I have ta'en
> Too little care of this! Take physic, pomp;
> Expose thyself to feel what wretches feel,
> That thou mayst shake the superflux to them,
> And show the heavens more just.[65]

As for Cordelia's wonder, it makes her question the established story of her genius (that she is pure empathy, a quality that cannot be put into words or embodied in land). Since she is not the focus of the play, we do not see her wonder develop on stage. But we do see that it has developed, for when she comes back on stage, she is a queen and soldier:

> MESSENGER: News, madam.
> The British powers are marching hitherward.
> CORDELIA: 'Tis known before; our preparation stands
> In expectation of them. O dear father,
> It is thy business that I go about;
>
> No blown ambition doth our arms incite,
> But love, dear love, and our aged father's right.[66]

A Dialectic of Wonders The play traces two developments: Lear's development from oracular destiny to being-toward and true speech, and Cordelia's development from raw empathy to political integrity. Both developments occur as a result of Lear's and Cordelia's encounter. The dream-logic of their geniuses is interrupted by the dislocating logic of wonder. They move from subconscious urges to the conscious urges of philosophy.

The two developments are related. What Lear and Cordelia need in order to develop is the truth of the other's genius, raised, through wonder, to consciousness. Each needs to *consciously* experience what the other's genius experienced *subconsciously.* Thus Lear needs to experience his self as purposiveness whose purpose has yet to be declared. He needs to be in touch with his existential condition, in which the future is undetermined

65. Ibid., 3.4.29–37, 2518.
66. Ibid., 4.4.21–29, 2533.

and yet nonetheless in need of articulation. He needs the qualitative side of experience. Cordelia, on her side, needs to experience the historically concrete forms of purpose that someone with an oracular, articulate, self-certain genius generates. Each needs to consciously develop the contradiction of purposiveness without a purpose (quality) and destiny or purposiveness with a purpose (quantity). They would each thereby complete their respective conceptual framework. For the truth about worth is that it *is* quantitative, but its distribution must be based on discussions of need according to agreed principles of equity; the truth about empathy is that it *does* defy any final quantification, but to be effective it must express itself concretely according to the particularity of circumstance.

Geniuses seek to get rid of one side of contradiction. But wonder is the urge of *consciousness* to embrace and overcome the contradiction.

Self-certainty and empathy together are the hallmark of humane reason. Each finds its completion only in and through the other. This occurs in and through the concrete self-understandings of a maturing spirit. Neither Lear nor Cordelia achieve the highest levels of such knowing (of Spirit—what Hegel calls "Absolute Knowing"). But by the end of the play, they have achieved the language necessary to begin that process.

The evidence is that near the end of the play, their speeches exhibit indifference to fate and a commitment to wonder. In the midst of terror, as they are taken to prison, they say:

> CORDELIA: We are not the first
> Who, with the best meaning, have incurred the worst.
> For thee, oppressèd King, am I cast down;
> Myself could else out-frown false Fortune's frown.
> LEAR: Come, let's away to prison.
> We two alone will sing like birds i'the cage.
> When thou dost ask me blessing, I'll kneel down,
> And ask of thee forgiveness. So we'll live,
> And pray, and sing, and tell old tales, and laugh
> At gilded butterflies, and hear poor rogues
> Talk of court news; and we'll talk with them too,
> Who loses and who wins; who's in, who's out;
> And take upon's the mystery of things,
> As if we were God's spies; and we'll wear out,
> In a walled prison, packs and sects of great ones,
> That ebb and flow by the moon.[67]

67. Ibid., 5.3.3–19, 2545.

Their dialogue is an achievement signaling that they have abandoned fate (and thus their geniuses). They are now wonder's captives. The world stands over against them as something to wonder at. This is an achievement against odds, for war is a captivation that usually destroys wonder as well as its participants. (We see that destruction in Macbeth: near the conclusion of that play, his imagination dies before he does.)[68] By the end of the play, Cordelia is no longer pure empathy, and Lear is no longer mesmerized by his oracle and its chorus.

Despite this dialect of wonders, the other logic, that of fate, develops. Let us look at another way in which fate and wonder work in the play.

The Language of Fate (Oracle) vs. the Language of Wonder (Witty Contradiction) in the Fool and Lear's Madness

The character who carries the language of wonder consistently through the play is the Fool. He helps Lear develop away from his genius toward consciousness. In the following passage, the Fool plays on Lear's narcissistic identification of quality and quantity. In one song, the Fool tries to show Lear how the language of "nothing" can make him "richer":

> Mark it, nuncle:
> Have more than thou showest,
> Speak less than thou knowest,
> Lend less than thou owest,
> Learn more than thou trowest,
> Set less than thou throwest,
> Leave thy drink and thy whore,
> And keep in-a-door,
> And thou shalt have more,
> Than two tens to a score.[69]

To this Kent replies: "This is nothing, fool." The Fool replies by making Lear wonder at Lear's earlier declaration to Cordelia that "Nothing will come of nothing."[70] That is, the Fool says to Lear: "Can you make no use of nothing [of my song], nuncle?" To which Lear replies: "Why, no, boy; nothing can be made out of nothing." The Fool then says

68. See my discussion of Macbeth in chap. 9 of *Hegel and Shakespeare on Moral Imagination.*

69. *Lear,* 1.4.100–10, 2493.

70. Ibid., 1.1.89, 2481.

to Kent: "Prithee, tell him, so much the rent of his land comes to. He will not believe a fool."[71] So far, Lear will not hear—will not be enriched by the wisdom—of the Fool's nothingnesses.

But Lear's language progressively becomes like the Fool's. The turning point occurs just before the heath, right after Lear's argument with Goneril and Regan about the number of attendants they will allow him. At the end of that torturous debate over quantity, Lear finally grasps the fallacy in his way of pairing love with quantity. To Regan's tormenting question "why [do you even need] one [man]?" he hollers "O, reason not the need! Our basest beggars / Are in the poorest things superfluous."[72] At this point, Lear's heart cracks and he begins speaking the language of contradiction. He heads to the heath. There, Lear becomes a contradiction: when Kent calls out "who's there?" the Fool replies ambiguously "Marry, here's grace and a cod-piece; that's a wise man and a fool."[73] Following a long rant, mad Lear, echoing both Cordelia and the Fool, contradicts his oracular self: "I will be the pattern of patience; I will say nothing."[74]

After the scene on the heath, Lear speaks through contradiction. For example, to blind Gloucester Lear says:

> LEAR: What, art mad? A man may see how this world goes with no eyes. Look with thine ears. See how yond justice rails upon yond simple thief. Hark, in thine ear. Change places and, handy-dandy, which is the justice, which is the thief?
>
> Get thee glass eyes;
> And, like a scurvy politician, seem
> To see the things thou does not.
> EDGAR: O, matter and impertinency mixed!
> Reason in madness!
> LEAR: If thou wilt weep my fortunes, take my eyes.
> I know thee well enough; thy name is Gloucester:
> Thou must be patient.[75]

In my Hegelian reading, Lear, in his madness, has passed from being dominated by his feeling soul's immediacy to the self-feeling soul's insanity. Lear's madness is therefore an advance: it is purgative and strangely insightful. He speaks of how contradictory the world appears (especially with regard to justice). He now knows that he is in a world of

71. Ibid., 1.4.113–16, 2493.
72. Ibid., 2.4.259–60, 2512.
73. Ibid., 3.2.37–39, 2515.
74. Ibid., 3.2.36, 2515.
75. Ibid., 4.6.142–71, 2537–38.

geniuses: "When we are born, we cry that we are come / To this great stage of fools."[76] Talking nonsense through contradictions is the only way to talk sense in a world of geniuses. The geniuses, however, cannot tolerate contradiction: they cannot "hear" the truth through contradictions. Their "eyes" fixate on one side. In their eyes, Lear is simply mad.

Hegel's discussion in the second section of the Feeling Soul in the *Encyclopedia Anthropology* concerns madness. He writes that, in madness, a higher level of mind sinks into the level of genius. But in Lear's case, madness is the language of a man attempting to exit the dream-world of geniuses. Lear's madness is like Hamlet's in this respect: the social world around him is a bad dream constituted by people's oracular authority; when someone like Hamlet or the Fool or Poor Tom or Lear himself pokes through to the waking world, their language is dissonant with that dream world. They speak in witty contradictions.

The language of contradictions is the language of wonder. It is the language of the urge to overcome the dreamscape in which the contradictions that constitute the social fabric are not recognized. This is why the theater players are so interesting to Hamlet: they have conscious control of the language of society and can turn that language on and off at will. According to Hegel, the ability to put on and take off a mask at will is the hallmark of comedy.[77] This is why the Fool's and Lear's and Poor Tom's (and Hamlet's) language is funny, even when deadly serious.

Kent's Urging of Lear to Overcome Contradiction

Kent and the Fool are the only characters who start out and remain outside of the illusory world of the geniuses. They both embrace contradiction in order to survive: the Fool is wise but must speak in confusing language; Kent is honest but must appear to be someone other than who he is. Kent also tries to bring Lear to his senses (literally, he tries to make Lear's feeling soul one that consciously feels rather than one that vibrates narcissistically). Here is an example of Kent's effort.

Early in the play, the banished, disguised Kent encounters Lear. Lear says: "Dost thou know me, fellow?" Kent replies: "No, sir; but you have that in your countenance which I would fain call master."[78] Hegel cites this passage as an example of the magical effect one person can have on another: "Among adults, a superior mind exercises a magical power over

76. Ibid., 4.6.176–77, 2538.

77. See Hegel, *Aesthetik,* on comedy, 1220–22.

78. *Lear,* 1.4.24–25, 2491.

weaker minds; thus, for example, Lear over Kent, who felt himself irresistibly drawn to the unhappy monarch because the king seemed to him to have something in his countenance which he, as he puts it, 'would fain call master.'"[79]

I disagree with Hegel here. I think that Kent is trying to get Lear to feel Lear's own authority rather than to construct it from the choruses that chime in with his genius. Kent sees something in Lear's countenance and in saying so invites Lear to look to himself to see it. Far from succumbing to magical influence from Lear, Kent is helping Lear *out* of Lear's magical thinking. Kent's words draw Lear away from the oracular toward feeling his body (rather than the words of others) as the site of authority. Kent is helping Lear toward "seeing the world feelingly," that is, toward a wonder that leads to proper self-knowledge. Kent is pointing Lear toward true mastery (his consciousness of the authority that is embodied in him).

Kent tries to make Lear wonder, but fails, because Kent's language is too easily appropriable by Lear's narcissism: to Lear, it is just more chorus. Hegel makes the mistake of interpreting Kent's words the way Lear hears them.

Fate and Wonder: Two Logics of Contradiction

The difference between violent contradiction and sublation of contradiction lies in a character's level of cognitive development. The check that inaugurates the urge to overcome contradiction (rather than violent reaction against it) has to be a result of otherness that invites rather than destroys. Cordelia invites, her sisters destroy. Similarly, Lear invites Cordelia insofar as he refers to her as the one he had loved most of all. That underlying love is what makes Lear wonder at himself and not just at Cordelia.

Contradiction from other geniuses is not enough to initiate wonder. Nor is mere vibration sufficient. Love is not just vibration: it seeks to know the other. And without love, self-knowledge is self-destruction.

The soul longs to vibrate in complete unity with its other. But the soul cannot have that unity, because it is always already different from its genius. Contradiction at this level makes the soul (i.e., the genius) seek to erase difference in order to return to its vibrations. But that vibration is particular vibration, not unity with being. By contrast, *consciousness's*

79. Hegel, *Encyclopedia Philosophy of Mind,* 97, Zusatz to para. 405.

urge to overcome contradiction shares in *being,* because the urge is becoming. A particular vibration is a destiny; sublation is eternity.

We can articulate this in terms of the contradictory relationship of quality and quantity. At the level of genius, the contradiction is catastrophic: for it is equally true that quality *is* quantity *and* that quality *cannot be* quantity. The genius who holds to one side of this contradiction cannot admit to the truth of the other side. For that genius, the destruction of the other side is the only solution. But at the level of consciousness, this contradiction is recognized as a real one, and the effort is made to overcome it.

The logic of fate is contradiction at the level of genius. It is a bad dream in which all the players act as if they are sleepwalking. For example, in act 1, scene 4, when Lear arrives at Goneril's castle, he is all of a sudden treated rudely by the steward.[80] Lear reacts angrily and exclaims in amazement "Ho? I think the world's asleep."[81] As the play progresses, there are more and more direct affronts against Lear's genius by the other (dreaming) geniuses. We noted above that this culminates in the absurd discussion of the number of men he is allowed to keep.

The logic of wonder, on the other hand, is driven by the urge to overcome contradiction by sublating it. We have traced that development in Cordelia and Lear. It culminates in a viewpoint from which they can dispassionately discuss the measure of things.

Let us look at quality vs. quantity in terms of subject vs. object. In Hegel's *Aesthetics,* the contradiction is spelled out as one between subject and substance. More specifically, it is a contradiction between our subjective apprehension and our objective condition. We can distill this down further, to a contradiction between ourselves as knowers and ourselves as bodies.

Feeling souls try to negate the contradiction that other bodied selves present to their genius. The genius's arena of contradiction is that of bodies and organs (by extension, people as functions of destiny).

By contrast, consciousness is the urge to overcome the contradictions of embodied subjectivity, and contradictions of social embodiment. Its effort and arena are incipient Spirit.

The tragedy of the play *Lear* is that the logic of fate organizes against the bodies even as the logic of wonder educates their minds.

80. *Lear,* 1.4.40ff, 2491.
81. Ibid., 1.4.42, 2491.

Blindness and Insight

In tragedy, the moment of overcoming contradiction is often accompanied by the destruction of organs. The removal of eyes is made the symbol of a character's transition from subconscious destiny to self-recognition. Real eyes are replaced by what Aristotle calls "prudence, that eye of the soul."[82]

In *Lear,* the character who symbolizes this is Gloucester. He shifts from having the sight of genius to the insight of consciousness, from seeing falsely to "seeing the world feelingly." He loses his eyes and, at that very moment, it is revealed to him that he had seen things all wrong.

Gloucester's insight at that point is not just that Edmund is bad and Edgar is good. It is that Gloucester's earlier way of seeing was faulty: "I stumbled when I saw."[83] When he had sight, he did not realize that it was an obvious contradiction that the son whom he loved hated and plotted against his life. Nor did he try to move beyond this contradiction. Gloucester was led by the genius of Edmund and followed the logic of geniuses, chasing out Edgar. Later, when blinded, Gloucester comes to "see the world feelingly."[84]

In this context, seeing the world feelingly is better than sight. On the one hand, this is just a metaphor for insight as opposed to seeing falsely. On the other, the "feeling" quality has to do with the urge to overcome contradiction. The danger of sight is that it can obscure the urge for philosophy. The danger of mere feeling is that the urge has nothing to see.

Gloucester's blinding foreshadows and symbolizes the tragic development of the play as a whole. It illustrates how fate and wonder unite tragically: insight is gained at the cost of the organs of sight; the beginning of philosophy is arrived at, at the cost of the bodies that would know. The entire play, from Lear's encounter with Cordelia forward, is an expanded moment of tragic self-recognition.[85]

Lear also starts out seeing falsely. Like Oedipus, when Lear truly

82. Aristotle, *Nicomachean Ethics,* 2nd ed., trans. Terence Irwin (Indianapolis, Ind., and Cambridge, Mass.: Hackett, 1999), 144a30, 98.

83. *Lear,* 4.6.145, 2537.

84. Gloucester's love for Edgar (like Lear's for Cordelia) makes his traumas subject to wonder and personal growth.

85. The loss of the bad way of seeing while keeping one's eyes is good. We the audience walk home, organs intact. Hopefully, the tragedy we have seen has instructed us how to see differently.

comprehends how genius works, he withdraws from the sighted world. He is swallowed up in what the geniuses around him take to be a mad view of the world.

But Lear's dislocation of his genius does not undo the powers of destruction unleashed by his earlier oracle. Hegel's insight about the nature of speculative knowledge is that "the Owl of Minerva flies at dusk."[86] *Lear* dramatizes how this truth can be *tragic*.

There is some (hellish) justification for what happens to Gloucester. But of tragedy in general we must ask: why can we not make the movement to seeing properly without destruction? Why, for example, does Oedipus take vengeance upon the eyes as though his genius, at its own demise, vengefully shouts "okay, but with me goes the possibility of sight!"? Is it consciousness that attacks the organs, mistaking them for the evil geniuses that led to consciousness's horrible condition? If that is the case, why does consciousness, at the moment of self-recognition, collapse back into the genius's logic that one should attack the organ that contradicts?

Why does the beginning of philosophy so often sabotage the body? How can the urge to know agency and the urge to purge agency coincide? What paradox is this at the beginning of philosophy?

We see here why Schmitz is right: in order to avoid tragedy at the birth of consciousness, philosophy must recover a wonder that is also a metaphysics of things. A pure metaphysics of *subjectivity* attacks bodies. It does because, in their very usefulness, bodies contradict the authority of subjectivity. This is Hegel's point about the Enlightenment—pure insight leads to the Terror of the French Revolution.[87] As Schmitz points out, we need to wonder at things and bodies, not just at our own subjectivity.

To avoid being tragedy, the beginning of philosophy must equally be the recovery of subjectivity and of being. With regard to being, philosophy must recover the luminous and original potential of the organs of sight; it must recover organs that are indifferent to the destinations to which the subject makes them look. It is to recover, as Kent says, "The true blank of thine eye."[88]

86. *Hegel's Philosophy of Right*, trans. T. M. Knox (London, Oxford, and New York: Oxford University Press, 1967), 13.

87. I discuss this in chap. 12 of Bates, *Hegel and Shakespeare on Moral Imagination*.

88. *Lear*, 1.1.158–59, 2483.

Conclusion: Tragedy and Recovery

On the one hand, the tragedy is personal, "modern," due to the pathos of Lear's (and Cordelia's) geniuses. At this level, the tragedy purges us of the particular failures of those kinds of geniuses: too much unconscious egoism, just like too raw an empathy, leads to trouble. On the other hand, the *Tragedy of King Lear* is something bigger than Lear or Cordelia. It is the clash of the universal forces of fate (destiny) and wonder (philosophy).[89] *This* is the reason the end of the play is so desolate.

The play is tragic because we feel that the logic of *wonder*, not the logic of fate, ought to win. The logics of Lear's and Cordelia's geniuses were overcome: they had moved beyond the language of their "inner oracles." These predestined souls had begun to be philosophically self-determinate. The tragedy is that they did so only when their destiny had unraveled too far: the very moment that Cordelia and Lear speak the language of an emerging, properly political, ethically sensitive order, their geniuses' political landscape destroys them.

If we do not react with the indifference of geniuses in the face of the destruction of other geniuses, it is because we love what Lear and Cordelia have come to represent to us over the course of the play. That is the check that moves us. We feel the urge(ncy) to move beyond genius and destiny to conscious ethical judgment. The play shows what is at stake: if we do not begin philosophy, we remain in a hellish dreamscape of geniuses.

This tragedy of wonder is therefore, traumatically, our recovery of wonder. Thanks to Hegel, we know that this is just the beginning. Thanks to Schmitz, we know why we must love our eyes and the things we see, as our insight develops.

89. In this respect, the play is like Hegel's conception of ancient tragedy; see Hegel, *Aesthetik*, 1222–23, for Hegel's distinction between modern and ancient tragedy.

Jude P. Dougherty

12. SCIENCE AND THE SHAPING OF MODERNITY

The Reciprocal Influence of Science and Culture

Cultural historians necessarily deal in broad generalizations. Whatever is affirmed of a period, a people, or a nation, no matter how well-grounded by factual study and reflection, is subject to qualification. Exceptions to broad characterizations may always be found without mitigating the value of the broader insight. We grasp something when an author refers to the Greeks, to Roman civilization, to the Hellenic period, to Christendom, to the Benedictines, to the Renaissance, or to the Enlightenment. These designations, all generalizations formed by an examination of a host of particulars, indeed refer to something intelligible, something quite apart from the mind.[1] Generalization, of course, can be misleading or false as well as perceptive and true. There is always the danger of unscrupulous forces manipulating history for present purposes. Then, too, in the study of history there is always the propensity to judge the past in the light of contemporary categories of experience. It is axiomatic that one must banish from the mind the customary con-

1. Lynn White, Jr., reminds us of the Herculean task awaiting the cultural historian. He writes "History is being made faster than we can absorb it.... As yet no mind, not even Arnold Toynbee's, has really digested the new material." Lynn White, Jr., "The Changing Past," in *Frontiers of Knowledge in the Study of Man,* edited by Lynn White, Jr. (New York: Greenwood Press, 1969), 68.

ceptions of one's own period before one can rightly understand the past. With that caveat in mind, this essay purports to examine with the aid of a host of distinguished twentieth-century scholars the reciprocal influence of science and culture, with particular attention to the role of religion at the birth of modern science.

Detached narrative is rare, yet, for example, those acquainted with the lifelong work and studied objectivity of Christopher Dawson are likely to give credence to his insight when he speaks of the great movement of thought that passed over the ancient world about the middle of the first millennium B.C. "that turned away men's minds from the world of human experience to the contemplation of absolute and unchanging Being, from Time to Eternity."[2] There are few readers who are in a position to render the same judgment unaided. Similarly, Dawson is convincing when he writes that with the advent of Christ, "the Absolute and the Finite, God and the World were no longer conceived as two exclusive and opposed orders of being standing over and against one another in mutual isolation. The two orders interpenetrated one another."[3] Dawson's judgment is an invitation to reflection. He makes a like generalization about the advent of modern science and its medieval antecedents. Scholars are nearly unanimous in recognizing that something dramatic occurred in the culture of Europe around the turn of the eleventh century. Explanations vary, with some emphasizing technological advancement, others the recovery of Greek learning, still others the practical influence of Christianity.

In 1925 the distinguished American philosopher Alfred North Whitehead delivered the prestigious Lowell Lectures at Harvard University, lectures subsequently published as *Science and the Modern World*.[4] Those lectures were significant because Whitehead, for a predominately American audience, challenged the Enlightenment view that only with the repudiation of a religious world view could modern science have emerged from a dark age. Whitehead, it must be noted, was writing a generation before the in-depth studies of Marshall Clagett, A. C. Crombie, and Anneliese Maier, and before the monumental work of Pierre Duhem became available in English translation. Examining the relation between science and culture, Whitehead put to himself a fundamental

2. Christopher Dawson, *Progress and Religion* (Garden City, N.Y.: Doubleday Image, 1960), 123.

3. Dawson, *Progress and Religion*, 126–27.

4. Alfred North Whitehead, *Science and the Modern World* (New York: Macmillan, 1925); also published as a Mentor Book, fourth printing, 1953.

question: Why did modern science emerge in the West during the sixteenth and seventeenth centuries, when all the conditions required for its birth were seemingly in place in classical antiquity? That question has entered public consciousness again with the reemergence of militant Islam. Contemporary scholars, in their attempt to understand an adversarial Islam, ask why the scientific revolution that we associate with Europe bypassed Islam, when for centuries Islam was in many respects at the forefront of human civilization and achievement. Bernard Lewis, the noted Middle East scholar, pointedly asks, what went wrong?[5] He writes, "In the course of the twentieth century it became abundantly clear in the Middle East and indeed all over the lands of Islam that things had indeed gone badly wrong. Compared with its millennial rival, Christendom, the world of Islam had become poor, weak, and ignorant."[6] "Why," he asks in a subsequent passage, "did the great scientific breakthrough occur in Europe and not as one might reasonably have expected in the richer, more advanced, and in many respects more enlightened realm of Islam?"[7]

Putting aside for the moment Lewis's somewhat romantic view of the "Golden Age of Islam," his question has been addressed, perhaps never more authoritatively, by A. C. Crombie.[8] In the same vein, a more recent account of the development of modern science, one that we will subsequently discuss, is that of Stephen Gaukroger.[9] Crombie's research led him to the conclusion that the new science that began to percolate into Western Christendom in the twelfth century, although largely Arabic in form, was founded on the works of the ancient Greeks. The Arabs, Crombie relates, preserved and transmitted to medieval Europe a large body of Greek learning, adding to it, to be sure, but what they added to its content was perhaps less important than the change they made in the conception and purpose for which science ought to be studied. The speculative or theoretical aspect of science interested them less than its application. In the judgment of Crombie, the most important and original contributions that the Arabs made to the history of European science

5. Bernard Lewis, *What Went Wrong?* (Oxford: Oxford University Press, 2002).

6. Ibid., 151.

7. Ibid., 156.

8. A. C. Crombie, *Medieval and Early Modern Science,* 2 vols.: vol. 1, *Science in the Middle Ages: V–XIII Centuries,* and vol. 2, *Science in the Later Middle Ages and Early Modern Times: XIII–XVII Centuries* (Garden City, New York: Doubleday Anchor Books, 1959).

9. Stephen Gaukroger, *The Emergence of a Scientific Culture: Science and the Shaping of Modernity, 1210–1685* (Oxford: Clarendon Press, 2006).

were those of alchemy, magic, and astrology. This was due partly to the Arabic approach to the study of nature, where power over nature, rather than rational explanation of fact, led inquirers to seek "the Elixir of Life," the magic properties of plants and minerals, instead of the causes of the properties of the things they experienced.[10]

It has been well documented that the Arabs themselves acquired their knowledge of Greek science from two sources: initially from Syriac intermediaries, but later directly from the Greeks of the Byzantine Empire. Their first encounter with Greek learning came from the Syriac-speaking Nestorian Christians of Eastern Persia.[11] The role that the Arabs played in the transmission of Aristotle to the West is an interesting and complicated story in itself and cannot be recounted here, but this much needs to be said: with the rapid expansion of Islam after Muhammad's death in 632, regions where Greek learning had previously been deposited came under Islamic domination. Under the Abbasid caliphs after 749, Muslims established contact with both Christians and hellenized Persians. The Abbasid caliphs and other patrons of translating activity were primarily interested in works of immediate practical utility, that is, technical treatises on medicine, astrology, logic, and the mathematical sciences.[12] "Partly through the growth of scholastic theology," David Lindberg tells us, "Islamic interests quickly expanded to encompass the whole of Platonic and Aristotelian philosophy. Texts already available in Syriac, the language of the Nestorian Christian community, were translated into the Arabic. Works not available in Syriac were rendered directly from Greek into Arabic."[13] The high-water mark of translations from Arabic to Latin came during the twelfth century. Lindberg finds that the story of the transmissions of Greek learning to the West is largely a tale of individual scholars responding in personal ways to unique historical circumstances. Yet there were important centers, such as Toledo and Palermo, where significant if not cooperative work was being

10. Crombie, *Medieval and Early Modern Science* 1:52.

11. Cf. David C. Lindberg, "The Transmission of Greek and Arabic Learning to the West," in *Science in the Middle Ages*, edited by David C. Lindberg (Chicago: Chicago University Press, 1978).

12. Ibid., 56. For an alternative account, one written from an Islamic perspective, see George Saliba, *Islamic Science and the Making of the European Renaissance* (Cambridge, Mass.: MIT Press, 2007); Saliba confirms with considerable textual evidence Crombie's account of the westward transmission of astronomical data from the world of Islam and makes the case that Copernicus's heliocentric view of the universe was largely indebted to Arab sources.

13. Ibid.

done. In 1250, for example, the provincial chapter of the Dominicans in Toledo sent eight friars to the *studium arabicum* in Tunis. By that time the works of Aristotle were diffused and understood throughout the Latin West. Interest in Aristotle was accompanied by interest in the philosophical works of the great speculative thinkers al Kindi, al-Farabi, and Avicenna, all Persians. The most influential Arabic thinker of the period was undoubtedly Averroes (1126–1198), who was regarded as the interpreter of Aristotle par excellence and was frequently referred to simply as the "Commentator."

Perhaps the better focus, unlike that of Lewis, should be not upon what went wrong in Arabia, but what went right within Christendom. Whitehead provides this insight: "My explanation is that the faith in the possibility of science, generated antecedently in the development of modern scientific theory, is the unconscious derivative from medieval theology."[14] "The Middle Ages, "Whitehead claims, "formed one long training of the intellect in Western Europe in the sense of order. There may have been some deficiency with respect to practice. But the idea never for a moment lost its grip. It was predominantly an epoch of orderly thought, rationalistic through and through."[15] Yet for science, something more is necessary than a general sense of the order of things. Equally important is the habit of definite and exact thought, which Whitehead attributes to the Greek philosophers, a legacy carried through the Middle Ages. Whitehead, in this passage, is less interested in the metaphysics that undergirds induction than he is in the impact of technological advance and the reciprocal influence of the theoretical and the practical. "We owe to St. Benedict," he writes, "that the monasteries were the homes of practical agriculturalists, as well as saints, and artists and men of learning. The alliance of science and technology, by which learning is kept in contact with irreducible and stubborn facts, owes much to the practical bent of the early Benedictines. Modern science derives from Rome as well as from Greece and this Roman strain explains its gain in an energy of thought kept closely in contact with the world of facts."[16]

The medieval historian Lynn White, Jr., later develops this theme in an article entitled "The Dynamo and the Virgin Reconsidered." Like Whitehead, he calls attention to the significant role that the Benedic-

14. Whitehead, *Science and the Modern World*, 14.
15. Ibid., 12.
16. Ibid., 16.

tines played in the history of Western technology, saying of St. Benedict that he was probably "the pivotal figure in the history of labor."[17] White, in comparing the status of labor in ancient Greece with its status in the later Middle Ages, finds that in the classical tradition, there is scarcely a hint of the dignity of labor. The civilizations of ancient Greece and Rome had rested on the backs of slaves. Reversing this Greek attitude toward labor was St. Benedict, by making labor part of the corporate life of his monastery, by adopting it not merely as a regrettable necessity but rather as an integral and spiritually valuable part of monastic discipline. White suggests that the Benedictine regard for the dignity of labor "marks a revolutionary reversal of the traditional attitude to labor: it is the high peak along the watershed separating the modern and ancient world.... Moreover, although St. Benedict had not intended that his monks should be scholars, a great tradition of learning developed in the abbeys following his *Rule:* for the first time the practical and the theoretical were involved in the same individual. The monk was the first intellectual to get dirt under his fingernails. He did not immediately launch into scientific investigation, but in his very person he destroyed the old artificial barrier between the empirical and the speculative, the manual and the liberal arts, and thus helped to create a social atmosphere favorable to scientific and technological development."[18]

What Whitehead dimly saw, Crombie makes explicit in his well-documented *Medieval and Early Modern Science,*[19] a history of science from Augustine to Galileo, from its decay after the collapse of the Roman Empire in the West to its full flowering in the seventeenth century. He emphasizes what he believes are the two most significant results of twentieth-century scholarship: the essential continuity of Western scientific traditions from Greek time to our own, and the significance of medieval discussions of scientific methodology. Crombie's wide study has convinced him that the most significant changes in the history of science are always brought about by new conceptions of scientific procedure. It is Crombie's thesis that if modern science owes most of its success to the use of inductive and experimental procedure, then it owes a great deal to the philosophers of the thirteenth and fourteenth centuries, who first produced an understanding of that experimental procedure. He credits

17. Lynn White, Jr., "The Dynamo and the Virgin Reconsidered," *American Scholar* 27 (1958): 187.

18. Ibid., 188–89.

19. Crombie, *Medieval and Early Modern Science.*

them with transforming the Greek geometrical method into the experimental science of the modern era. Although the conception of scientific explanation accepted by Galileo, Harvey, and Newton is a theory of formal proof developed by Greek geometers and logicians, the distinctive feature of the seventeenth century, Crombie writes, is non-Greek in origin. It is a scientific method based on "a conception of how to relate a theory to observed facts it explained, the set of logical procedures ... for constructing theories and for submitting them to experimental tests."[20] Whereas Aristotle distinguished natural science on the basis of subject matter, deriving three orders of abstraction—physics, mathematics, and metaphysics—the medieval mind tended to look upon this distinction as not one of subject matter but method of inquiry. The philosophers of the thirteenth century distinguished clearly among the kinds of questions to be asked under each level of inquiry. Crombie likens this to the role of linguistic analysis in our own time. The object of the experimental method worked out during this period was to discover and to define the conditions necessary and sufficient to uncover the experiential data. It was recognized that a theory defining these conditions could never be certain: it was necessary to "save the appearance," but it may not be "necessarily true" in the sense of being a *demonstrated* conclusion. The effect of this tendency to regard mathematics as a method rather than a domain or province of study was to change the kind of questions asked. Interest gradually shifted from the physical or metaphysical to the kind of question that could be answered by a mathematical theory within reach of experimental verification. The history of medieval science shifts to the working out of the consequences of this new approach to nature. Examples of this shift are seen in the sciences of statics, optics, and astronomy.[21]

Crombie is not alone in his view. Whitehead and Dawson imply as much.[22] Lynn Thorndike[23] and W. C. Bark [24] take similar views. Dawson makes much the same point when he compares the utilitarian view of science propounded by Roger Bacon in the fourteenth century with

20. Crombie, *Robert Grosseteste and the Origins of Experimental Science, 1100–1700* (Oxford: Oxford University Press, 1971), 1.

21. Ibid., 2–3.

22. Whitehead, *Science and the Modern World*, 12.

23. Lynn Thorndike, *A History of Magic and Experimental Science*, 8 vols. (New York: Columbia University Press, 1923–58).

24. See especially W. C. Bark, *Origins of the Medieval World* (New York: Doubleday Anchor, 1960), 115 ff.

the speculative view of science entertained by the Greek mind. Bacon is obviously closer to the modern mind than to the Greek when he makes science an instrument of world conquest and exploitation. Dawson suggests that both the utilitarian view and the Greek view of science contributed to the European scientific tradition: "The pragmatic experimentation of the Baconian ideal could have borne no fruit apart from the intellectual training and discipline which were provided by Aristotelian scholasticism."[25]

Other scholarship suggests that it is from Robert Grosseteste that Bacon derived his distinctive philosophical and scientific views.[26] Both Dawson and Crombie accord Grosseteste a major role in the history of scientific theory, using Grosseteste as a symbol of the fusion of two traditions. Crombie writes: "From the almost pure empiricism of such practical sciences of the twelfth century as practical mathematics, astronomy, and medicine, and the almost pure rationalism of theoretical speculation in contemporary philosophy on scientific method, he [Grosseteste] produced a science in which he tried to show the principles according to which the world of experience could be experimentally investigated and rationally explained."[27] Other important elements of Grosseteste's thought are his conception of physical nature, in which the essence or "form" is mathematically determined, and his conception of the immediate objective of inquiry as mathematical and predictive laws instead of Aristotelian essential definition. These concepts, Crombie maintains, were not without their effect, for in the fourteenth century we find developments of mathematical technique designed to take advantage of the new methodology and conceptions of explanation. At the same time, extension of the use of experiment and mathematical abstraction had begun to produce results so striking that this movement in itself could well be called a scientific revolution.

Benjamin Farrington similarly attributes the success of Renaissance science to the technological revolution of the Middle Ages.[28] According to Farrington, when the classic works arrived in the West, the West was prepared. Medieval man had learned the use of natural re-

25. Christopher Dawson, "The Origins of the European Scientific Tradition: St. Thomas and Roger Bacon," *Clergy Review* 2 (1931): 193–205.

26. Cf. Pearl Kibre and Nancy Sirasi, "The Institutional Setting of the Universities," in *Science and the Middle Ages*, edited by David C. Lindberg, 128–29 (Chicago: University of Chicago Press, 1978).

27. Crombie, *Robert Grosseteste*, 43.

28. Benjamin Farrington, *Greek Science* (London: Penguin, 1952), 307ff.

sources, and upon this had built a society in which humans were free from a large part of their former drudgery. Technical advance had led to social change. The slave had been replaced by the serf and the craftsman.[29] Concerning the relation of the new technology to slavery there are a number of theses. Lynn White, who has directed considerable attention to the subject, suggests that the development of medieval technology owes its impetus to the Christian teaching of the infinite worth of the individual and the Church's opposition to slavery. In his article "The Dynamo and the Virgin Reconsidered," White notes that whereas Henry Adams can symbolize an age by the concept of "dynamo," the early Middle Ages can be characterized by the devotion shown to Our Lady. "St. Bernard's Cistercian monks were so devoted to the Virgin that every one of their hundreds of monasteries was dedicated to her; yet these White Benedictines seem often to have led the way in the use of power."[30] In a seminal article entitled "Technology and Invention in the Middle Ages," White argues:

> The chief glory of the later Middle Ages was not its cathedrals or its epics or its scholasticism: it was the building for the first time in history of a complex civilization which rested not on the backs of sweating slaves or coolies but primarily on non-human power.... The labor saving power machines of the later Middle Ages were produced by the implicit theological assumptions of the infinite worth of even the most degraded personality, by the intrinsic repugnance towards subjecting any man to monotonous drudgery which seems less human in that it requires the exercise neither of intelligence nor choice. It has often been remarked that the Latin Middle Ages first discovered the dignity and spiritual value of labor—that to labor is to pray. But the Middle Ages went further: they gradually and very slowly began to explore the practical implications of an essentially Christian paradox: that just as the heavenly Jerusalem contains no temple, so the goal of labor is to end labor.[31]

In defending this thesis, White is developing Lefebvre des Noëttes's argument that the new inventions destroyed slavery by making it unnecessary and undesirable.[32] On the other hand, the French medieval

29. Ibid.

30. White, "The Dynamo and the Virgin Reconsidered," 190.

31. White, "Technology and Invention in the Middle Ages," *Speculum* 15 (1940): 156.

32. The medieval contribution to technology gained recognition as a result of the researches of Commandant Lefebvre des Noëttes, a one-time cavalry officer who, upon retirement from military life, turned his professional attention to account by making a historical study of animal power. This work, published in the early 1930s, eventually led him to accumulate an impressive body of evidence on medieval technical developments and

historian Marc Bloch has argued that the end of slavery came first and created a necessity to which such devices as the new harness and water mill were the response.[33] Both Crombie and Bark nevertheless defend the view that the Church, although it never succeeded in completely stamping out slavery, was greatly aided in its opposition to slavery by the new labor-saving devices.

In the opinion of Pierre Duhem (1861–1916), author of the classic ten-volume history of the physical sciences from Plato to Copernicus, *Le Systeme du monde*,[34] if we had to assign a date to the birth of modern science, we would be compelled to choose the year 1277, when Etienne Tempier, Bishop of Paris, solemnly condemned 219 philosophical and theological propositions then currently entertained within the Arts Faculty and the Faculty of Theology of the University of Paris. His example was followed in the same year by the Archbishop of Canterbury, John Pecham. From the vantage point of Duhem, it was significant that the condemnations undermined the authority of Aristotle insofar as they condemned the Peripatetic theory of place, and everything that Aristotle's *Physics* asserted about infinity, place, time and the possibility of a void.

It is to be remembered that Aristotle arrived in Paris with considerable baggage, imperfect translations, to be sure, but more damaging were the often misleading commentaries of Averroes. Of the 219 theses condemned by Tempier, many were Averroistic in nature. Although no names were mentioned in the condemnations,[35] many were presumably held by Siger of Brabant and Boethius of Dacia. Some of the condemned theses were held by Albertus Magnus and Thomas Aquinas. Just how many of them were clearly Thomistic depends, Gilson remarks, on

their social consequences. The result of his work has been praised as one of the capital historical discoveries of the early twentieth century; cf. Lefebvre des Noëttes, *l'Attelage et le cheval de selle à travers les âges* (Paris: 1931); des Noëttes, *De la marine antique à la marine moderne* (Paris: 1935).

33. Cf. Marc Bloch, *Feudal Society*, trans. L. A. Manyon (Chicago: University of Chicago Press, 1961).

34. Pierre Duhem, *Le Système du monde: Histoire des doctrines cosmologiques de Platon à Copernic*, originally published in French by Hermann, éditeurs des sciences et des arts (Paris); selections from Duhem's massive work have been translated and made available by Roger Ariew, *Medieval Cosmology: Theories of Infinity, Place, Time, Void, and Plurality of Worlds* (Chicago: University of Chicago Press, 1985); cf. also Stanley Jaki, *Uneasy Genius: The Life and Work of Pierre Duhem* (Dordrecht: Martinus Nijhoff, 1984).

35. For an authoritative account of the condemnation, cf. John F. Wippel, "The Condemnations of 1270 and 1277 in Paris," *Journal of Medieval and Renaissance Studies* 7 (1977): 169–201; also Wippel, "Thomas Aquinas and the Condemnation of 1277," *Modern Schoolman* 72 (1955): 233–72.

whether the list "is compiled by a Franciscan or a Dominican."[36] William A. Wallace provides a cautionary note when he writes, "It is generally agreed that Duhem's thesis is extreme, for there is no indication of a spurt in scientific thought or activity following 1277, and it is doubtful whether any authoritarian restriction on cosmological teachings could have stimulated that free spirit of inquiry that is generally seen as characteristic of modern science."[37] Yet Wallace concedes, "It is undeniable that the condemnation of 1277 had an effect on the development of medieval science, although not as profound as was maintained by Pierre Duhem."[38] Clearly the condemnation did not seriously affect the study of Aristotle. With Albert and Thomas, scholars began to sort out what in Aristotle was merely outmoded science or cosmology from the time-transcendent value of his philosophy of nature and its supporting metaphysics. It is not an exaggeration to claim that Aristotle's philosophy of science remains viable in the twentieth century. Whereas Gilson speaks of the 1277 condemnation as a "landmark," Stephen Gaukroger employs the notion of a "paradigm shift" to suggest the magnitude of the change.

The investigation of the physical world and natural philosophy were regarded until the thirteenth century as part of a single philosophical activity. There purpose was to discover the enduring and intelligible reality behind the changes perceived though the senses. With the condemnation of the deterministic (Averroistic) view of Aristotle, the authority of Aristotle was challenged, thus undermining confidence in his entire system. In the judgment of Crombie, the natural philosophers of the thirteenth century, "because of the skepticism of Christian theologians," were freed from the authority of Aristotle and thus free to develop the empirical habit of mind, but within a rational framework.[39]

Cultural historians agree that since classical antiquity there have been a number of civilizations that have witnessed a scientific revolution. Stephen Gaukroger,[40] whose work we will now consider, speaks of the "rich productive scientific cultures, in which fundamental and especially intractable, physical, medical, astronomical, and other problems

36. Etienne Gilson, *History of Christian Philosophy in the Middle Ages* (New York: Random House, 1955), 728.

37. *William A. Wallace,* "Philosophical Setting of Medieval Science," in *Science in the Middle Ages,* edited by David C. Lindberg, 105–6 (Chicago: University of Chicago Press, 1978).

38. Ibid., 105.

39. Crombie, *Medieval and Early Modern Science* 1: 64.

40. Graukroger is writing some eighty years after Whitehead and fifty years after Crombie. Specialized studies subsequently written abound, yet the basic facts as well as most interpretations remain unchanged; cf. Gaukroger, *Emergence of a Scientific Culture.*

are opened up and dealt with in an innovative and concerted fashion, producing cumulative results over several generations."[41] Besides Greece and the Hellenic diaspora, he identifies these as the Arab/Islamic North Africa/Near East/Iberian Peninsula in the ninth, tenth, and eleventh centuries, Paris and Oxford in the thirteenth and fourteenth centuries, and China from the twelfth to the fourteenth century.[42] The scientific revolution of seventeenth- and eighteenth-century Europe is something different, he thinks, insofar as the uninterrupted and cumulative growth of the early modern period breaks with the boom/bust pattern of earlier cultures. Not only that, but the scientific revolution was so spectacular that it not only displaced competing accounts but was extrapolated to all cognitive disciplines. In a relatively short period of time, Copernicanism and Darwinism came to replace firmly held philosophical and theological views concerning nature and the order in nature that had persisted since biblical times.

Stephen Gaukroger, like Whitehead, takes exception to what he calls the "Enlightenment interpretation," namely, that the scientific revolution occurred as a result of Western science's ability to disassociate itself from religion. Vigorously challenging that "self-serving account," he writes: "Far from science breaking free of religion in the early modern era, its consolidation depended crucially on religion being in the driver's seat: Christianity took over natural philosophy in the seventeenth century, setting its agenda and projecting it forward in a way quite different from that of any other scientific culture."[43] Gaukroger's strong claim is defended in what promises to be a multi-volume study, the first of which is entitled *The Emergence of a Scientific Culture: Science and the Shaping of Modernity, 1210–1685*.

In demonstrating the continuity of science and technology through the later Middle Ages into modernity, Gaukroger contrasts the progress of science in the West with that in the cultures of Islam and China. "Arab-Islamic science," he writes,

> had two distinctive features. The first is that there was no institutional support available for scientific work that was not motivated by extra-scientific concerns.... Second, the way in which the achievements of Greek philosophers, and Greek and Alexandrian mathematicians, were 'naturalized' in the Arab-Islamic culture is distinctive. They were domesticated, incorporated into an indigenous culture and philosophical system, rather

41. Ibid., 17.
42. Ibid., 18.
43. Ibid., 23.

than being institutionalized in such a way that they carried "their own specific gravity of autonomy and legitimacy, independent of the moral and religious scruples of the surrounding culture." The consequence of these two institutional features of Arab-Islamic civilization is that while it was occasionally possible for innovations to be made in astronomy, optics, and even metaphysics, there was no way in which they could be followed up in a systematic manner.[44]

With respect to China, the situation was almost the reverse. "If Arabic-Islamic culture could initiate scientific developments but not follow them up, China had an extensive network of communication, and this acted in such a way as to foster scientific and technological achievement. In the Sung and Ming dynasties we find inventions such as mechanical clocks, moveable type, and seismographs that predate developments in the West by a couple of centuries, and we find significant advances in observational astronomy and medicine."[45] Yet there were serious obstacles to innovation that were not practically oriented. The bureaucratic structure of Chinese society was a crucial factor. Then, too, traditions of philosophical disputation are relatively marginal in Chinese intellectual culture. Adherence to tradition plays a crucial role in all artistic and intellectual pursuits, with the result that there was a strong sense that scholarship rather than innovation is the path to wisdom. This was reinforced by the Confucian tendency to self-effacement and avoidance of contentiousness, as well as a strong commitment to outward obedience to public authorities. This Chinese respect for authority formed a sharp contrast with Greek models of confrontational debate.[46]

Crombie's study is reinforced by Gaukroger when he writes that "In the thirteenth century, natural philosophy was transformed from a marginal enterprise into one that was to provide the principal point of entry into understanding of the natural world and our place in it."[47] The engine of transformation was Aristotle's natural philosophy, in spite of the condemnations. Gaukroger thinks the significant event is not Etienne Tempier's condemnation of 1277 but the much earlier Paris condemnation of Aristotle in the year 1210. He uses that date as a starting point as he traces the development of natural philosophy from the Scholasticism of the early thirteenth century, through the corpuscularism and atomism associated with Gassendi and Mersenne, to Descartes' cosmology and to Hobbes's mechanism. The year 1685 Gaukroger uses to mark the

44. Ibid., 33.

45. Ibid.

46. Ibid.

47. Ibid.

twilight, if not the demise, of Aristotelian natural philosophy and the ascendancy of a period dominated by the works of Locke, Newton, and Leibniz. He maintains that from the thirteenth to the sixteenth century two models had provided the unity of knowledge: one was the Aristotelian notion of *scientia*, the other the Christian idea of a universe designed and created ex *nihilo* by a single God as an abode for human beings. In the seventeenth century both were confronted by *nominalistic* and mechanistic interpretations of nature. Copernicus was thought to displace a man-centered universe, Darwin to displace *Genesis*, and Hobbes's mechanism to displace the recognition of design in nature.

The shift from an Aristotelian world view to modernity, although gradual, was radical. Pagan philosophers had made natural philosophy the basis of moral philosophy. Aristotelian categories had been employed by the early Church Fathers as they interpreted the texts of the Gospel. Justin Martyr, Marius Victorinus, and Clement of Alexandria recognized that Aristotelian natural philosophy, while not intrinsically Christian, was nevertheless not inherently pagan. Aristotelian natural philosophy, although not without rivals, notably those of the neo-Platonic and Augustinian schools, held sway until it gave ground to mechanistic interpretations of nature in the seventeenth century, notably that advanced by Pierre Gassendi (1592–1655). It is Descartes and his artificially created "mind-body problem" that stimulated Gassendi to address the age-old problem of universals and the relation between sense and intellectual knowledge.[48] In his criticism of Descartes, he writes, "When you say that you are simply a thing that thinks, you mention an operation that everyone was aware of but you say nothing about the substance carrying out this operation: What sort of substance it is, What it consists in, how it organizes itself in order to carry out its different functions."[49] Gassendi's atomism in its pre-Newtonian form is an attempt to explain macroscopic phenomena by means of the microscopic. Presented as a matter theory inspired by the Greek atomists, when combined with the doctrine of primary and secondary qualities, it undermined the Aristotelian concept of "nature" and, with it, teleology. But those implications and others are not what he intended. It is a small step from Gassendi's atomism to Auguste Comte's positivism.

Science in the Aristotelian sense and above all an acknowledgment

48. Cf. the excellent study of Antonia Lolordo, *Pierre Gassendi and the Birth of Early Modern Philosophy* (Cambridge: Cambridge University Press, 2006).

49. As quoted by Lolordo, *Pierre Gassendi*, 228.

of its scholastic roots suffer greatly at the hands of Renaissance humanists. A number of scholars are of the opinion that the fifteenth-century humanism that arose in Italy and spread northward was an interruption of the development of science. The so-called revival of letters deflected interest from content to literary style, and in turning back to classical antiquity, many humanists affected to ignore the progress of the previous three centuries. Unaware of how much they owed to their immediate predecessors, these humanists, by their contempt of Scholasticism, did much to initiate the Dark Age myth that the *philosophes* of the French Enlightenment were happy to perpetuate. Crombie suggests that "The same absurd conceit that led the humanists to abuse and misrepresent their immediate predecessors for using Latin constructions unknown to Cicero and to put out the propaganda, which in varying degrees has captivated historical opinion until quite recently, also allowed them to borrow from Scholasticism without acknowledgment. The habit affected almost all the great scientists of the sixteenth and seventeenth centuries, whether Protestant or Catholic, and it has required the labors of Duhem and Maier to show that their statements on matters of history cannot be accepted at face value."[50]

Whitehead is convinced that the natural scientists of the sixteenth and seventeenth centuries were anti-intellectualists in the same way as the religious reformers were anti-intellectualists.[51] Herbert Butterfield recalls how the humanists of the Renaissance, Erasmus included, were accustomed to complaining of the boredom of scholastic lectures and suggests that this was due to the ignorance of the humanists more than anything else.[52] The humanists derided their scholastic teachers, but these despised scholastic disciplines now hold a remarkable key position in the story of the evolution of the modern mind. Butterfield writes: "Perhaps the lack of mathematics or the failure to think of mathematical ways of formulating things was partly responsible for what appeared to be verbal subtleties and an excessive straining of language in these men who were yearning to find the key to the modern science of mechanics."[53]

The Renaissance attitude took hold and has held sway since. For complex reasons positivism has come to be associated with modern sci-

50. Crombie, *The History of Science from Augustine to Galileo,* 2nd ed. (New York: Dover, 1996), 268–69; also cf. Charles B. Schmitt's extended treatment, *Aristotle and the Renaissance* (Cambridge, Mass.: Harvard University Press, 1983).

51. Whitehead, *Science and the Modern World,* 12.

52. Herbert Butterfield, *Origins of Modern Science* (New York: Macmillan, 1957), 2.

53. Ibid.

ence. Positivism, insofar as it restricts knowledge to that attained by physico-mathematical methods, in effect reduces science to description and prediction. With remarkable insight, Christopher Dawson, writing three-quarters of a century ago, commented, "The disease of modern civilization lies neither in science nor in machinery but in the false philosophy with which they have been associated.... Though these ideas accompanied the rise of the machine order, they are in reality profoundly inconsistent with that order and with scientific genius."[54] Elsewhere he remarks that "we cannot be sure that the world which science has made will be as favorable to the production of scientific genius as the world that made science."[55]

Karl Popper likewise indicts the positivistic attitude toward science in which the emphasis is placed on description and practical results: "Instrumentalism," Popper maintains, "is unable to account for the importance to pure science of severely testing even the most remote implications of its theories since it is unable to account for the pure scientist's interest in truth and falsity. In contrast to the highly critical attitude requisite in the pure scientist, the attitude of instrumentalism (like that of applied science) is one of complacency at the success of application. Thus it may well be responsible for the recent stagnation in theoretical physics."[56]

We began not with Bernard Lewis's question of what went wrong in the Islamic world, but shifted the discourse to what went right within Christendom. As contemporary Europe struggles with its identity, Dawson's work is there to remind us: "Europe is not a group of people held together by a common type of material culture; it is a spiritual society that owes its existence to the religious tradition which for a thousand years molded the beliefs, the ideals, and the institutions of European peoples."[57] Dawson adds a frightening thought: "If modern Europe falls either through internal revolution or through loss of her world leadership, modern civilization falls with her. For that civilization was entirely a European creation, and there is no force outside Europe to-day capable of carrying on her work, whatever the case a century or two hence."[58]

54. Dawson, *Christianity and the New Age* (London: Sheed and Ward, 1931), 102.

55. Dawson, *The Modern Dilemma* (London: Sheed and Ward, 1933), 49.

56. Karl Popper, *Contemporary British Philosophy* (New York: Macmillan, 1960), 381.

57. Dawson, *Progress and Religion*, 173.

58. Ibid., 171.

Daniel O. Dahlstrom

13. SCHELER ON THE ESSENCE OF CHRISTIAN RELIGIOUS CONSCIOUSNESS

One of Kenneth Schmitz's major and undoubtedly lasting accomplishments is his demonstration of the distinctive contribution made by Karol Wojtyla to philosophy. In Schmitz's masterful expositions, Wojtyla's philosophical project comes alive as an effort to understand action phenomenologically and realistically, as something that proceeds from and reveals, not consciousness, but the whole person "as a being among other beings."[1] In this connection, among other things, Schmitz corrects a common misunderstanding of the extent of Wojtyla's philosophical debt to Scheler's thought. To be sure, Wojtyla plainly acknowledges the importance to him of both Scheler's critique of Kant's ethics and its basis in a phenomenological analysis of the affective experience of values. However, Schmitz ably shows how Wojtyla also takes Scheler to task for failing to give an adequate account of the entire phenomenon of the person in ethical action, the sort of account only a realistic metaphysics of the person can provide.[2]

1. Kenneth L. Schmitz, *At the Center of the Human Drama: The Philosophical Anthropology of Karol Wojtyla: Pope John Paul II* (Washington, D.C.: The Catholic University of America Press, 1993), 65f; see, too, Kenneth L. Schmitz, "Jacques Maritain and Karol Wojtyla: Approaches to Modernity," in *The Bases of Ethics,* edited by William Sweet, 127f (Milwaukee: Marquette University Press, 2000).

2. While Wojtyla advances these criticisms principally in his *Lublin Lectures,* they are not absent from *The Acting Person,* a dozen years later; see Karol Wojtyla, *The Acting Person,* trans. Andrzej Potocki (Dordrecht: Reidel, 1979), 178, 233; for the acknowledgment of a debt to Scheler, see ibid., viii, xiii–xiv, 302 n. 8. For Schmitz's discussion of Wojtyla's *Lublin*

The following paper makes no attempt to defend or refute either Wojtyla's criticisms of Scheler or Schmitz's rendering of them. However, it does attempt to provide some context for further consideration of them by reviewing what Scheler takes to be Christianity's revolutionary conception of the relation between love and knowledge.[3] In Scheler's essay *Liebe und Erkenntnis,* he identifies "the essence of Christian religious consciousness" by contrasting its conception of love's relation to knowledge with other traditions' conceptions. While rhetorically effective, the contrast is made with such broad strokes that it begs various questions regarding the expansive meanings and varieties of love and knowledge, not least in regard to philosophy itself. We can begin to get a clearer picture of Scheler's general thesis by taking a look at his various independent considerations of love and knowledge. When we do so, we find that this general thesis is no less problematic than it is radical and, indeed, problematic for reasons that, one might argue, converge with some of Wojtyla's concerns. In fact, it is not difficult to imagine that Wojtyla was motivated by Scheler's masterful portrayal of the essence of Christian religious consciousness to come up with ways to resolve these very problems.

The following chapter accordingly examines Scheler's account of the significance of the essence of Christian religious consciousness, in light of some of his own specific treatments of love and knowledge. The chapter is divided into four sections. The theme of the first section is Scheler's general thesis in *Liebe und Erkenntnis* about the revolutionary Christian conception of the relationship of love and knowledge. In an attempt to specify the sense of love supposed by that general thesis, I turn in the second section to the Christian idea of love outlined by Scheler in his rebuttal of Nietzsche's charge that Christian religious consciousness is the product of *ressentiment.* The subject of the third section is Scheler's

---

Lectures and the criticisms of Scheler voiced therein, see *At the Center of the Human Drama,* 42–56.

3. The importance of this line of Scheler's thinking for Wojtyla's development has been relatively neglected. It does not figure, for example, in the following accounts of Wojtyla's critical appropriation of Scheler's thought: Rocco Buttiglione, *Karol Wojtyla,* trans. Paolo Guietti and Francesca Murphy (Grand Rapids, Mich.: Eerdmans, 1997), 54–82; and George Williams, *The Mind of John Paul II* (New York: Seabury, 1981), 131–35. Schmitz does qualify his exposition by noting that he does not intend to evaluate the accuracy of Wojtyla's understanding of Scheler's positions; at the same time, it is abundantly clear that Schmitz considers Wojtyla's criticisms on target and, indeed, that Schmitz endorses a Thomistic conception of the complementarity of love and knowledge, something that, at least in its Aristotelian form, is one of the objects of Scheler's criticism; see Kenneth Schmitz, *The Texture of Being* (Washington, D.C.: The Catholic University of America Press, 2007), 160ff, 193, 196, 266f.

account of knowing, the other component of that relation essential to Christian consciousness. In this connection I consider specifically Scheler's differentiation of the forms of knowledge, based principally on his late lecture, *Die Formen des Wissens und die Bildung.* In conclusion, I summarize the problems, identified in the chapter, with Scheler's account of Christian religious consciousness and suggest how some of these problems converge with Wojtyla's misgivings about Scheler's philosophy.[4]

The General Thesis: The Christian Revolution

The general thesis of Scheler's essay *Liebe und Erkenntnis* is that Christianity represents a radical revolution in human culture, so radical that we have barely come to grips with it, not least because it completely debunks many of our most entrenched prejudices about the relationship between love and knowledge. One such popular prejudice, a staple of modernity, he notes, is the view that love is blind and "all genuine knowledge of the world can be found only by means of the most extreme *withholding* of emotional acts" (*LE,* 5). This modern prejudice has, Scheler points out, a surprising confluence with Indian and Greek thinking, for which value is a function of nonbeing or being, and love a function of knowing.

The Indian and Greek traditions are distinct, to be sure, but their different takes on the ontological status of values are, Scheler submits, precisely what allows the similarity of their views on the relation of love and knowledge to emerge so clearly. For the Indian tradition not-being is the highest value, and the world is at once real and impoverished, the

4. The first three parts of the chapter draw heavily on three republished texts: *Liebe und Erkenntnis, Das Ressentiment im Aufbau der Moralen,* and *Bildung und Wissen;* all can be found in volumes of Scheler's *Gesammelte Werke* (Bern: Francke, 1954–1986; Bonn: Bouvier, 1985–present), cited herafter as *"GW,"* followed by volume and page number. "Liebe und Erkenntnis" was first published in *Krieg und Aufbau* (Leipzig: 1916), later in *Moralia* (Leipzig: 1923) and, posthumously, in *Liebe und Erkenntnis* (Munich: Francke, 1955). I cite hereafter from the 1955 edition; in the body of the chapter, I refer to it as *"LE,"* followed by the page numbers. The fact that Scheler republished the essay in the early 1920s lends some support to treating it in conjunction with work from that period. When I cite *Das Ressentiment im Aufbau der Moralen* (hereafter *R*), I refer to the pagination of its republication in *Vom Umsturz der Werte,* Band I, Zweite durchgelesene Auflage (Leipzig: der neue Geist, 1919), 43–236. I cite the posthumous publication *Bildung und Wissen* (Frankfurt am Main: Schulte-Bulmke, 1947) as *"BW"*; this posthumous edition contains a slightly edited version of the 1925 publication, *Die Formen des Wissens und die Bildung* (Bonn: Cohen, 1925). On the periodization of Scheler's work, see Manfred Frings, *Max Scheler,* 2nd ed. (Milwaukee, Wisc.: Marquette University Press, 1996), 6f. Because Scheler in the texts under consideration does not sharply distinguish *Erkenntnis* and *Wissen,* indeed, often using them as synonyms, I do not translate them differently (e.g., "cognition" and "knowing"), as is sometimes done; see Frings, *Max Scheler,* 131f. For Scheler's differentiation of the two notions, see GW 8: 200–11.

more passionately it is desired. Indeed, the difference between real and unreal is only a difference for us as driven, volitional agents of action, "not for us as purely *knowing* spirits" (*LE,* 7). Thus, knowledge in this Indian tradition is a matter of overcoming the desires and actions that bind us to real things, overcoming them by way of objectifying them. So, too, the objective content of love in this context is the progressive diminishing of the world, its transformation into a mere image, and the emotion of love itself is "nothing self-sufficient, no original act of the spirit, but only the *process* of the growth of the respective knowledge" (*LE,* 7). Scheler notes the structural similarities of this basic viewpoint with Plato's view of *nous* and *eros,* where love is also depicted as a striving for knowledge, as the dynamics of the transition from lesser to greater knowledge, from sensory things suffused with not-being to the idea of the good, the being of beings. In Plato's account, only philosophers (lovers of wisdom) truly love, but gods (perfect knowers) cannot love. For this Greek tradition no less than for the Indian one mentioned, love is a consequence, an epiphenomenon of knowledge. Moreover, knowledge is superior to love, indeed, love's ultimate aim.

Probably because Scheler's overriding purpose is to stress the basic continuity between these two traditions, he also points out the obvious differences between them on the matter of the relation between love and knowledge. In particular, he notes two features distinctive of the Buddhist-Indian tradition that stand in stark contrast to the Greek tradition. Inasmuch as love for the Buddhist takes the form of a denial of one's individual bodily self as well as the world, its call for an indiscriminate love of otherness, exemplified by its vegetarianism, is not so much a movement toward others as it is a movement away from oneself. So, too, in the face of the doctrine of reincarnation, a commonplace in the Indian world, Buddha proclaims a redemption in the form of a genuine, definitive death, thanks to the knowledge of the utter "*nothingness* of the individual-personal *form of existence in general*" (*LE,* 10). In these respects the contrast with the Greek tradition is patent and patently enormous. Whereas knowledge and love for the Buddhist are essentially directed at "not-being," the Greek tradition construes knowledge and love as related in progressively positive ways to ever more fecund degrees of being, where "not-being" is a lack and positive values are a function of the fullness of being. "Analogously, love (subjectively) is a primary turning toward a *positive* value, i.e., to a form of being of a certain fullness; it is *not* some primordial turning away from such" (*LE,* 11). From Empedocles to Plato and Aristotle, love is conceived as a cosmic agent, "a principle of *generation* and production of ever newer and richer forms of being" (*LE*, 11).

Yet despite these formidable differences, the Greek tradition retains a basic affinity with the Indian tradition, and that affinity is the already mentioned construal of love as a consequence and epiphenomenon of knowledge.

> Wherever in history this twofold determination of love recurs, such that it does not dynamically precede but instead follows knowledge and such that it teleologically is only a path, a method to the goal of increasing knowledge, there the theological conclusion is always the heathen illusion of that rigid divinity, shining only within itself, a divinity that does not love back, that is only an *object* of creatures' adoration, but not the cooperating *subject* of that "intimate conversation of the soul with God," as Gregory of Nyssa defines Christian prayer (*LE*, 13).

Scheler's account of these traditions is abbreviated but sufficient to make his central point about how radically their common view of the connection between love and knowledge differs from the Christian account. In the Christian view, divine love and love of one's neighbor have an equally original or even more original role than knowledge. In Christianity an act of love stemming from someone outside human beings originally redeems human beings; redemption is an act of love that transcends the individual—the individual can never redeem himself through an act of knowledge. Accordingly, Christianity has a savior, the Indian tradition sages or wise men. "Indeed, in contrast to knowledge that one has found oneself, each communication of a knowledge necessary for salvation would have to be already founded on the love of the one communicating for those who receive the communication" (LE, 8). Nor is the individual, in the Christian view, dissolved in pure contemplation of the *ontos* on or not-being, as in the Greek and Indian views respectively. Hence, Scheler's simple but profound contention: the priority of love before knowledge is (part of) the essence of Christian religious consciousness.[5]

5. Scheler, *Liebe und Erkenntnis*, 21. A separate investigation is necessary to examine the trenchancy of the reasons that Scheler gives for the philosophical failure to come to grips with the radical novelty of the Christian experience. Because Christians of the first century supposedly possessed neither the training nor the disposition of philosophers, the eventual demands of the struggle with other sects forced them, Scheler submits, to have recourse for the most part to the extant conceptual framework of Greek philosophy. Even Augustine, a notable exception here in some ways, is betrayed by his profound dependence on neo-Platonism, Scheler claims. But if Christianity in fact makes this historical turn, that is to say, if early Christians found it possible to articulate their religious experience in Greek philosophical terms, on what basis can Scheler claim that this turn is tantamount

Yet the contention, as such, is underdetermined. To get a clearer idea of Scheler's account of the essence of Christian religious consciousness, we need to examine what he means more precisely by love, knowledge, and the priority of the former over the latter.

As for the first of these themes, what Scheler means by love in this connection, he tells us explicitly where to look. Thus, in the course of recounting the "inversion in the movement of love," effected by the Christian revolution, in contrast to the Greek conception of love, he refers his readers for more details to his earlier discussion of this topic in *Das Ressentiment im Aufbau der Moralen* (*LE*, 18). Accordingly, with the aim of specifying more precisely the sense of "love" at work in what Scheler calls "the essence of Christian religious consciousness," I turn briefly to the account of Christian love in *Ressentiment*.

Scheler on the Christian Idea of Love

In the *Ressentiment* essay Scheler sheds light on what he means by the Christian idea of love in the course of contrasting it first with the ancient idea of love and then with the modern, humanistic idea of love. The aim of the contrast is to demonstrate, among other things, how and why Nietzsche confuses the Christian idea with a modern, humanistic idea of love that is in fact rooted in the phenomenon of resentment. Nietzsche's criticism is extremely paradoxical at first glance, given the enormous change from the ancient *eros* and *amor* to Christian *agape* and *caritas*. Inverting the ancient conception of love as an erotic movement from lower to higher, motivated by want and consumed in its satisfaction, Christianity conceives love as something that originates from a surfeit of nobility and blessedness, extends itself alike to friend and foe, good and evil, and grows in the process (*R*, 107–12). Because resentment is born, not of strength, fecundity, and self-love, but of weakness, want, and self-hatred, Nietzsche errs in explaining Christian love as an expression of resentment. Jesus says that we are not to fret about food and drink, not because life and its preservation are unimportant to him but because he sees in all our concerns about our own physical well-being "a *vital* weakness" (*R*, 116). Nor is love the supreme Christian value because of its beneficial or benevolent effects or, in short, because of its utility.

to philosophy failing Christianity—particularly if this basis is to be construed in ways at a supposedly innocuous distance from the Greek philosophical heritage? In some respects this claim seems counterintuitive precisely for someone with Scheler's intuitions. For it is Scheler who emphasizes the inescapable necessity of tradition in all its particularity (see *GW* 3: 97f).

There is no direct correlation between love and utility. "Helping is an immediate and adequate *expression* of love, not its 'purpose' and sense" (*R*, 121).

But if Christian love is diametrically opposed to resentment, what prompted Nietzsche to equate them? The answer to this question lies to a great extent, as already suggested, in a confusion of modern and Christian views of love.[6] According to the former view (or at least a typically modern view), love is to be directed, not at what is divine in human beings, but at human beings merely as human beings, those respectively present and visible, limited and earthly members of the species. Just as humanity, in this restricted view, is cut loose from the divine realm, so, too, is it cut loose from the rest of nature and, indeed, not only nature but also the entire realm of the departed souls. In place of Christianity's basic concept of "love of neighbor" in all its particularity, modern humanism substitutes love of humanity as a collective sum of human individuals (*R*, 152).

In place of the distinctive action and movement that Christianity understands by "love," modern humanism substitutes feelings. Drawing on his earlier work on the phenomenology of feelings of sympathy, Scheler notes how modern moral-sense philosophers, from Hutcheson to Bain and Rousseau, attempt to ground love in sympathy and the latter in the contagiousness of anguish and joy.[7] What facilitated the various

6. Scheler accounts for how Nietzsche missed this point philosophically as well as historically and culturally (*R*, 1; 138–42). According to Scheler, Nietzsche mistakes the essence of Christian love by measuring it against a false criterion of value. Thus, Christian love is tied to the kingdom of God and, whatever its effect on life, its value lies not in life, the living body, or the living as such, but instead in something beyond life. Nietzsche's mistaken criterion is "the maximal advancement of life" and, measured against this criterion, all Christian values appear as values of the downfall of life (*R*, 140; see, too, *R*, 2: 142–50). The Christian idea of love is intrinsically related to the idea of the kingdom of God and, as such, is not bound up with a specific form of political institution or socioeconomic structure (*R*, 142f); nor is the image of Jesus to be associated with "certain forms of the modern social and democratic movements" (*R*, 145). Important in this connection, too, is Scheler's discussion of ascetic ideals in Christianity, "insofar as they were not influenced by a Hellenistic philosophy of decadence" (*R*, 135f).

7. Scheler articulates various reductive accounts of compassion in modernity. Compassion is reduced to an artificial transportation into someone else's mental state, in accordance with the question "what would you feel if that happened to you?"—in effect, a reproduction of one's own states of feelings, experienced in analogous circumstances. He also finds it reduced to the process of being thrust or transported into the state of feeling of someone else in a kind of "hallucination of feelings" or an empathy of one's own reproduced experiences of feeling, immediately incited (without any transportation) by imitation of someone else's expression of feeling. It is also reduced to a mental epiphenomenon of impulses to action, useful to the species, as a consequence of a herd drive already per-

reductions of sympathy and compassion to "mechanics of necessary deceptions" among the moderns, not least Darwin, is the demotion of love to refinements of an animal drive advantageous to a species and the elevation of feelings to the core component of love. Love descends "from the height, symbol, and sign of a supernatural order, indeed, from being the *power-stream* within the kingdom of God" to the sort of feelings and drives, shared with herd animals, that are propitious to the human species (*R*, 155).

Having differentiated Christian and humanistic ideas of love in terms of the respective objects and states of the subject involved in those ideas, Scheler also notes the different value that love has for the Christian and the modern humanist. For the latter, the value of love consists, not in securing the salvation of lover and beloved, but in advancing "common well-being" (*R*, 156). Whereas Christianity values love for its own sake and, indeed, as the supreme value, love is one value among others for the humanist, valuable only for its capacity to enlarge general well-being, understood as the largest possible number of individuals achieving their egoistic goals.

For all these reasons, Scheler maintains that modern humanism is a thinly veiled egoism and its universalistic pretensions are, as Nietzsche concluded, an expression of resentment. The claims of both philosophers strike me as unfair and forced, probably the result of their considerable rhetorical skills getting the better of a concern for argumentative precision. Without differentiating among modern humanists or offering in a specific case a demonstration of the egoism and resentment allegedly motivating them, Scheler apes Nietzsche's annoying, metaphysical habit of lumping all humanists together. Nevertheless, these reservations do not gainsay the poignancy of Scheler's sketch of the considerable social and cultural changes, made in the name of humanity at the cost of traditional values and institutions and, most of all, the persons themselves closest at hand in the form of family and community. It is hardly a coincidence, he rightly submits, that these changes value what is universally human, namely, what human beings share biologically with animals, a frequent source of all-too-human frailties that can be "understood" and "excused." This "modern love of man" in fact express-

---

ceivable in the animal kingdom; see *GW* 3: 98; see also "Verhältnis der Lieben zum Mitgefühl," in *Wesen und Formen der Sympathie,* fünfte Auflage, A, vol. 11: 152–57 (Frankfurt am Main: Schulte-Bulmke, 1948). Scheler's contrast of the active character of Christian love with mere feelings, including shared feelings or sympathy, is in alignment, at least in this respect, with Wojtyla's ideas.

es hatred of positive higher values, the "fatherland," and even God himself (*R*, 158–65). As Scheler puts it:

> That the core to the movement of modern universal love of mankind rests on resentment is already obvious from the fact that this social-historical movement of the mind rests in no way on an original, spontaneous *movement up to a positive value,* but instead on a *protest,* on a *counter-impulse* (hate, envy, revenge, and so forth) against dominating minorities whom one knows to be in possession of positive values (*R*, 162).

Altruism is a modern phenomenon and, to his credit, Nietzsche made us aware of how the pathos of the modern flight to others can also be a symptom of a resentful self-disgust and self-hatred. I have already alluded to the fact that I think that Nietzsche plainly overreaches—as does Scheler—by insisting that this modern flight not merely can be, but is a symptom of resentment. But, more important for our purposes is Scheler's diagnosis of Nietzsche's mistake of having identified the degeneracy of this sociopsychological phenomenon with the Christian love of one's neighbor.[8]

It seems to me that Scheler's case against Nietzsche is trenchant when it comes to the Christian *idea* of love. The idea supposes the very opposite of resentment, and there is considerable evidence, with some exceptions noted by Scheler, that early Christianity, from the evangelists on, did, indeed, understand love as an expression of strength and fullness, not weakness and want. But this historical fact is, as Scheler is also quite aware, insufficient to make the case against Nietzsche, for the Christian idea of love could be itself a veil or mask of resentment, largely unknown to the very Christians who blithely wore them. The deeper issue, in other words, is whether Christian love is more than an idea, whether it is in fact a reality, whether, in contrast to Greek and modern European interpretations, including Nietzsche's, Christianity existentially embodies and, in this embodiment, expresses a viable, that is to say, a philosophically adequate interpretation of love.

However, if we put the issue in these terms, as Scheler himself does, we immediately run up against a further fundamental difficulty. For "philosophy" is itself the love of wisdom and, hence, built into the very

8. Scheler recognizes that, despite the basic differences in the nature and origins of the Christian and the modern ideas of love, history shows concrete combinations of them. Scheler devotes the rest of the fourth section of *Das Ressentiment im Aufbau der Moralen* to discussion of these combinations by way of the many different forms of "ascesis" (*R*, 169–82). The discussion is meant to explain but not justify Nietzsche's identification of the two ideas.

supposition of it as a criterion is a foregoing understanding and realization of the relation of love and knowledge of one sort or the other. Even if we presume that we can bracket the meanings of the Greek roots of the term "philosophy," we seem to find ourselves in an uncomfortable circle, uncomfortable not least because the circularity suggests a certain smug insularity as well. The point about the circularity is not simply that a philosophical interpretation of the relation of love and knowing supposes a conception of philosophy, but that a conception of philosophy itself entails a conception of knowing, if not wisdom, and, at its best, a conception and, even more, an actual instance of love.

This difficulty is fundamental for any philosophical treatment of the relation of love and knowing, but it takes on an added severity, it seems to me, in the case of treating the essence of a Christian religious consciousness, as Scheler describes it. By the added severity I do not mean simply the fact that a philosophy of a Christian religious consciousness or the Christian conception of the relation of love and knowledge is an oxymoron if we attend to historical senses of the term "philosophy." I mean something much simpler and, for that reason, more obstinate, namely, the sense in which Christian religious consciousness is *sui generis* and, hence, understandable only on its own terms. If this sense obtains, then it is impossible to give a philosophically adequate account of the essence of Christian religious consciousness precisely because the Christian understanding of the relation of love and knowing involves a commitment, a commitment based upon faith, to the supernatural order of things. Here the potential philosophical circularity besetting a philosophical interpretation of love, knowledge, or their distinctive combination in a Christian religious consciousness is in danger of being replaced by the circularity of a loving, religious self-understanding.

Yet in raising these points, I am clearly getting ahead of myself when it comes to Scheler's view of the matter. For up to this point we have only focused on his conception of the Christian idea of love. In order to do justice to his conception of the essence of the Christian religious consciousness (*Bewußt-sein*), particularly in regard to the issues just mentioned, we have to take a closer look at what he means by "knowing" (*Wissen*).

Scheler on Knowing

In giving his own account of knowing (*Wissen*), Scheler takes over Husserl's basic insight that knowing is marked by the experience of the coincidence of intuitive content and a meaning independent of it (*die Deckung eines anschaulichen Gehalts mit einer von ihm unabhängigen Bedeutung*). Yet, while requiring the input of intuition and thinking (the two main classes of mental acts), knowing as the experience of this coincidence (*Deckungserlebnis*) or evidence, as he also calls it, is not to be confused with either of them. This irreducibility of knowing to other forms of consciousness is, again, a central theme in Husserl's work.

However, in the interest of avoiding circularity, Scheler also demands that knowing be defined by "purely *ontological* concepts," thereby ruling out attempts such as Husserl's to explain knowing by way of consciousness, since consciousness (*Bewußt-sein*) is a particular form of knowing (*BW,* 24). The ontological concepts employed by Scheler are, however, mereological concepts (reminiscent of Husserl's third *Logical Investigation*). Knowing is a relation between entities x and y in which x has a part of what it is for y to be such and such, having it in such a way that leaves x and y completely undisturbed.[9] With this last qualification, Scheler again shows his phenomenological colors as he emphasizes that what is so known is an *ens intentionale,* in contrast to the *ens reale* or existence that lies beyond any epistemic relation.

According to Scheler, love as a manner of giving oneself over to the other is the root of knowing, as just described. It is instructive that he infers from this loving basis that what is known must enjoy the dual existence already indicated, *ens intentionale* and *ens reale.*[10] Yet, as a relation between entities, the goal of knowing is a becoming, that is, a coming to be other, that involves a value and an ultimate, ontic sense (*BW,* 25). There seems to be an unresolved tension, if not contradiction, here that I would like to mention merely in passing.[11] On the one hand, as the invocation of *ens intentionale* is meant to underscore, Scheler makes the intuitively plausible observation that knowing, despite being a kind of sharing in and having part of another (*teilnehmen und teilhaben*), is not such that knower and known or, more precisely, lover and beloved, in any way become real parts of one another. Yet, on the other hand, he

9. There is some ambiguity here as to whether Scheler means for both the knower and the known to be left undisturbed. Insofar as the known is left undisturbed, his account of knowing can be read as anti-idealist. Yet, if he follows Husserl's reduction, then both are left undisturbed and there is a kind of idealism or anti-realism at work.

10. Note, too, that Scheler describes knowing, so grounded in love, as "ecstatic," thereby underscoring that it is not simply a standing out from but also a standing out toward and, indeed, toward a specific sort of being; ecstasy is not rapture.

11. This tension may, indeed, motivate Wojtyla's attempts to criticize Scheler's phenomenology from the standpoint of a metaphysical realism.

clearly conceives the love of human beings as part of a universal force, effective in everything. Thus, in general terms, he observes that "love is the tendency or, respectively, the act that seeks to lead each thing into the direction of the perfection of the value peculiar to it—and does lead it if not hindered. It is, hence, the edifying and *constructive* action in and beyond the world, that we determined to be the essence of love" (GW 10: 355). Yet this characterization of love, a characterization that Scheler gives by way of introduction to his account of knowledge's origins in love, is difficult to square with his emphasis on the purely intentional existence of the known.

Setting this considerable problem aside for the moment, we encounter other problems in the inference that Scheler draws from the origination of knowing in love. That origin, he infers, rules out the idea of pure theory for its own sake. *Science pour la science* is no less a fiction than *l'art pour l'art* and, indeed, Scheler notes, Epicurus had already panned such a pursuit as sheer vanity. Yet if knowledge is not pursued for its own sake, then the question arises of what it is for. Scheler poses this very question (as well as the question of whose becoming it is and what it comes from—a question that takes us back to the problem broached in the previous paragraph).[12]

Scheler proposes three goals that knowing can and should serve: domination, edification, and salvation. These goals distinguish irreducible ways of knowing. Domination is the goal served by pragmatic knowing, the sort of knowing that serves human aims, enabling us to change the world and accomplish various practical purposes. Edification is the goal of education, the full unfolding of the person, through which an individual expands herself into a "microcosm" and seeks to gain some share in the world's totality, albeit from the perspective of her unique individuality. Salvation is the goal of the sort of knowing by which a person attempts to participate in the supreme being and ground of the world in its totality. Or, equivalently, the goal of this salvific or redemptive knowing is that becoming, free of time, in which "the supreme ground of things, insofar as it 'knows' itself and the world in us and through us, arrives itself at a becoming, free of time, as first Spinoza, later Hegel and Eduard von Hartmann taught—some sort of unification with itself, salvation from a 'tension' and 'primordial opposition' placed in it" (*BW*, 26f).

12. Scheler, *Bildung und Wissen*, 26: "Dann ergibt sich die Frage: Dem Werden *wovon*, dem Werden *wessen*, dem Werden *wozu?*"

Of the three ideals of knowing, knowledge for the sake of work and domination has taken precedence over the other two in the West and, indeed, Scheler submits, principally with respect to outer nature, though he is quick to add that a strong movement oriented toward technologies of the inner life of the soul is beginning to take hold. In what is surely an oversimplification, he regards the development of the types of knowledge in Eastern cultures as the inversion of this development in the West and contends that each of the major cultural traditions has developed a respective form of knowing in a "one-sided" way: India has thus developed salvific knowing, China and Greece edifying knowing, and the West pragmatic knowing (*BW*, 27, 31).

Although Scheler thinks that pragmatism and positivism are "merely the very one-sided philosophical formulations of the actual condition of modern Western culture, both making science relative to work [*Arbeitswissenschaft*] the only possible knowing at all," he gives credit to pragmatism, in contrast to positivism, for at least recognizing the purposes served by the modern sciences. He also considers positivism the more dangerous of the two, since its pretensions to a purely contemplative "theoretical" science leave no place for edifying or redemptive knowledge. Scheler accordingly considers it necessary to emphasize the superiority of pragmatism to positivism as a means of enabling the recovery of the other sorts of knowing from "the ruins of a civilization devoted to work and success" (*BW*, 28).

Philosophy, for Scheler, is a form of edifying knowledge. Its goals and criteria are directly opposed to those of science, despite the inner cooperation between philosophy and science. While philosophy begins in the wonder of why anything exists at all (to pose the question in its traditional metaphysical garb), science is motivated by the need to be able to predict or bring about the course of things. Science proceeds by means of observation and measurement, together with mathematical inference; its object is the world of what is contingently such-and-such and its respective laws. In short, science investigates the world with respect to its existence. If something novel or surprising can be subsumed under general laws as their consequence in given circumstances (Scheler is, in effect, presenting a version of the covering law model of explanation), then science is satisfied. By contrast, philosophy is concerned precisely with what things are—their essences, what causes things of this sort, and what the things mean, independently of their relation to the make-up of the knowing subject (e.g., its sensorimotor functions). To this end, philosophy begins by suspending any technical principle for selection of the objects of knowing in terms of a potential for dominating them and by suspending every mental stance motivated by desires or practical intent. In other words, philosophy suspends a stance in which, as he puts it, "the contingent, actual being, only the reality of things is given" (*BW*, 29).

Yet Scheler appears to regard philosophy not only as an edifying, but also as a redemptive, form of knowing. For he explicitly identifies two criteria that are decisive for it and that correspond respectively to the criteria of edifying and redeeming forms of knowing. The criterion of edifying forms of knowing is the a priori or essential, precisely what is allegedly not accessible by means of the observational and metric methods of the sciences. The criterion of redemptive knowing is the absolute level of being of the object of the knowledge or, in effect, metaphysical knowledge, demanding that we know the existence, essence, and value of what is absolutely real in all things. Note that here the attention shifts back to existence and, presumably, the individual, albeit the individual not alone, but in communal dialogue. Scheler makes this point in the course of emphasizing the difference between the Indian-Greek view of redemption as the dissolution of the individual through knowledge found by the individual and the Christian view of a knowing in need of salvation that is communicated and leads to love of the person communicating it (*LE*, 8).

If philosophy is both edifying and redemptive, its status is a complicated one, especially since Scheler considers the three forms of knowing to be, as noted earlier, irreducible to one another. Indeed, identifying knowing exclusively with only one of the forms and, in effect, supplanting and suppressing the others is, Scheler submits, extremely harmful to human existence. He accordingly indicts the scientific hegemony in the present age. Yet, given the irreducibility of the three forms of knowing, the antidote cannot take the form of some romantic denial of science in favor of a form of knowing that edifies. Instead, Scheler proclaims that the future of human culture will arise—and I take it that he means thereby that a genuine future only can arise—from the complementary development of all three forms of knowing.

Concluding Questions

But this emphasis on complementarity is largely programmatic and accordingly underdetermined to a fault. Even if we set aside for the moment the question of the nature and role of philosophical knowledge within this conception, we have to find a way to reconcile this acknowledgment of complementarity with Scheler's insistence on a hierarchy among the three forms of knowing. Thus, he subordinates scientific knowledge to edifying cultural knowledge, and the latter to redemptive or salvific knowing. I stress this problem because it brings us back to the question of the alleged priority of love to knowing that defines "the essence of Christian religious consciousness." For while each form of knowing is said to originate generally in love, Scheler does not indicate whether there is a particular form of love that corresponds to each form of knowing (as its motivating basis) or whether some general conception of love is meant to suffice and, in any case, whether some version of the Christian form of love serves a special function here, as one might expect. Christian love, I take it, must not only be a source of an individual's motivation for knowing, but also the *ordo amoris* animating the entire process of knowing and, ultimately, the nature of what is known. In short, what is left unexplained in the texts reviewed here are precisely the nature and import of the love in all the respects and levels that encompass the complementarity and hierarchy of the forms of knowing. One might, as Manfred Frings has plausibly done, retrieve the account of the three forms of love distinguished in *Wesen und Formen der Sympathie,* namely, vital, mental, and spiritual, and line them up with the three forms of knowing.[13] But again, we are still left with the question of the full reach of the Christian revolution, that inversion of the traditional conception of the relation of love and knowledge that is the essence of the Christian religious consciousness.

These problems converge with the question of the status of volitional phenomena in Scheler's account of the Christian revolution, a question that brings us back to Wojtyla's concerns, for Scheler's conception of that revolution in terms of the relation of love and knowledge bypasses considerations of normativity, rationality, and decision-making as such.[14] At the very least, Scheler owes us an account of these phenomena in the light of the priority that Christianity in a revolutionary way, in his view, accords to love over knowledge. He owes us an account, since there may well be reasons, grounded in the phenomenology of the acting person, to regard decision-making as something irreducible to either love or knowledge.

13. Scheler, *Wesen und Formen der Sympathie,* part A, chap. 11, 152–58, 182ff; Frings, *Max Scheler,* 48f.

14. See Buttiglione, *Karol Wojtyla,* 72, 133, 142, 142 n. 26, 163, and 274f.

In this paper, I have tried to sketch three themes: first, what Scheler takes to be the essence of Christian religious consciousness—namely, a consciousness that love is a condition for knowing; second, his distinctive understanding of Christian love, not as a lack, but as an act of fullness and strength, thus the very antithesis of feelings and relationships born of resentment; and third, his mature conception of the forms of knowing. Several problems have been raised along the way: the problem of a philosophy of religion, given Scheler's account of the essence of religious consciousness; the problem of reconciling the intentional character of the known with the loving foundation of knowledge and reality; the problems presented by the three forms of knowing both among themselves (e.g., in what sense is our knowledge of these three types and their supposed complementarity and hierarchy pragmatic, edifying, and/or redemptive?) and in relation to the love and the forms of love (e.g., is redemptive knowledge necessarily rooted in Christian love or something akin to it?); and, not least, the problem of the status of decision-making in the context of Christian love, given the priority that Scheler assigns to love over knowledge. Some of these problems are no doubt less intractable than others; some may even be resolvable. But they have a focal point, namely, the challenge that the Christian revolution presents to philosophy, as traditionally conceived. For the fact that love is not a lack, but the fullness or, at least, participation in the fullness of the possession of wisdom, entails that the love of wisdom (in effect, a philosophy in the wake of the Christian religious experience), in some fundamental respect is no longer a quest, no longer a question. But, then, should we retain the word "philosophy" for this redemptive knowing at all? Or should we reconcile ourselves to the fact that a Christian philosophy is an oxymoron, a fatal hybrid of Athens and Jerusalem that Scheler cannot escape in his valiant attempt to come to terms philosophically with the essence of the Christian religious consciousness?

Thomas C. Anderson

14. THE PERVASIVE PRESENCE OF THE SPIRITUAL IN GABRIEL MARCEL'S WORLD

I imagine that Ken Schmitz was responsible for a number of his students pursuing the exalted vocation of philosopher. That was certainly true in my case. I was an engineering student when I took my first philosophy course from him, and it was the beginning of my life-long pursuit of wisdom and my affection for Dr. Schmitz.

This chapter dealing with Gabriel Marcel's investigations into the spiritual dimensions of reality is, I believe, particularly appropriate as a tribute to Ken, for it was he who first introduced me to Marcel's thought. In addition, his own investigations into the nature of the spiritual, which make frequent use of Marcel's ideas, have enabled me to deepen my understanding and appreciation of the French philosopher's insights and, more personally, have helped me recognize the pervasive presence of the spiritual in my own experience. Although what follows is an exposition of Marcel's views, I must acknowledge the debt that this paper owes to Schmitz's work and inspiration.

Self and World

Although I had read it innumerable times, until recently it never seemed important that Gabriel Marcel himself described his Gifford lectures, *The Mystery of Being,* as "an investigation into the essence of spiritual reality."[1] Still, I thought it might be interesting to reread this work and many of his other works from that perspective, namely, as investigations into spiritual reality. When I did so, I found that remarks about the spiritual and all kinds of spiritual entities pervade Marcel's writings, so much so that I would now suggest that for him the world of our experience is fundamentally spiritual in nature. In what follows I will try to make that case.

If Marcel believes that reality is fundamentally spiritual, that goes a long way toward explaining why in many works he critiques the rampant materialism of Western culture.[2] Philosophically speaking, that materialism holds that everything, including human beings and their societies, consists at bottom of various arrangements of atoms, strings, or some other subatomic physical entities. The human mind or consciousness is the physical brain, and our thoughts, desires, choices, sensations are "brain events or acts," that is, physical, biochemical, electrical phenomena located in our body and particularly in our head. As a recent *Popular Science* article put it, "sensation is at its core just neurons firing" in our brain.[3] That materialism coupled with the glorification of technology leads to the belief that the right scientific-technological procedures, that is, the right manipulations of matter, can solve all human problems from birth to death. If there are some problems such techniques can't resolve, those problems have no solution and so are not worth dealing with.

The logical result of materialism, Marcel observes, is that human fulfillment comes to be considered as consisting in pleasure and satisfactions on a material level, which naturally requires the unending accu-

1. Gabriel Marcel, *The Mystery of Being*, vol. 1, *Reflection and Mystery*, trans. G. S. Fraser (South Bend, Ind.: St Augustine's Press, 2001), 1–2 [cited hereafter as *Mystery*]; *Mystery*, vol. 2, *Faith and Reality*, trans. René Hague (South Bend, Ind.: St Augustine's Press, 2001); in his final summary chapter, Marcel states that these lectures of his attempted to describe "the spiritual attitudes" we need to adopt today (*Mystery* 2:167).

2. To mention two of the main ones: *Mystery* 1: chap. 2 and Marcel, *Man Against Mass Society*, trans. G. S. Fraser (Chicago: Regnery, 1962) [hereafter *Man Against*], especially part 1, chap. 3 and 4; part 2, chap. 5; Marcel actually connects materialism to the worship of technology in Western society. He also grants that many are materialists "by default," inasmuch as matter is the only reality they can imagine.

3. Sara Seager, "Head Games," *Popular Science* (October 2007): 66; note too, Francis Crick, *The Astonishing Hypothesis* (N.Y.: Scribner, 1994), 3: "The Astonishing Hypothesis is that 'You,' your joys and your sorrows, your memories and your ambitions, your sense of personal identity and free will, are in fact no more than the behavior of a vast assembly of nerve cells and their associated molecules." I thank Professor Brendan Sweetman for this reference and for his helpful comments on this chapter.

mulation of amusements and possessions (hence lavish consumerism). The need for and the joys of a rich spiritual life dedicated to spiritual goods such as truth, justice, fidelity, and other virtues tend to be minimized or ignored. Likewise, our desire for something that transcends the physical world, some reality that could provide ultimate meaning and justification for our existence, is dismissed as a remnant of ancient prescientific superstition or is interpreted psychologically as a childish father fixation.[4] Finally, since death terminates our brief physical existence, "a widely diffused pessimism,"[5] Marcel says, tends to consider life itself "a dirty joke"[6] and an "incomprehensible calamity,"[7] because in the final analysis it is a meaningless "tale told by an idiot."[8]

To counter this, as I've said, Marcel focuses his investigations on spiritual dimensions of reality. However, before going into any of his analyses, let us briefly remind ourselves that Marcel's method of investigation is phenomenological.[9] His philosophizing is not an attempt to demonstrate truths logically, rationally, about the real, but to describe concrete features of human existence and of the world as we actually live and experience them, in order to grasp their essential structures. Also, by reflecting deeply on particular experiences, he attempts to uncover the ontological conditions that make them possible. This will become clearer as we go on.

Turning first to his analysis of human consciousness, Marcel states that "Descartes was right," "consciousness is essentially something that is the contrary of a body, of a thing," and, "whatever the ultimate nature of consciousness may be it obviously cannot be considered as a body."[10] Recall that Descartes says in his *Meditations*, chapter 6, that we can grasp clearly and distinctly that mind does not have the essential characteristic of body, which is extension, and includes size, shape, location in space and time, and motion. (As a phenomenologist who reflects on ordinary human experience, Marcel would add to that list other bodily features, such as odor, texture, color, temperature, mass.) And bodies in turn do

4. *Man Against*, 55–57, 93–97; Marcel, *Tragic Wisdom and Beyond*, trans. Stephen Jolin and Peter McCormick (Evanston, Ill.: Northwestern University Press, 1973), 176 [hereafter *Tragic Wisdom*].

5. *Mystery* 1:167.

6. Ibid., 170.

7. *Man Against*, 94.

8. Marcel, "On the Ontological Mystery," in *The Philosophy of Existentialism*, trans. Manya Harari, 14 (New York: Citadel, 1956) [hereafter "Ontological"].

9. "Ontological," 128; *Tragic Wisdom*, 14, 229; *Mystery* 1:41, 45–48, 51–52, 54–56, 94.

10. *Mystery* 1:50.

not have the essential characteristic of mind, namely, thought in its various forms: sensing, feeling, desiring, imagining, remembering, understanding, choosing.[11] One way to express Descartes' insight might be as follows. It seems bizarre to refer to bodies or parts of bodies, like atoms and electrons, as insightful or superficial, logical or illogical, as worrying, perplexed, loving, hating, joyful, or in despair. Yet we use all these terms to describe our conscious acts. And it seems equally bizarre to refer to conscious acts of thinking, wondering, desiring, choosing in bodily terms, as green or smelly or triangular or weighing two grams or measuring three centimeters in length, as having a positive or negative electric charge, and as moving with a certain velocity. Actually, Marcel himself contrasts consciousness and body using the categories of permanence and impermanence. To consider consciousness itself bodily, he says, raises "insoluble difficulties ... the most serious of these have to do with the word itself. The word implies a permanence ... and it does not seem that one can attribute this attribute to body as such ... by reason of its very mutability [it] has no self. It is selfless by definition."[12]

His point is that I am in some real sense the same self I was at age eight or age forty-eight. I have had many different experiences and performed many different activities in the course of my life—yet I am the same me, the same individual person, Tom Anderson, through them all. However, in my seventy-plus years my body has changed thoroughly at the cellular and molecular levels. It has no cells and no molecules today that it had when I was eight or twenty-eight or fifty-eight. Therefore, it cannot be that same self that I have been and am from birth up to today. Accordingly, Marcel designates the persisting self that I am as spiritual[13] and even as "supratemporal" and "eternal," insofar as it transcends the continual temporal flow and changing elements of my "life-processes."[14] I should add that it is only because I am (at least implicitly) aware of the persisting, eternal, spiritual dimension of my self, a dimension that tran-

11. Professor Lance Richey remarks that Marcel apparently considers Descartes' categories of physical and spiritual to be unproblematic. He (Richey) suggests, however, that on a nonreflective level of experience, consciousness does not differentiate itself from its objects using spiritual and physical as categories. Accordingly, Richey states that Marcel needs to provide a phenomenological account of human experience that explains how reflective consciousness generates those two classes to deal with experience. I agree with Richey and I thank him for his incisive comments on this chapter.

12. My translation from *Le Mystère de l'Être* (Paris: Aubier, 1951), 60; see also *Mystery* 1:51.

13. *Mystery* 1:184–91.

14. *Mystery* 1:194; Marcel, *Being and Having*, trans. Katherine Farrer (New York: Harper and Row, 1965), 20, 42.

scends time, that I am able to pledge my self to be always faithful to another human being. (More on fidelity later.)

Moreover, it isn't just that I *am* the same self throughout my life, I am *aware* that I am the same self. Marcel defines a self as "a being capable of saying I who can posit itself or be posited as an I."[15] A self for him is a being who is conscious of having an inner life of its own and of being a center or source of acts. It is conscious of its freedom to choose its own attitude toward and live its own life.[16] Thus a self for Marcel is a spiritual, self-conscious being capable of experiencing and asserting that it is the same free center and source of acts, the same I, through all the changes it undergoes. The self I am is *primarily* spiritual in nature, since it, not the body, is what I continue to be throughout my entire life.

Of course, Marcel insists that I am also a physical body; but, if I may say so, I am a "spiritualized" body. I use this term because the spiritual self I am permeates my body. My body is not just a physical thing with objective features such as size, color, shape, composed of molecules and atoms like any other body. My feelings reveal that I *am* my body.[17] I feel my body in pain to be *me* in pain; I experience my eyes seeing the tan wall as *me* seeing that tan wall. Materialism ignores feeling, Marcel says; it replaces it with some organic event (e.g., nerves firing) going on in my body that I do not feel and am not even aware of.[18] The cells, atoms, strings, forces, whatever, of my body are not just cells, atoms, strings, and forces found in every physical thing. The spiritual self that I am infuses and transforms them. Since they are part of me, and I am primarily a spiritual self, they are spiritualized. But that way of putting it tends to view me from the ground up, that is, as matter or a body (noun) that has spiritual features (adjectives). I would suggest that the more accurate Marcelian way to view my self and my body is to say (and he does) that I am an enfleshed or incarnated spirit, making spirit the noun and incarnated and enfleshed its attributes.[19] I am, first and foremost, a spiritual being that also has features that can be perceived by the senses. And speaking of the senses, they too (as well as my brain) are not just cells, atoms, strings, but cells, atoms, and strings infused by the spiritual self

15. Marcel, *Creative Fidelity*, trans. Robert Rosthal (New York: Fordham University Press, 2002), 89.

16. *Mystery* 2:25, 55–57; *Creative Fidelity*, 96; Marcel, *Homo Viator*, trans. Emma Craufurd (New York: Harper and Row, 1962), 84.

17. *Mystery* 1:93, 97, 101.

18. *Being and Having*, 108.

19. *Mystery* 1:202–3; *Creative Fidelity*, 20.

that I am. I will return to this very important point when I discuss Marcel's view of sensation.

Needless to say, to the degree I am aware of the spiritual nature of my self, I can come to realize that I cannot be satisfied by a life centered on material possessions and pleasures, as materialism suggests. I can recognize my need for spiritual goods, such as knowledge and truth, virtue, freedom, love, meaning, and life eternal.[20] In fact, such spiritual entities embodied in physical things are the primary objects of most of my ordinary experiences. Love and justice, for example, are certain kinds of relations among human beings and human societies. Meanings are found in stop signs and sensible words and sounds. In fact, everything I experience possesses some degree of intelligibility and meaning. And it seems ludicrous to claim that those relationships and meanings as such are nothing but combinations of atoms, particles, strings, or forces. Surely on the macro level, the meanings of justice and friendship have no color, weight, odor, and shape, no more than do the meanings present in visible and audible words and sentences. Marcel refers to such meanings and relations as "intelligible" (not sensible) "essences" and "relations."[21] To take an obvious example, the reader experiences the visible marks on this page to be intelligible, to mean something. He or she experiences in physical things meanings that are not physical. In general, insofar as I experience things of my world to be intelligible and meaningful—and to some degree I always do—I experience my world to be spiritual through and through.[22]

To sum up this first point, for Marcel, I, my self, am primarily spiritual in nature, and the world of my everyday experience is permeated with intelligibility that is spiritual in nature, granted that both spiritual dimensions are embodied in matter.

Experience

Furthermore, since the conscious self is spiritual, *all* of its experiences are spiritual, according to Marcel, even its sense experiences of physical things. Contemporary materialism's description of experience,

20. Marcel refers to such spiritual entities in many places; see, for example, *Mystery* 2:167; *Tragic Wisdom,* 11, 31; *Man Against,* 22, 35, 147, 163, 209; *Being and Having,* 119, 208, 211.

21. *Mystery* 1:55, 53; *Man Against,* 115 and 169, also refer to essences as not empirical.

22. In Schmitz, *The Texture of Being* (Washington D.C.: The Catholic University of America Press, 2007), at 104–05, Kenneth Schmitz speaks of the intelligibility of things as a certain "generosity" written into being and points out that human cognition is rooted in this ontological generosity.

he complains, is "far too restrictive" and "robs experience of its true nature."[23] It *imagines* (and that word is very significant) both experience itself and the mind that experiences to be physical, in particular, to be processes in the brain. It considers experience to be a matter of ingesting or taking in something, such as images or stimuli, and consciousness to be a body-like container in which they reside. As a result, "all experience in the end comes down to a self's experience of its own internal states."[24] And that position logically devolves into solipsism, since all one can be conscious of are entities within his or her mind or head.[25] On the contrary, Marcel states, when, as phenomenologists, we reflect upon our ordinary lived experience, "unbiased reflection" will reveal that we are not aware of something inside of our consciousness or our brain;[26] but rather, to quote Marcel quoting Husserl, "before it is anything else consciousness is conscious of something other than itself."[27] I am conscious of all the books on my shelves ten feet in front of me, not of images or ideas of them within me, nor of stimuli transmitted from them to my brain. To deny my most basic and spontaneous experience, that I experience real things in a real world, is a mere "academic" exercise, he says.[28] It expresses "contempt"[29] for the most fundamental evidence of experience and the "continuous foundation of human knowledge."[30] Rather than experience bringing things or their images or stimuli into me, reflection on our experience reveals it to be a going out, a transcending of my self, opening me and throwing me into the world of other beings. My consciousness of things in the world involves my presence to them as they are *in the world* (and their corresponding presence to me).[31]

As I reflect more deeply on my experiential presence to things, I also find that in my experience I am not only presence to them but really united to them (and they to me). When I am aware of this chair, for example, the only object that is present in my experience is the chair itself. Experientially I become one with the chair, and that conscious union has to be a "spiritual unity" with it,[32] Marcel claims, because, unlike a physical union of things where one or both are physically changed and maybe even destroyed, my awareness of the chair does not modify its

23. *Mystery* 1:47, 55.

24. Ibid, 1:49.

25. Ibid., 1:110.

26. Marcel, *Metaphysical Journal*, trans. Bernard Wall (Chicago: Gateway, 1952), 320–21 [hereafter *Metaphysical*].

27. *Mystery* 1:52.

28. "Ontological," 17.

29. *Being and Having*, 56.

30. *Creative Fidelity*, 165.

31. *Mystery* 1:47.

32. *Man Against*, 217.

color or size or location or molecular structure or any of its physical features. Being conscious of the chair is a union of me and the chair that lets it be as it is physically; therefore, that union must be spiritual. As Kenneth Schmitz says, "knowing puts us in the world in a nonphysical immaterial way. I mean that precisely as knowing, it does not disturb the world."[33] And he adds that when I am aware of a physical thing, that thing itself is "converted," for it participates in and thereby becomes part of my spiritual being. In addition to its own physical being in the world, I cause the chair to have an immaterial, spiritual mode of being.[34] That is why it can affect me both physically and spiritually. Since we are spiritually one, the chair can modify me "inwardly," Marcel writes, in my thoughts, feelings, and choices.[35] If the chair is a handmade heirloom passed on to me from my great-grandparents, I may have deep affection for it and great sorrow if it is damaged or taken from me.

What Marcel says about experience in general, its transcending of self, opening onto the world, being present to things, uniting my self spiritually with the things I experience, all this is also true of sensation. Science's materialistic account of sensation is woefully inadequate, for it claims that sensation consists of the brain "interpreting" or "translating" stimuli received from my particular senses into my experiences of seeing a blue sky, hearing loud music, feeling a smooth cool surface. However, if sensation consists of interpreting, then the original uninterpreted stimuli I receive from objects are not themselves something I can sense nor, a fortiori, can I interpret or translate them.[36]

Let me add that the stimuli that travel from my different sense organs to my brain are essentially indistinguishable. All of them are nothing but weak electrical currents moving at different speeds along different nerve pathways. They never possess the sensible features I actually see or hear or smell or touch. Electric impulses that travel to the brain from my optic nerve are not blue or green, impulses from my olfactory organs have no odor, stimuli coming to the brain from my ears make no sound. How then can they be interpreted or translated into the perceptible objects outside my body that I actually sense: green grass, smelly

33. Schmitz, *The Texture of Being*, 195.

34. Schmitz has a much more thorough discussion of the spiritual union between the knower and the known than does Marcel; see chap. 10 of *The Texture of Being*. Although Marcel stresses the ontological unity between knower and known, he does not, to my knowledge, discuss the spiritual mode of being the object attains when it is known.

35. *Tragic Wisdom*, 154.

36. *Mystery* 1:105–10.

feet, Beethoven's Fifth Symphony? If, instead of adopting the scientific account, I reflect upon my ordinary sensory experiences, I will find them to be various ways I am consciously present to physical things. My seeing, hearing, and touching things do not take place within me or my brain, Marcel insists. Rather, "Sensation is in reality a mode of *being in the world*."[37] Seeing, hearing, touching are "avenues" by which I consciously unite with and participate in physical things. "Sensation," he writes, "involves the immediate participation of what we normally call the subject in a surrounding world from which no real frontier separates it."[38] By means of sensation, "I am really *attached* to and really adhere to all that exists."[39] For, "to experience a sensation is really to become in some manner the thing sensed ... a sort of temporary coalescence is established" between us.[40] Note that last quotation; to sense is to "become in some manner the thing sensed." That manner is *spiritual*, for unlike a physical union, our conscious union with the things we sense does not change them in any of their physical features. Nor do I physically become the thing sensed, even though I am really present and united to it, spiritually.

In all of the foregoing analyses Marcel warns us not to think of sensation or experience in general or the self as physical in nature. Don't try to *imagine* (that word again) any of them, he cautions; for if we do, we will inevitably consider them to be some kind of circumscribed bodily substance, however ethereal. But if experience or the self are some kind of bodies, how can they become aware of anything outside of their bodies?[41] No physical ray goes out from my eye or brain to the object I see, whether it is a tree ten feet away or the sun millions of miles away; nor does the tree or sun become part of me (or my brain) physically. Yet in sensing them I really do experience the tree and the sun and am joined to them, spiritually. I spiritually participate in their being and they in mine.

Human Dignity and Human Relations

Of course, the spiritual union that Marcel is most interested in is the union among two or more persons or spiritual selves, especially that union present in love. Love's union, he states, "really does bind" subjects together "at the ontological level, that is qua being," for lovers "negate themselves as simple, detached, items."[42] Once again that ontologi-

37. Marcel, *The Existential Background of Human Dignity* (Cambridge, Mass.: Harvard University Press, 1971), 45 [hereafter *Dignity*].

38. *Metaphysical*, 331–32.

39. *Metaphysical*, 274.

40. *Metaphysical*, 257.

41. *Mystery* 1:46–47, 52–53; 2:35.

42. See his whole discussion in *Mystery* 1:177–82; also see *Creative Fidelity*, 33–36, 91, 99.

cal bond must be spiritual, for of itself it does not modify either subject physically.[43] Of course their spiritual oneness can radically affect them "inwardly," for each lover identifies his or her self with the beloved and thereby participates in his or her life and experiences.[44] Her joys and sorrows, her worries, her search for meaning and happiness truly become part of me and my life. Yet at the same time, my love respects the beloved as she is; after all, it is *she* that I know and identify with. In other words, love's union preserves the integrity of the lover and the beloved at the same time that it amplifies and enhances their beings.[45] To paraphrase Erich Fromm, love is a spiritual union in which two beings become one and still remain two.[46] They remain two in the sense that love's "suprapersonal unity"[47] does not diminish or obliterate either lover but strengthens and enlarges them, since they are no longer alone but share each other's lives.

I have been talking about the spiritual relation of love; but, of course, there are all kinds of nonphysical spiritual relationships among people in society. All in the same country and culture to some extent share goals and values and customs and practices in their economic, political, religious, and social relationships. Those relationships have no atomic weight or mass, no electric charge, or color, or shape, or any physical feature, yet they are of paramount importance; for it is only because human beings enter into them that cultures and societies and religions come to be in the first place and continue to be.

In intersubjective relationships, the most important spiritual feature present in each person, Marcel believes, is his or her inherent dignity or value. To consider human beings to be only extremely complex physical organisms inevitably leaves that out. The value of purely material organisms must be measured by material standards such as power, wealth, output, and consumption, and he claims that is precisely what is happening in our materialistic Western culture. That explains why the last hundred years have witnessed the slaughter of human beings on an unprecedented scale. If humans are nothing but matter, once they become useless or become obstacles, they are destined for the scrap heap or crematorium.[48]

43. *Man Against*, 167–68.

44. *Creative Fidelity*, 84, 95; *Being and Having*, 225.

45. *Creative Fidelity*, 35, 136; *Mystery* 1:182; *Dignity*, 91–92, *Tragic Wisdom*, 39.

46. Erich Fromm, *The Art of Loving* (New York: Harper and Row, 1989), 19.

47. *Mystery* 1:182.

48. *Man Against*, 96, 174; "Ontological," 10–12.

Marcel finds evidence that human beings possess inherent dignity/value from his examination of ordinary human experiences such as love and fidelity. Since I have discussed his analyses in detail elsewhere, I will be brief here.[49] Marcel is struck by the fact that some people offer *unconditional* pledges of loving fidelity to other human beings.[50] What, he asks, can explain why some commit themselves without reservation to others, maybe even to the extent of offering them their lives? His answer is that their commitments are intelligible only if the individuals who make them experience, at least vaguely and nonreflectively, the presence of unconditional, eternal (that is, not temporally limited) value in those to whom they pledge unconditional love and fidelity.[51]

Still, he goes on, how can finite human beings possess unconditional eternal value and dignity? And he responds that it is only because they are "created in the image of God,"[52] a God who is a loving Father.[53] Even more, Marcel claims that only if we somehow, at least obscurely and implicitly, experience other persons to be *gifts* of Divine intelligence and will, and not merely blind accidents of cosmic evolution, can we experience them to possess intrinsic, unlimited dignity. Only if an Absolute Thou *reveals* himself to be its source can we feel confident that human life is a gift endowed with absolute value. He writes: "It is only in so far as I somehow become gratefully conscious of this revelation that I can come to apprehend life and my own life as a gift."[54] For that "revelation" (small "r") is that life is not meaningless nor absurd; it is not a tale told by an idiot, ultimately signifying nothing, as materialism logically implies. Marcel's startling claim, then, is that we can experience human life to be meaningful and possess unlimited intrinsic dignity only because in some way we are aware of God's revelation that life is his gift, not just a product of blind chance.[55]

Let me hasten to add that, in speaking of God's revelation with a

49. See my commentary on *Mystery* 1: chap. 9 and *Mystery* 2: chap. 5–10, in Thomas Anderson, *A Commentary on Gabriel Marcel's* The Mystery of Being (Milwaukee,Wisc.: Marquette University Press, 2006).

50. He also recognizes that people are faithful to causes such as freedom, justice, and peace; but says they (the causes) cannot be mere abstractions. They must be incarnated in concrete relations among human beings and human societies; see *Homo Viator*, 143–44, 155–57; *Creative Fidelity*, 37; *Tragic Wisdom*, 196–97.

51. This is a condensation of material in *Creative Fidelity*, chap. 6 and 8, and *Mystery* 2: chap. 5 and 8.

52. *Mystery* 2:148.

53. *Man Against*, 67, 258; *Tragic Wisdom*, 44; *Dignity*, 94–96, 133; *Homo Viator*, 46–47.

54. *Mystery* 2:122.

55. *Mystery* 2:118–22, 151.

small "r," Marcel makes it clear he is not referring to any particular historical religion or faith communities with their inspired books or creeds or traditions. The revelation he has in mind, while it comes from God, involves no particular religion or beliefs and no particular church, with its formulated creeds and sacred scriptures. It can be given even to those who are not explicitly aware of God's creative presence, even to professed atheists. Verbal atheism, proclaimed by persons whose lives bear witness to their deep conviction that human existence has ultimate meaning and dignity, is compatible, Marcel claims, with a very obscure, veiled, nonreflective experience of a loving Creator as its source. After all, it is not just avowed theists who faithfully and lovingly commit themselves without reservation, sometimes at great risk, to their fellow human beings. But, to repeat, such commitments make sense, he argues, only if those who pledge unconditional fidelity and love somehow or other experience the unconditional inherent dignity of those to whom they offer such fidelity and love. That in turn requires that they in some way experience that human life is not a freak accident of indifferent cosmic forces, but a meaningful gift from creative intelligence and will. Who other than the Creator himself could reveal that, albeit not clearly and distinctly, nor necessarily in words? Whether one reflectively explicitly recognizes it nor not, Marcel argues, only God can disclose the incomparable value and dignity of ourselves and others.[56] And, to repeat, that revelation is able to enlighten those "who are strangers to all positive religion of whatever kind."[57]

Needless to say, the experience that life is meaningful, that human beings possess inherent value because they are gifts of an absolute Thou, is spiritual in nature. The absolute value of human persons cannot be confirmed or even reached by either our senses or the instruments and methods of empirical science. Furthermore, it is not just human life that is a divine gift; according to Marcel, all life and all creatures are. In fact, human reality itself would be impossible without "an entire class of unspecifiable objects" necessary for its physical and biological existence.[58] God creates beings, not in splendid isolation, but *in the world,* that is, within a countless number of totally interdependent beings.[59]

56. In a number of works, Marcel distinguishes between professed and lived atheism; see *Mystery* 2:120–23; *Creative Fidelity,* 77–80, 182; *Tragic Wisdom,* 42-44, 166-69.

57. "Ontological," 46.

58. *Tragic Wisdom,* 105.

59. *Mystery* 2:122; Schmitz, *The Gift: Creation* (Milwaukee, Wisc.: Marquette University Press, 1982), 74–77, has an excellent discussion of this point. He writes, "The created

Obviously, to view all worldly things as gifts is very different from the way materialism views them. For the latter the world is simply, as Schmitz puts it, "a set of given facts (data)" that just happen to be there.[60] It is matter or, even better, raw material that can be used by human beings in any way they please. For Marcel, things are fundamentally gratuitous, unmerited, intrinsically good gifts purposely willed to be by an intelligent and loving Creator.[61] They embody the generosity of their giver. Indeed, generosity is the very "soul" (animating principle) of a gift, since what is offered is neither deserved nor necessary.[62] Moreover, like all gifts, they achieve their giver's intended goal when they are humbly accepted in gratitude, in delight, and in wonder.[63] To consider everything we are and have as divine gifts is to experience them as sacred and holy, Marcel adds, and, therefore, as deserving respect and reverence.[64] If I may say so, it is to experience them, only obscurely and confusedly, as sacramental realities, sacred windows through which we may glimpse the "Creative Spirit"[65] actively, intimately present at every moment within their innermost being.[66] It follows that our spiritual bond with everything we know and love is also, then, a union with an absolute Thou whose creative activity is always at work within all his creatures.

Finally, Marcel believes that we are part of an invisible "living reality ... which quite certainly surrounds us on all sides." That reality includes the dead "whom we have never ceased to love."[67] For, as we have seen, Marcel considers love to be a spiritual union with the spiritual dimension of another self, the self that possesses *eternal* dignity and value. It must be, therefore, a union that survives physical death.[68] Further-

world is the totality of all totalities, the most extensive dynamic plurality and their factors. Within it there is movement, interaction, communication, and, in the broadest and deepest sense, giving and receiving. For these are endemic to any dynamic plurality, and without them it can neither be established nor maintained" (76).

60. Schmitz, *The Gift*, 88–89.

61. Marcel cites *Genesis*, "God saw all that He had made and it was very good," in *Homo Viator*, 119.

62. *Mystery* 2:118–20.

63. *Being and Having*, 217; *Homo Viator*, 75, 119.

64. *Being and Having*, 220–21, 228; *Homo Viator*, 75; Tragic Wisdom, 114–16; *Mystery* 1:87.

65. *Being and Having*, 221; *Mystery* 2:35.

66. Schmitz refers to the "metaphysical interiority of nature ... a rich metaphysical texture grounded in the intimate presence of the creative cause to the things of nature" and says it accounts for nature's intelligibility, usefulness, and availability to art (Schmitz, *The Gift*, 90).

67. *Mystery* 2:186.

68. For more treatment of Marcel's belief in immortality and in the presence of the

more, even this side of the grave there are "infiltrations" of that invisible world and subtle "solicitations" from it.[69] Two that Marcel mentions are: (1) the feeling that we sometimes have that our dead loved ones continue to exert influence on our lives; that they "continue to make me what I am";[70] and (2) the feeling that we must be faithful to our deceased loved ones and never betray them. Marcel insists that such feelings can best be explained as experiences of the actual presence of our dead loved ones. A faint image of him or her in our memory is simply not powerful enough to account for our feelings.[71]

Concluding Review

I will conclude with a brief review. I have attempted to show that Marcel regards the world of our experience to be fundamentally (not entirely) spiritual. The continuous self-conscious being that I am is primarily spiritual in nature, as are all my experiences. Because it embodies and is me, my body is a spiritualized body. Likewise the physical world I experience is thoroughly spiritual, inasmuch as I find it to be intelligible and meaningful. Things are further spiritualized by being known and loved, for by consciously uniting with them, I cause them to participate in my spiritual reality. The world constituted by human beings entering into a multiplicity of relations with each other is also fundamentally spiritual. For the human beings themselves and their relationships (such as friendship, marital love, justice, freedom, democracy, employee-employer relations), while embodied in matter, are spiritual. The most important spiritual feature of each person is his or her inherent dignity; and to experience the eternal, intrinsic value of persons requires at least a vague, inexplicit awareness that they are gifts of a loving Creator. Indeed, all things are divine gifts, which means that the Creative Spirit is constantly within them, knowingly, lovingly, willing them to be at every moment. In order for us to experience creatures as gifts rather than as products of purposeless chance, we must in some way recognize that creative spiritual presence deep within them. Finally, we participate

---

dead, see Thomas Anderson, "Gabriel Marcel on Personal Immortality," in *American Catholic Philosophical Quarterly* (2006): 393–406.

69. *Mystery* 2:167.

70. Marcel, *Presence and Immortality*, trans. Michael A. Machado (Pittsburgh, Penn.: Duquesne University Press, 1967), 17, 80, 89, 177, 192, 238, 242–43.

71. In many places he claims that it is not the image of a deceased loved one that I experience but his or her actual presence; see *Presence and Immortality*, 73–82, 87–90, 144–45, 189–93; *Being and Having*, 97.

in a living spiritual reality composed of both the living and the dead.

Let me again suggest that if Marcel is correct, that the world of our experience is primarily and thoroughly spiritual, then we need to turn our normal way of looking at things upside down. It is not that we are first and foremost physical beings in a physical world that also contains some spiritual features. Rather we are first and foremost spiritual beings immersed in a spiritual world, and what we call physical is, Marcel states, "only the *one* aspect" of it "which is in tune with our organic- psychic structure."[72] To limit ourselves only to that single aspect has had, and will continue to have, dire consequences for the human spirit and for its relationship to an absolute Thou.

72. *Mystery* 2:157–58; emphasis mine.

Thomas W. Busch

15. JEAN-PAUL SARTRE

An Existentialist to the End?

Early in the 1960s, I had completed my first year of graduate study. While I found my professors to be good people, I was discouraged because none of the courses I had taken had gripped me to the point of personal involvement. I was beginning to wonder whether I had made a wise career choice. Then this blast of fresh air from Canada arrived on the scene and abruptly reassured me. Professor Kenneth Schmitz introduced me to Kierkegaard, Jaspers, Heidegger, Marcel, and Sartre. I just had to go on in philosophy. What a role model this man was: brilliant, scholarly, a super teacher, humble, and hospitable. I know he had the same effect on my fellow students. Looking back, I can only say with gratitude that I was in the right place at the right time. What follows grew out of Schmitz's introduction to Sartre.

It has been just over thirty years since Sartre's death, and it looks like his legacy, at this point in time, remains that of the philosopher of subjectivity, an existential Cartesian ("I consider myself a Cartesian philosopher, at least in *L'Etre et le Néant*").[1] Sartre had insisted in an interview late in his career about how "my outlook changed so fundamentally after the Second World War."[2] In the same interview he is specific

1. Michel Contat, Oreste Pucciani, and Susan Gruenwald, "Interview with Sartre," in *The Philosophy of Jean-Paul Sartre,* edited by Phillip Schilpp (LaSalle, Ill.: Open Court Press, 1981), 8.

2. Sartre, "The Itinerary of a Thought" (interview), in *Between Existentialism and Marxism,* trans. John Mathews (New York: Morrow, 1974), 33.

about how subjectivity is an important factor in this change: "Thus, in *L"Etre et le Néant,* what you could call 'subjectivity' is not what it would be for me now, the small margin in an operation whereby an interiorization re-exteriorizes itself in an act. But 'subjectivity' and 'objectivity' seem to me entirely useless notions today, anyway."[3] However, by this time other philosophical fashions were obsessing readers, and they had moved on without giving equal time to the later work. When he became aware that he was being known in terms of *Being and Nothingness* alone,[4] Sartre was disappointed: "But they all stop too soon. I think that a study of my philosophical thought should follow its evolution. But no, they don't do it. It's odd."[5] A complete and fair assessment of his work would require setting *Being and Nothingness* and *The Family Idiot* side by side for comparison.[6] When one does so, the question arises as to whether or to what extent Sartre can be said to be an existentialist at all in his final work.

Sartre insisted in his early work upon the centrality of the *cogito,* albeit a revised understanding of it. This was the intent of his *The Transcendence of the Ego,* subtitled "an existentialist theory of consciousness."[7] His existentialist view attempted to avoid the dangers of immanence and substantialism by reference to a prereflective *cogito.* Descartes, according to Sartre, failed to see that his *cogito* (I doubt, therefore I am), which had the effect of sealing consciousness and its immanent contents off from the world, was founded upon a prereflective *cogito* that discovers itself always already and inescapably in the world. Descartes' *cogito* is a consciousness of consciousness, whereby an act of consciousness (reflecting) takes as its object another act of consciousness (doubting), which becomes the reflected-on. Sartre points out that the act of reflection depends upon the prior, in this case, doubting consciousness. The doubting consciousness, in its actuality as doubting (the "lived" doubting), is a consciousness that intends objects given as dubious. The focus of the doubting consciousness is not itself, but something other than itself (the dubious objects). Such a consciousness is "outside" itself in its

3. Contat, "Interview with Sartre," 38.

4. Jean-Paul Sartre, *Being and Nothingness,* trans. Hazel Barnes (New York: Philosophical Library), 1956.

5. See "Interview with Sartre," 12–38.

6. Jean-Paul Sartre, *The Family Idiot,* 5 vols., trans. Carol Cosman (Chicago: University of Chicago Press, 1981–93).

7. Jean-Paul Sartre, *The Transcendence of the Ego,* trans. Forrest Williams and Robert Kirkpatrick (New York: Noonday, 1957).

intending. While the doubting consciousness is in its "lived" condition of actually doubting, it is not intentionally or focally aware of itself. Its focus is upon the dubious objects. With an act of reflection the scene changes, as the doubting consciousness is pulled from its ecstatic involvement with the dubious objects, to become itself an object for a new consciousness, the reflecting consciousness. Sartre points out that when the reflecting consciousness itself is actually reflecting (in the "lived" act of reflecting), it is intentionally focused upon the consciousness reflected on and is not focused upon itself. Thus, whether in a prereflective state (doubting) or in a reflective state (reflecting on the doubting), consciousness is intentionally focused upon an object, and not on itself. At this point Sartre asks whether this means that in its "lived" condition, not focusing upon itself, consciousness (whether prereflective or reflective) is unconscious of itself. He answers by resisting any notion of an unconscious. Instead, he posits what he calls a "non-positional" self-consciousness, a nonfocal, tacit self-awareness, a "sense" of self. Thus, in doubting or reflecting on one's doubt, while focally intending an object, consciousness is nonfocally, nonpositionally self-conscious. In fact, this nonpositional consciousness is what creates a "self," one that resists objectification. Objectification, turning reflectively upon ourselves, creates what Sartre calls the "ego."

The ego is an objective representation, or picture, of oneself, a fixed identity. He gives us the example of a young wife who considered herself to be "faithful" and is overcome by anxiety when she experiences that she could act unfaithfully to her husband. If she really were "faithful" in a deep sense of essence, Sartre claimed that she could only act within the limits of that essence which would ground her actions. In experiencing anxiety, the young woman, to her shock, realized that her "self" was beyond essence, and thus radically free. What one calls "essence," or identity, is for Sartre a creation of one's radically free self. Sartre remarks on how people seem so invested in deep identity, how people create these representations of themselves and try to hide in them, thus setting the stage for his pursuit of this issue (in forms of bad faith) in *Being and Nothingness.* Sartre, thus, thinks that he has purged the *cogito* of immanence, since, in both reflective and prereflective forms, consciousness ecstatically opens upon its other (for reflective consciousness the prereflective, and for prereflective consciousness its objects), and as well as desubstantializing the *cogito* by denying it any deep, essential identity.

In *Being and Nothingness,* Sartre provides an ontological understanding of the cogito that privileges subjectivity, appearing now as "being-for-itself," as the author of meaning and value. Sartre had established in *The Transcendence of the Ego* that there was a single structure of consciousness, whether on the prereflective or reflective levels, and he reiterates that structure in the "Introduction" to *Being and Nothingness:* "every positional consciousness of an object is at the same time a non-positional consciousness of itself."[8] Ontologically, to be conscious of an object, to intend an object, for Sartre, assumes that consciousness *is not* that object. "Presence incloses a radical negation as presence to that which one is not. What is present to me is what is not me."[9] Intentionality is not fusion with an object, but rather differentiation from it. The differentiation is possible because of the nonpositional self-awareness of the intentional act, which, so to speak, bends the act upon itself to create a subject/object relationship. In the *cogito* there appears a breaking apart of being: "The presence of being to itself implies a detachment on the part of being in relation to itself."[10] The nonpositional self-awareness that is a dimension of all consciousness marks the place where this "fissure" in being occurs, constituting subjectivity itself: "What can properly be called subjectivity is consciousness (of) consciousness."[11] The subjective self is a relation to itself, a presence to itself, differentiating it from all that is its other, splitting being into subjective and objective modes (being-for-itself and being-in-itself). The splitting itself, according to Sartre, is due to *nonbeing:* "The being of consciousness qua consciousness is to exist *at a distance from itself* as a presence to itself, and this empty distance which being carries in its being is Nothingness."[12] This disruption of being from coincidence with itself bears the existential consequences of temporalizing the being of consciousness, of emptying the being of consciousness from identity with itself, of throwing consciousness into and haunting it by the imaginary. Exiled from the fullness of being, being-for-itself is condemned to rush into the unknown future, create and support identities, and project meaning and value. "In anguish I apprehend myself at once as totally free and as not being able to derive the meaning of the world except as coming from myself."[13]

Sartre once said that it is necessary to create a synthesis of Husserl and Heidegger, and indeed these two major influences are apparent in *Being and Nothingness*. Husserl and the *cogito* tradition are apparent in the

8. Sartre, *Being and Nothingness*, liii.
9. Ibid., 133.
10. Ibid., 77.
11. Ibid., lxi.
12. Ibid., 78.
13. Ibid., 40.

philosophy of consciousness that dominates the ontology, whereas Heidegger is present in the emphasis upon situatedness and facticity. Sartre repeatedly insists upon the situatedness of the for-itself, and this builds a tension that runs through his ontology. In order to protect freedom and autonomy, Sartre adopts the discourse of the *cogito* tradition with its metaphor of distance (as in Descartes' doubt and Husserl's *Epoche*). The power of consciousness over the given is guaranteed by the "break in being" that occurs in the nonpositional self-awareness, which creates a "rupture," "detachment," "fissure" between subjectivity and its situation. Heidegger, of course, is notorious for his critique of the *cogito* tradition, by emphasizing the belongingness of *Dasein* to its situation and the sheer worldliness of subjectivity. Given Sartre's dedication to protecting a radical freedom, it is not surprising that, when push comes to shove, he sides with Husserl, the *cogito* and the metaphor of distance. While Husserl had "shut himself up inside the *cogito*" (something Sartre had remedied through his prereflective *cogito*), Heidegger "begins with the existential analytic without going through the *cogito*," with the result that "*Dasein* has from the start been deprived of the dimension of consciousness [and] can never regain this dimension."[14] In turn, the result of this loss is that the "ekstatic character of human reality will lapse into a thing-like, blind in-itself, unless it arises from the consciousness of ekstasis."[15] In other words, Heidegger's thought cannot support radical freedom.

Sartre's ontology guarantees freedom with the "break in being," (*le Néant*) that is apparent in the nonpositional self-consciousness. In his early work this break is represented as a clean one. In depicting the relation between the present moment of consciousness and the past in *The Transcendence of the Ego,* Sartre used the expression "creation *ex nihilo,*"[16] and depicting the same relation in *Being and Nothingness,* he refers to "the *absolute distance* which cuts [the past] from me and makes it fall out of my reach, without contact, without connections."[17] In the same vein, in discussing language, Sartre tells us that, in speaking, the speaking subject is "beyond" the structure of language (including its "syntax" and "morphemes"): "This 'beyond' is enough to assure its *total independence* in relation to the structures which it surpasses."[18] Indeed, when dealing with

14. Ibid., 73.
15. Ibid., 73.
16. Sartre, *Transcendence of the Ego,* 99.
17. Sartre, *Being and Nothingness,* 118; emphasis added.
18. Ibid., 520; emphasis added.

the relation between the for-itself and a given situation, Sartre consistently portrays a one-sided relationship, wherein the for-itself surpasses a given situation "as a pure and simple negation of the given":

> But if consciousness exists in terms of the given [there must be a given to surpass], this does not mean that the given conditions consciousness; consciousness is a pure and simple negation of the given, and it exists as the disengagement from a certain existing given and as an engagement toward a certain not yet existing end.[19]

For sure, this understanding of the nihilation of the given preserves the autonomy and radical freedom of the for-itself from determination by any given state of affairs. Sartre, however, goes further in denying that subjectivity is "conditioned" by its given situation, leading one to question how deeply situated subjectivity really is, promoting the general impression of a philosophy dominated by the power of subjectivity.

Sartre, we have noted, assures us that subsequent to *Being and Nothingness* he "changed ... fundamentally," attributing the reason for this to his experience of the Second World War, which taught him "the force of circumstances." On more than one occasion, he said that the best formulation of what he means by freedom is his book *Saint Genet:* "Perhaps the book where I have best expressed what I mean by freedom is, in fact, *Saint Genet.*"[20] In this work, I believe the crucial point of difference from *Being and Nothingness* is that Sartre treats of the childhood of Genet. There is no developmental approach to subjectivity in *Being and Nothingness.* Being-for-itself appears to be adult (classless and genderless) and knows itself to be radically free, a situation that it can assume in authenticity or flee in bad faith. In dealing with Genet's childhood, Sartre is led to speak of the vulnerability of the child, the child's susceptibility to socially shaping influences; in fact and surprisingly to readers of *Being and Nothingness,* he speaks of "the making of Genet."[21] The child Genet was illegitimate and his actions twisted by adults into rendering him a "thief." He was "provided with a monstrous and guilty 'ego.'"[22] Whereas the emphasis in *The Transcendence of the Ego* and *Being and Nothingness* was on a radical freedom that forged its own identity, the Genet book acknowledges the power of social processes in identity formation. The

19. Ibid., 478.

20. Jean-Paul Sartre, *Saint Genet: Actor and Martyr,* trans. Bernard Frechtman (New York: Pantheon, 1963); see also "Itinerary of a Thought," 35.

21. Sartre, *Saint Genet,* 23.

22. Ibid., 18.

child Genet would not so easily fit into the framework of *Being and Nothingness,* because there Sartre presumed one's knowledge of radical freedom, leaving only the options of authenticity and bad faith. The child Genet did not reflectively know that he was free, and his ignorance in this regard could not be construed as a form of bad faith, which presupposes that one knows what one is hiding from oneself.

Genet, of course, is not a thing, with the identity of a thing. He can only exist at being a thief as a project. Even if he believes himself to be a thief on the authority of others, he has to make himself a thief, and eventually, in the process, comes to recognize himself as a "making" and not a "being." Language plays a decisive role in this transformation. Early in his life, Genet's relation with words is poor: "Genet is on the side of the objects named, not those who name them.... [I]t is as if a page of a book suddenly became conscious and felt itself *being read aloud* without being able *to read itself.*"[23] Later, when he is moved to write of his life, he becomes aware of the power of words to affect others and in the process learns of his own freedom, discovers himself as a subject.

Whereas *Being and Nothingness* was all about the power of subjectivity to make itself by its choices, *Saint Genet* is very much about how one is made by one's environment. From now on Sartre will depict freedom as the process whereby "a man can always make something out of what is made of him."[24] He now admits that one is "conditioned" by one's situation, something he avoided in *Being and Nothingness:* "But freedom is simply the fact that ... choice is always unconditioned."[25] Sartre, faithful to his commitment to phenomenology, does not attempt to explain conditioning by a causal action, but rather as a dialectic, whereby one "interiorizes" one's exterior environment and "exteriorizes" oneself back into the environment:

> The individual interiorizes his social determinations: he interiorizes the relations of production, the family of his childhood, the historical past, the contemporary institutions, and then re-exteriorizes these in acts and options which necessarily refer us back to them. None of this existed in *L'Etre et le Néant.*[26]

In the dialectical relation, subjectivity as being-for-itself is replaced by "praxis" and objectivity as being-in-itself is replaced by the "practico-inert." Praxis includes the "distance" that is "nonpositional" self-

23. Ibid., 41.
24. Sartre, "Itinerary of a Thought," 35.
25. Sartre, *Being and Nothingness,* 479.
26. Sartre, "Itinerary of a Thought," 35.

consciousness, so that "existentialism" is not abandoned. People are not things. But subjectivity is no longer "everything" it was in *Being and Nothingness,* being now "a moment in the objective process (that in which externality is internalized)."[27] In developing a dialectical methodology, no longer is the emphasis upon reconciling Husserl and Heidegger, but upon appropriating Marx and Freud. As is apparent in *Search for a Method,*[28] while preserving the distance/negation at the heart of subjectivity, Sartre adds an additional emphasis absent in *Being and Nothingness.* Beyond its "pure and simple" negation, he adds negation as retention: "In relation to the given, the *praxis* is negativity;... [but] the project retains and unveils the surpassed reality."[29] Subjectivity as praxis is marked by the very given it surpasses in the form of "traces," "inscriptions," and "colorations." Our childhood and subsequent transactions with the natural and social environment create an inevitable baggage of our lives, infecting the very apprehension and interpretation of ourselves and others: "To surpass ... is also to preserve.... We shall think *with* these original deviations, we shall act *with* these gestures which we have learned."[30] Self-transformation is always possible, but it must be mediated through the possibilities inherent in the baggage that we are. His model for transformation is the spiral: "A life develops in spirals; it passes again and again by the same points but at different levels of integration and complexity."[31] New experience, the contingencies of life, put continual stress on our attempt to form coherent selves, a process Sartre now insists is "a long work."

The other of subjectivity as praxis is the practico-inert, not the simple object-being of being-in-itself, but objectivity as worked-over matter, matter inscribed with sedimented meanings. "Matter" comprehends not only matter in the commonly accepted sense, but also cultural institutions (primary of which is language). As laden with meaning, the practico-inert constitutes the objective possibility of thought and action: "The material conditions of his existence circumscribe the field of his possibilities.... One must consider this field "as a strongly structured region."[32] The result for the dialectical understanding of freedom is that "the most individual possible is only the internalization of a social possible."[33] The structured

27. Ibid.

28. Jean-Paul Sartre, *Search for a Method,* trans. Hazel Barnes (New York: Random House, 1958).

29. Ibid., 92.

30. Ibid., 101.

31. Ibid., 106.

32. Ibid., 93.

33. Ibid., 75.

situation grounds a sense of "exigency," "necessity," and "predestination." Imperatives spring up everywhere to guide thought and action. Predestination is not determinism, for options always remain, but the options are narrowed by one's situation. One is predestined in the sense that one is situated in practico-inert structures that offer only certain options, given one's place in the structure (a place also defined by structures).

Sartre's unfinished study of Flaubert in *The Family Idiot* was an attempt to apply these newly developed notions in order to understand a life. Early on, Sartre dwells on the "making" of Flaubert in the context of his family, of his relations with his parents and siblings. Of crucial importance was the relationship of mother and son, a relationship that constituted Flaubert as a "passive" character and indelibly marked his future. Gustave's passivity had a devastating effect on his relationship to language and thus on his sense of subjectivity/agency. He never realized a sense of agential power in the real world, which resulted in a flight into the imaginary. Sartre then brilliantly places family existence in broader social, political, and economic contexts. Putting together these various sides (subjective and objective) of the constitution of Flaubert, one wonders what role is left for freedom. Indeed, if one were to immediately follow up a reading of *Being and Nothingness* with that of *The Family Idiot,* one would, I think, be very puzzled and tempted to conclude that Sartre was rejecting his existentialism. But to conclude that would be a mistake, and perhaps a consideration of Sartre's attitude toward structuralism can best confirm this.

Sartre's emphasis in his later work on the situation as "a strongly structured region" overlaps with the emergence of the structuralist movement. Levi-Strauss's attack on Sartre and Foucault's rejection of the existential subject left Sartre and many others with the impression that structuralism and existentialism were incompatible. Peter Caws appropriately remarked that "all [Sartre's] major criticisms of the structuralists turn on their failure to make room for human subjectivity and praxis."[34] Sartre's attitude toward structuralism parallels his attitude toward a certain form of historical materialism that features objective processes without a subject. On the other hand, it is important to realize that Sartre does not reject structures, systems, economies, and institutions that

34. Peter Caws, "Sartrean Structuralism?" in *The Cambridge Companion to Sartre,* edited by Christina Howells, 297 (Cambridge: Cambridge University Press, 1992). For Sartre's relation to Foucault in particular, see Thomas R. Flynn, *Sartre, Foucault and Historical Reason,* vol. 2: *A Poststructuralist Mapping of History* (Chicago: University of Chicago Press, 2005).

are composed of internal and self-referential relationships and their constraint on thought and action. His quarrel, he affirms, is with the methodology of structuralism that constructs pure objectivities (totalities) in abstraction from the realm of their functioning by means of human activity (totalization). Concretely, structures must be understood in the dialectical context of ongoing internalization and externalization: "I am in complete agreement that social facts have their own structures and laws that dominate individuals, but I only see in this the reply of worked matter to the agents who work it."[35] Sartre agrees with Merleau-Ponty's observation that structures, while constraining and limiting thought and action, also enable subjective agency in terms of the language in which one thinks, the body in which one acts, the tools that extend one's bodily capacities, and the institutions that define our relationships to others. (It is in this sense, I think, that we should understand Sartre's claim that "the most individual possible is only the internalization and enrichment of a social possible.")[36] In internalizing structures, in living them, praxis opens, temporalizes, and translates totality into totalization, into project and work. Structures are opened to a future in becoming tasks; they encounter the contingencies of life, other lived structures engaging the subject, and result in creative deformations instead of mechanical repetitions.

In *The Family Idiot,* Sartre frames the issue of structure and subject in terms of the singular universal. Structures are universal, for they link lives and experiences. They have their own intelligibility, and they can be studied in their own right, but to concretely understand them, they must be seen in the context of their operation in praxis. Language is an example that Sartre often uses to show this. Language as a system is self-referential, and it is intelligible in terms of lawful necessities. Language as spoken brings language into existence, into life as lived, and therefore into various contingencies of time, place, and circumstance. Sartre thus differentiates between *signification,* the meaning immanent to the system, and *sens,* the meaning in existential usage. Instantiated as an expression of lived experience, one cannot deduce the singular from the universal, nor is the singular merely an example of the universal, but a mingling of both universal and singular in a nonreductive relationship, in

35. Sartre, "Itinerary of a Thought," 55.

36. Sartre, *Search for a Method,* 95.

a particular adventure, whose point of departure is a set of socio-economic, cultural, moral, religious and other relations, which proceeds with whatever means are to hand, that is to say within the limits of these relations, and which gradually becomes inscribed in the same set.[37]

Freedom appears in the singular as "the limit I would today accord to freedom: the small movement which makes of a totally conditioned social being someone who does not render back completely what his conditioning has given him."[38]

So, in the end, is Sartre an existentialist? I think so, if we understand his existentialism in terms of what he himself called the "spirals" of the development of our lives. He continually remained committed to freedom, responsibility, and contingency, but expressed this commitment in different paradigms. At one time his existentialism was formulated in terms of phenomenology, with stress on the constitutive power of subjectivity, and then his life experience, the spirals of his singular adventure, led him to express his existentialism in terms of structures. At the end I would call him an "existential structuralist," which is, I believe, a stronger defense of existentialism than he made in his earlier work.

37. Jean-Paul Sartre, "Kierkegaard: The Singular Universal," in *Between Existentialism and Marxism,* trans. John Mathews (London: NLB, 1974).

38. "Itinerary of a Thought," 35.

John Deely

16. THE UNMASKING OF OBJECTIVITY

Professor Kenneth Schmitz and I developed a friendship as senior to relatively junior member of the academic world with a common interest in Heidegger, Aquinas, and matters metaphysical and epistemological, which came increasingly to mean for me semiotics.

Probably the main event that cemented our friendship and intellectual relationship was the review he wrote for the University of Toronto Press concerning my then-manuscript *Four Ages of Understanding,* purporting to be a new map of the history of philosophy, removing the gap between Ockham and Descartes by redefining the Middle Ages as rather "the Latin Age," wherein the first general conception of *signum* was established between the late-fourth-century work of Augustine (*De doctrina christiana*) and the early-seventeenth-century work of Poinsot (*Tractatus de signis*). Schmitz opened his review with the statement that what he had to say below is to be read in the light of his opinion that this work "simply must be published"; and he then proceeded to make more than thirty single-spaced pages of suggestions for improving the text, the majority of which would require interlibrary loan.

The Press gave me a contract and free hand in taking account of or ignoring all particular suggestions; but with the Schmitz suggestions I could not but treat them with the care they deserved. Accordingly, I cut short my European travels in the summer of 1998 to return immediately from teaching in the Imatra Semiotics Summer School (rather than visit Constantinople/Istanbul) to begin work on the Schmitz suggestions. The work took not only the rest of June, but the whole summer and three months into the fall. As I completed each point, I would check it off on the Schmitz review, annotate, and date it, and in the end sent the checked, dated, and annotated list to Schmitz so that he would know that his efforts had been treated with the same seriousness of purpose and spirit in which they had been proposed.

I have since been a house guest with Ken in Toronto, and he with me in Houston. Those days were what I can only imagine what it must have been like to dialogue with Plato. It is a pleasure and a privilege to participate in the volume being published to honor a great scholar and philosopher of our age.

Professors who have some familiarity with the thought of the Middle Ages are often enough heard to remark that the terms "objective" and "subjective" underwent a kind of reversal of meaning in modern philosophy. The several times that I have heard such a remark made, the professors made clear from their expression and tone—zoösemiotically, as it were—that they considered themselves to have imparted with this remark a true gem of wisdom hardly in need of further explanation. Well, certainly the trajectory of Scholastic realism in the Latin development from the time of Albert the Great's commentaries on the full range of Aristotle's writings and the taking of those same writings as the Curriculum of Arts for the newly emergent universities marked a very different trajectory than that of the early modern mainstream development in the national languages after Descartes. But whatever the comparative reversal of "object" and "subject" in the two cases of philosophical development may have been, if the noting of it is some gem of wisdom, it is a rough-cut gem indeed; for nowhere in the earlier Latin mainstream do we find a full and thematic development of the thing/object distinction accomplished, and certainly the professors imparting this gem so far have failed to provide one.

Nonetheless, an older contemporary of Ken Schmitz, Jacques Maritain, without succeeding fully to spell out why, nonetheless remarked correctly in his work on *The Degrees of Knowledge* that this matter of the relation between thing and object is the nub of the "critical problem," the problem, that is to say, of reconciling Scholastic realism with the demands modern philosophy made central in its "turn to the subject." That is the matter I want to address in this chapter: a full and thematic clarification of the thing/object distinction, perforce in postmodern rather than simply medieval or modern terms.

Why So Long in Abeyance?

My hypothesis as to why the clarification of this crucial distinction has yet so long lain in abeyance is quite simple. The distinction requires for its final clarification a more sophisticated understanding of the subject of *relation*—more specifically, *relatio secundum esse,* in the term of Aquinas central for this purpose—than was commonly achieved among Latin thinkers;[1] and though the later moderns, most specifically Charles Sanders Peirce in his semiotic writings and, on the British side (though to a *much* lesser extent), Bertrand Russell, did indeed achieve an understanding of relation approaching the sophistication necessary, no one before Poinsot or since Maritain has actually brought the understanding of relation directly to bear upon the thing/object distinction, till now. And without that bearing, there is no chance whatever of getting much beyond nominalism in discussing the thing/object distinction, as became clear in the writings of John Poinsot cast aside by modernity.

In short, Poinsot, more than anyone among the Latins, points the way to the possibility of actually explaining the thing-object distinction, and Maritain more than anyone among the moderns points to the desperate need for such an explanation. But the explanation is not to be found either by going back to the Latins or by searching among the moderns, down to their dying breath. The explanation, if it is to be given, then, will be perforce a *postmodern* accounting, as we shall see.

"Objectivity" as a Modern Development

In the matter of relation, the modern development has been bedeviled throughout by Ockham's claim that there are no relations in the order of *ens reale,* only in thought through comparisons among objects made by the mind. Against this background, we have Descartes' equation of objects with ideas, an equation affirmed also by Locke, though shifting his emphasis from ideas of reason to ideas of sense. And on this common modern assumption that all objects are self-representations formed by

1. Poinsot's report in the first two articles of his second preamble, "On Relation," for his *Tractatus de signis*, trans. and ed. by John Deely in collaboration with Ralph Austin Powell (Berkeley: University of California Press, 1985) shows the utter chaos surrounding the usage of this term among the Latin authors, including the would-be followers of Thomas (e.g., article 1, page 80, line 12, through page 81, line 44; article 2, page 89, line 24, through page 91, line 28, and again page 93, line 17, through page 96, line 36).

the mind, we have Kant's synthesis of post-Cartesian "Rationalism" with post-Lockean "Empiricism," distinguishing *objects* as vessels of necessity, such as is required for the success of thought scientific in the modern sense, from subjective ideas as no more than *founding* the relation to objects, wherein alone reason achieves its distinctive awareness and mastery.

Thus Kant accomplishes a successful replacement of the subjective idealism of his modern predecessors with his own objective idealism, and it is this notion of "objectivity" as *the way things must be for thought become sufficiently aware* that has descended into common speech by the time modernity in philosophy reached the twentieth century. Of course, the "elephant in the room" throughout this later, "objective" modern development was Kant's accompanying doctrine: that objectivity does not concern the things in themselves, because it can't, things in themselves being unknowable. But this central tenet of the Kantian system is so obnoxious and impractical in its application that only a very few, as Bertrand Russell noted,[2] even in philosophy, respect its implications. Whence the "objective" in common speech—"natural language," as is said in some linguistic circles—has come to mean not merely what must be thought by the scientific observer, but more simply *the way things are* once all individual bias—all "subjective opinion"—has been overcome and set aside.

The authority of *The New Oxford American Dictionary* shows well just how deeply sedimented this modern understanding of objectivity has become since the halcyon days of Descartes' *Discourse on Method* and *Meditations on First Philosophy.* Something is "objective," this dictionary tells us, when it is "not dependent on the mind for existence"; when it is "actual." And persons are "objective" when their judgment is "not influenced by personal feelings or opinions."[3]

Whence this authoritative work identifies this word "objective" as in binary opposition to "subjective," by which is meant, we are told,[4] anything "dependent on the mind or an individual's perception for its existence"; anything "based on or influenced by personal feelings, tastes, or opinion"—which has to mean, of course, everything actually experienced!

2. For the majority, he considered, prefer more sentiment of their fellows than logic of their philosophers, particularly when that logic (as in the case of modern "critical philosophy" or "epistemology") entails solipsism; see Bertrand Russell, *My Philosophical Development* (New York: Simon and Schuster, 1959), 25–26 and *passim.*

3. Elizabeth Jewell and Frank Abate, eds., *The New Oxford American Dictionary,* 1st ed. (Oxford University Press, 2001), 1180.

4. Ibid., 1694.

So we are not surprised to find that an "object," when it is not "a goal or purpose," is, for philosophy, "a thing external to the thinking mind or subject" (the famous modern "external world," of course—unknowable anyway, according to Kant, except as to the bare fact of its existence), and, more specifically, as also for modern common-sense usage, an object is "a material thing that can be seen and touched." All this derived, we are told, "from medieval Latin *objectum* 'thing presented to the mind,' itself a nominative usage derived from the Latin verb '*obicere*,' from *ob-*, 'in the way of,' and *jacere*, 'to throw.'"

So what do we learn from this consultation with one of the latest of English dictionaries? Pretty much what any late modern speaker of English intuitively (by reason of the habit structure of the language at this historical juncture) already "knows," namely, that there is practically no such thing as "objective thought," and that "object" and "thing" are pretty much synonyms, being two ways of saying the same.

What interests me in all this is that this established common usage of the terms "object" and "subject," with their derivatives, is the outcome of three centuries of modern thought, wherein philosophy thought to distinguish so-called "epistemology" from "ontology" in order to show that the former alone could establish the foundations for human knowledge from purely within the knowing subject. In taking this turn, modern philosophy and the current usage of the terms "subject" and "object" it sedimented in "ordinary language" did not "derive from" the Latin usage, but rather *dissociated itself* from the Latin medieval development, which itself was far from complete in this area of the understanding of human knowledge, but which was definitively moving in an opposite direction from the turn modernity took in and after the work of, first, Ockham, as above mentioned, and then, more decisively, Descartes and Locke, "synthesized by Kant."[5]

"Objectivity" at the End of Latin Times

In the medieval understanding, far from being independent of finite mind, an "object" to be such had to be something present or presented to mind, whether or not it was (in addition to existing within awareness) a thing not dependent upon the mind for existing in its own right, that is, subjectively or intersubjectively (in the case of categorial relations) in the order of *ens reale*. Thus the later Latins, in contrast with the later mod-

5. But on the basis of an unexamined common assumption, as noted above.

erns, had an "intuitive" grasp of the difference between a thing, *aliquid* or *res,* which exists whether or not anyone is aware of it, and an object, *objectum,* which cannot be as object outside of or apart from awareness. In fact, they were quite explicit about this. Every object, they had come to hold, as object, is either *also ens reale* (a mind-independent being) *as well as* an object, *only* an object (which is the fullest meaning of "*ens rationis*" or mind-dependent being), or (more commonly), objectivity is *an admixture* of *entia realia* and *entia rationis.*[6]

Now this Latin Age or "medieval" understanding of the distinction between object and thing is clearly far from complete. It remained far from something established in principle and fully thought through, although things were fast moving in that direction when the whole Latin Scholastic and Aristotelian tradition came a-cropper over the case of Galileo, the case where the difference in principle between object and thing could hardly be more crucial or complete, yet never came to be viewed in that light. The reverberations and irony of the "Galileo affair" will no doubt continue as long as earthlings continue to inquire into the affairs of nature and culture. But that it involved centrally a matter of relations makes no small part of its importance for intellectual culture, as I hope here shortly to show.

So, as usual in postmodern affairs, there can be no question of a simple "going back to" or "restoration of" an earlier standpoint in the question before us. No. The medieval development of the distinction between objects and things, as I say, was far from completely worked through. At the time of Poinsot, Galileo's contemporary and author of the first systematic *Treatise on Signs,* which demonstrated the unified subject matter of semiotic inquiry, it was only beginning to emerge that "object" is a synonym for "significate" (*signatum seu significatum*), such that to say something is an "object" or to say that something is an "object signified" is to say the same thing. This is exactly what I mean in speaking of the *unmasking* of objectivity: seeing the objective for what it is, as *neither* opposed to subjectivity *nor* ever in principle wholly reducible to the status of things, *but always and throughout presupposing "semiosis,"* the peculiar, indirect sort of "causality" that has come to be known as "semiosis," or the action of signs.[7]

6. See Poinsot, *Tractatus de signis,* 48/1–49/26.

7. See Poinsot's *Tractatus de signis,* esp. book 1, question 5, "Whether to signify, formally considered, is to cause something in the order of productive causality?" 166–92; and, *inter alia,* John Deely, "How Do Signs Work?" in *New Beginnings: Early Modern Philosophy*

The Singularity of Relation: Three Steps to Its Recognition

The most advanced discussion of the thing/object distinction in that development of philosophy called the "mediaeval period" or, more accurately, the Latin Age, is very likely what is to be gathered from John Poinsot's 1632 *Tractatus de signis,* with its first preamble on *ens rationis,* or mind-dependent being, and second preamble on relation.[8] It is no coincidence in this matter that this work of Poinsot, *Tractatus de signis,* is also the first to latch on to the singularity of relation already identified by Aquinas,[9] albeit somewhat obscurely,[10] but now to realize the central role of relation in making full sense of the thing/object distinction as involving an action of signs.

Where, then, according to this late Latin tradition, do we find objectivity in its most irreducibly distinctive condition, so to say, in its *purest form?* Not at all in the "external world," as modernity has accustomed us to think. Poinsot's answer is quite straightforward and to the contrary, hence somewhat surprising for modern ears accustomed to understanding objectivity as "the way things are," apart from all subjective biases. What depends upon the human understanding as object, Poinsot tells us,[11] is above all what needs to have *no existence whatever* independently of the understanding, and what is objective in this sense stands in contrast to the whole order of mind-independent being, which is never more than partially objective, even when it is cognized or known in its own right—that is to say, in its character as mind-independent. Thus Poinsot contrasts purely objective reality with the subjective and inter-

---

and Postmodern Thought (Toronto: University of Toronto Press, 1994), 151–82; and Deely, "The Full Vista of the Action of Signs," in *Basics of Semiotics,* 5th expanded ed. (Tartu, Estonia: Tartu University Press, 2009), 233–75, esp. sect. 4.3, 261–69.

8. As typical of his time, Poinsot's treatment of relation is primarily focused on the order of *ens reale.* He is careful to note that Thomas uses the expression *relatio secundum esse* not simply as a synonym for *relatio praedicamentalis seu realis,* but rather to identify the *singularity* of relation wherein it alone has a positive essence or being equally verifiable when it is *ens reale* and when it is *ens rationis,* indeed; yet not until he actually undertakes to establish the standpoint of its own required by semiotics in book I, question 1, of his *Tractatus de signis,* does he explicitly underline the *sharp contrast* of this standpoint to the preoccupations heretofore of Latin tradition: see esp. 117/20–118/18, esp. 118/7–18.

9. Aquinas 1266: *Summa theologiae, prima pars,* question 28, article 1.

10. See Poinsot's survey of discussion on this point in his *Tractatus de signis,* second preamble, article 2, page 93, line 16, through page 96, line 36.

11. "Quod autem secundo modo ab intellectu dependet, scilicet ut obiectum, dicitur proprie ens rationis, ut pertinet ad praesens, quia nullum esse habet extra rationem, sed solum obiective dicitur esse in ipsa, et sic opponitur enti reali" (*Tractatus de signis,* 48/17–22).

subjective realities that *wholly* constitute the order of *ens reale*, but only *partially* the order of *ens rationis*.

It is in this way that he approaches the sign—or rather, and more exactly,[12] it is in this way that he says the sign *must* or *has to be* approached if there is to be any hope of coming to understand how signs succeed in their distinctive work. We need to understand how the sign as an instrument or tool of knowledge works within our experience to lead us through the entire world of what is or can be known, and so permeates the objective order in its entirety, the realm of falsehoods as well as truths, the realm of reality that is socially constructed no less than what is hardcore, giving us access to *ens reale*, yes, but no less also to *ens rationis*, to objective realities lacking subjective counterpart, as is not the case with objective realities in the order of *ens reale* (although we can well be mistaken about what *actually does* belong to *ens reale*, as anyone falsely convicted of a crime can tell you—at least, before they are executed for the non-deed).

And just how is it that signs can lead us "everywhere in nature, even where humans have never set foot," as a later semiotician summarized?[13] Because, Poinsot tells us, they *consist* in their *proper and formal being* of *relations*, and relations alone among all the forms of being identified by Aristotle in his list of the categories or types of *ens reale* (or τὸ ὄν, as he called it, the thematic distinction between *ens reale* and *ens rationis* not yet having been drawn in his time). Not that all relations *eo ipso* are sign relations, for relations can be merely dyadic as well as triadic, while relations of sign perforce are always triadic; but that is a further story, and the point here simply is that triadic relations to be relations exhibit the *suprasubjectivity* that we will see is the defining feature of *relatio secundum esse* and the reason for the *singularity* of relation among the modes of being, as we shall also see.

The First Step toward Recognizing the Singularity of Relation

Relation *does not belong under a division between being in se and being in alio.*

This is a stunning point to grasp, the more so when we consider that it has not been grasped at all to speak of over the entire history of philosophy, from the time Aristotle first drew up his "list" of catego-

12. Poinsot, *Tractatus de signis*, 118/1–18.

13. Claus Emmeche, *The Garden in the Machine* (Princeton, N.J.: Princeton University Press, 1994), 126.

ries to the twentieth-century end of modern times. Indeed, the problem begins with Aristotle himself, the first to thematize the notion of relation as constituting an irreducible category or type of being. It took him three tries,[14] and even when he finally got it right, he blurred his own point by burying relation's irreducible difference in foregrounding the division of subjective being into "categories" as either substance, *ens in se,* or accident, *ens in alio.*

But relation is not itself an *ens in alio.* It depends upon an *ens in alio,* yes, as the foundation or ground upon which it rests and from which it provenates, but it *is not* an *ens in alio.* It is—and it alone is—an *ens ad aliud,* a being toward or between another than the individual substance upon whose accidents (whose intrinsic or inherent characteristics) the relation depends. As *ens reale*—relation is neither in itself nor in another (as Aristotle's opening distinction to present the list of categories tacitly implies and historically has [mis]led the majority of his readers to consider). To the contrary, relation in its being as relation is over and above the substances it links and obtains invisibly *between* them, not *in* either one of them. Relation is, as later authors would say, when they did not wind up denying the distinctive reality of relations as distinct from their *inesse* fundaments or grounds, an *intersubjective* mode of being, over and above the subjects of existence that it links—without realizing that, in speaking this way, just as to begin the discussion with the *in se/in alio* substance/accident distinction buries and hides the *uniqueness* of relation among the categories, so, too, calling relation "intersubjective" is to background and hide from view the *singularity* of relation as an *ens reale* vis-à-vis *ens rationis.*

Thus the first correction called for in the traditional presentation of the categories of *ens reale*—namely, to bring the uniqueness of relation in that order out from behind the subjective division of being into substance and accident, and to foreground instead the contrast between subjective and intersubjective being, all the while maintaining in that very foreground the double dependency that relation has—which is why St. Thomas identified it as *ens minimum* in the order of finite *ens reale*—not only upon substance, but also upon the characteristics of substance as existing in this or that way—is crucial, yes, but no more than a *first*

14. The detailed story in the Greek texts is told in Deely, the "Editorial Afterword," subsection "The Secundum Dici–Secundum Esse Couplet: The Fundamental Architecture of the Treatise on Signs," in *Tractatus de Signis: The Semiotic of John Poinsot,* edited and translated by John Deely, 472–79, esp. the Greek text in nn.112–14 (Berkeley: University of California Press, 1985); this is the bilingual critical edition of Poinsot 1632.

FIGURE 1 **The Categories of *Ens Reale***

- being
  - toward or between (*ad esse*)
  - in (*inesse*)
    - another (*esse in alio*, accident)
    - itself (substance, *esse in se*)

LINE OF DEPENDENCY in finite being, of relations upon inherent attributes or accidents, and of inherent accidents upon substances

step. At least that first step can be achieved with a simple diagram, replacing the "being in itself/being in another" traditional starting point for discussing *ens reale* with a "being in/being toward" initial distinction, as in figure 1 above.

The Second Step toward Recognizing the Singularity of Relation

The paths of non-being interweave with those of being.

With this first step we see already the justice of Ratzinger's claim that "the undivided sway of thinking in terms of substance is ended; relation is discovered as an equally valid primordial mode of reality."[15] That is quite an important step, indeed, but, as already mentioned, it is only a *first* step, one that clarifies the status of relation in the order of *ens reale,* but that still requires at least two steps further fully to bring out the *singularity* of relation vis-à-vis the *ens reale/ens rationis* divide. Let us move on to step two.

Aquinas pointed out (only to be largely ignored upon the point in the twentieth-century fixation of Neothomism upon "realism"—i.e., the ability of human understanding to come to know things as they are in their subjective constitution, apart from our relation to them in awareness) that "being as first known" by the human intellect (*ens primum cognitum*) is not simply *ens reale* but an irreducible admixture of *something* of *ens reale* (far from the whole of it), objectified only in part through sensations, and *ens rationis* added to sensations in order to present the surrounding environment (so far as we are aware of it within animal awareness), *organized* as objects to be sought, avoided, or safely ignored.[16]

15. Joseph Ratzinger, *Introduction to Christianity,* trans. J. R. Foster (New York: Herder and Herder, 1970), 132.

16. For details of this initial concept-formation in the zoösemiosis of animals (human and brute indifferently according to Aquinas), see John Deely, *Intentionality and Semiotics: A*

Little realized is the fact that, for Aquinas, *ens rationis* in this distinction under *ens primum cognitum* is a synonym for nonbeing, non *ens;* and Maritain has said that the failure among followers of Thomas today to realize this point has made of them "Cyclopeans,"[17] would-be philosophers who have only an eye for *ens reale,* thus failing to see that the reality of experience involves nonbeing no less fundamentally, that "the paths of non-being, once one has, by a kind of inverted intuition, become conscious of it and of its formidable role in reality, are as difficult as those of being."[18] Thus the question of signs and objectivity concerns not only being, but nonbeing as well—and even, to some extent, *equally*—given the human animal's proneness to hasty judgments and outright mistakes, as the witches of Salem along with many of their kin in Europe before them learned the hard way.

Among the Latins there were many and complex discussions about the divisions or types of *ens rationis* within objectivity, but Aquinas argued that an exclusive and exhaustive division of *ens rationis* could be made on the basis of whether the experienced *ens realis,* after or upon which an *ens rationis* is formed, belongs to the *ens reale* category of *inesse* or *adesse:* if the former, then the *ens rationis,* being what its pattern is not, is a *negation;* if the latter, then the *ens rationis,* being what its pattern also is, is a *relation.* Poinsot's analysis of this very point, however, goes on to reveal an even more important underlying point: Just as Descartes' emphasis on ideas of reason in contrast to Locke's emphasis on ideas of sense should not allow us to overlook (as did apparently Kant) the more fundamental point that both agree on in identifying the direct objects of experience with ideas or mental representations, just so Aquinas' emphasis on the difference in the patterns after which animal awareness forms *entia rationis* should not make us overlook the more fundamen-

---

Story of Mutual Fecundation (Scranton, Penn.: University of Scranton Press, 2007); and Deely, "Animal Intelligence and Concept-Formation" (fourth reading), in *Realism for the 21st Century: A John Deely Reader,* ed. Paul Cobley (Scranton, Penn.: University of Scranton Press, 2009).

17. Jacques Maritain, *God and the Permission of Evil* (Milwaukee: Bruce, 1966), 32.

18. Precisely here is the place where semiotics assimilates the ethical insights of Emmanuel Levinas (*Autrement qu'être ou au-dela de l'essence* [The Hague: Nijhoff, 1974]) that, in Susan Petrilli's summary ("On Communication," *American Journal of Semiotics* 24 [2008]: 203), "the being of social communication has an *otherwise than being,*" where "being" means *ens reale,* and "otherwise than being" means, above all, the element of *ens rationis* essential to the constitution of every Umwelt in its difference from the physical environment; see now "The Ethical Entailment of Semiotic Animal, or the Need to Develop a Semioethics," in John Deely, *Semiotic Animal* (South Bend, Ind.: St Augustine's Press, 2010), 107–25.

tal point that (if negations and relations exhaust the possible varieties of nonbeing) *all entia rationis without exception* consist in a *being-patterned-after,* and so have as their positive essence or being one and the same *esse ad,* which sets intersubjective being apart from the varieties of subjective being in the order of *ens reale,* but does yet fail to set relation as relation (*relatio secundum esse*) apart from *ens rationis.*[19] In short, "intersubjective," while accurate and adequate to describe relation as an *ens reale,* a "categorical" or "predicamental" mode of being, is insufficient to describe the fact that every relation, whether *ens reale* or *ens rationis,* is always suprasubjective, regardless of whether or not it is intersubjective; for the "being intersubjective" of relations depends upon surrounding circumstances external to the being of relation as such, while the "being suprasubjective" is a characteristic without which there is no relation at all, as Aquinas and Poinsot say, "secundum esse". The order of *ens rationis,* in short, consists of relations and nothing else besides relations, while the order of *ens reale* consists of relations, yes, but not only of relations, and not of relations most fundamentally, but rather of substances—of individuals with their individual characteristics upon which relations, all relations, including those consequent upon interactions no less than those invented by the animal to orientate itself in a world of objects,[20] depend for their being.

The Final Step in Recognizing the Singularity of Relation

The main story of relation goes beyond intersubjectivity.

This brings us four-square before what is different about relations within *ens primum cognitum* as the formal object distinguishing human understanding from the estimative powers and imaginations of other animals: in recognizing the difference between being and nonbeing, between what reduces to our experience of it (like the boundaries between states) and what transcends our experience of it (like the connection between smoke and burning), the human animal tacitly recognizes not only the reality of things, but also the difference between relations and what (objects or things) is related. Thus the last step in recognizing

19. Deely, *Purely Objective Reality* (Berlin: Mouton de Gruyter, 2010).

20. Here again we encounter a revolutionary point in the *Tractatus* of Poinsot, the explicit recognition that, while brute animals cannot cognize relations in their distinction from things related, they nonetheless depend in their behavior upon *relatio utens,* that is, on forming *relationes rationis* in order to organize their world of experience; see Poinsot, *Tractatus de signis,* First Preamble, article 3, "By what powers and through which acts do mind-dependent beings come about?" 65–76, esp. 66/46–68/35.

the singularity of relations is the first step toward recognizing the being proper to signs and the action uniquely consequent thereon, yes, and in that sense also is the first step toward the rational animal becoming more fully the semiotic animal,[21] with all the consequences for a global human responsibility "without excuses" that that awareness will entail.

But what is decisive for our purposes is the recognition that is now possible of the fact that *intersubjectivity is not enough* to characterize or define the being proper and singular to relation. For intersubjective relations depend wholly upon the subjects that they are between existing, and hence those relations themselves come and go with the individuals related. Yet mind-dependent relations, relations that are *entia rationis* from the start, or that once were *entia realia* but (by reason of changed circumstances) are so no longer, relations without which an animal could not orient itself within its environment in order to hunt down prey and find its way "home," may or may not be intersubjective; and even when they are not they remain as relations *suprasubjective.*

The Singularity of Relation Recognized

So we see then full-blown, as it were, the *singularity* of relation: relation is the *only* form or mode of being that is verified in its positive and proper "essence" or ontological structure, *both* in the order of *ens reale and* in the order of *ens rationis;* so that *one and the same relation*, as Poinsot puts it, can be verified under one set of circumstances as an *ens reale* and under another set of circumstances (a changed set of circumstances) as an *ens rationis*. When Heidegger asked in 1930, "How is it possible for there to be a correspondence between thought and things? What is the prior possibility for truth as correspondence?"[22] he was pointing us in the very direction of having to realize the singularity of relation as capable, essence unchanged, to be one-time real being and one-time nonbeing within the experience of human animals, according to circumstance.

While it is the singularity of relation, then, positively to exist in the order of being as *ens reale* and in the order of nonbeing as *ens rationis,* in-

21. See John Deely, Susan Petrilli, and Augusto Ponzio, *The Semiotic Animal* (Ottawa: Legas Publishing, 2005); Deely, "Defining the Semiotic Animal: A Postmodern Definition of Human Being Superseding the Modern Definition "Res Cogitans,'" *American Catholic Philosophical Quarterly* 79 (2005): 461–81; and Deely, *Semiotic Animal* (2010).

22. Martin Heidegger, *Vom Wesen der Wahrheit* (Frankfurt: Vittorio Klostermann, 1954; actual composition 1930); see the English translation by R. F. C. Hull and Alan Crick, "On the Essence of Truth," in *Existence and Being,* ed. Werner Brock (Chicago: Gateway, 1949), 292–324.

tersubjective in the first case whether or not also objective, suprasubjective in the second case and always functioning objectively in the structuring of the objects of awareness as transcending things, yet it is the functioning of relation throughout the order of objectivity, both insofar as it contains something of *ens reale* and insofar as it transcends that order in rendering the physical surrounding *meaningful* to the particular type of animal species inhabiting a given ecological niche, that is crucial for the understanding of objectivity. In a word, as we will now go on to see, relation is decisive for the understanding of objectivity precisely because the singularity of relation is what makes semiosis possible in the first place—the singularity of relation (as Heidegger might put it) alone constitutes directly the basis for the prior possibility of an action of signs, which in turn births the order of "being as objective" and the possibility of a conformity or coincidence of thought with things, while yet transcending their subjective limitations.

Objectivity Unmasked: The Postmodern Understanding

Having seen the modern understanding of what is "objective," and having contrasted that understanding with the understanding of the Latin Age, we are now in a position perhaps to pick up the loose threads of the discussion overall and to fashion or weave therefrom an integral understanding of what objectivity is that can not only overcome the antinomies of the modern understanding, but can even for the first time thematically clarify the notion in a way that has the possibility of changing over time even the common usage of the term as it has become miserably sedimented in natural language from the perverse, almost antisemiotic (Sebeok called it "cryptosemiotic") turn that modern philosophy took in its needlessly but understandably—sickened at the fate suffered by Bruno, Galileo, and others at the hands of the "scholastic masters" in concert with their religious authorities in scripture and theology—extreme break with the Latin Age.[23]

The Distinguishing Feature of Relation Determining the Difference between Objects and Things

We will oversimplify things a little, but not a lot, if we say that, as far as human experience goes, the difference between objects and things is that, in general, objects are but things are not necessarily involved in a re-

23. Deely, *Medieval Philosophy Redefined* (Scranton, Penn.: University of Scranton Press, 2010), esp. chap. 9, "The Crash and Burn of Scholasticism, c.1600–1650," 381–84.

lation to a finite knower. Now a relation in relation to the case of a knower is not a complicated form or mode of being to dissect prescissively: (1) there is the subjective element or aspect of the cognizant individual (its "accidental" feature or features) upon which the relation is founded; (2) there is the relation itself, which is over and above the subjectivity of the individual related; and (3) there is the terminus itself of the relation, that at which the relation the relation terminates in the other related.

Thus when we say in general (allowing for exceptions in particular cases) that an object is necessarily while a thing is not necessarily involved in a relation to a knower, we have only to decide in which position it is that the object as object stands: is it the foundation, or the relation itself, or the terminus of the relation? And it should not be hard to decide that, when we say an object is necessarily involved in a relation with a cognizing subject, we are saying that an object as such is always the *terminus* of the cognitive relation, not the relation itself nor the fundament (the subjective ground) upon which the relation depends.

And here we have to note a subtle but important point that is not generally considered (at least not in any literature on the subject of relation familiar to me)—namely this: it is the existence of the relation itself that makes a fundament to be a fundament and a terminus to be a terminus, which is somewhat surprising, but may be shown as follows. Take the case of a categorial relation, a relation in Aristotle's sense of an intersubjective connection or link between two subjects, two individual "substances"—two triangular-shaped entities, let us say, that are "similar" to one another on the basis of their shape. The shape of A founds a relation of similarity that terminates at B in its triangularity, and conversely. Now let us suppose that B is destroyed. A is no longer similar to B, for there is no B to be similar to. Yet note this: the *shape* of A in its subjectivity has not been in any way affected by the destruction of B, yet that shape *is no longer either a fundament or a terminus of a relation.*

The point is quite general: a fundament *qua* fundament and a terminus *qua* terminus, whatever may be its subjective status or being in the order of *ens reale* as an inherent accident of an individual, can be a fundament or a terminus as long and only as long as the relation itself exists; and, in the order of *ens reale,* mind-independent being, the relation can exist as long and only as long as *both* of the individuals related, the related subjects, also exist. That is the distinguishing feature of relation as intersubjective, as we have seen, but it is not the distinguishing feature of relation simply as relation.

The distinguishing feature of relation as relation is *supra*subjectivity, whether or not it is *also inter*subjective. A relation as *adesse* has to be suprasubjective, and it *can* (if circumstances allow) but *need not* be intersubjective as well. Intersubjectivity is essential not for relation as *adesse,* but only for relation to belong to the order of *ens reale,* for relation as a mind-independent being here and now. Every relation in a given respect is *either* mind-independent *or* mind-dependent, yes, but *which* a given relation may be here and now is not determined by the being proper to relation, but wholly and only by the *circumstances* under which the relation here and now obtains.

The Psychological Source of Intentionality Respecting Objectivity

Here we come up against the distinctive feature of intentionality: a psychological state (this is true of cathectic no less than of cognitive states, to be sure; but let us not be distracted, and for the moment confine our consideration to the cognitive states) differs from a physiological condition of the body in that the psychological state, unlike the physiological state, *cannot exist except* as giving rise to a relation as such—that is to say, to relation as suprasubjective, whether or not it be also intersubjective; and this unavoidable relation in turn makes the subjective psychological state, on the one side, to be the *fundament* of the cognitive relation, and gives rise on the other side to a *terminus* of that same cognitive relation, and it is precisely this terminus that we call an object.

Now think back on the matter of a categorial relation, a relation obtaining under conditions that make the relation belong to the order of *ens reale,* of mind-independent being. In that order of being (rather plainly), nothing prevents a terminus from *also* being a subjective feature of being, an element existing as *ens reale.* In fact, even when the thing to which some other thing is here and now mind-independently related terminates the relation in one or another of its features, that terminus is not only "also" a subjective feature of being, it is *necessarily also* a subjective feature of being, not as terminus simply, to be sure, but as terminus *of a relation in the order of ens reale.*

Thus, while a terminus as terminus depends on there being here and now a relation, nothing precludes or prevents that a terminus as terminus be *more than* a terminus, that a terminus be *also* a subjective element or feature of *ens reale.* Nothing requires it, and nothing prevents it—nothing on the part of the relation itself, that is, as *adesse, but* only on the part of the relation as belonging to the order of *ens reale:* and that is up to the circumstances alone.

And this is true no less when the relation in question happens to be a *cognitive* relation. In that case, the terminus as terminus is always an object, but nothing prevents it from being *more than* a mere object; nothing prevents the object from *also* being or *further* being a thing that does not depend upon being an object in order to be. But nothing in the relation as suprasubjective *requires* it, either.

So again, in this case of the cognitive relation, since the psychological state upon or from which the cognitive relation depends and provenates cannot be without giving rise to that relation suprasubjective respecting the idea or cognitive fundament, neither in turn can that cognitive relation exist without giving rise to the third of the three elements or factors necessary for any relation, namely, a terminus—in this case an *objective* terminus, that is to say, a terminus of which the animal cognizing has some awareness: and this, note carefully, whether the object in question here and now *also* has a subjective existence in *ens reale* or *only* has an objective existence—a purely objective existence in that case, note—as terminating the relation in *ens rationis.*

We see, then, in a sense for the first time, how and why an object can be public regardless of its reality: because it always if not only in awareness terminates a suprasubjective mode of being. It may do more. It may terminate as an intersubjective mode of being. But this is not owing to its positive and distinctive, let alone its singular, being as a relation, but owing to the circumstances of its provenation.

Completing the Unmasking

To complete the unmasking of objectivity there remains only to show that every object as such is a significate, a "product" of the action of signs.[24] Not only are objects not merely things "said another way," but to say "object signified" is actually a redundancy, for there is no other kind of object than that of something signified.

Let me emphasize this point as firmly as I can. Once it becomes clear that "all thought is in signs" (the realization first formulated by

24. I place the word "product" here in quotation marks because, strictly speaking, a product is usually the result of Secondness, efficient causality, whereas the action of signs is not in that order mainly, but rather in the order of Thirdness as a formal causality extrinsic to whatever things are involved in a physical interaction at the time of the semiosis; see Deely, "How Does Semiosis Effect Renvoi?" the Thomas A. Sebeok Fellowship Inaugural Lecture from October 22, 1993, published in *The American Journal of Semiotics* 11 (1994): 11–61.

Poinsot's teachers, the Conimbricenses, but credit for which these days[25] is assigned customarily to Peirce),[26] it becomes further clear that all objects are objects signified, or, to suppress the redundancy, that all objects are significates. Not all *things* are significates, but all *objects* are. In other words, to say "significate" is to say clearly what "object" says obscurely and confusedly—and in the late modern habits of English usage sedimented from modern philosophy, perhaps, not at all.

Now that is a point that I do not believe has ever been made before, but is a point that, unless and until it be made, the way to understanding thematically the object/thing distinction remains effectively barricaded.

It is quite interesting that, in modern English, there was early considerable resistance to the entry of the term "significate" into the dictionary as a legitimate item of common usage. In fact, in the authority I am using for the present writing, "significate" is still not an entry at all.[27] Yet—so I hope to have shown—significate is a synonym of the correct understanding of object, saying clearly what the latter term has said all along mutely, as it were, for only in the most obscure fashion. (So the resistance to the term "significate" among the modern English makers of dictionaries provides a kind of index pointing to how far off the way of signs the mainstream of modern philosophy carried the English-speaking peoples, as national language traditions carried peoples of the post-Latin age generally.)

In Summary and Conclusion

The road to the postmodern understanding of objectivity as, quite simply, whatever exists as apprehended or "known," has been a long and winding one. The human animal awoke to the awareness that there are signs only fitfully and with many distractions.

In the world of ancient Greece, thinkers saw signs only in nature and in the divination of mysteries bordering or thought to border upon the supernatural. With Augustine they awakened to the fact that any

25. The early postmoderns generally have a long way to go in shriving the antihistorical attitude and consciousness of the late moderns, particularly those influenced by inhabitants of that house of cards known as "analytic philosophy."

26. John P. Doyle, ed. and trans., *The Conimbricenses: Some Questions on Signs* (Milwaukee, Wisc.: Marquette University Press), question 2, article 3 (bilingual critical edition of *Conimbricenses 1607*); see also Peirce, "Questions concerning Certain Faculties Claimed for Man," *Journal of Speculative Philosophy* 2 (1868): 103–14, as reprinted in *The Collected Papers of Charles Sanders Peirce*, vol. 5, para. 213–63; and Poinsot, *Tractatus de signis* (1632), book 2, question 2, 240/1–253/37, and question 5, esp. 271/28–35.

27. *New Oxford American Dictionary*, 1, 588.

material object can and does become a sign rather quickly in the course of experience, once it has entered that path as a known thing.[28] Much more slowly, after Aquinas and Roger Bacon,[29] did they make their way to realizing that psychological states too, and not only material objects, are vehicles of significations, and are so even more fundamentally than material objects can become signs, for unlike material things, ideas or concepts within the mind do not need first to become objects in order to function as signs.

With the Conimbricenses and their star pupil, Poinsot, the Latins realized near the end of their time that what makes *anything* be a sign is not directly its subjective constitution, but rather its occupation of the foreground position of representing another than itself to or for some third, so that, strictly speaking, anything visible or tangible or audible that we *call* a sign is in reality but the vehicle of a signification that consists, formally and strictly, not in anything directly sensible at all, but always and only in a triadic relation, connecting in one single unity sign vehicle, significate, and interpretant.

This last term, interpretant (as distinguished from an interpreter),[30] comes not from the Latins, but from Charles Peirce, the last of the moderns and first of the postmoderns,[31] the first to pick up from the Latins the threads of semiotic consciousness they had so carefully woven[32] with their arguments and analyses that first compelled the conclusion that signs strictly and formally are not particular things at all, but the triadic relationships, suprasubjective like all relationships, and hence participating in the singularity by which relation alone transcends all subjective and intersubjective divisions of *ens reale* to constitute an objective world that includes something of, but never wholly reduces to, the order of things as *ens reale*.

Reality, too, is a word, and we have to learn that it includes what has

28. Deely, *Augustine and Poinsot: The Protosemiotic Development* (Scranton, Penn.: University of Scranton Press, 2009).

29. Deely, "The Role of Thomas Aquinas in the Development of Semiotic Consciousness," *Semiotica* 152 (2004): 75–139; and Deely, "The Semiosis of Angels," *The Thomist* 68, no. 2 (April 2004): 205–58.

30. Deely, "Peirce's Grand Vision," in *Peirce's Doctrine of Signs,* edited by Vincent M. Colapietro and Thomas M. Olshewsky, 45–67 (Berlin: Mouton de Gruyter, 1996). See also "Physiosemiosis and Phytosemiosis," in any edition of Deely, *Basics of Semiotics.*

31. Deely, *Four Ages of Understanding: The First Postmodern Survey of Philosophy from Ancient Times to the Turn of the Twenty-First Century* (University of Toronto Press, 2001), chap. 15.

32. See Mauricio Beuchot and John Deely, "Common Sources for the Semiotic of Charles Peirce and John Poinsot," in *Review of Metaphysics* 48 (1995): 539–66.

subjective and intersubjective existence without necessarily relating to a finite knower. And so is objectivity, too, a word, and we may say that we have finally learned that an object is something only insofar as it presupposes the action of signs that make of it, even when it is also a thing, more than a thing. For not every thing presupposes a sign, but every object does.[33] And it is only thus that Hamlet and Napoleon, witches and bitches, Olympian gods and Allah, are equally objective, however unequal they may be as things "in themselves."

33. Deely, "A Sign Is *What?*" (presidential address to the Semiotic Society of America's 26th Annual Meeting), *Sign Systems Studies* 29 (2001): 705–43; reprinted as "Dramatic Reading in Three Voices: 'A Sign Is *What?*'" *American Journal of Semiotics* 20 (2004): 1–66; also "How Does Semiosis Effect Renvoi?" referenced in note 22 above, reprinted in Deely, *New Beginnings: Early Modern Philosophy and Postmodern Thought* (Toronto: University of Toronto Press, 1994), 201–44.

PART 3

THEMES IN THE SPIRIT OF KENNETH L. SCHMITZ

John C. McCarthy

17. SEEING THE UNSEEN

It was as an undergraduate student that I incurred my first debts to Kenneth Schmitz. In the years since, my obligations to him have steadily mounted, and in ways that I could not possibly have anticipated on that bright September afternoon, now decades ago, when I found myself sitting in a wood-paneled classroom at Trinity College, the University of Toronto, as he outlined the task of the semester ahead: a reading of the *Critique of Pure Reason*. The course had been highly recommended by friends, as was its sequel, an introduction to the *Phenomenology of Spirit*. In conformity with the anglophilic observances prevailing at Trinity, Professor Schmitz sported an academic robe while he lectured. His was rather threadbare, as I recall, and lightly dusted with chalk. It thereby lent to the proceedings an air of easy and unruffled sobriety at equal remove from the College's ritual attachment to the old forms and our dogmatically uncertain rejection of them. Certainly there was nothing in the least theatrical about his performance. His lucidity as an expositor, and the depth of learning that marked his engagement with those demanding works, were quite sufficient to make the year's experience an exhilarating one. What most impressed me about his approach to the titans of German idealism was something else, however. Someone had told me that he had begun his studies as a medievalist, under the tutelage of the great Étienne Gilson. And from occasional remarks he made during the course of his lectures I thought I could glimpse something of his ongoing allegiance, so to say, to the thought of Thomas Aquinas. It was perfectly clear, nevertheless—I adopt the adversative conjunction that seemed to me appropriate at the time—that his overriding purpose was to introduce us to the thought of Kant and Hegel in a genuinely critical fashion, which is to say, sympathetically, and with the utmost attention to their own chosen terms, but with an eye principally to understanding the world that is our common inheritance. In effect, what most impressed me that year was his uncommon capacity to observe the Pauline injunction to "test everything" and "hold fast to what is good" (1 Thes 5:21). For as I gradually came to see, his openness, which was anything but naïve, was of a piece with the charity of his bearing toward a frequently quite demanding body of students.

Later I came to appreciate how much he had taken to heart the Christian doctrine of creation *ex nihilo*. Indeed, one would exaggerate only slightly, I think, were one to describe it as the great theme of his life. It is no exaggeration at all to say that in his writing and teaching, but above all in his very person, he is a wise and generous witness to the truth of creation. With this, I hope to have acknowledged, in a manner suitable to the occasion, the extent of my debt to Kenneth Schmitz. The following chapter provides at best a small payment on the accrued interest.

"Ever since the creation of the world His invisible [or unseen] things ἀόρατα, namely, His eternal power and divinity, have been clearly seen καθορᾶται, being understood νοούμενα in the things that have been made" (Romans 1:20).[1] Throughout the long and controversial history of reflection on the relation between Christian faith and human reason, few propositions have figured so prominently as this memorable claim from the Letter to the Romans, not infrequently by inspiring believers to attempt a demonstrative argument for the God whom they also in faith adore. I say "inspired" because, of course, the letter's author, conscious that he has been charged with a far greater task,[2] does not himself pause to work out such an argument for his readers. To be sure, we are told that the apostle to the gentiles did engage in a dialectical apology on behalf of his Lord during his stay in Athens. On St. Luke's telling, however, the evangelical consequences of that brief exchange seem to have been rather modest.[3] All the more striking, then, is St. Paul's willingness

1. Romans 1:20; numerous anticipations of this claim are to be found in the Jewish scriptures, for which see, for example, Job 12:7–10, Psalms 19:1–6, and Psalms 104:24; see also Wisdom 13:1–9; and Sirach 42:15–19.

2. Romans 1:1–6.

3. Acts 17:16–34. Notably, St. Paul fared no better in Lystra, where he attempted to

in his brief to "God's beloved in Rome," to put the matter so tersely. Nor, it must be said, has his claim come to acquire, in the nearly two millennia since he first made it, the patina of obviousness that is the mark of commonly acknowledged truths.

It is not my intention, however, to complete an argument one might suppose to be lacking in the writings of St. Paul; I shall not rehearse any of the traditional proofs for God's existence; still less do I mean to hazard one of my own devising.[4] I propose, instead, to take at face value the locutionary form, so to say, of Romans 1:20, which suggests rather a different sort of question. Let me begin by underlining a fact that will be obvious to any comer: namely, that the first and longest of St. Paul's epistles is addressed, at least in the first instance, to a community of readers who already share the faith that he preaches—as is the case with every other Pauline letter that has come down to us. Almost everyone knows, moreover, that it is in Romans that the apostle develops his most extensive reflections on the nature of that faith. Nevertheless, it is precisely there that we find him insisting that the evidence of God's eternal power and divinity is available in principle to all human beings, even those who have never heard the words God has spoken about himself "to our fathers by the prophets" and "in these last days to us by his Son."[5] In light of considerations such as these, one is naturally led to wonder about the saint's purpose. Why should it matter to him, or to any other believer, for that matter, that the reality of the unseen God is, as he maintains, always and everywhere to be seen? Of what possible interest can purportedly manifest truths about God be to those who have been accorded—albeit "in a mirror, dimly"—"all the riches of assured understanding, for the knowledge of the mystery of God, Christ, in whom are hidden all the treasures of wisdom and knowledge"?[6]

Although the question is one in which the scripture scholars might well take some interest, it surely does not fall exclusively, or even pri-

respond, in words, to fervent expressions of a gentile piety quite unmarked by the quasi-philosophical leanings of his interlocutors on the Areopagus, for which see Acts 14:8–19.

4. Elsewhere I have discussed several impediments to the rational acceptance of the claim of Romans 1:19–20; I there propose, in response, not a demonstration that God exists, but some reasons for holding that faith does not overstep its "bounds," so to say, in conceiving of reason as it does in that text; see John C. McCarthy, "The Reach of Reason," in *Ethics and Theological Disclosures: The Thought of Robert Sokolowski*, edited by James Hart and Guy Mansini, O.S.B., 102–34 (Washington, D.C.: The Catholic University of America Press, 2003).

5. Hebrews 1:1.

6. 1 Corinthians 13:12; Colossians 2:2–3.

marily, within their competence. For St. Paul's remarkable assertion has been reiterated on numerous occasions, in a variety of settings, and above all by figures who understand themselves to have been entrusted with superintendence of the very same Christian community for whom his missive to "the Romans" was originally composed. Consider, for example, the first of two documents to issue from the First Vatican Council, the "Dogmatic Constitution of the Catholic Faith," *Dei Filius* (April 24, 1870). There the Council Fathers solemnly proclaim, with explicit reference to Romans, that "God, the origin [*principium*] and end [*finem*] of all things, can be certainly known from created things by the natural light of human reason." The peculiar literary form in which they restate St. Paul's teaching undoubtedly reflects something of the unusual rhetorical stance of the original, as is evident especially from the concluding section of the document, wherein its authors warn that "if anyone should say that God, one and true, our creator and Lord, cannot from the things that have been made be certainly known by the natural light of human reason, let him be anathema."[7]

In keeping with its dogmatic form, the Council's teaching has been authoritatively reaffirmed on several occasions since, most recently in the *Catechism of the Catholic Church* and in Pope John Paul II's 1998 encyclical, *Fides et Ratio*.[8] Not that canonical reiteration of Romans 1:20 amounts to a mechanical repetition of the same, as the various differences between these texts makes clear. Kenneth Schmitz has called attention to a "new element" in *Fides et Ratio,* for example, an element that is not explicit in the teaching of Vatican I. He notes that while the church speaks authoritatively in both documents, in the recent encyclical the "attitude" of the teacher is much less that of a "judge" of the world, and much more of a "pilgrim" within it. This is reflected, he observes, in

7. First Vatican Council, *Dei Filius,* in *Enchiridion Symbolorum,* edited by Heinrich Denzinger and Adolf Schönmetzer (Freiburg, Basel, Rome, and Vienna: Herder, 1997).

8. John Paul II, *Fides et Ratio: On the Relation of Faith and Reason* (Boston: Pauline Books and Media, 1998) refers expressly to *Dei Filius* at §§8–9, 52–53, 55, 57, 67, 83, and 100; and see §§5, 13, 19, 22, 24, 33–34, 36, 41–42, 43, 84–85, 97, and 106; also see *Catechism of the Catholic Church (*New York: Random House, 1995), part 1, sect. 1, chap. 1, subsect. 3 §36 and note 11. Other notable reiterations of the Conciliar teaching include: St. Pius X's 1907 encyclical *Pascendi domenici gregis* ("De falsis doctrinis modernistarum"), in *Enchiridion Symbolorum*, 2072; Pius X's 1910 "Motu proprio" (*Iusiurandum contra errores modernismi*), in ibid., 2145; Pius XII's 1950 encyclical *Humani Generis,* in ibid., 2305, 2318, 2325 ; and the Second Vatican Council's "Dogmatic Constitution on Divine Revelation," *Dei Verbum*, chapt. 1, §6 in *Vatican II: The Conciliar and Post Conciliar Documents*, new rev. ed., edited by Austin Flannery, O.P. (Boston: St. Paul Books and Media, 1992).

the encyclical's "more direct" engagement with the world, as also in its "tone," which is "at once ... more bold and more hopeful" than the conciliar pronouncement of the century before. He associates these changes with an increased "sensitivity to time and history" on the church's part, and correlatively, with a marked decline in confidence in the power of reason almost everywhere else. Finally, he underlines what he describes as the "remarkable expansion in the sense of truth" operative in the encyclical, whereby the pursuit, attainment, and communication of truth are not merely "a matter of theory alone," but concern "above all the vocation that calls each person to a way of life."[9] Differences of the sort Schmitz identifies do not signify a break with the past. To the contrary, they enable what is living in the past to speak more persuasively to the present. Because the formulations of *Dei Filius* could not help but be conditioned in some respects by the preoccupations and polemics of what is for us now largely a bygone era,[10] it is only by developing the constant teaching of the Christian tradition, which necessarily entails a reiteration of St. Paul, that the church can restate that teaching. Repetition here means the liberation of what is essential, so that it can be appropriated in the present time, which is always inflected by opportunities and oppositions all its own.

That said, *Dei Filius* does possess one quality sorely undervalued in our prolix age, namely, a penchant for formal clarity and concision. And precisely in the trenchant economy of its expression it makes salient, in a way that *Fides et Ratio* perhaps does not, something of the paradoxical character of St. Paul's claim. Hence, having identified the possibility of a rational cognizance of the divine, it immediately goes on to insist on the superiority of the knowledge of God available in faith. That knowledge is superior, the Council teaches, not only because it concerns truths

9. Kenneth L. Schmitz, "Faith and Reason: Then and Now," *Communio: International Catholic Review* 26 (1999): 595–608; see also Avery Cardinal Dulles, S.J., "Faith and Reason: From Vatican I to John Paul II," in *The Two Wings of Catholic Thought: Essays on* Fides et Ratio, edited by David Ruel Foster and Joseph W. Koterski, S.J., 193–208 (Washington, D.C.: The Catholic University of America Press, 2003), which builds upon Schmitz's analysis. The link between the truths of faith and the practice of life has long been of a subject of some interest to Schmitz, for which see, inter alia, "Faith and Practice: The Nature and Importance of Religious Activities," in *The Life of Religion: A Marquette University Symposium on the Nature of Religious Belief*, edited by Stanley Harrison and Richard Taylor, 591–98. Lanham, Md.: University Press of America, 1986.

10. On this dimension of Vatican I, see Hans Urs von Balthasar, *The Theology of Karl Barth: Exposition and Interpretation*, trans. Edward T. Oakes, S.J. (San Francisco: Ignatius Press, 1992), 303.

about God otherwise quite hidden from rational view. Faith also knows better than reason alone because, the text pronounces in an unmistakable allusion to St. Thomas Aquinas, it allows "those divine things not impervious to human reason" to be known by "all," and not only some talented few, and known "quickly, with firm certitude, and mixed with no error."[11] With all the more reason, then, might we wonder why Christianity should accord so much importance to the very possibility of a strictly rational theology. To what end does Christian faith trouble itself to defend a mode of knowing God that is, from its vantage point, beneath it?

Before I outline a doubtless very partial response to the difficulty just raised, I should like briefly to consider a second, and in a sense more obvious, question provoked by the claim of Romans 1:20, namely, what business has Christian faith to speak in any case about the power of human reason as such? Christians engaging in political activity are frequently accused, and still more frequently suspected, of seeking to impose Christian moral commitments upon their non-Christian fellow citizens. *Dei Filius* and other such statements might well seem to be guilty of a far more unreasonable form of presumption: that of the acolyte who would hold a taper to the sun. The *Summa theologiae* reminds us that, according to Boethius, there is no argument weaker than an argument from authority.[12] Yet at Vatican I, and repeatedly thereafter, the church advances what presents itself as an authoritative interpretation of an earlier authority, according to which no argument from authority is necessary to attain to certain knowledge of God. Does this teaching not work, *in actu exercito,* at cross-purposes to what it expresses *in actu signato?*

A variety of considerations may be educed to show that, when considered on its own terms, Vatican I's Pauline understanding of reason makes a certain sense. Note, to begin, that the Council does not target reason wholly as such. It defends, instead, the possibility of a rational apprehension of the divine *as distinguished from* what is revealed about God in faith. And precisely because it involves the formulation of a distinction, the claim of *Dei Filius* is meaningful only insofar as both terms are affirmed, which is to say, only if Christian "belief"—to use a common but here potentially misleading term—is received and understood as a form of knowledge in its own right (as opposed, say, to some venera-

11. First Vatican Council, *Dei Filius,* 1786.

12. Aquinas, *Summa theologiae* I 1.8, obj. 2.

ble but nevertheless unsettled theological opinion). The distinction is already implicit, of course, in the phrase "certain knowledge of God by the natural light of human reason," which in any setting other than that established by biblical faith would be a bundle of tautology and pleonasm. It is not, in sum, despite but precisely because *Dei Filius* means to be a "Dogmatic Constitution of the Catholic Faith," that it can presume to speak as it does about reason. Only because St. Paul and his successors were occupied with that alone for which they bore particular responsibility could they have ventured a definitive judgment concerning that for which they could otherwise claim no special competence.

Further clarity about the meaning of "reason" in this context may be gained by recalling a discussion by St. Thomas Aquinas of a distinct but closely related matter. Several times over the course of his career, St. Thomas considers whether there is any place for believing truths about God that might also be known by rational demonstration; and while the several responses he provides to this question differ in some interesting particulars, he answers unvaryingly in the affirmative; what is more, he consistently holds that belief in such truths is "necessary." In his confidence in the natural reach of human intelligence, Aquinas had and has few equals. All the same, he was convinced that our capacity to exercise our highest powers to their fullest is, for a variety of reasons, sorely compromised. As he argues in the first article of the first question of the *Summa,* because we commonly find ourselves without the talent, the leisure, or the inclination prerequisite to the acquisition of a thoroughly rational apprehension of things divine, it is reasonable that we should accept on the word of another what we might, at least in principle, have discovered about God by our own devices. Otherwise such knowledge "would occur [*proveniret*]" only "to a few, after a long time," and even then, "mixed with many errors." The necessity of belief is, therefore, conditional on his account. Yet what makes this necessity less than absolute is not, as one might suppose, the presence of one or more of the impediments to natural theology he enumerates. It is conditioned, rather, by a supposition of an entirely different character, namely, "salvation" or "beatitude." This unexpected and wholly unmerited gift, freely bestowed upon the believer by God, is indispensable for the knowledge at issue.[13] As already indicated, the *Summa*'s opening discussion of faith, reason, and their relation,

13. Ibid. I 1.1c, to which we are directed by a footnote to *Dei Filius,* 1786; see also *Summa theologiae* II-II 2.4c; *Questiones disputatae de veritate* 14.10; *Super Boetium de Trinitate* 3.1; *Summa contra gentiles* I.4. In the *Commentaries* on the *Sentences* and on Boethius's *De Trini-*

was very much on the minds of the some 500 bishops who gathered in Rome for Vatican I.[14] And since there is not the slightest reason to think that they regarded themselves as an assembly of philosopher-prelates, able to think through for themselves what the great mass of their fellow believers are advised to take on their word, we may safely infer that they themselves had, as a body, taken on faith what they insist, with one voice, is rationally accessible to human beings without benefit of the Gospel. Surely the Council Fathers never once ventured beyond their Christian faith when they spoke with such confidence of human "reason."

Little in the way of dialectical skill would appear to be needed, however, in order to turn the argument of St. Thomas against itself: the obstacles that he identifies to a strictly rational theology could be used, it might seem, to fashion a blade toothful enough to saw away the very branch upon which his argument, and the Council's claim, appear to be seated. Does Christian certainty about reason's powers have, or even require of itself, any rational basis? Is there any reason for the church's great faith in reason? A glance at the historical record lends additional force to the question. If for no other reason than owing to the contingencies attending their origin, the writings left to us by the philosophers of classical antiquity afford us the strongest empirical evidence we are ever likely to have of the shape theological reasoning is capable of assuming when human intelligence proceeds without conscious recourse to divine assistance. In even the most penetrating of those writings, however, the evidence is at best equivocal whether ancient philosophy ever once came to conceive of the divine as both origin and end of all else that exists. And if that be granted, is it not fatal for the traditional Christian view of "natural reason"?

In truth, the church's teaching need in no way be threatened by the ambiguous textual legacy of pagan philosophizing, so long as it is under-

tate, as also in the *De veritate*, St. Thomas identifies Maimonides as a primary source for his discussion (for which see *Guide of the Perplexed* I c.33), whereas in both the *Summa contra gentiles* and the *Summa theologiae*, the debt to the great Jewish thinker goes unmentioned. Even in the earlier works, Aquinas' argument differs in important respects from that of Maimonides; but in his most mature treatments of the issue, Thomas' divergence from Maimonides is sufficiently pronounced that it is not unfitting that he pass over in silence what he owes to his predecessor.

14. See note 13 above. The relevant text from *Summa theologiae* was summarized in the *Schema* that the Council Fathers had received in preparation for the Council. The *Schema* adds the precision that a supernatural revelation of rationally accessible truths was "morally necessary," for which see the second of the "Adnotationes" to the *Schema constitutionis dogmaticae de doctrina catholica contra multiplices errores ex rationalismo dervivatos patrum examini popositum;* in Jean-Michel-Alfred Vacant, *Études Théologiques sur les Constitutions du Concile du Vatican d'après les actes du Concile*, vol. I (Paris and Lyon: Delhomme et Briguet, 1895), 588.

stood, once again, on its own terms. Consider an additional piece of the historical record. Although several participants at Vatican I urged that reference be made in *Dei Filius* to the natural theology of one or another pre-Christian thinker in support of its claim, their recommendation was decisively rejected. The capacity that the Council Fathers confidently ascribe to human intelligence is secured without any appeal to the history of its self-actualization. As Hans Urs von Balthasar observes, "as clearly as the Council decided the *de jure* question" about the God of reason, it "just as clearly left the *de facto* [question] open."[15] In this case, an argument from silence is fully justified: by prescinding from any particular human achievement, or state of human existence, actual or (theoretically) possible, the Council, in speaking of "certain knowledge of God by the natural light of reason," quite deliberately assumes a standpoint that is not simply formal, but formal in a highly unusual sense. What "reason" signifies in this context is thus only analogous to the sense that the term normally carries, either in common usage or among the philosophers.

To this one can imagine an objection issuing from another quarter. On behalf of the Christian theological tradition someone might possibly object that, even if ancient philosophy never did quite manage to live up to the church's standard of a fully rational theology, this does not mean that the standard is unrealistic or unreasonable. After all, "success" in this regard could never be more than partial, and would be achieved only by the few human beings able and willing to expend the necessary effort. Yet this hardly signifies that the culmination of rational inquiry is humanly unattainable—a point we must readily concede. Our interlocutor might then go on to argue, in support of the transparently rational character of the church's understanding of reason, by appealing to one or more of the various demonstrations for God's existence that have been devised over the centuries by professed Christians. Far be it from me to question the cogency of any argument of that sort. Even so, it bears mentioning that the Fathers of Vatican I also entertained, but ultimately rejected, the suggestion urged by some that *Dei Filius* document its teaching with examples of such demonstrations. I might also note that the frequent disputes that have erupted between thoughtful and well-meaning believers over the interpretation, and even the soundness, of putative demonstrations of God's existence developed within

15. *The Theology of Karl Barth*, 306–7; see also Vacant, *Études Théologiques*, 1, 288–91; and Roger Aubert, "Le concile du Vatican et la connaissance naturelle de Dieu," *Lumière et vie*, n. 14 (1954): 21–52.

the Christian tradition—to say nothing of recent grumbling about the "ontotheological" confusion allegedly infecting the whole enterprise—strongly suggest that St. Thomas's account of the limitations of an exclusively rational theology deserves more attention than philosophically inclined Christians have generally accorded it.

Be that as it may, there are grounds for thinking not only that the church speaks of reason as such only from within her faith, but also that she could not possibly have done otherwise. After all, even unbelievers will sometimes allow that the world and its history have been indelibly marked by two millennia of Christianity, not the least through its effects, both manifest and occult, on the common opinions that provide the inevitable starting point for every philosophical inquiry. But if one is not persuaded by Nietzsche that Christianity is merely vulgarized Platonism, or by some theogony akin to his, in which case the point here at issue is clearly moot, then in a world so shaped by Christian words and deeds it may be doubted whether *any* exercise of reason, much less one whose ambition is theological, could justly be described as wholly "natural" in the relevant sense, in which case it is by no means clear how an individual believer could ever really know what he *might* have known about the divine had he chanced to live at a time and in a place that had heard nothing about the God of Abraham, Isaac, and Jacob.[16] Moreover, even if, for purely speculative reasons, he were temporarily able not only to suspend his assent to the church's creed but also to bracket off all awareness of it—both of which may doubted—his doing so would scarcely be consistent with the demands of Christian fidelity. When Christ says to his friends that "He who is not with me is against me,"[17] I take it that he is only telling them what they must already have intuited: that having met him, there could be no turning back, no pretending that nothing had really changed, and thus no refuge in what they might be sometimes tempted to regard as an "innocent" ignorance about him. It is, I think, above all on these grounds that we must regard the church's conception of reason as necessarily part and parcel of her faith.

If it is wholly within her faith that the church speaks of reason and its proper scope, one would expect ecclesial pronouncements on the

16. See Hebrews 11:3: "By faith we understand that the world was created by the word of God, so that what is seen τὸ βλεπόμενον came to be out of things not appearing φαινομένων."

17. Matthew 12:30; Luke 11:23.

theme to be somehow in service of her faith. But how? In view of the relative poverty of reason's theological capacities when compared to what Christian faith discloses about the divine, the significance of the doctrine we have been considering has sometimes been construed in terms of its implications for Christian foreign policy, so to say. Romans 1:20 is then taken chiefly to be a spur to rational apologetics, as though the command to "Go into the whole world and proclaim the gospel to the whole of creation"[18] would best be observed by first seeking to establish a rational common ground with unbelievers before any explicit appeal be made to the God of faith. To be sure, the example set by St. Paul himself does afford a notable warrant for attempts to articulate a rational theological protreptic. Believing himself "under obligation both to Greeks and to barbarians," he endeavored to be "all things to all men," including those talkative and idly curious souls he chanced upon in Athens.[19] On the other hand, it would be manifestly at odds with the plain sense of scripture to treat rational certainty about the divine as an indispensable precondition for Christian faith. It was, after all, the same St. Paul who observed that "since, in the wisdom of God, the world did not know God through wisdom, it pleased God through the folly of what we preach to save those who believe"—and as is clear from the context, it is chiefly the "Greeks" he has in mind when writes ironically of God's "folly."[20] One must also allow that strictly rational arguments for the traditional *praeambula fidei* entail peculiar rhetorical difficulties. Among other things, the attempt to use reason in this way could easily appear, to unbelieving eyes, as a mere pretext, or an exercise in special pleading.

Whatever eventual consequences the doctrine under consideration may have for Christian evangelization, that which I have called the locutionary form in which it finds classical expression suggests that it is believers who are in the first instance to benefit from it. But that makes sense only on the supposition that they are at times inclined to forget, or disposed to doubt, or even tempted to deny, that certainty about God is rationally within their reach. In order more fully to appreciate the point of the teaching, it would therefore be useful to ask why that should be.

18. Mark 16:15.

19. Romans 1:14 and 1 Corinthians 9:20–22, with Acts 17:16–34.

20. 1 *Corinthians* 1:17–25. It is not at all unlikely that as he penned these words to the church in Corinth, he was thinking especially of his recent experience in nearby Attica, for which see Acts 18:1, and 18:24–19:7 with 1 Corinthians 1:10–12. As regards the missionary value of a strictly rational account of the divine, see also 2 Corinthians 4:3–6; Colossians 2:8; Hebrews 11:3 and 6.

We already have a partial answer at hand in the variety of all-too-human limitations that would impede even believers from the pursuit of natural theology. Because Christian faith always involves, moreover, "mysteries hidden in God which, unless they are divinely revealed, are incapable of being known,"[21] a strictly rational illumination of the divine cannot help but seem, by comparison, a much dimmer light than it would otherwise be. The road up and the road down are not, from the Christian theological point of view, one and the same. It is thus hardly surprising that Christians should require instruction or reminders that the God of their faith is also the God of reason. Yet the failure within faith to acknowledge the rational evidence of the divine may also be due to something accidental to Christian belief, so to say, namely, that the believer be encumbered by a distorted conception of faith (and thereby also of reason), or of reason (and thereby also of faith). *Dei Filius* and *Fides et Ratio* both came about largely as a response to confusions of this sort.[22] Legion, no doubt, are the ways a believer here can err. For present purposes it suffices simply to identify the two basic forms of error to which faith, as an act of mind, can fall prey—call them "rationalism" and "fideism" if you will.[23] To insist upon the possibility of a strictly natural theology is especially timely whenever confusions of this sort threaten to compromise Christian belief.

In order better to grasp how, in a general way, the teaching of Romans 1:20 might serve the life of faith, we must take up a phrase that we have to this point ignored, "the things that have been made." Up until now we have approached St. Paul's celebrated statement as though its primary concern were the uppermost natural limits of our cognitive powers, but as these words make clear, it is as much, or even more, a claim about what it means to be. For of course, by "the things made" the apostle does not intend an ordinary, albeit fundamental, term of distinction (as opposed, say, to "the things by nature"); he means anything and everything that we encounter, or could encounter, within the world; hence, as *Dei Filius* translates, "all things."[24] To be (or to be related to) a being in this sense is to be (or to refer to) a "creature," that which ultimately owes both *what* and *that* it is wholly to God's creative initiative.[25]

21. First Vatican Council, *Dei Filius,* 1796.

22. For an enumeration of the particular confusions to which each text seeks to respond, see Schmitz, "Faith and Reason: Then and Now," 600, notes 11 and 12.

23. Aubert, 165–66, calls "agnosticism" and "traditionalism" the two principal targets of Vatican I.

24. And see Ephesians 3:9; Colossians 1:15–17; Hebrews 1:3; 2:10; 11:3.

25. Although in this case "wholly" does not signify "exclusively," as the scholastic

The doctrine we are considering goes on to assert that worldly things are, in the form and facticity of their being, a *sign* of their divine origin. The Christian tradition's insistence upon the innately theological capacity of human reason is, in a word, inseparable from its conviction that the beings clearly visible to all are constituted in such a way as clearly to point to the God hidden from every view. Yet this clearly means in turn that the real focus of the teaching is neither ontological nor anthropological. What is ultimately at issue for St. Paul and his successors is the nature of the divine.

To elaborate upon this last remark, if creatures have been created in such a way as to point to their Creator, and if the human creature has been fashioned so as to be capable of following up on their lead, then notwithstanding the distinction commonly drawn between "reason" and "revelation," it must be said that creation is itself a revelation, an act of divine self-disclosure. And, in fact, the text of Romans is particularly emphatic on this point. Every reader of St. Paul is familiar with his insistence, further on in the letter, that it is by "faith alone," and not by dint of his own efforts, that any human being has ever been "justified."[26] Yet even in describing what can be known about God through his creation, the apostle stresses, not our native capacities, but what God has already accomplished. As the apostle puts it in the verse immediately preceding the one that has chiefly concerned us, the theological truth "manifest φανερόν" to human beings is so "because God has manifested ἐφανέρωσεν it to them."[27]

This link between creation, reason, and revelation has recently been highlighted to great, not to say notorious, effect by Pope Benedict XVI in the lecture he delivered in Regensburg on September 12, 2006, under the title "Faith, Reason, and the University: Memories and Reflections." The first biblical text the Pope cites on that occasion is the opening verse of the prologue to the Gospel of St. John, "In the beginning was the λόγος," the significance of which he interprets as follows:

---

notion of "secondary causality" takes pains to insist. Because the Christian God is neither a part of "the whole" nor identical with it, Christianity can speak meaningfully of God's causing things wholly to be without thereby excluding, which is to say competing with, things in their worldly causal interrelations.

26. See, inter alia, Romans 3:21–30, 4:5–16, 5:1, 9:30, 10:6.

27. Romans 1:19. Similarly, in the sequel (1:20–32) he goes on at some length to charge the gentiles with a culpable failure—"they are without excuse"—to do justice to the theological abilities and insights that were accorded to them as human beings.

Logos means at once reason and word—a reason which is creative and capable of self-communication [or that can share itself: *sich mitteilen kann*], precisely as reason. John has thereby imparted to us the final word on the Biblical conception of God, in which all the often toil-some and tortuous ways of Biblical faith reach their destination [*Ziel*] and find their synthesis.[28]

Pope Benedict's purpose, in context, is to indicate the "profound harmony" that exists between the "idea" of the divine nature at work in Greek philosophy and "the Biblical understanding of faith in God."[29] But one might well go on to say, on the basis of his exegetical observations, that from a biblical point of view, so far is "reason" from being distinct from "revelation" that it is best conceived as but an image of, or a participation in, the very nature and self-expression of God himself.

At this juncture we might profitably appeal to the account of the "metaphysics of creation" set forth at length, and in telling detail, by Kenneth Schmitz in his 1982 Aquinas lecture, *The Gift: Creation*. As he there brings masterfully to the fore, creation means that every existing thing, as having been brought freely into being from out of nothing, is truly a gift. Things owe their origin to a divinely superabundant generosity, with which they are suffused, and to which they attest.[30] Now it

28. Pope Benedict XVI, "Meeting with the Representatives of Science, Lecture of the Holy Father, Aula Magna of the University of Regensburg, September 12, 2006: Faith, Reason and the University: Memories and Reflections," http://www.vatican.va/holy_father/benedict_xvi/speeches/2006/september/documents/hf_ben-xvi_spe_20060912_university-regensburg_en.html. I have attempted to bring the English somewhat closer to the German original (for which see http://www.vatican.va/holy_father/benedict_xvi/speeches/2006/september/documents/hf_ben-xvi_spe_20060912_university-regensburg_ge.html). Neither version enumerates the paragraphs of the text, but this is easily done, and facilitates references to it (hence, in the present instance, para. 5).

29. Ibid., para. 5; as is clear from the lecture's title, it differs from every other ecclesial pronouncement to which I have hitherto made reference in *not* being addressed primarily to Christians. Delivered at the University of Regensburg, the English translation, skirting over the well-known difficulty in rendering "Wissenschaft," introduces it as a "Meeting with Representatives of Science [*aus dem Bereich der Wissenschaften*]." This all but inevitable linguistic imprecision in the translation bears mentioning because a, or rather the, leading theme, of the lecture is the "broadening [*Ausweitung*] of our conception of reason" (see paras. 13, 15–16), where "our" is clearly to be taken in the most comprehensive sense, namely, as referring to "humanity" in this day and age. Hence the other audience specifically envisaged for the lecture, albeit in an indirect fashion, is the contemporary Muslim world: to each body he urges, though on contrary grounds, that "theology belongs in the university, and within the broad [or wide-ranging: *weiten*] dialogue of the sciences ... precisely as theology" (15).

30. See Kenneth L. Schmitz, *The Gift: Creation* (Milwaukee, Wisc.: Marquette University Press, 1982), *passim*. Schmitz returns extensively to this theme in his Gilbert Ryle lectures, delivered at Trent University in 1997, and subsequently published under the title *The*

is true that we sometimes speak of what is given (the *data*), which cannot or should not be changed, but is to be accepted or acknowledged for what it is.[31] Much more to the point, however, it is not uncommon that people who do not suppose themselves to be particularly "religious" should occasionally be moved to a sense of gratitude for their existence, and even for the existing whole to which their particular existence somehow contributes. Schmitz helps us to see how much the Christian doctrine of creation fully ratifies such apprehensions, no matter how vague, or intermittent, or fragile they may be. By virtue of their very being, things really do elicit and so merit our gratitude. But Romans 1:19–20 suggests an addendum to Schmitz's account, namely, that creation affords us reason to be thankful, not only *for* the world but also *to* its source. For if creation rationally signifies its own origin and end, then the hidden God, in freely creating things to be, also freely announces himself. In the superabundant generosity of creation, God also generously introduces himself by making himself knowingly available to us.[32]

Recovery of Wonder: The New Freedom and the Asceticism of Power (Montreal and Kingston: McGill–Queen's University Press, 2005), especially 29–49, 104–5. In the latter work Schmitz refers approvingly to Robert Sokolowski's philosophical and theological reflection on creation, *The God of Faith and Reason: Foundations of Christian Theology* (Notre Dame, Ind.: University of Notre Dame Press, 1982; reprint, Washington, D.C.: The Catholic University of America Press, 1995), which initially appeared in the same year as Schmitz's Aquinas lecture.

31. Even more common is talk of the "facts," which one might construe as a remote echo of St. Paul, but improbably. The Oxford English Dictionary traces its roots to *facere*, in the sense of "to do" and not "to make," and identifies a relatively early use of the word in a passage from Bacon: "Men are to be admonished that, as they are not to mistake the causes of these operations, so much less they are to mistake the fact or effect." As is clear from the context, however, the "operations" Bacon has in mind are those of the "imagination," and pointedly do not concern the things "made" by the Creator, for which see *Sylva sylvarum*, X §903, in *The Works of Francis Bacon*, edited by James Spedding, Robert Leslie Ellis and Douglas Denon Heath, vol. 2 (London: Longman, 1859), 642. For a suggestive reflection on Machiavelli's contribution to "fact" in this sense, see Harvey C. Mansfied, "Nature and Fact in Tocqueville's *Democracy in America*, in *Nature in American Philosophy*, edited by Jean De Groot, Studies in Philosophy and the History of Philosophy 42 (Washington, D.C.: The Catholic University of America Press, 2004), 111–12. The "given" is of a much more recent vintage. The OED identifies its first appearance in the relevant sense in an 1879 essay by William James. All the more unlikely is its provenance biblical, therefore. Much more plausible is a mathematical derivation, as in "Given that X = . . ."

32. If, according to the Scholastic dictum, "omne agens agit sibi simile"—see, e.g., *Summa contra gentiles* II c. 16 n.6; II c. 21, n. 9; II c. 24 n.3—it would seem to follow that God, in freely bringing things to be, brings about that which is necessarily somehow like him. But whether or not this were to entail that God could have created a world that would not be revelatory of him is immaterial to the claim I am advancing here, which is that the Creator freely and so generously discloses himself already by virtue of his freely and so generously causing the world to be.

What, though, has any of this to do with Christian faith as such? To conclude this chapter, I shall limit myself to a single suggestion. If it is true that in the act of creating God declares himself, then, following Pope Benedict, we could say that the creation itself is a kind of linguistic expression, uttered in a "language" in which the Creator alone is perfectly fluent. Correlatively it might be said that creation is expressed in a language of which the human being possesses the verbal and syntactic rudiments. In other words, the rational animal, the only creature born with the capacity to think and to speak, is by nature the theological animal.[33] This means in turn that when God addresses himself to human beings in that unforeseen and unforeseeable way that is his divine Word made human flesh, he will not inevitably be wasting his breath; his Word will not necessarily fall on deaf ears: because we are naturally equipped to recognize God in and through his creation, on the day that he begins to address us in and through Christ's utterly distinctive but fully human voice, we are able to attend to and understand in some measure what he says, or rather who he is. In affirming Romans 1:20, the church affirms that Christian faith is not incoherent because it is not inhuman, and that it is not inhuman because it is not incongruous with reason, the mark of our humanity. As St. Augustine noted long ago, "we could not believe at all if we did not have rational souls."[34]

All of this is bears greatly upon the way Christian faith is lived. One could easily gain the impression from certain forms of devotional art—although also, truth to tell, from the words and deeds of many believers—that the eyes of faith should somehow be fixed infinitely beyond the visible world. We may be grateful that "otherworldliness" is far less common among the pious than it once was. What one often finds in its stead nowadays is a vaguely personal "spirituality," whose attention appears to be directed somewhere deep within the individual, there to await the consolation, if not quite the illumination, afforded by an incommunicable religious sentiment. Now, it is true that assent to Christian teaching is an eminently personal affair; it is also true that, according to its own terms, the fullness of biblical revelation cannot be fully contained or disclosed by the world around us. On the other hand, the

33. It would seem to follow that, according to the biblical understanding of the divine, as distinct from that of Greek philosophy, "theology" is at every level primarily a subjective genitive; compare, e.g., Plato, *Republic* 2.380d–383c and Aristotle, *Metaphysics* 12.9 1074b15–35.

34. St. Augustine, *Letters*, vol. 2 (83–130), translated by Sr. Wilfred Parsons, S.N.D. (Washington, D.C.: The Catholic University of America Press, 2008), "Letter 120: To Consentius," 302.

focus of Christian belief is neither upon some infrapsychic "world," nor some extraterrestrial one, as is clear from the opening words of the first letter of John:

> That which was from the beginning, which we have heard, which we have seen with our eyes, which we have looked upon and touched with our hands, concerning the word of life—the life was made manifest, and we have seen it and testify to it, and proclaim to you the eternal life that was with the Father and was made manifest to us—that which we have seen and heard we proclaim also to you.[35]

According to tradition, the evangelist wrote these words as an old man, looking back. But what he looks back to is what he once saw before his eyes: a man like himself, who used human words and gestures in an eminently human way to make known to others the way the things of the world appeared to him and who thereby also made known who he took himself to be. In assuming human flesh, the divine Word, though wholly irreducible to the language spoken by God in and through his creation, freely adapted himself to, indeed freely submitted to, the created world and its terms. In sum, the theological truths made manifest in and by Christ's person are at once unmixed with and inseparable from his humanity, itself bound up in turn with the human world in which he lived, and moved, and breathed. And since God pronounces both the things that may commonly be known about him, and the things he has reserved exclusively for his "chosen" ones, within one and the same visible order, it is precisely there that Christians must look if they are to see and believe all that St. John had seen and believed long before them.

It is along the lines just stated that *Fides et Ratio* advances what is surely intended as an amplification of the teaching of *Dei Filius* on the superiority of faith's knowledge to that obtainable by the natural light of reason. After noting that "It is within time that the whole work of creation and salvation comes to light," the encyclical goes on to observe that with the Incarnation, God "touches us in the things most familiar to us and most easily verified [*ad demonstrandum facilia*], because they constitute the stuff of our everyday life [*cotidiana nostra adiuncta*]."[36]

35. 1 John 1:1–3.

36. *Fides et Ratio*, §§11–12. As Robert Sokolowski notes in *The God of Faith and Reason*, 31–41, only a God who is no part of the world could use worldly realities to manifest himself historically in Christ. In the pagan way of thinking, the divine is what it is as distinct from other parts of the whole, and so could not be made "one" with any other part without

But this is to say, once again, that it is by looking squarely at the world around him that a Christian can reasonably hope to see "beyond" it, which makes sense, as we have argued, only because the world as such, far from being an impediment to "theology," exists in such a way as both to elicit from us a question—"God?"—and point us to the answer it poses—"God!"

A few words must now suffice for what can in no way ever be concluded. A reasonable unbeliever might well regard Christian faith in human reason as worthy of modest commendation. But it must also cause him some perplexity, especially in view of the challenge that it has often posed even to those who count themselves Christians. On this point at least, the believer would probably help his unbelieving neighbors best by helping himself first: in the measure that he neglects reason's tireless quest truly to understand the reality that encompasses him, he effectively deprives himself of his native capacity to seek, to encounter, to acknowledge and to respond to the human and divine source of his faith, in the Word made flesh, who dwells among us. Moreover, just as the distinction between "natural" and "revealed" theology does not signify the existence of two deities, but two distinct approaches to the one God, so the distinction between "faith" and "reason" does not deny but rather presupposes their identity-in-difference in the life of the one reasoning and believing human being. If, in sum, the natural culmination of human reason is theological, then surely one who aspires to love God with all his heart, soul, mind, and strength has better reason than anyone else to welcome reason's every achievement.

---

compromise to that part's integrity. The creator God does not compete with his creation in that way.

Robert E. Wood

18. HUMAN NATURE, CULTURE, AND THE DIALOGICAL IMPERATIVE

Kenneth Schmitz is my teacher. His courses on existentialism, on modern philosophy, and on Hegel and Nietzsche had a decisive impact on my own subsequent approach to philosophy. Existentialism and its background in phenomenology, as well as both Nietzsche and Hegel, continue to be focal points in my own studies. His interest in Paul Weiss led me to Weiss's systematic approach to philosophy; his interest in the aesthetics of Hans Urs von Balthasar led me to a comprehensive review of *The Glory of the Lord* that was linked to my own writings on aesthetics.[1]

Schmitz's class presentations were models of unscrupulous fairness to the thinkers upon which he focused. That was in marked contrast to what was an all-too-common polemical approach to other thinkers on the part of those trained in Scholastic thought. For Schmitz, every thinker had something positive to teach us, a different angle in approaching matters philosophical. The history of philosophy was a gold mine rather than a mine field. His appreciation of modern thought found an echo in the work of John Paul II, who spoke of "the precious and seminal insights" in modern thought.[2] (Schmitz devoted a notable book to John Paul.) Following Schmitz's lead, I have continued to learn through a lifelong study of a select number of thinkers, from the early Greeks to

1. Robert E. Wood, "Philosophy, Aesthetics and Theology: A Review of Hans Urs von Balthasar's *The Glory of the Lord*," *American Catholic Philosophical Quarterly* 47 (1993): 355–82.

2. John Paul II, *Fides et Ratio: On the Relation of Faith and Reason* (Boston: Pauline Books and Media, 1998), sect. 4 and 64.

those from more recent times. In fact, when I became editor of the *American Catholic Philosophical Quarterly,* the new policy of dedicating every third issue to a positive treatment of figures from the history of thought moved in the direction Schmitz had given us.

The following essay, which attempts to present the grounds for pluralism, individual and cultural, that calls for dialogue parallels Schmitz's own "Philosophical Pluralism and Philosophical Truth" and his central focus upon the notion of Being.[3]

The Contemporary Situation

The horizon of contemporary discussion includes a rejection of human nature that stands in tension with attempts to revive the notion within the context of dialogue. Lyotard considers the notion of human nature as a construct of the Enlightenment, a blanched, one-leveled notion that destroys the plurality of cultural experiences. He reaffirms the plurality of Wittgensteinian language games. And he rejects the Habermasian search for consensus by calling attention to the dissension from dominant paradigms that leads to scientific expansion.[4] Habermas claims that the structure of language implies a decentered subjectivity in a community underpinned by language and aimed at an ideal consensus to be sought through dialogue governed by the power of the stronger argument.[5] Heidegger lays the grounds for that possibility through his questioning of Being as the ground for the emergence of collective worlds of meaning.[6] Derrida also argues for the priority of the notion of Being as opening up fields of discourse,[7] but argues against a logocentric understanding of it. By logocentrism he understands both the dominance of logic, which presupposes translogical starting points for its machinery to work upon, and the *logos*-centrism of Heidegger's reading of Heraclitean gathering.[8] For Derrida the logos is disseminated and *différance* takes

3. Schmitz, "Philosophical Pluralism and Philosophical Truth," in *Philosophy Today* 10, no. 1 (Spring 1966): 3–16.

4. Jean-François Lyotard, *The Postmodern Condition: A Report on Knowledge,* trans. Geoffrey Bennington and Brian Massumi (Minneapolis: University of Minnesota Press, 1984), 503.

5. Jürgen Habermas, "Discourse Ethics: Notes on a Program of Philosophical Justification," in *Moral Consciousness and Communicative Action,* trans. Christian Lenhardt and Shierry Webster Nicholsen, 43–115 (Cambridge, Mass.: MIT University Press, 1990).

6. Martin Heidegger, *Being and Time,* trans. John Maquarrie and Edward Robinson (New York: Harper and Row, 1962), 2–35.

7. Jacques Derrida, "The Supplement of the Copula: Philosophy Before Linguistics," in *Margins of Philosophy,* trans. Alan Bass, 194–205 (Chicago: University of Chicago Press, 1982).

8. Derrida, *Of Grammatology,* trans. Gayatri Chakravorty Spivak (Baltimore: Johns Hopkins University Press, 1976), 3, 23, 74.

center stage as metaphysics is "sent packing."[9] Derrida in effect rejected a proposed dialogue with Gadamer who, following Heideggerian *Logos*-Being, seeks a *Horizont-Verschmelzung* with other thinkers.[10]

On the other hand, Levinas, like Kierkegaard, claims there is a basic totalitarianism implicit in the notion of Being, whether given a Hegelian or a Heideggerian reading. He favors an Infinity "beyond Being" that transcends the enclosed universe of Being and leaves Its trace in the face of the human Other. Levinas would replace ontology, understood as a comprehensive "physics," with metaphysics as a disciplined attention to what is "*meta*," beyond.[11]

In relation to this situation, I will argue, against Lyotard, that there is a human nature that has a peculiar bipolar character: it is biologically grounded and ontologically referred. The ontological reference is shared in different ways by Heidegger and Derrida, the latter of whom attempts to occupy a ground between Heidegger and Levinas.[12] I would claim that the grounding in ontological reference is precisely the basis for openness to the mystery of the Beyond that is both revealed and concealed in the present epiphany of the face of the human other upon which Levinas is focused. I would claim that, by reason of its bipolarity, human nature is culture-creating, establishing a second nature on top of the first. Its bipolar character gives human activity its unitary ground; its culture-creating consequence gives that activity its diversity and concreteness. But that unitary ground entails several positive and negative imperatives that center upon inquiry and freedom and impel us to dialogue, thus furnishing the grounds for the Habermasian and Gadamerian projects.

Human Bipolarity

Attend then to the bipolarity of human nature.[13] At one pole, human nature is set on an animal base. It is the locus of a field of awareness that

9. Derrida, "Difference," in *Speech and Phenomena and Other Essays,* trans. David B. Allison (Evanston, Ill.: Northwestern University Press, 1973), 129–60; Derrida, *Of Spirit: Heidegger and the Question,* trans. Geoffrey Bennington and Rachel Bowlby (Chicago: University of Chicago Press, 1989), 75.

10. Cf. Diane P. Michelfelder and Richard E. Palmer, eds., *Dialogue and Deconstruction: The Gadamer-Derrida Encounter* (Albany: SUNY Press, 1989); Hans-Georg Gadamer, *Truth and Method* (New York: Crossroads, 1975), 273ff, 337ff.

11. Emmanuel Levinas, *Totality and Infinity,* trans. Alphonso Lingis (Pittsburgh, Penn.: Duquesne University Press, 1969), 33–52.

12. Derrida, "Violence and Metaphysics," in *Writing and Difference,* trans. Alan Bass (Chicago: University of Chicago Press, 1978), 79–153.

13. I have previously treated this in slightly different ways: in Robert E. Wood, *A Path*

is a synesthetic-orectic-kinesthetic circle displaying relational features of an environment of goods, threats, and neutralities in relation to the achievement of the immanent goals of the organism for growth, sustenance, reproduction, and the fostering of offspring, as well as for defense against predators. At the other pole, peculiar humanness is open to the whole scheme of things via the notion of Being that includes everything; but, as given by our nature, the notion of Being is, as Hegel claimed, only empty reference.[14] It begins as Nietzsche's "last trailing cloud of evaporating reality."[15] That sets up the human being as the locus of the question of Being. This being-open means that the Whole is pregiven as a question: What's it all about? What is "the scheme of things"? How does humanness fit within that scheme? Religions (as inspired and proclamatory pronouncements about the Whole) and philosophies (as critical and systematic claims about the Whole) attempt to fill in what is an initially empty reference to that totality.

"Scheme of things" suggests an outline. How is that possible? Granted that it is a human construct, is it only a human construct? Scheme is already entailed in the character of the animal base. The appetites and sensory powers involved are concrete universals, oriented toward specific kinds of achievement in relation to aspects and types of environmentally given entities. Native powers are both *individual* aspects of *individual* things and *universal* orientations toward the *kinds* of individuals in the environment that could activate them. As concrete universals, they sublate the distinction between individual and universal. An organism that cannot distinguish instances of the type (*eidos*) "food" or "enemy" will perish—perishing being a *type* of event overtaking the *type* called living.[16]

The concretely available scheme of things is present in the food chain. Humans sit at the top of a hierarchy as omnivores who subsume carnivores, herbivores, plants, and aspects of the nonliving environ-

into Metaphysics (Albany: SUNY Press, 1991), I provided an approach parallel to "Plato's Cave" by using the model of multidimensional space provided by Edwin Abbott's *Flatland: A Romance in Many Dimensions* (Amherst, N.Y.: Prometheus Books, 2005); in Wood, *Placing Aesthetics: Reflections on the Philosophic Tradition* (Athens: Ohio University Press, 1999), I explored the structure of the field of experience as a way into the study of select highpoints in the history of thought on matters aesthetic.

14. G. W. F. Hegel, *Hegel's Science of Logic,* trans. A. V. Miller (London: George Allen and Unwin, 1969), 82.

15. Friedrich Nietzsche, *Twilight of the Idols,* trans. R. J. Hollingdale (Baltimore: Penguin, 1968), 3:4.

16. See Wood, "Potentiality, Creativity, and Relationality: Creative Power as a 'New' Transcendental?" *The Review of Metaphysics* 59 (2005); this paper was originally delivered at the John Paul II Institute at a symposium in honor of Kenneth Schmitz.

ment. Carnivores subsume herbivores, who, in turn, consume plant life. And plant life subsumes aspects of the nonliving environment. And the nonliving forms each consist of determinate powers of acting and being acted upon that link them together in various systems. One could say, with Plato's Eleatic Stranger, that the definition of being is the power of acting and being acted upon.[17]

Now what that involves is that each individual, manifest in the environment as individual and actual, contains underlying powers as universal orientations toward the kind of things correlative to it: those things upon which it can act and that can act upon it. So individuals are not simply other than the universals we use to describe them; they are themselves the loci of concrete, that is, *individual* powers that themselves are *universal* orientations. They mesh with their kind of environment, and ultimately with the cosmos itself.

What throws us off is that sensory appearance is misleading theoretically. It misleads us into thinking that all that is is individual and actual. But reflection shows that individuals are the loci of powers as *universal* orientations. They each contain concrete universals peculiar in their interrelation to a given type of individual. And that the individuals are instances of types is not only something we add to them by abstraction and classification; at least in the case of living things, by way of reproduction each organism is an instance of the type of its progenitors and offspring.

The distance from the environmentally and intra-organically manifest afforded by orientation toward the Whole makes possible reflection upon those concrete universals, grasping their repeatability any time and any place the conditions for their activation are met. Reference to the Whole solicits the attempt to link them together in systematic ways, paralleling, in the distinctively human in relation to its world, the systematicity that is involved in the organism in itself and in its relation to its environment.

Reference to the Whole as reference to Being sets up a tension between organ-based appearance, a selective filter in relation to the whole of what appears in service of biological needs, and the encompassing Whole—in such a way, however, that the appearance *expresses* for us the character of that Whole. This calls for interpretation that may stay at the level of reading how the given affords occasions for identifying support-

17. Plato, *Sophist,* 247E, in Plato, *Theaetetus, Sophist,* trans. Harold North Fowler (Cambridge, Mass.: Harvard University Press, 1977).

ive, threatening, or neutral aspects of the manifest environment. On the other hand, guided by the notion of Being, it might advance, in a purely theoretical way, through inference and the invention of appropriate methods and instruments, into the character of what underlies the initial appearance.

That same reference that solicits interpretation also, as Sartre put it, condemns us to choose from among the possibilities for action demanded by our animal nature and opened up by the interplay of sensory manifestness and historically situated interpretation.[18] Referred to the Whole, we are pried loose at the deepest level of ourselves from the partially manifest and are thus able and even required to choose among the options as we come to understand them. As in our case, sexuality drives male and female together but also poses problems not solved by sheer natural drive—namely, how shall we care for the offspring that emerge from that togetherness? And subsequently, how shall we conceive of the relation of our freedom to choose and that natural drive? Nature addresses humankind in terms of problems not solved by nature; nature presses human freedom for decisions. The cluster of decisions provided by humankind in response to these questions as they pass on to others constitutes the history of the institutions of marriage and child-rearing. Feelings of possessiveness and power, grounded in nature but focused by the sedimentation of decisions we call institutions, cluster about mates and offspring to furnish a second level, beyond natural organic feelings, of felt reverberations in the presence of *sensa*.

The togetherness of the family makes collective the first problem posed by nature—namely, how do I get enough to eat and drink? and how do I protect myself against the threats posed by the environment, natural and human? Actually, because human beings are not born even relatively self-sufficient but require years of care, these questions an individual might ask actually originate from the questions, how do *we* get enough to eat? and how do *we* protect ourselves against the environment? As larger conglomerations of humans form, the sedimentation of decisions in this realm gives rise to the history of institutions of production and exchange. The plurality of humans poses the problem of how we relate to others in and beyond those relations of mate and offspring grounded in sexuality, and eventuates in determinate social practices. Of course, involved in all of this is the problem of authority: Who makes the

18. Jean-Paul Sartre, "Existentialism Is a Humanism," in *Existentialism from Dostoevski to Sartre,* ed. and trans. Walter Kaufmann (New York: Meridian, 1956), 287ff.

decisions? And how do we pass on the results of these processes to those who follow us? This introduces not only the dialectic between individuals and groups who are coexistent, but, perhaps even more powerfully, that between the live community and the tradition of folkways, the sedimented set of decisions, now become second nature, that have allowed the community to survive against the more or less frequent hostility of the environment, natural and social. The answers we give to the questions posed by nature and by our sedimented responses to nature are not just *ad hoc* solutions, but involve the establishment of anticipated possible regularities of response that could apply anywhere and any time we meet the same situations. By our decisions we help establish or disestablish both individual and collective principles for action.

But the questions posed to our freedom by our nature in relation to the natural and social environment are not the only questions. Our nature as oriented toward the Whole of being poses to us the basic question of *the meaning of the Whole* as object of our deepest human desire.[19] It may not be the most immediately overpowering desire; but the former ultimately pales into insignificance without some sense of its relation to the Whole. After the height of orgasm one could readily ask if it "means" anything. And meaning, we suggest, is a matter of seeing and indwelling in the belonging together of humans and other entities within the Whole. So we not only have to make fundamental decisions as to how we are to respond to the basic questions posed by nature in the realm of practice, we also stand under the requirement of certain interpretative decisions regarding the meaning of each entity within the Whole. That they are, in a sense, decisions seems clear from the fact that there is a plurality of them. Yet neither type of decision—interpretive or practical—can be simply arbitrary and unconstrained, since they will not hold over time unless they are in some way compatible with the totality of what is given, both in terms of the encountered and in terms of our own needs, individual and collective. They are deeply tied to the sedimented history of decisions of those long dead that constitute the institutions within which a We exists. Fundamental decisions are responses to directions we are invited to walk, presented by the concrete situation in which we find ourselves, insofar as such decisions involve our place in the whole scheme of things.[20]

19. Cf. Heidegger's notion of *Dasein* in *Being and Time*, 27.

20. On "decision" in this regard, see Heidegger's *Contributions to Philosophy: From Enowning*, trans. Parvis Emad and Kenneth Maly (Bloomington: Indiana University Press, 2000), 66–69.

It is out of the ground of this question about the Whole that the most powerful and sophisticated of all institutions emerges: namely, the institution of language. In the first place, that structure makes possible the functioning of each individual entity given in the sensory field as an icon of the Whole. Further, the factual reoccurrence, spatially and temporally, of *types,* of *kinds* of entities as necessary correlates to our native powers mediates the mode of manifestation in the individual's relation to the Whole. It is language that allows us to retain our awareness of types. And in its mediation, language functions fundamentally in opening up the space from which decisions come, the space of meaning that emerges from the wedding between immersion in the problems posed by the sensory Now and our fundamental reference to the encompassing Whole of being. Focus upon the rude artifacts from prehistorical times that archaeologists discover often makes us forget that so-called primitive peoples for millennia were developing that most sophisticated of instruments to which we are still necessarily beholden: language.[21] Language, initially incarnated in the flow of sound generated by our lips, gathers about the immediately given *sensa* the Whole as known, as inferred and as imagined. It endows the objects presented with emotional reverberations of extreme depth and subtlety, upon which the arts play in their reconstruction of the sensory. Language binds together a people over space and time; but at the same time it separates those people from all others.

This binding is made possible by the extraction of an interrelated set of vowels, consonants, and phonemes that play in relation to one another, from the indeterminate number of sounds made possible by the structure of the human oral cavity. Such units are eidetic constants, humanly constructed identities over against the plurality of their sensory instances. To give an instance of writing that involves the same observation: it is the same "a" that is repeated again and again in the differing spaces of this page and generated during different aspects of the time span within which I am writing. But it would be the same eidetic "a" if it is written as A or as a/A, a/A, a/A and the like. The intelligible/sensible distinction is present in the formation of words as sensibly present individuals—abstracting from the fact that the words so formed incarnate the apprehension of universal terms. The components of words are themselves exhibitions of a culturally formed eidetic alphabet.

The accumulation of observations, interpretations, and choices sedi-

21. Cf. Lewis Mumford, *The Myth of the Machine: Technics and Human Development* (New York: Harcourt, Brace, and World, 1976), 79.

ments into a habituated world that is shared by others and passed on to offspring. It fills the initially empty space of meaning between the animal Now and our empty, founding orientation toward the Whole. It stamps those who enter into it as "the way things are." As the Latins would have it, *cultura fit secunda natura:* culture becomes second nature. On top of the spontaneities afforded by the two poles constituting human nature, habituation, culturally stamped and individually chosen, adds another set of spontaneities.

It is not until people confront the differently sedimented worlds of interpretation and action coming out of different traditions or out of the past of their own tradition that they are forced to come to terms with real human otherness. Prior to that, the stamp of tradition is so strong that individual otherness is a minor variation on a cultural theme. One traditional way of coming to terms with otherness is condemnation of the others and exaltation of one's own—until one begins to understand something of the origins and sedimented character of one's own. Then we first meet the conditions for genuine dialogue. This is especially the case in religion that develops a system of legitimation so powerful that the individual fears—and is strongly encouraged to fear—even raising questions with regard to that religion. It is only relatively recently that religions have dared to enter into real dialogue, have dared to question their own legitimation structures. This occurs against the background of the emergence of religious freedom through the separation of religious understanding and political power and with the common threat to irrelevance posed by the developing secular world of science, technology, economics, and democratic government.

Individual, Culture, and the Heart

Once again, it is our contention that the natural human structure, what Hegel calls the structure of "subjective spirit," consists of ontological reference as founding empty intention of the totality, playing in tandem with the ever-manifest sensory emergence from the organic pole.[22] This structure places the human being on the level of ontological reference at an infinite distance from biological givenness and makes descriptive eidetic inventory, interpretation, and choice possible. Out of those

22. On the notion of "Objective Spirit," see *Hegel's Philosophy of Mind,* trans. William Wallace (Oxford: Clarendon Press, 1971); for a fuller treatment, see G. W. F. Hegel, *Elements of the Philosophy of Right,* ed. Allen W. Wood, trans. H. B. Nisbet (Cambridge: Cambridge University Press, 1991).

possibilities built into human structure emerge the multiplicity of cultural traditions, the plurality of the works of Hegelian "objective spirit" that stamp the individuals raised within them. This sets up a tension between nature and culture. But ontological distance also creates another tension: that between the individual, on the one hand, and the nature-culture tension, on the other.

At the individual level the founding structure of "subjective spirit" makes possible the distinction between I and Me. The Me is everything about myself from which I, as the conscious and initiating I, can gain distance. It includes the genetically grounded set of individual possibilities and the cultural opening and closure of those possibilities by the stamp I have received from my primary caregivers and from the impact of those who have surrounded and continue to surround me. Like the founding structure of human nature, both the genetic and the initial cultural stamp are features about which I have no choice. But when I initially came into the capacity to stand at an inward distance from those factors and determine myself by choosing from among the options they afforded, I began to determine the Me for which I am increasingly responsible. At any given moment of lucid wakeful awareness I have to decide what to do with Me, with the sedimented resultant of genetic, cultural, and personal-historical factors that afford me my real possibilities for choice now.[23]

We would have then within the Me a series of zones of greater and lesser proximity to the I. At the outermost zone, setting the framework for all achievements, would be the genetic. Closer to the I would be the cultural stamping one has received and continues to receive, and closer still the habit structure one has cooperated in forming on the basis of the other two. The biological pole provides a given set of proclivities for action. The way I come finally to take them up and set them in relation to the other features of my experience establishes that multiple set of proclivities that sediment into what a long tradition calls "the heart." The heart is the unique center formed by the meeting of my given and chosen proclivities. It sets close to me the things and persons and the lines of action I am spontaneously inclined to take in relation to those things and persons; it sets other things and persons and lines of action further from me. The heart determines significant presences that solicit my action. But as a creature of ontological distance I am still remote

23. On the I-Me relation, see Wood, *Placing Aesthetics*, 11–12.

from that which spontaneously solicits my attention and action. Consequently I still have to ask myself, "Where is my heart? And is it where it should be?" The founding ontological reference has its own natural proclivity, leading to that curious expression "in my heart of hearts" as a center of desire beyond the center constituted by my past history of passive stampings and active choices.[24]

Just as sexual desire is an expression, as Plato's Diotima would have it, of "the desire of the mortal for the immortal,"[25] even though such underlying desire is not that to which the one experiencing that desire usually attends, so there is a natural "desire for the Totality" following from the all-encompassing notion of Being that leads us to ask how what we do fits within the largest possible Whole, even though such underlying desire is also not something to which one usually attends. It is interpreted religiously as the thirst for the presence of God as all-encompassing. Augustine would say "our hearts are restless until they rest in God."[26]

Cultural Pluralism

The structure of the human individual sets the conditions for the possibility for different developments. The structure of the human race, whose basic features we have presented in the first part, sets the general frame of distinctively human possibilities. The genetic structure of each individual specifies the general limits for that individual's possibility of development within that more generalized structure. And the type and level of the culture further sets the concrete institutional parameters within which the most general and the most genetically specific can operate.

The history of the race necessarily ramifies into the history of different cultures with their own ways of understanding and acting, within which, collectively, the possibilities of humanness can be discovered and the understanding of our place in the scheme of things expanded.

24. On the notion of the heart, see Wood, "Hegel on the Heart," *International Philosophical Quarterly* 41 (2001): 131–44; see also Stephan Strasser, *Phenomenology of Feeling: An Essay on the Phenomena of the Heart,* trans. and introduction by Robert E. Wood; preface to the English edition by Paul Ricoeur (Pittsburgh: Duquesne University Press; New York: Humanities Press, 1977); and Paul Ricoeur, *Fallible Man,* trans. Charles Kelbley (Chicago: Regnery, 1965), 122–202.

25. Plato, *Symposium* 206C–208B, in *Lysis, Symposium, Gorgias,* trans. W. R. M. Lamb (Cambridge, Mass.: Harvard University Press, 1975).

26. Augustine, *Confessions* 1:1, trans. William Watts (Cambridge, Mass.: Harvard University Press, 1977).

At a certain level, the contacts between cultures led to comparisons and attempts at synthesis, with the search for standards of comparison and evaluation. The founding level of human nature affords the basis for understanding the necessity of the plurality of cultures and of individual lifestyles within cultures; but it also affords the basis for evaluation of the resultant ways of understanding and differentiation of practices as it affords us the drive toward synthesis.

At an earlier stage, realization of the fact that a culture provides the concrete possibilities for human thought and action led to the priority of the disposition of *pietas,* a sense of unpayable indebtedness to one's parents for life and upbringing, to the culture for the way of life, and to the divine for the whole context of existence.[27] And the three tended to bond together in the projection of the notion of the father from the family to the head of the group and on to the ground of being itself. Fathers determined the occupation and the marriage partners of their children, and the king-father commanded the group, while the Father in heaven backed up the institutional arrangement.

With the emergence of the study of comparative cultures and the search for measures that transcend cultures, one measure of a culture became the degree to which it fosters such inquiry. Inquiry takes place by means of individuals standing at the level of ontological reference, pried loose from both biology and culture and taking their measure from what emerges through inquiry. This establishes a certain dignity to the individual human being. Though at one level that dignity was deeply ingrained in the religious tradition of the West, at the same time freedom of choice and of inquiry were severely restricted by the alliance of that tradition with political power. A first step was the separation of religion from political power and thus freedom of choice in religion, which, when it emerged, was viewed as an extreme act of impiety.[28] Thomas Aquinas held that one is obliged to follow one's conscience; but, on the other hand, he held that the civil power is responsible to see to it that the true faith rules the realm and that heretics are to be persuaded, if possible, but excised, if necessary.[29] After the fracturing of political unity under the legitimation structure of religion, freedom of inquiry was followed by free-

27. Thomas Aquinas, *Summa theologica,* II-II, q. 103, a. 3, ad 1.

28. See Pius IX, *Quanta Cura and the Syllabus of Errors: The Pope Against Modern Errors,* ed. A. Minoni (Rockford, Ill.: Tan Books, 1999), especially 17, 24, 77; and John Locke, "An Essay Concerning Toleration," 184–209, and "A Letter Concerning Toleration," 390–435, in *Political Writings of John Locke,* ed. David Wooton (London: Penguin Books, 1993).

29. Aquinas, *Summa theologica,* II-II, q. 10, a. 8 and q. 11, a. 3.

dom of dissemination of the results of inquiry, freedom of assembly, free election of leaders, and free enterprise.[30] This was allied with what were viewed as acts of impiety toward the family through free choice of marriage partners and occupations. The fathers no longer dominated the marriages and lifework of their children; the father-king was subject to his subjects' elective choice and no longer determined enterprise; and the Father in heaven no longer directly supported the paternal regime.

"Freedom" is the watchword of the modern world, its one absolute, in spite of, indeed as a major cause of, the claim to ethical and cognitive relativism. The advancement of freedom to the center of human existence is perhaps *the* achievement, the true glory of modernity, but also its central problem.[31] It emerged at the expense of that *pietas* that held the premodern world together. Is there any possibility of a rapprochement between these two views?

Earlier, Martin Buber wrote on "the dialogical principle" and claimed that our epoch afforded the situation for a real dialogue between religions, rather than polemically speaking past one another as they always have. The dialogue must be rooted in a real meeting with the Other, a dialogue first of all of life-to-life with deepest respect and the capacity to respond from the depth of one's being, with the possibility of a move from communication to communion. Traditions necessarily degenerate from original Presence to morality and religion as objectifications and hardenings. And "just as nothing can hide from us the face of our fellow man as morality can, so nothing can hide from us the face of God so much as religion can."[32]

The Dialogical Imperative

The bipolar structure of human nature grounds cultural and individual diversity and calls forth intelligence and creativity, but it also grounds critique of individual and cultural understanding and practice. It imposes a dialogical imperative: to seek the other, to understand the

30. Grounding such rights is at the center of Hegel's *Philosophy of Right:* on love, conscience, and inquiry, Hegel, *Elements of the Philosophy of Right,* §124, 151–52; on conscience, §137/201–2; on choice of marriage partners, §162/201–2; on religion, §270/291ff; on speech and the press, §319/355–58; on property, §41ff; on occupation, §254/272.

31. On Hegel's notion of freedom see *Hegel's Philosophy of Mind,* 481–82, 238–40; and Hegel, *Lectures on the Philosophy of World History,* trans. H. B. Nisbet (Cambridge: Cambridge University Press, 1975), 47–55 and *passim.*

32. Martin Buber, "Dialogue," in *Between Man and Man,* trans. Ronald G. Smith (Boston: Beacon Press, 1955), 1–39, and esp. 54.

other, to let the self and the other be measured by what emerges from the dialogue. It aims at an ideal consensus open to its own correction through dissensus, which, contrary to Lyotard, only makes sense in terms of an aim at a richer consensus. Difference is not a final aim, except as a contribution to identity. The difference of cultures is their contribution to humanity.

Reference to the Whole sets us at a distance from all putative claims to theoretical and practical completion. Human nature at its deepest level generates and transcends the second natures we have produced on its basis. It raises in principle questions with regard to the final adequacy of given ways of understanding and consequent ways of life. In fact it poses the demand that questioning go forward.[33] Rather than letting us rest complacently with our individual and cultural proclivities, it puts them all into question. Indeed, as the condition for the possibility for all responsible questioning, it puts oneself into question first of all. Where should my heart be? Ultimately in that place where it is respectful of all beings, most respectful of all humans, founded upon respect for oneself as responsible openness to the Whole.

And though one's first measures for that self-questioning are culturally provided, the power of the questioning can then be focused upon the cultural measures themselves. If humility consists in letting oneself be measured, a deeper humility lets one's measures be measured. In fact, the claim to having the final measures too often tends to make one arrogant and closed. The vehicle of such questioning is dialogue: the opening out of oneself to the other for mutual testing and consequently mutual refutation and/or confirmation. The dialogical imperative is rooted in the sense of our own individual and collective questionability on the one hand and an appreciation for one's own and one's culture's achievements on the other: freedom of inquiry—and the imperative of inquiry—on the one hand and *pieta* towards one's tradition on the other. We can understand and act and question the adequacy of our ways of understanding and acting, not only because of our common human nature, but also because we are the recipients of specific ways of understanding and acting, including the tradition of questioning the adequacy of our ways of understanding and acting.[34] In dialogue we "bear witness" to

33. See Charles Peirce's imperative: "Do not block the way of inquiry," "The Scientific Attitude and Fallibilism,"in *Philosophical Writings of Peirce,* ed. Justus Buchler (New York: Dover, 1955), 54.

34. This moves in the direction of Alasdair MacIntyre's notion of tradition-bound

ourselves and our traditions as well as submit them and ourselves with them to a questioning that is not only self-generating, but that comes from the testimony of the other, inside and outside our specific tradition. In virtue of our common human nature, oriented toward a totality that we do not and cannot fully possess, we are essentially "on the way," in the tension between the past and the future, between *pietas* and freedom, in the tension between the self and the other, in the tension between bearing witness and questioning, both individually and collectively. Human nature generates culture, transcends any given culture, and imposes the dialogical imperative involved in the plurality of cultural modes and modes of transcendence.

---

inquiry, but gives it a ground; see MacIntyre's "The Rationality of Traditions," *Whose Justice, Which Rationality?* (Notre Dame, Ind.: University of Notre Dame Press, 1988), 349–69.

A CHRONOLOGICAL BIBLIOGRAPHY OF WORKS BY KENNETH L. SCHMITZ

Monographs

Art and Logic in Hegel's Philosophy. Edited by Kenneth L. Schmitz and Warren E. Steinkraus. Atlantic Highlands, N.J.: Humanities Press; Sussex: Harvester Press, 1980.

What Has Clio to Do with Athena? Etienne Gilson: Historian and Philosopher. The Etienne Gilson Series 10. Toronto: Pontifical Institute of Mediaeval Studies, 1987.

At the Center of the Human Drama: The Philosophical Anthropology of Karol Wojtyla/Pope John Paul II. Washington, D.C.: The Catholic University of America Press, 1993.

The Gift: Creation. The Aquinas Lecture. Milwaukee, Wisc.: Marquette University Press, 1982. Translated by Sebastian Greiner into German as *Das Geschenk des Seins: die Schopfüng.* Einsiedeln: Johannes Verlag, 1995.

The Recovery of Wonder: The New Freedom and the Asceticism of Power. Montreal and Kingston: McGill-Queen's University Press, 2005.

The Texture of Being: Essays in First Philosophy. Edited by Paul O'Herron. Studies in Philosophy and the History of Philosophy 46. Washington, D.C.: The Catholic University of America Press, 2007.

Contributed Chapters in Books

"Towards a Metaphysical Restoration of Natural Things." In *An Etienne Gilson Tribute,* edited by Charles O'Neill. Milwaukee, Wisc.: Marquette University Press, 1959.

"Max Picard and the World of Silence." In *Masterpieces of Catholic Literature,* edited by Ian McCreal. New York: Salem Press, 1966.

"Phenomenology and the Notion of Person." In *Current Issues in Modern Philosophy: New Departures in Colleges and Seminaries,* edited by George McLean. Washington, D.C.: The Catholic University of America Press, 1969.

"Sport and Play: Suspension of the Ordinary." In *Sport and the Body,* edited by Ellen Gerber. Philadelphia: Lea and Febiger, 1972. Reprinted in *Sport in the Sociocultural Process,* edited by Marie Hart. Dubuque, Iowa: W.C. Brown, 1972–1976.

"The Conceptualization of Religious Mystery: An Essay in Hegel's Philosophy of Religion." In *The Legacy of Hegel: Proceedings of the Marquette Hegel Symposium,* edited by Joseph J. O'Malley, Keith W. Algozin, Howard P. Kainz, and Lee C. Rice. The Hague: Martinus Nijhoff, 1973.

"Human Nature, History and the Transcendental Character of Being." In *Scholasticism in the Modern World: Proceedings of the American Catholic Philosophical Association* 40, edited by George McLean. Washington, D.C.: American Catholic Philosophical Association, 1966.

"Hegel's Philosophy of Religion." In *Religion in Contemporary Thought,* edited by George McLean. New York: Alba House, 1973. Revised version printed as "Hegel's Philosophy of Religion: Typology and Strategy." In *Review of Metaphvsics* 23 (1975):717–36.

"Shapes of Evil in Mediaeval Epics: A Philosophical Analysis." In *The Epic in Medieval Society,* edited by Harald Scholler. Tübingen: Max Niemeyer, 1977.

"The Given and the Gift: Two Different Readings of the World." In *The Human Person and Philosophy in the Contemporarv World,* edited by Joseph M. Zycinski. Krakow: Pontifical Faculty of Theology/Philosophical Section, 1980.

"Hegel's Assessment of Spinoza." In *The Philosophy of Baruch Spinoza,* edited by Richard Kennington. Studies in Philosophy and the History of Philosophy 7. Washington, D.C.: The Catholic University of America Press, 1980.

"Natural Imagery as a Discriminatory Element in Religious Language." In *Experience, Reason and God,* edited by Eugene T. Long. Studies in Philosophy and the History of Philosophy 8. Washington, D.C.: The Catholic University of America Press, 1980.

"The Element of Mystery in the Conception of God." In *The Challenge of Religion Today,* edited by Frederick Ferre, Joseph Kockelmans, and John E. Smith. New York: Seabury, 1982.

"Philosophy of Religion and the Redefinition of Philosophy." In *The Challenge of Religion Today,* edited by Frederick Ferre, Joseph Kockelmans, and John E. Smith. New York: Seabury, 1982.

"The Restitution of Meaning in Religious Speech." In *The Challenge of Religion Today,* edited by Frederick Ferre, Joseph Kockelmans, and John E. Smith. New York: Seabury, 1982.

"Analysis by Principles and Analysis by Elements." In *Graceful Reason: Essavs in Ancient and Mediaeval Philosophy,* edited by Lloyd Gerson. Toronto: Pontifical Institute of Medieval Studies, 1983.

"A Question of Duration: Timelessness and Timefulness. In *In Spirit and in Truth: Essays Dedicated to Fr. Ignatius Hirudayam, S.J.,* edited by Ignatius Viyagappa, S.J. Madras, India: Aikiya Alayam, 1985.

"Gibt es für den Menschen Wichtigeres, als zu überleben? Das Erbe Griechenlands: Rationalität." In *Das Europaische Erbe und Seine Christliche Zukunft,* vol. 16, edited by Nicholas Lobkowicz. Cologne: Hans Martin Schleyer-Stiftung/Pontificium Consilium pro Cultura, 1985.

"Hegel on Kant: Being-in-Itself and the Thing-in-Itself." In *The Philosophy of Immanuel Kant,* edited by Richard Kennington. Studies in Philosophy and the History of Philosophy 12. Washington, D.C.: The Catholic University of America Press, 1985.

"Temporal Integrity, Eternity and Implicate Order." In *Beyond Mechanism: The Universe in Recent Physics and Catholic Thought,* edited by David L. Schindler. New York: University Press of America, 1986.

"La transcendance coincidente: Fondement de l'interrogation religieuse." In *Urgence de la Philosophie,* edited by Thomas De Koninck and Lucien Morin. Quebec: Les Presses de 1'Universite Laval, 1986.

"Faith and Practice: The Nature and Importance of Religious Activities." In *The Life of Religion: A Marquette University Symposium on the Nature of Religious Belief,* edited by Stanley M. Harrison and Richard C. Taylor. Lanham, Md.: University Press of America, 1986.

"Hegel on War and Peace." In *Conceptions de la paix dans 1'histoire de la philosophie,* edited by Venant Cauchy, 127–40. Montreal: Editions Montmorency, 1987.

"Why Philosophy Must Have a History: Hegel's Proposal." In *Doing Philosophy Historically,* edited by Peter Hare. Buffalo: Prometheus Books, 1988.

"Some Cultural Implications of Technology." In *Servo Veritatis.* Krakow: Uniwersytet Jagielionski, 1988.

"Paradigms of Nature in Western Thought." In *Man and Nature: The Chinese Tradition and the Future,* edited by Tang Yi- Jie, Li Shen, and George McLean. New York: University Press of America, 1989.

"Sources of Community: Reflections on America." In *Catholicism and Secularization in America: Essays on Nature, Grace, and Culture,* edited by David L. Schindler. Huntington, Ind.: Our Sunday Visitor; Notre Dame, Ind.: Communio, 1990.

"Is Liberalism Good Enough?" In *Liberalism and the Good,* edited by R. Bruce Douglass, Gerald M. Mara, and Henry S. Richardson. New York and London: Routledge, 1990.

"The Unity of Human Nature and the Diversity of Cultures." In *Relations between Cultures,* edited by George McLean and John Kromkowski. Washington, D.C.: Council for Research in Values and Philosophy, 1991.

"The Bounds of Art." In *Philosophy and Art,* edited by Daniel O. Dahlstrom. Studies in the Philosophy and the History of Philosophy 23. Washington, D.C.: The Catholic University of America Press, 1991.

"Theological Clearances: Foreground to a Rational Recovery of God." In *Prospects for Natural Theology,* edited by Eugene T. Long. Studies in the Philosophy and the History of Philosophy 25. Washington, D.C.: The Catholic University of America Press, 1992.

"Trans-Formal Mediation in Responsibility and Authority." In *Conflict and Community: New Studies in Thomistic Thought,* edited by Michael Lukens. New York and Frankfurt am Main: Peter Lang, 1992.

"From Anarchy to Principles: Deconstruction and the Resources of Christian Philosophy." In *The Philosophy of Person: Solidarity and Cultural Creativity,* edited by Jozef Tischner, Joseph M. Zycinski, and George F. McLean. Washington, D.C.: Paideia Publishers and the Council for Research in Values and Philosophy, 1994.

"The Root and Branch of St. Thomas's Thought." In *Thomas Aquinas and His Legacy,* edited by David M. Gallagher, 1–15. Studies in the Philosophy and the History of Philosophy 28. Washington, D.C.: The Catholic University of America Press, 1994.

"Naming God: Analogical Negation." In *Christian Spirituality and the Culture of Modernity: The Thought of Louis Dupré,* edited by Peter J. Casarella and George P. Schner. Grand Rapids, Mich., and Cambridge: Eerdmans, 1998.

"Lessing at God's Left Hand." In *Modern Enlightenment and the Rule of Reason,* edited by John C. McCarthy. Studies in the Philosophy and the History of Philosophy 32. Washington, D.C.: The Catholic University of America Press, 1998.

"The Future of the Family in the Light of its Past." In *The Family of the Future, The Future of the Family: Proceedings of the ITEST Workshop.* St. Louis, Mo.: ITEST Faith/Science Press, 1999.

"The Idealism of the German Romantics." In *The Emergence of German Idealism,* edited by Michael Baur and Daniel O. Dahlstrom. Studies in the Philosophy and the History of Philosophy 34. Washington, D.C.: The Catholic University of America Press, 1999.

"Jacques Maritain and Karol Wojtyla: Approaches to Modernity." In *The Bases of Ethics,* edited by William Sweet. Milwaukee, Wisc.: Marquette University Press, 2000.

"The Personalist Philosophy of Karol Wojtyla." In *New Catholic Encyclopedia: The Jubilee Years.* Washington, D.C.: The Catholic University of America Press, 2001.

"One Hundred Years of German Catholic Thought." In *One Hundred Years of Philosophy,* edited by Brian Shanley, O.P. Studies in the Philosophy and the History of Philosophy 36. Washington, D.C.: The Catholic University of America Press, 2001.

"God, Being and Love: New Ontological Perspectives coming from Philosophy." In *La Razon Creyente: Actas del Congreso Internacional sobre la Enciclica Fides et Ratio,* edited by J. Pradez and J. Ma. Magaz. Madrid: Studia Theologica Matritensia, 2002.

"The Apostolicity of the Eucharist and of the Church." In *At the Altar of the World: The Pontificate of John Paul II through the lens of L'Osservatore Romano and the Words of Ecclesia de Eucharistia.* Washington, D.C.: Pope John Paul II Cultural Center, 2003.

"The Integration of History and Metaphysics." In *Approaches to Metaphysics,* edited by William Sweet. Dordrecht: Kluwer Academic Publishers, 2004.

"The Lustrous Power of Beauty." In *To the Mountain: Essays in Honor of George F. McLean,* 233–45, edited by William Sweet and Hu Yeping. Taiwan: Fu Jen Catholic University Press, 2004.

"Contemporary Philosophy of Action." In *The Person and the Polis,* edited by Craig Steven Titus. Arlington, Va.: Institute for the Psychological Sciences, 2006.

"Death and the Rebirth of Man." In *The Texture of Being,* edited by Paul O'Herron. Studies in Philosophy and the History of Philosophy 46. Washington, D.C.: The Catholic University of America Press, 2007.

"The Witness of Beauty: The Profile of God." In *The Texture of Being,* edited by Paul O'Herron, 300–15. Studies in Philosophy and the History of Philosophy 46. Washington, D.C.: The Catholic University of America Press, 2007.

"Josef Pieper and the Concept of Tradition." In *A Cosmopolitan Hermit: Modernity and Tradition in the Philosophy of Josef Pieper,* edited by Bernard N. Schumacher. Washington, D.C.: The Catholic University of America Press, 2009.

Articles

"The Primacy of Christian Wisdom." *El Plavano: Education Issue* 9 (1955–56): 3–7.

"Natural Wisdom and Some Recent Philosophy Manuals." *The Role of Philosophy in the Catholic Liberal College: Proceedings of the American Catholic Philosophical Association* 30 (1956): 181–90.

"Knowing and Redeeming: A Reason for Studying." *Centre* (1961): 5–13.

"The Redemptive Role of the Knowledge of Nature." *Franciscan Studies Annual* 24 (1964): 223–60.

"Weiss and Creation." *Review of Metaphysics* 18 (1964): 147–69.

"The New Freedom and the Integrity of the Profane." *Proceedings of the Society for Catholic Teachers of Sacred Doctrine* 11 (1965): 13–38.

"Philosophical Pluralism and Philosophical Truth." *Philosophy Today* 10 nos. 1–4. (1966): 3–16.

"Father Richardson, S.J., on Heidegger." *The Modern Schoolman* 44 (1967): 247–59.

"Authority, Community, Communication." *Cross Currents* 17 (1967): 468–87.

"The Modes in Process." *Review of Metaphysics* 21 (1967): 310–42.

"The Philosophy of Religion and the Redefinition of Philosophy." *Man and World* 3 (1970): 54–82.

"Hegel's Philosophy of Religion: Typology and Strategy." *Review of Metaphysics* 23 (1970): 717–36.

"A Gloss on Being, Immediacy and Articulation." *Review of Metaphysics* 25 (1971): 112–18.

"Hegel's Attempt to Forge a Logic for Spirit." *Dialogue: Journal of the Canadian Philosophical Association* 10 (1971): 653–72.

"Art and Existence: Reflections on Paul Weiss's Modal Philosophy of Art." *Review of Metaphysics:* Twenty- fifth Anniversary Supplement 25 (1972): 71–93.

"Hegel and the Philosophy of Religion: The Wofford Symposium." *The Owl of Minerva* (1973).

"Idealism and Utopia: The Background of Hegel's Political Thought, by George Armstrong Kelly." *Catholic Historical Review* (1973).

"Scrutinizing the Inscrutable." *Review of Metaphysics* 27 (1973): 346–70.

"Enriching the Copula." *Review of Metaphysics* 27 (1974): 492–512.

"Another Look at Objectivity." *Thomas and Bonaventure: Proceedings of the American Catholic Philosophical Association* 48 (1974): 86–98.

"Restitution of Meaning in Religious Speech." *International Journal for Philosophy of Religion* 5 (1974): 131–51.

"Immanuel Kant (1724–1804): Philosopher of Reason." *The German-Canadian Year Book* 2 (1975): 253–64.

"Embodiment and Situation: Charles Taylor's *Hegel.*" *Journal of Philosophy* 73 (1976): 710–23.

"Entitative and Systemic Aspects of Evil." *Dialectics and Humanism: New Polish Philosophical Quarterly* 5 (1978): 149–61.

"Divine Initiative and Christian Praxis." *Communio: International Catholic Review* 5 (1978): 44–52.

"Immateriality Past and Present." *Immateriality: Proceedings of the American Catholic Philosophical Association* 52 (1978): 1–15.

"A Religious and Philosophical Use of the Past." *A Filosofia e as Ciencias* 4 (1978): 54–56.

"The Pluralism of Methods in Theology." *Communio: Approaches to the Study of Theology* 4 (1979): Foreword.

"Intimacy and the Knowledge of Persons." *Presenca Filosofica* 5 (1979): 45–50.

"A Moment of Truth: Present Actuality." *Review of Metaphysics* 33 (1980): 673–88.

"Ritual Elements in Community." *Religious Studies* 17 (1981): 163–77.

"Transcendental and Empirical Pressures in Human Subjectivity." *Thought: Hegel Commemorative Issue* 56 (1981): 272–86.

"An Original Mode of Communication: Vicariosity." *Filosofia e Communicacio* 7 (1981): 44–47.

"The Secularization of Western Culture and the Catholic College and University." Coauthored with Jude P. Dougherty, Thomas Langan, and Desmond Fitzgerald. *Current Issues in Catholic Higher Education* 2 (1981): 7–23.

"Community: The Elusive Unity." *Review of Metaphysics* 37 (1983): 243–64.

"Word and World in Theophany." *Faith and Philosophy* 1 (1984): 50–70.

"Natural Value." *Review of Metaphysics* 38 (1984): 3–15.

"Joachim Ritter, Hegel and the French Revolution: Essays on The Philosophv of Right." *Journal of the History of Philosophy* 12 (1984): 493–94.

"The Roots of Catholic Intellectuality." In *Catholic Commission on Intellectual and Cultural Affairs Annual 1984*. Washington, D.C.: Catholic Commission on Intellectual and Cultural Affairs, 1984.

"The Authority of Institutions: Meddling or Middling?" *Communio: International Catholic Review* 12 (1985): 5–24.

"The Geography of the Human Person." *Communio: International Catholic Review* 13 (1986): 27–48.

"Enlightenment Criticism and Embodiment of Values: The Hegelian Background to a Contemporary Problem." *Indian Philosophical Annual* 18 (1986): 33–53.

"Metaphysics: Radical, Comprehensive, Determinate Discourse." *Review of Metaphysics* 39 (1986): 675–94.

"Purity of Soul and Immortality." *Monist* 69 (1986): 396–415.

"Truths of Nature, Truths of Culture, Truths of Faith." *Philosophy and Theology* 1 (1986): 173–96.

"Substance Is Not Enough—Hegel's Slogan: From Substance to Subject." *Metaphysics of Substance: Proceedings of the American Catholic Philosophical Association* 61 (1987): 52–68.

"Concrete Presence." *Communio: International Catholic Review* 14 (1987): 300–15. Translated by Mireille de Maistre as "Presence concerte." *Revue Catholique Internationale Communio* 1 (1988): 95–114.

"Neither With nor Without Foundations." *Review of Metaphysics* 42 (1988): 3–25.

"Traces of Eternity." *Communio: International Catholic Review* 15 (1988): 294–304. Translated as "Vestigios de eternidad." *Communio: Revista Catolica Internacional* 2 (1989): 163–72.

"The History of Philosophy as Actual Philosophy." *Journal of Philosophy* 85 (1988): 673–74.
"From Anarchy to Principles: Deconstruction and the Resources of Christian Philosophy." *Communio: International Catholic Review* 16 (1989): 69–88.
"Postmodern or Modern-plus?" *Communio: International Catholic Review* 17 (1990): 152–66.
"Selves and Persons: A Difference in Loves?" *Communio: International Catholic Review* 18 (1991): 181–206.
"Natural Religion, Morality and Lessing's Ditch." *Religions and the Virtue of Religion: Proceedings of the American Catholic Philosophical Association* 65 (1991): 57–73.
"Foreword to the Special Issue on Hegel." *American Catholic Philosophical Quarterly* 65 (1991): 423–427.
"Catholicism in America." In *Communio: International Catholic Review* 19 (1992), 474–77.
"The Fortunes of Philosophy Within the Association." *Proceedings of the Catholic Philosophical Association* 66 (1992): 13–28.
"St. Thomas and the Appeal to Experience." *Catholic Theological Society of America* 47 (1992): 1–20.
"Gott mit Namen nennen." *Internationale katholische Zeitschrift Communio* 22 (1993): 3–22.
"The God of Love." *Thomist* 57 (1993): 495–508.
"On a Resistant Strain within the Hegelian Dialectic." *Owl of Minerva* 25 (1994): 147–54.
"What Happens to Tradition when History Overtakes It?" *Reason in History: Proceedings of the American Catholic Philosophical Association* 68 (1994): 59–72.
"Modernity Meets Tradition: The Philosophical Originality of Karol Wojtyla." *Crisis: A Journal of Lay Catholic Opinion* (1994): 30–36.
"The First Principle of Personal Becoming." *Review of Metaphysics* 47 (1994): 757–74.
"The Language of Conversion and the Conversion of Language." *Communio: International Catholic Review* 21 (1994): 742–64.
"Liberal Liberty and Human Freedom." *Chesterton Review* 20 (1994): 213–27.
"The Passage of Love: Wojtyla's Radiation of Fatherhood." *Communio: International Catholic Review* 22 (1995): 99–106.
"La Naturaleza Actual de la Filosofia se revela en su Historia." *Revista Latinoamericana de Filosofia* 22 (1996): 97–109.
"Created Receptivity and the Philosophy of the Concrete." *Thomist* 61 (1997): 339–71.
"The Transfiguration of Gnosis in Late Enlightenment German Thought." *Communio: International Catholic Review* 24 (1997): 691–712. Translated as "Gnostizismus im Denken der deutschen Aufklärung." *Internationale katholische Zeitschrift Communio* 26 (1997): 525–42.
"An Addendum to Further Discussion." *American Catholic Philosophical Quarterly* 73 (1999), 277–90.
"Postmodernism and the Catholic Tradition." *American Catholic Philosophical Quarterly* 73 (1999): 233–52.

"Reconstructing the Person: A Meditation on the Meaning of Personality." *Crisis: A Journal of Lay Catholic Opinion* 28 (1999): 135–38.

"From Convertibility to Convergence: The Absoluteness of Truth and the Realization of the Person in God's Plan." *Anthropotes* 15 (1999): 369–73.

"Faith and Reason: Then and Now." *Communio: International Catholic Review* 26 (1999): 595–608.

"Dies, el ser y el amor: nuevas perspectivas ontoldgicas procedentes de la filosofia." *Revista espanola de teolosia* 9 (2000): 303–29.

"A Not Uncritical Harmony." *Catholic Social Science Review* 5 (2000): 17–22.

"The Solidarity of Personalism and the Metaphysics of Existential Act." *Fides Quaerens Intellectum* 1 (2001): 183–99. Republished in *The Texture of Being*, edited by Paul O'Herron, 132–45. Studies in Philosophy and the History of Philosophy 46. Washington, D.C.: The Catholic University of America Press, 2007.

"Who Has Seen the Father?" *Josephinum Journal of Theology* 9 (2002): 56–73.

"The Ontology of Rights." *Ave Maria Law Review* 3 (2005): 275–88.

"Transcendentalism or Transcendentals? A Critical Reflection on the Transcendental Turn." *Review of Metaphysics* 58 (2005): 537–60.

"The Ingathering of Being, Time and Word, and the Inbreaking of a Transcendent Word." *Nova et Vetera* 4 (2006): 799–814.

Nonprint Media

St. Thomas Aquinas. Text by Kenneth. L. Schmitz. Narration by Charlton Heston. The Giants of Philosophy series. Ashland, Oreg.: Knowledge Products, 2006.

BIBLIOGRAPHY

Abbott, Edwin. *Flatland: A Romance in Many Dimensions.* Amherst, N.Y.: Prometheus Books, 2005.

Adorno, Theodor W. *Hegel: Three Studies.* 1963, 1971. Reprinted Cambridge, Mass.: MIT Press, 1993.

———. "Skoteinos, or How to Read Hegel." In *Hegel: Three Studies.* 1963, 1971. Reprinted Cambridge, Mass.: MIT Press, 1993).

Anderson, Thomas. *A Commentary on Gabriel Marcel's* The Mystery of Being. Milwaukee, Wisc: Marquette University Press, 2006.

———. "Gabriel Marcel on Personal Immortality." *American Catholic Philosophical Quarterly* (Summer 2006): 393–406.

Anselm. *Proslogion.* In *The Library of Christian Classics,* translated by Eugene Fairweather. Vol. 10, *A Scholastic Miscellany: Anselm to Ockham.* Philadelphia: Westminster Press, 1956.

Aquinas, Thomas. *De aeternitate mundi contra murmurantes.* Translated by Ralph McInerny. In *Thomas Aquinas Selected Writings.* London: Penguin Classics, 1998.

———. *In Boethiium de Trinitate Expositio.* Edited by P. Ucelli. Rome, 1880.

———. *On Truth.* Translated by R. W. Mulligan. Chicago: Regnery, 1952.

———. *Questiones disputatae de veritate.* Translated and edited by Raymundi M. Spiazzi. Turin and Rome: Marietti, 1949.

———. *Scriptum super Sententiis.* Piana edition. Rome: 1570. Books III and IV (dist. 1–21). Moos edition. Paris: 1933, 1947.

———. *Summa contra gentiles.* 5 vols. Translated by Anton C. Pegis, James F. Anderson, Vernon J. Bourke, and Charles J. O'Neil. Notre Dame, Ind.: University of Notre Dame Press, 1978.

———. *Summa theologiae.* Leonine edition. Rome, 1888–1903. Translated by the English Dominican Fathers. 5 vols. New York: Christian Classics, 1981.

Ariew, Roger. *Medieval Cosmology: Theories of Infinity, Place, Time, Void, and Plurality of Worlds.* Chicago: University of Chicago Press, 1985.

Aristotle. *Aristotle's Metaphysics.* Revised text with introduction and commentary by W. D. Ross. 2 vols. Oxford: Clarendon Press, 1958.

———. *The Complete Works of Aristotle: The Revised Oxford Translation.* Edited by Jonathan Barnes. 2 vols. Princeton, N.J.: Princeton University Press, 1984).

———. *De Anima*. With translation, introduction, and notes by R. D. Hicks. Cambridge: Cambridge University Press, 1907.

———. *De Anima*. Edited with an Introduction and Commentary by Sir David Ross. Oxford: Clarendon Press, 1961.

———. *Metaphysics*. Translated by Hippocrates G. Apostle. Grinnell, Iowa: Peripatetic Press, 1979.

———. *Metaphysics*. In *The Complete Works of Aristotle: The Revised Oxford Translation*. Vol. 2, edited by Jonathan Barnes. Princeton, N.J.: Princeton University Press, 1984).

———. *Nicomachean Ethics*. In *The Complete Works of Aristotle: The Revised Oxford Translation*. Vol. 2, edited by Jonathan Barnes. Princeton, N.J.: Princeton University Press, 1984).

———. *Nicomachean Ethics*. 2nd ed. Translated by Terence Irwin. Indianapolis, Ind., and Cambridge, Mass.: Hackett, 1999.

———. *On the Heavens*. In *The Complete Works of Aristotle: The Revised Oxford Translation*. Vol. 2, edited by Jonathan Barnes. Princeton, N.J.: Princeton University Press, 1984).

———. *On the Soul*. In *The Complete Works of Aristotle: The Revised Oxford Translation*. Vol. 1, edited by Jonathan Barnes. Princeton, N.J.: Princeton University Press, 1984).

———. *Politics*. In *The Complete Works of Aristotle: The Revised Oxford Translation*. Vol. 2, edited by Jonathan Barnes. Princeton, N.J.: Princeton University Press, 1984).

———. *Posterior Analytics*. In *The Complete Works of Aristotle: The Revised Oxford Translation*. Vol. 2, edited by Jonathan Barnes. Princeton, N.J.: Princeton University Press, 1984).

Aubert, Roger. "Le concile du Vatican et la connaissance naturelle de Dieu." *Lumière et vie*, no. 14 (March 1954): 185.

Augustine. *City of God*. Translated by Henry Bettenson. London: Penguin Books, 1981.

———. *Confessions*. 2 volumes. Translated by William Watts. Cambridge, Mass.: Harvard University Press, 1977.

———. *Letters*, vol. 2 (83–130). Translated by Sr. Wilfred Parsons, S.N.D. Washington, D.C.: The Catholic University of America Press, 2008.

Bacon, Francis. *Sylva Sylvarum*. In *The Works of Francis Bacon*, vol. 2. Edited by James Spedding, Robert Leslie Ellis, and Douglas Denon Heath. London: Longman, 1859.

Baiins, Paul. *The Primacy of Semiosis: An Ontology of Relations*. Toronto: University of Toronto Press, 2006.

Bark, W. C. *Origins of the Medieval World*. New York: Doubleday Anchor, 1960.

Bates, Jennifer. *Hegel and Shakespeare on Moral Imagination*. Albany: State University of New York Press, 2010.

———. *Hegel's Theory of Imagination*. Albany, N.Y.: State University of New York Press, 2004.

Bateson, Gregory. *Steps to an Ecology of Mind: Collected Essays in Anthropology, Psychiatry, Evolution, and Epistemology*. Northvale, N.J., and London: Aronson, 1987.

Benedict XVI. "Meeting with the Representatives of Science, Lecture of the Holy Father, Aula Magna of the University of Regensburg, September 12, 2006: Faith, Reason and the University: Memories and Reflections." Available at http://www.vatican.va/holy_father/benedict_xvi/speeches/2006/september/documents/hf_ben-xvi_spe_20060912_university-regensburg_en.html.

Benveniste, Emile. *Problèmes de linguistique générale*. Vol. 1. Paris: Gallimard, 1966.

Berti, Enrico. *Struttura e significato della Metafisica di Aristotle*. Rome: Edizioni Università della Santa Croce, 2006.

Betz, John R. "Beyond the Sublime: The Aesthetics of the Analogy of Being (Part One)." *Modern Theology* 21 (2005), 367–411.

———. "Beyond the Sublime: The Aesthetics of the Analogy of Being (Part Two)." *Modern Theology* 22 (2006): 12–50.

Beuchot, Mauricio, and John Deely. "Common Sources for the Semiotic of Charles Peirce and John Poinsot." *Review of Metaphysics* 48 (1995): 539–66.

Bloch, Marc. *Feudal Society*. Translated by L. A. Manyon. Chicago: University of Chicago Press, 1961.

Boethius. *Consolation of Philosophy*. Translated by Joel C. Relihan. Indianapolis, Ind., and Cambridge, Mass.: Hackett, 2001.

Boswell, James. *Life of Johnson*. Edited by R. W. Chapman. Oxford: Oxford University Press, 1980.

Brentano, Franz. *Psychologie von Empirischen Standpunkt*. 1874. Translated by Linda McAlister, Antos C. Rancurello, and D. B. Terrell as *Psychology from an Empirical Standpoint*. New York: Humanities Press, 1963.

Buber, Martin. "Dialogue." In *Between Man and Man*, translated by Ronald G. Smith, 1–39, 54. Boston: Beacon Press, 1955.

Burbidge, John W. "Hegel's Absolutes." *Owl of Minerva* 29, no. 1 (1997): 23–37.

———. *Hegel's Systematic Contingency*. Basingstoke: Palgrave Macmillan, 2007.

———. *The Logic of Hegel's Logic: An Introduction*. Peterborough, Ont.: Broadview Press, 2006.

Butterfield, Herbert. *Origins of Modern Science*. New York: Macmillan, 1957.

Buttiglione, Rocco. *Karol Wojtyla*. Translated by Paolo Guietti and Francesca Murphy. Grand Rapids, Mich.: Eerdmans, 1997.

Cassiodorus. The *Institutiones* of *Cassiodorus Cassiodori Senatoris Institutiones*. Edited by Roger A. B. Mynors. Oxford: Clarendon Press, 1937.

Catechism of the Catholic Church. New York: Random House, 1995.

Cavarnos, Constantine. *The Classical Theory of Relations: A Study in the Metaphysics of Plato, Aristotle, and Thomism*. Belmont, Mass.: Institute for Byzantine and Modern Greek Studies, 1975.

Caws, Peter. "Sartrean Structuralism?" In *The Cambridge Companion to Sartre*, edited by Christina Howells, 293–317. Cambridge: Cambridge University Press, 1992.

Chenu, Maria-Dominique. *The Scope of the Summa of St. Thomas*. Translated by Robert E. and Albert M. Landry. Washington, D.C.: The Catholic University of America Press, 1958.

———. "The Symbolist Mentality." In *Nature, Man, and Society in the Twelfth*

Century, edited and translated by Jerome Taylor and Lester K. Little, 99–145. Toronto: University of Toronto Press, 1997.

Chrétien, Jean-Louis. "The Wounded Word: Phenomenology of Prayer." In *Phenomenology and the Theological Turn: The French Debate,* translated by Bernard G. Prusak, 147–75. New York: Fordham University Press, 2000.

Collingwood, Robin G. *The Principles of Art.* Oxford: Clarendon Press, 1938.

Collins, James. "Przywara's 'Analogia Entis.'" *Thought* 65 (1990): 266–77.

Connor, Peter Tracey. *George Bataille and the Mysticism of Sin.* Baltimore: Johns Hopkins University Press, 2000.

Contat, Michael, Oreste Pucciani, and Susan Gruenwald. "Interview with Sartre." In *The Philosophy of Jean-Paul Sartre,* edited by Phillip Schilpp, 8. LaSalle, Ill.: Open Court Press, 1981.

Cornell, Drucilla. *The Philosophy of the Limit.* New York: Routledge, 1992.

Crick, Francis. *The Astonishing Hypothesis.* New York: Scribner, 1994.

Crombie, A. C. *The History of Science from Augustine to Galileo.* 2nd ed. New York: Dover, 1996.

Crombie, A. C. *Medieval and Early Modern Science.* Vol 1, *Science in the Middle Ages: V–XIII Centuries;* vol. 2, *Science in the Later Middle Ages and Early Modern Times: XIII–XVII Centuries.* Garden City, N.Y.: Doubleday Anchor Books, 1959.

———. *Robert Grosseteste and the Origins of Experimental Science, 1100–1700.* Oxford: Oxford University Press, 1971.

David, Anthony. "Hamlet, Prince of Denmark." In *The Oxford Companion to Shakespeare,* 179–83. Oxford: Oxford University Press, 2001.

Davies, Paul. "This Contradiction." In *Futures: Of Jacques Derrida,* 18–64. Stanford, Calif.: Stanford University Press, 2001.

Dawson, Christopher. *Christianity and the New Age.* London: Sheed and Ward, 1931.

———. *The Modern Dilemma.* London: Sheed and Ward, 1933.

———. "The Origins of the European Scientific Tradition: St. Thomas and Roger Bacon." *The Clergy Review* 2 (1931): 193–205.

———. *Progress and Religion.* Garden City, N.Y.: Doubleday Image, 1960.

Deely, John. "Animal Intelligence and Concept-Formation." Fourth Reading. In *Realism for the 21st Century: A John Deely Reader,* edited by Paul Cobley. Scranton, Penn.: University of Scranton Press, 2009.

———. *Augustine and Poinsot: The Protosemiotic Development.* Scranton, Penn.: University of Scranton Press, 2009.

———. "Defining the Semiotic Animal: A Postmodern Definition of Human Being Superseding the Modern Definition 'Res Cogitans.'" *American Catholic Philosophical Quarterly* 79 (2005): 461–81.

———. "Editorial Afterword" and "Critical Apparatus" to *Tractatus de Signis: The Semiotic of John Poinsot.* Edited and translated by John Deely. Berkeley: University of California Press, 1985.

———. "The Ethical Entailment of Being a Semiotic Animal, or Why the Semiotic Animal Needs to Develop a Semioethics." In John Deely, *Semiotic Amimal: A Postmodern Definition of Human Being Transcending Patriarchy and Feminism,* 107–25. South Bend, Ind.: St. Augustine's Press, 2010.

———. *Four Ages of Understanding: The First Postmodern Survey of Philosophy from Ancient Times to the Turn of the Twenty-First Century.* Toronto: University of Toronto Press, 2001.

———. "The Full Vista of the Action of Signs." In *Basics of Semiotics.* 5th expanded edition, 233–75. Tartu, Estonia: Tartu University Press, 2009).

———. "How Do Signs Work?" In *New Beginnings: Early Modern Philosophy and Postmodern Thought,* 151–82. Toronto: University of Toronto Press, 1994.

———. "How Does Semiosis Effect Renvoi?" Thomas A. Sebeok Fellowship Inaugural Lecture from October 22, 1993. *American Journal of Semiotics* 11 (1994): 11–61.

———. *The Impact on Philosophy of Semiotics: The Quasi-Error of the External World, with a Dialogue between a "Semiotist" and a "Realist."* South Bend, Ind.: St. Augustine's Press, 2003.

———. *Intentionality and Semiotics: A Story of Mutual Fecundation.* Scranton, Penn.: University of Scranton Press, 2007.

———. *Medieval Philosophy Redefined.* Scranton, Penn.: University of Scranton Press, 2010.

———. *New Beginnings: Early Modern Philosophy and Postmodern Thought.* Toronto: University of Toronto Press, 1994.

———. "The Nonverbal Inlay in Linguistic Communication." In *The Signifying Animal,* edited by Irmengard Rauch and Gerald F. Carr. Bloomington: Indiana University Press, 1980.

———. "Peirce's Grand Vision." In *Peirce's Doctrine of Signs,* edited by Vincent M. Colapietro and Thomas M. Olshewsky, 45–67. Berlin: Mouton de Gruyter, 1996.

———. "Physiosemiosis and Phytosemiosis." In *Basics of Semiotics.* Bloomington, Ind.: Indiana University Press, 1990.

———. *Purely Objective Reality.* Berlin: Mouton de Gruyter, 2010.

———. "The Role of Thomas Aquinas in the Development of Semiotic Consciousness." *Semiotica* 152 (2004): 75–139.

———. "The Semiosis of Angels." *The Thomist* 68, no. 2 (April 2004): 205–58.

———. "Semiotic and the Controversy over Mental Events." In *Immateriality: Proceedings of the American Catholic Philosophical Association* 52 (1978): 16–27.

———. "Semiotics and Jakob von Uexküll's Concept of Umwelt." *Sign System Studies* 32, nos. 1–2 (2004): 11–34.

———. "A Sign Is *What?*" Presidential Address to the Semiotic Society of America's 26th Annual Meeting. *Sign Systems Studies* 29, no. 2 (2001): 705–43. Reprinted as "Dramatic Reading in Three Voices: 'A Sign Is *What?*'" *The American Journal of Semiotics* 20 (2004): 1–66.

———. "The Thomistic Import of the Neo-Kantian Concept of Umwelt in Jakob von Uexküll." *Angelicum* 81, no. 4 (2004): 711–32.

———. "Umwelt." *Semiotica* 134, nos. 1–4 (2001): 125–35.

Deely, John, Susan Petrilli, and Augusto Ponzio, eds. *The Semiotic Animal.* Ottawa: Legas Publishing, 2005.

De Lubac, Henri. *Augustinianism and Modern Theology.* Translated by Lancelot Sheppard. New York: Crossroad, 2000.

———. *Catholicism*. London: Burns and Oates (Universe Book Editions), 1962.

———. "Retrieving the Tradition: On Christian Philosophy." *Communio: International Catholic Review* 19 (1992): 478–506.

De Montheux, Pierre Guillet. *The Art Firm: Aesthetic Management and Metaphysical Marketing*. Stanford, Calif.: Stanford Business Books, 2004.

Derrida, Jacques. "Difference." In *Speech and Phenomena and Other Essays*, translated by David B. Allison, 129–60. Evanston, Ill.: Northwestern University Press, 1973.

———. *Of Grammatology*. Translated by Gayatri Chakravorty Spivak. Baltimore: Johns Hopkins University Press, 1976.

———. *Of Spirit: Heidegger and the Question*. Translated by Geoffrey Bennington and Rachel Bowlby. Chicago: University of Chicago Press, 1989.

———. "The Supplement of the Copula: Philosophy Before Linguistics." In *Margins of Philosophy*, translated by Alan Bass, 194–205. Chicago: University of Chicago Press, 1982.

———. "Violence and Metaphysics." In *Writing and Difference*, translated by Alan Bass (Chicago: University of Chicago Press, 1978.

Descartes, Rene. *Discourse on Method*. In *The Philosophical Writings of Descartes*. Translated by John Cottingham, Robert Stoothoff, and Dugald Murdoch. Cambridge: Cambridge University Press, 1985.

Des Noëttes, Lefebvre. *l'Attelage et le cheval de selle à travers les ages*. Paris: 1931.

———. *De la marine antique à la marine moderne*. Paris: 1935.

Donougho, Martin. "Art and History: Hegel on the End, the Beginning, and the Future of Art." In *Hegel and the Arts*, edited by Stephen Houlgate, 179–215. Evanston, Ill.: Northwestern University Press, 2007.

———. "Hegel, Philosopher of the Secular [*irdischen*] World: On the Dialectics of Narrative." In *Hegel and the Tradition: Essays in Honour of H. S. Harris*, edited by Michael Baur and John Russon. Toronto: University of Toronto Press, 1998.

———. "Hegel's Art of Memory." In *Endings: Questions of Memory in Hegel and Heidegger*, edited by Rebecca Comay and John McCumber, 139–59, 229–36. Evanston, Ill.: Northwestern University Press, 1999.

———. "Hegel's Pragmatics of Tragedy." *Idealistic Studies* 36, no. 3 (2006): 153–68.

———. "On the Hegelian Sublime: Paul de Man's Judgment Call." *Philosophy and Rhetoric* 34, no. 1 (2001): 1–20.

Duhem, Pierre. *Le Systeme du monde: Histoire des doctrines cosmologiques de Platon à Copernic*. Paris: Hermann.

Dulles, Avery Cardinal, S.J. "Faith and Reason: From Vatican I to John Paul II." In *The Two Wings of Catholic Thought: Essays on* Fides et Ratio, edited by David Ruel Foster and Joseph W. Koterski, S.J., 193–208. Washington, D.C.: The Catholic University of America Press, 2003.

Dupré, Louis. *Passage to Modernity*. New Haven: Yale University Press, 1993.

Emmeche, Claus. *The Garden in the Machine*. Princeton, N.J.: Princeton University Press, 1994.

Fairweather, Eugene. *The Library of Christian Classics*. Vol. 10, *A Scholastic Miscellany: Anselm to Ockham*. Philadelphia: Westminster Press, 1956.

Farrington, Benjamin. *Greek Science*. London: Penguin, 1952.

Fichte, Johann Gottlieb. *Science of Knowledge*. Edited and translated by Peter Heath and John Lachs. Cambridge: Cambridge University Press, 1982.

First Vatican Council. *Dei Filius*. In *Enchiridion Symbolorum*, edited by Heinrich Denzinger and Adolf Schönmetzer. First published in 1785 and 1806. Freiburg, Basel, Rome, and Vienna: Herder, 1997.

Flynn, Thomas R. *Sartre, Foucault and Historical Reason*. Vol. 2, *A Poststructuralist Mapping of History*. Chicago: University of Chicago Press, 2005.

Franks, Angela Franz. "Trinitarian *Analogia Entis* in Hans Urs von Balthasar." *The Thomist* 62 (1998): 533–59.

Frege, Gottlob. *The Foundations of Arithmetic*. Translated by J. L. Austin. New York: Harper, 1960.

———. "Letter to Husserl (1906)." In The *Frege Reader*, edited by Michael Beaney, 301–7. Oxford: Blackwell, 1997.

———. "On *Sinn* and *Bedeutung*." In *The Frege Reader*, edited by Michael Beaney, 151–71. Oxford: Blackwell, 1997.

———. "Review of Husserl's *Philosophie der Arithmetik*." Reprinted in *Translations from the Philosophical Writings of Gottlob Frege*, edited by Peter Geach and Max Black, 79. Oxford: Blackwell, 1966.

Freud, Sigmund. *The Ego and the Id*. New York: W. W. Norton, 1962. Reprinted as Standard Edition. Edited by James Strachey, with an Introduction by Peter Gay. New York: W. W. Norton, 1994.

Frings, Manfred. *Max Scheler*. 2nd ed. Milwaukee: Marquette University Press, 1996.

Fromm, Erich. *The Art of Loving*. New York: Harper and Row, 1989.

Gadamer, Hans-Georg. *Truth and Method*. New York: Crossroads, 1975.

Gaukroger, Stephen. *The Emergence of a Scientific Culture: Science and the Shaping of Modernity, 1210–1685*. Oxford: Clarendon Press, 2006.

Gibson, James J. *The Ecological Approach to Visual Perception*. New York: Houghton Mifflin, 1979.

Gilson. Étienne. *History of Christian Philosophy in the Middle Ages*. New York: Random House, 1955.

Gredt, Josephus. "De Cognitione Sensuum Externorum: Inquisitio psychologico-criteriologica circa realismum criticum et objectivitatem qualitatum sensibilium." Rome: Desclée and Socii, Editores Pontificii, 1924.

———. *Elementa Philosophiae Aristotelico-Thomisticae*. 2 Vols. Barcelona: Herder, 1899–1901.

Guardini, Romano. *World and Person*. Translated by Stella Lange. Chicago: Regnery, 1939.

Habermas, Jürgen. "Discourse Ethics: Notes on a Program of Philosophical Justification." In *Moral Consciousness and Communicative Action*, translated by Christian Lenhardt and Shierry Webster Nicholsen, 43–115. Cambridge, Mass.: MIT University Press, 1990.

Hanslick, Eduard. *On the Musically Beautiful*. Translated and edited by Geoffrey Payzant. Indianapolis, Ind.: Hackett, 1986.

Hart, Kevin. *The Dark Gaze: Maurice Blanchot and the Sacred*. Chicago: University of Chicago Press, 2004.

Hay, Jonathan. "Interventions: The Mediating Work of Art." *Art Bulletin* 89 (2007): 435–59.

———. Review of *Ten Thousand Things,* by Lothar Ledderose. *Art Bulletin* 86 (2004): 381–84.

Hegel, G. W. F. *Ästhetik. Bände 1 and 2.* Nach der zweiten Ausgabe von H. G. Hothos (1842). Edited by Friedrich Bassenge. Frankfurt am Main: Europäische Verlagsanstalt, 1955.

———. *Elements of the Philosophy of Right.* Edited by Allen W. Wood. *Translated by* H. B. Nisbet. Cambridge: Cambridge University Press, 1991.

———. *The Encyclopaedia Logic.* Translated by T. F. Geraets, W. A. Suchting, and H. S. Harris. Indianapolis, Ind., and Cambridge, Mass.: Hackett, 1991.

———. *Encyclopaedia Philosophy of Mind.* Translated by William Wallace. With Zusätze in Boumann's Text (1845). Translated by A. V. Miller. Oxford: Clarendon Press, 1971.

———. *Grundlinien der Philosophie des Rechts.* Hamburg: Verlag von Felix Meiner, 1955.

———. *Hegel's Aesthetics: Lectures on Fine Art.* Vols. 1–2. Translated by T. M. Knox. Oxford: Clarendon Press, 1975.

———. *Hegel's Logic: Being Part One of the Encyclopaedia of Philosophical Sciences.* Translated by William Wallace. Oxford: Clarendon Press, 1975.

———. *Hegel's Phenomenology of Spirit.* Translated by A. V. Miller. Oxford, New York, Toronto, and Melbourne: Oxford University Press, 1977.

———. *Hegel's Philosophy of Mind.* Translated by William Wallace. Oxford: Clarendon Press, 1971.

———. *Hegel's Philosophy of Right.* Translated by T. M. Knox. London, Oxford, and New York: Oxford University Press, 1967.

———. *Hegel's Science of Logic.* Translated by A. V. Miller. London: Allen and Unwin, 1969.

———. *Hegel's Systematic Contingency.* Basingstoke, UK: Palgrave Macmillan, 2007.

———. "Introduction to the Philosophy of Nature." In *Philosophy of Nature,* translated by Michael John Petry. London and New York: Humanities Press, 1970.

———. *Lectures on the Philosophy of World History.* Translated by H. B. Nisbet. Cambridge: Cambridge University Press, 1975.

———. *The Logic of Hegel. Translated by* William Wallace. London: Oxford University Press, 1965.

———. *Phänomenologie des Geistes.* Frankfurt am Main: Suhrkamp Verlag, 1973.

———. *Philosophy of Nature.* Translated by Michael John Petry. London and New York: Humanities Press, 1970.

———. *Vorlesungen über die* Ästhetik. Vols. 1–3. In *Hegels Werke in Zwanzig Bänden,* vols. 13–15, edited by Eva Moldenhauer and Karl Markus Michel. Frankfurt am Main: Suhrkamp Verlag, 1970.

———. *Wissenschaft der Logik.* In *Werke in Zwanzig Bänden.* Edited by Eva Moldenhauer and Karl Markus Michel. Frankfurt am Main: Suhrkamp Verlag, 1986.

———. *Wissenschaft der Logik. Bände 1 and 2.* Edited by Georg Lasson. Leipzig: Felix Meiner, 1948.

Heidegger, Martin. *Basic Writings*. Edited by David F. Krell. Translated by William Lovitt. New York: Harper and Row, 1977.

———. *Being and Time*. Translated by John Maquarrie and Edward Robinson. New York: Harper and Row, 1962.

———. *Contributions to Philosophy: From Enowning. Translated by* Parvis Emad and Kenneth Maly. Bloomington: Indiana University Press, 2000.

———. "On the Essence of Truth." In *Existence and Being*, edited by Werner Brock, translated by R. F. C. Hull and Alan Crick, 292–324. Chicago: Gateway, 1949.

———. *Poetry, Language, Thought*. Translated by Albert Hofstadter. New York: Harper and Row, 1971.

———. *Vom Wesen der Wahrheit*. Frankfurt: Vittorio Klostermann, 1954; written in 1930.

Henrich, Dieter. "Anfang und Methode der Logik." In *Hegel im Kontext*, edited by Dieter Henrich, 73–94. Frankfurt am Main: Suhrkamp Verlag, 1971.

———. "Formen der Negation in Hegels Logik." In *Seminar: Dialektik in der Philosophie Hegels*, edited by Rolf-Peter Horstmann, 213–29. Frankfurt am Main: Suhrkamp Verlag, 1978.

———. "Hegels Logik der Reflexion: Neue Fassung." In *Die Wissenschaft der Logik und die Logik der Reflexion*, edited by Dieter Henrich, 203–24. *Hegel-Studien, Beiheft 18*. Bonn: Bouvier Verlag, 1978.

Henrici, Peter. "The Philosophy of Hans Urs von Balthasar." In *Hans Urs von Balthasar: His Life and Work*, edited by David Schindler, 149–67. San Francisco: Communio, 1991.

Houlgate, Stephen. *The Opening of Hegel's Logic: From Being to Infinity*. West Lafayette, Ind.: Purdue University Press, 2005.

Hume, David. *A Treatise of Human Nature*. Edited by Páll S. Árdal. London: Fontana/Collins, 1972.

Hyppolite, Jean. *Logic and Existence*. Translated by Leonard Lawlor and Amit Sen. Albany: State University of New York Press, 1997.

Jaki, Stanley. *Uneasy Genius: The Life and Work of Pierre Duhem*. Dordrecht: Martinus Nijhoff, 1984.

John Paul II. *Fides et Ratio: On the Relation of Faith and Reason*. Boston: Pauline Books and Media, 1998.

Johnson. Mark. *Moral Imagination: Implications of Cognitive Science for Ethics*. Chicago: University of Chicago Press, 1993.

Kant, Immanuel. *Critique of Judgment*. Translated by Werner Pluhar. Indianapolis, Ind.: Hackett, 1987.

———. *Critique of Pure Reason*. Translated by Paul Guyer and Allen Wood. Cambridge: Cambridge University Press, 1998.

———. *Critique of Pure Reason*. Translated by Norman Kemp Smith. New York: St. Martin's, 1929.

———. *Critique of Pure Reason*. Translated by Werner S. Pluhar. Introduction by Patricia W. Kitcher. Indianapolis, Ind., and Cambridge, Mass.: Hackett, 1996.

———. *Kritik der reinen Vernunft*. Edited by Raymond Schmidt. 1956. Hamburg: Felix Meiner, 1976.

———. *Kritik der Urteilungskraft.* Edited by Karl Vörlander. 1924. Reprint Hamburg: Felix Meiner Verlag, 1974.

Kehl, Medard. "Hans Urs von Balthasar: A Portrait." In *The Urs von Balthasar Reader,* edited by Medard Kehl and W. Loser; translated by R. Daly and F. Lawrence, 17–22. Edinburgh: Crossroad, 1985.

Kibre, Pearl, and Nancy Sirasi. "The Institutional Setting of the Universities." In *Science and the Middle Ages,* edited by David C. Lindberg, 128–29. Chicago: University of Chicago Press, 1978.

Kleist, Henrich von. *Penthesilea.* In Kleist's *Werke in einem Band,* edited by Helmut Sembdner, 249–342. Munich: Carl Hanser, 1966.

———. *Plays.* Edited by Walter Hinderer. Translated by Peggy Meyer Sherry. New York: Continuum, 1982.

———. *Prince of Homburg.* In Kleist, *Plays,* edited by Walter Hinderer, translated by Peggy Meyer Sherry, 269–341. New York: Continuum, 1982.

———. *Werke in einem Band.* Edited by Helmut Sembdner. Munich: Carl Hanser, 1966.

Kojève, Alexandre. *Introduction to the Reading of Hegel: Lectures on the* Phenomenology of Spirit. Translated by J. Nichols. Ithaca: Cornell University Press, 1969.

Koselleck, Reinhart. *Futures Past: On the Semantics of Historical Time.* Translated and with a foreword by Keith Tribe. Cambridge, Mass.: MIT Press, 1990.

Koyré, Alexander. "Note sur la langue et la terminologie hégéliennes." In *Études d'histoire de la pensée philosophique.* Paris: Gallimard, 1971.

Kull, Kalevi, ed. "Jakob von Uexküll: A Paradigm for Biology and Semiotics." *Semiotica* 134, nos. 12–4 (2001).

Lacan, Jacques. *Four Fundamental Concepts of Psychoanalysis.* New York: W. W. Norton, 1979.

Lampert, Jay. *Deleuze and Guattari's Philosophy of History.* London: Continuum, 2006.

Laycock, Stephen William. "Introduction: Towards an Overview of Phenomenological Theology." In *Essays in Phenomenological Ontology,* edited by Stephen William Laycock and James Hart, 1–22. Albany: State University of New York Press, 1986.

Leibniz, Gottfried Wilhelm. *La Monadologie.* In *Opera Philosophica,* edited by J. E. Erdmann (Berlin, 1940), enlarged with a preface by Renate Vollbracht. Meisenheim and Glan: Scientia Aalen, 1959.

Levinas, Emmanuel. *Totality and Infinity.* Translated by Alphonso Lingis. Pittsburgh, Penn.: Duquesne University Press, 1969.

Lewis, Bernard. "Philosophical Setting of Medieval Science." In *Science in the Middle Ages,* edited by David C. Lindberg. Chicago: University of Chicago Press, 1978.

———. *What Went Wrong?* Oxford: Oxford University Press, 2002.

Lewontin, Richard Charles. *Biology as Ideology: The Doctrine of DNA.* San Francisco: HarperPerennial, 1993.

Lindberg, David C. "The Transmission of Greek and Arabic Learning to the West." In *Science in the Middle Ages,* edited by David C. Lindberg. Chicago: Chicago University Press, 1978.

Locke, John. "An Essay Concerning Toleration." In *Political Writings of John Locke,* edited by David Wooton, 184–209. London: Penguin Books, 1993.

———. "A Letter Concerning Toleration." In *Political Writings of John Locke,* edited by David Wooton, 390–435. London: Penguin Books, 1993.

Lolordo, Antonia. *Pierre Gassendi and the Birth of Early Modern Philosophy.* Cambridge: Cambridge University Press, 2006.

Lonergan, Bernard. *Insight: An Essay on Human Understanding.* London: Longmans Green, 1957.

Longuenesse, Béatrice. *Hegel's Critique of Metaphysics.* Translated by Nicole J. Simek. Cambridge: Cambridge University Press, 2007.

Lopez, Antonio. "Eternal Happening: God as an Event of Love." In *Communio: International Catholic Review* 32 (2005): 214–45.

Luhmann, Niklas. *Art As a Social System.* Stanford, Calif.: Stanford University Press, 2000.

———. *The Differentiation of Society.* New York: Columbia University Press, 1982.

———. *Essays on Self-Reference.* New York: Columbia University Press, 1990.

———. *Die Gesellschaft der Gesellschaft.* Frankfurt am Main: Suhrkamp, 1997.

———. "Identity—What or How?" Translated by Joseph O'Neill and Elliott Schreiber. In *Theories of Distinction: Redescribing the Descriptions of Modernity.* Stanford, Calif.: Stanford University Press, 2002.

———. *Die Kunst der Gesellschaft.* Frankfurt am Main: Suhrkamp, 1995.

———. *Love as Passion: The Codification of Intimacy.* Translated by Jeremy Gaines and Doris Jones. Cambridge, Mass.: Harvard University Press, 1986; Stanford, Calif.: Stanford University Press, 1998.

———. "The Medium of Art." *Thesis Eleven* 18, no. 19 (1987): 101–13.

———. "Paradigm Lost: On the Ethical Reflection of Morality." *Thesis Eleven* 29 (1991): 82–94.

———. *Political Theory in the Welfare State.* New York: de Gruyter, 1990.

———. *Social Systems (Writing Science).* Stanford, Calif.: Stanford University Press, 1996.

———. *Soziale Systeme: Grundriss einer allgemeinen Theorie.* Frankfurt am Main: Suhrkamp, 1984.

———. *Theories of Distinction: Redescribing the Descriptions of Modernity.* Stanford: Stanford University Press, 2002.

Luhmann, Niklas, and Kathleen Cross. *The Reality of the Mass Media.* Stanford, Calif.: Stanford University Press, 2000.

Lyotard, Jean-François. *The Postmodern Condition: A Report on Knowledge.* Translated by Geoffrey Bennington and Brian Massumi. Minneapolis: University of Minnesota Press, 1984.

MacIntyre, Alasdair. "The Rationality of Traditions," *Whose Justice? Which Rationality?* Notre Dame, Ind.: University of Notre Dame Press, 1988.

Mansfield, Harvey C. "Nature and Fact in Tocqueville's *Democracy in America.*" In *Nature in American Philosophy,* edited by Jean De Groot, 109–26. *Studies in Philosophy and the History of Philosophy* 42. Washington, D.C.: The Catholic University of America Press, 2004.

Marcel, Gabriel. *Being and Having.* Translated by Katherine Farrer. New York: Harper and Row, 1965.

———. *Creative Fidelity.* Translated by Robert Rosthal. New York: Fordham University Press, 2002.

———. *The Existential Background of Human Dignity.* Cambridge, Mass.: Harvard University Press, 1971.

———. *Homo Viator.* Translated by Emma Craufurd. New York: Harper and Row, 1962.

———. *Man Against Mass Society.* Translated by G. S. Fraser. Chicago: Regnery, 1962.

———. *Metaphysical Journal.* Translated by Bernard Wall. Chicago: Gateway, 1952.

———. *Le Mystère de l'Être.* Paris: Aubier, 1951. Translated as *The Mystery of Being.* Vol. I translated by G. S. Fraser. Vol. II translated by R. Hague. South Bend, Ind.: St Augustine's Press, 2001.

———. "On the Ontological Mystery." In *The Philosophy of Existentialism,* translated by Manya Harari, 9–46. New York: Citadel, 1956.

———. *The Philosophy of Existentialism.* Translated by Manya Harari. New York: Citadel, 1956.

———. *Presence and Immortality.* Translated by Michael A. Machado. Pittsburgh: Duquesne University Press, 1967.

———. *Tragic Wisdom and Beyond.* Translated by Stephen Jolin and Peter McCormick. Evanston, Ill.: Northwestern University Press, 1973.

Maritain, Jacques. *Distinguish to Unite, or The Degrees of Knowledge.* Translated under the supervision of Gerald B. Phelan. New York: Scribner's, 1959.

———. *God and the Permission of Evil.* Milwaukee: Bruce, 1966.

———. "Language and the Theory of Sign." In *Frontiers in Semiotics,* edited by John N. Deely, Brooke Williams, and Felicia E. Kruse. Bloomington: Indiana University Press, 1986.

Maurer, Armand A. "Some Aspects of Fourteenth-Century Philosophy." *Medievalia et Humanistica* 7 (1976): 175–88.

McCarthy, John C. "The Reach of Reason." In *Ethics and Theological Disclosures: The Thought of Robert Sokolowski,* edited by James Hart and Guy Mansini, O.S.B, 102–34. Washington, D.C.: The Catholic University of America Press, 2003.

McCumber, John. *Poetic Interaction: Language, Freedom, Reason.* Chicago: University of Chicago Press, 1989.

McInerny, Ralph. *Boethius and Aquinas.* Washington, D.C.: The Catholic University of America Press, 1990.

———. *Aquinas against the Averroists: On There Being Only One Intellect.* West Lafayette, Ind.: Purdue University Press, 1993.

———. *Thomas Aquinas: Selected Writings.* London: Penguin Classics, 1998.

Michelfelder, Diane P., and Richard E. Palmer, eds. *Dialogue and Deconstruction: The Gadamer-Derrida Encounter.* Albany: SUNY Press, 1989.

Moeller, Hans-Georg. *Luhmann Explained: From Souls to Systems.* Chicago: Open Court, 2006.

Mumford, Lewis. *The Myth of the Machine: Technics and Human Development*. New York: Harcourt, Brace, and World, 1976.

Mure, G. R. G. *Aristotle*. London: Ernest Benn, 1932.

Nancy, Jean-Luc. *The Speculative Remark (one of Hegel's Bons Mots)*. Translated by Celine Surprenant. Stanford, Calif.: Stanford University Press, 2001.

Nietzsche, Friedrich. *Twilight of the Idols*. Translated by R. J. Hollingdale. Baltimore: Penguin, 1968.

Oakes, Edward T. "Erich Przywara and the Analogy of Being." In *Pattern of Redemption: The Theology of Hans Urs von Balthasar*, 15–43. New York: Continuum, 1997.

Oakes, Edward T., and David Moss, eds. *The Cambridge Companion to Hans Urs von Balthasar*. Cambridge: Cambridge University Press, 2004.

Oberman, Heiko A. *The Harvest of Medieval Theology: Gabriel Biel and Late Medieval Nominalism*. Durham, N.C.: Labyrinth, 1983.

———. "Some Notes on the Theology of Nominalism: With Attention to Its Relation to the Renaissance." *Harvard Theological Review* 53 (January1960): 47–76.

O'Meara, Thomas F., O.P. *Erich Przywara, S.J.: His Theology and His Word*. Notre Dame, Ind.: University of Notre Dame Press, 2002.

Owens, Joseph. "Aristotelian Soul as Cognitive of Sensibles, Intelligibles, and Self." In *Aristotle: The Collected Papers of Joseph Owens*, edited by John R. Catan, 96. Albany: State University of New York Press, 1981.

———. *Aristotle: The Collected Papers of Joseph Owens*. Edited by John R. Katan. Albany: State University of New York Press, 1981.

———. *The Doctrine of Being in the Aristotelian Metaphysics*. Toronto: Pontifical Institute of Medieval Studies, 1951.

Peirce, Charles Sanders. "How to Make our Ideas Clear." In *Collected Papers of Charles Sanders Peirce*, edited by Charles Hartshorne and Paul Weiss. Cambridge, Mass.: Harvard University Press, 1934.

———. "The Scientific Attitude and Falliblism,"in *Philosophical Writings of Peirce*, edited by Justus Buchler. New York: Dover, 1955.

Peperzak, Adriaan. *Philosophy between Faith and Theology: Addresses to Catholic Intellectuals*. Notre Dame, Ind.: University of Notre Dame Press, 2005.

———. *Reason in Faith: On the Relevance of Christian Spirituality for Philosophy*. New York: Paulist Press, 1999.

———. *Thinking: From Solitude to Dialogue and Contemplation*. New York: Fordham University Press, 2006.

Petersen, Aage. "The Philosophy of Niels Bohr." In *Niels Bohr: A Centenary Volume*, edited by Anthony Philip French and P. J. Kennedy, 299–310. Cambridge, Mass.: Harvard University Press, 1985.

Pius IX. *Quanta Cura and the Syllabus of Errors: The Pope Against Modern Errors*. Edited by A. Minoni. Rockford, Ill.: Tan Books, 1999.

Pius X. *Pascendi domenici gregis* ("De falsis doctrinis modernistarum"). In *Enchiridion Symbolorum*. Edited by Heinrich Denzinger and Adolf Schönmetzer. Freiburg, Basel, Rome, and Vienna: Herder, 1997.

———. "Motu Proprio" (*Iusiurandum contra errores modernism*). In *Enchiridi-*

on Symbolorum. Edited by Heinrich Denzinger and Adolf Schönmetzer. Freiburg, Basel, Rome, and Vienna: Herder, 1997.

Pope Pius XII. *Humani Generis*. In *Enchiridion Symbolorum*. Edited by Heinrich Denzinger and Adolf Schönmetzer. Freiburg, Basel, Rome, and Vienna: Herder, 1997.

Plato, *Republic*. In *The Complete Works of Plato*. Edited by John Cooper and Douglas Hutchinson. Indianapolis, Ind., and Cambridge, Mass.: Hackett, 1997.

———. *Sophist*. In *Theaetetus, Sophist*. Translated by Harold North Fowler. Cambridge, Mass.: Harvard University Press, 1977.

———. *Symposium*. In *Lysis, Symposium, Gorgias*. Translated by W. R. M. Lamb. Cambridge, Mass.: Harvard University Press, 1975.

———. *Theaetetus*. In *The Complete Works of Plato*. Edited by John Cooper and Douglas Hutchinson. Indianapolis, Ind., and Cambridge, Mass.: Hackett, 1997.

Poinsot, John. *Cursus Philosophicus Thomisticus*. 3 vols. Edited by B. Reiser. Turin: Marietti, 1930, 1933, 1937.

———. "Tractatus de Angelis." In *Joannis a Sancto Thoma Cursus Theologicus*, 4:441–835. Paris: Desclée, 1946.

Popper, Karl. *Contemporary British Philosophy*. New York: Macmillan, 1960.

———. *Tractatus de Signis: The Semiotic of John Poinsot*. Edited and translated by John Deely. Berkeley: University of California Press, 1985.

Priest, Graham. *Beyond the Limits of Thought*. Cambridge: Cambridge University Press, 1995.

Prufer, Thomas. *Recapitulations: Essays in Philosophy*. Studies in Philosophy and the History of Philosophy 26. Washington, D.C.: The Catholic University of America Press, 1993.

Przywara, Erich, S. J. *Polarity: A German Catholic's Interpretation of Religion*. Translated by A. C. Bouquet. London: Oxford University Press, 1935.

Ratzinger, Joseph. *Introduction to Christianity*. Translated by J. R. Foster. New York: Herder and Herder, 1970.

Ricoeur, Paul. *Fallible Man*. Translated by Charles Kelbley. Chicago: Regnery, 1965.

Rilke, Rainer Maria. *Duino Elegies*. Translated by David Young. New York: W. W. Norton, 1978.

Rist, John M. "Notes on Aristotle's *De Anima* 3.5." *Classical Philology* 61 (January 1966): 8–20.

Ross, Sir David. *Aristotle*. London: Methuen, 1930.

———. *Aristotle: De Anima*. Edited with an Introduction and Commentary by Sir David Ross. Oxford: Clarendon Press, 1961.

Russell, Bertrand. *My Philosophical Development*. New York: Simon and Schuster, 1959.

Russon, John. "Absolute Knowing: The Structure and Project of Hegel's System of Science." In *Reading Hegel's Phenomenology*. Bloomington, Ind.: Indiana University Press, 2004.

———. *Reading Hegel's Phenomenology*. Bloomington, Ind.: Indiana University Press, 2004.

———. *The Self and Its Body in Hegel's Phenomenology of Spirit.* Toronto: University of Toronto Press, 1997.

Saliba, George. *Islamic Science and the Making of the European Renaissance.* Cambridge, Mass.: MIT Press, 2007.

Sartre, Jean-Paul. *Being and Nothingness.* Translated by Hazel Barnes. New York: Philosophical Library, 1956.

———. "Existentialism Is a Humanism." In *Existentialism from Dostoevski to Sartre,* edited and translated by Walter Kaufmann. New York: Meridian, 1956.

———. *The Family Idiot.* 5 vols. Translated by Carol Cosman. Chicago: University of Chicago Press, 1981–93.

———. "The Itinerary of a Thought" [interview]. In *Between Existentialism and Marxism.* Translated by John Mathews. New York: Morrow, 1974.

———. "Kierkegaard: The Singular Universal." In *Between Existentialism and Marxism: Sartre on Philosophy, Politics, Psychology, and the Arts,* translated by John Matthews, 141–69. Pantheon, 1983.

———. *Saint Genet: Actor and Martyr.* Translated by Bernard Frechtman. New York: Pantheon, 1963.

———. *Search For A Method.* Translated by Hazel Barnes. New York: Random House, 1958.

———. *The Transcendence of the Ego.* Translated by Forrest Williams and Robert Kirkpatrick. New York: Noonday, 1957.

Scheler, Max. *Bildung und Wissen.* Frankfurt am Main: Schulte-Bulmke, 1947.

———. *Die Formen des Wissens und die Bildung.* Bonn: Cohen, 1925.

———. *Gesammelte Werke.* Bern: Francke, 1954–1986; Bonn: Bouvier, 1985–present,

———. *Liebe und Erkenntnis.* Munich: Francke, 1955.

———. *Das Ressentiment im Aufbau der Moralen.* In *Vom Umsturz der Werte.* Band I, Zweite durchgelesene Auflage. Leipzig: der neue Geist, 1919.

———. *Wesen und Formen der Sympathie.* Frankfurt am Main: Schulte-Bulmke, 1948.

Schelling, Friedrich Wilhelm Joseph. *Philosophie der Kunst.* 1859. Reprint, Darmstadt: Wissenschaftliche Buchgesellschaft, 1980.

———. *The Philosophy of Art.* Translated by Douglas W. Stott. Minneapolis: Minnesota University Press, 1989.

Schiller, Friedrich. *On the Aesthetic Education of Man, in a Series of Letters.* Translated by Elizabeth M. Wilkinson and L. A. Willoughby. Oxford: Clarendon Press, 1968.

Schmitt, Charles B. *Aristotle and the Renaissance.* Cambridge, Mass.: Harvard University Press, 1983.

Schmitz, Kenneth L. "An Addendum to Further Discussion." *American Catholic Philosophical Quarterly* 73 (1999), 277–90.

———. "Analysis by Principles and Analysis by Elements." In *Graceful Reason: Essays in Ancient and Mediaeval Philosophy Presented to Joseph Owens, CSSR,* edited by Lloyd Gerson, 315–30. Toronto: Pontifical Institute of Mediaeval Studies, 1983.

"Another Look at Objectivity." *Thomas and Bonaventure: Proceedings of the American Catholic Philosophical Association* 48 (1974): 86–98.

———. *At the Center of the Human Drama: The Philosophical Anthropology of Karol Wojtyla/Pope John Paul II*

———. "The Authority of Institutions: Meddling or Middling?" In *Communio: International Catholic Review* 12 (1985), 5–24.

———. "The Bounds of Art." In *Philosophy and Art,* edited by Daniel O. Dahlstrom, 143–59. Studies in the Philosophy and the History of Philosophy 23. Washington, D.C.: The Catholic University of America Press, 1991.

———. "Catholicism in America." In *Communio: International Catholic Review* 19 (1992), 474–77.

———. "Community: The Elusive Unity." *Review of Metaphysic* 37 (1983): 243–64.

"The Conceptualization of Religious Mystery: An Essay in Hegel's Philosophy of Religion." In *The Legacy of Hegel: Proceedings of the Marquette Hegel Symposium,* edited by Joseph J. O'Malley, Keith W. Algozin, Howard P. Kainz, and Lee C. Rice. The Hague: Martinus Nijhoff, 1973.

———. "Concrete Presence." *Communio: International Catholic Review* 14 (1987): 300–15.

———. "Created Receptivity and the Philosophy of the Concrete." *Thomist* 61 (1997), 339–71.

———. "Death and the Rebirth of Man." In *The Texture of Being,* edited by Paul O'Herron. Studies in Philosophy and the History of Philosophy 46. Washington, D.C.: The Catholic University of America Press, 2007.

"Divine Initiative and Christian Praxis." *Communio: International Catholic Review* 5 (1978): 44–52.

———. "Enlightenment Criticism and Embodiment of Values: The Hegelian Background to a Contemporary Problem." *Indian Philosophical Annual* 18 (1986): 33–53.

———."Enriching the Copula." *Review of Metaphysics* 27 (1974): 492–512.

———."Entitative and Systemic Aspects of Evil." *Dialectics and Humanism: New Polish Philosophical Quarterly* 5 (1978): 149–61.

———."Faith and Practice: The Nature and Importance of Religious Activities." In *The Life of Religion: A Marquette University Symposium on the Nature of Religious Belief,* edited by Stanley M. Harrison and Richard C. Taylor. Lanham, Md.: University Press of America, 1986.

———. "Faith and Reason: Then and Now." *Communio: International Catholic Review* 26 (1999): 595–608.

———. "The First Principle of Personal Becoming." *Review of Metaphysics* 47 (1994): 757–74.

———. "The Fortunes of Philosophy Within the Association." *Proceedings of the Catholic Philosophical Association* 66 (1992): 13–28.

———. "From Anarchy to Principles: Deconstruction and the Resources of Christian Philosophy." In *The Philosophy of Person: Solidarity and Cultural Creativity,* edited by Jozef Tischner, Joseph M. Zycinski, and George F. McLean. Washington, D.C.: Paideia Publishers and the Council for Research in Values and Philosophy, 1994. Also published in *Communio: International Catholic Review* 16 (1989): 69–88.

———. "The Geography of the Human Person." *Communio: International Catholic Review* 13 (1986), 27–48.

———. "Gibt es für den Menschen Wichtigeres, als zu überleben? Das Erbe Griechenlands: Rationalität." In *Das Europaische Erbe und Seine Christliche Zukunft*, vol. 16, edited by Nicholas Lobkowicz. Cologne: Hans Martin Schleyer-Stiftung/Pontificium Consilium pro Cultura, 1985.

———. *The Gift: Creation*. Milwaukee, Wisc.: Marquette University Press, 1982.

"God, Being and Love: New Ontological Perspectives coming from Philosophy." In *La Razon Creyente: Actas del Congreso Internacional sobre la Enciclica Fides et Ratio,* edited by J. Pradez and J. Ma. Magaz. Madrid: Studia Theologica Matritensia, 2002.

———. "The God of Love." *Thomist* 57 (1993): 495–508.

———. "Hegel on Kant: Being-In-Itself and the Thing-In-Itself." In *The Philosophy of Immanuel Kant*, edited by Richard Kennington. Studies in Philosophy and the History of Philosophy 12. Washington, D.C.: The Catholic University of America Press, 1985.

———. "Hegel on War and Peace." In *Conceptions de la paix dans l'histoire de la philosophie,* edited by Venant Cauchy. Montreal: Éditions Montmorency, 1987.

———. "Hegel's Attempt to Forge a Logic for Spirit." *Dialogue: Journal of the Canadian Philosophical Association* 10 (1971), 653–72.

———. "Hegel's Philosophy of Religion: Typology and Strategy." *Review of Metaphysics* 23 (1975): 717–36.

"Human Nature, History and the Transcendental Character of Being." In *Scholasticism in the Modern World: Proceedings of the American Catholic Philosophical Association* 40, edited by George McLean. Washington, D.C.: American Catholic Philosophical Association, 1966.

———. "The Idealism of the German Romantics." In *The Emergence of German Idealism,* edited by Michael Baur and Daniel O. Dahlstrom, 176–97. Studies in Philosophy and the History of Philosophy 34. Washington, D.C.: The Catholic University of America Press 1999.

"Immateriality Past and Present." *Immateriality: Proceedings of the American Catholic Philosophical Association* 52 (1978): 1–15.

———. "Is Liberalism Good Enough?" In *Liberalism and the Good,* edited by R. B. Douglass, G. M. Mara, and Henry S. Richardson, 86–104. New York and London: Routledge, 1990.

———. "Jacques Maritain and Karol Wojtyla: Approaches to Modernity." In *The Bases of Ethics,* edited by William Sweet, 127f. Milwaukee: Marquette University Press, 2000.

———. "The Language of Conversion and the Conversion of Language." *Communio: International Catholic Review* 21 (1994): 742–64.

———. "Lessing at God's Left Hand." In *Modern Enlightenment and the Rule of Reason,* edited by John C. McCarthy, 213–31. Studies in Philosophy and the History of Philosophy 32. Washington, D.C.: The Catholic University of America Press, 1998.

———."The Lustrous Power of Beauty." In *To the Mountain: Essays in Honor of George F. McLean,* 233–45, edited by William Sweet and Hu Yeping. Taiwan: Fu Jen Catholic University Press, 2004.

———. "Metaphysics: Radical, Comprehensive, Determinate Discourse." *Review of Metaphysics* 39 (1986), 675–94.

———. "The Modes in Process." *Review of Metaphysics* 21 (1967): 310–42.

———. "A Moment of Truth: Present Actuality." *Review of Metaphysics* 33 (1980): 673–88.

———."Naming God: Analogical Negation." In *Christian Spirituality and the Culture of Modernity: The Thought of Louis Dupré,* edited by Peter J. Casarella and George P. Schner. Grand Rapids, Mich., and Cambridge: Eerdmans, 1998.

———. "Natural Imagery as a Discriminatory Element in Religious Language." In *Experience, Reason, and God,* edited by Eugene T. Long. Studies in Philosophy and the History of Philosophy 8. Washington, D.C.: The Catholic University of America Press, 1980.

———. "Natural Value." *Review of Metaphysics* 38 (1984): 3–15.

———."Natural Wisdom and Some Recent Philosophy Manuals." *The Role of Philosophy in the Catholic Liberal College: Proceedings of the American Catholic Philosophical Association* 30 (1956): 181–90.

———. "Neither With nor Without Foundations." *Review of Metaphysics* 42 (1988), 3–25.

———. "On a Resistant Strain within the Hegelian Dialectic." *Owl of Minerva* 25 (1994), 147–54.

———. "The Ontology of Rights." *Ave Maria Law Review* 3 (2005): 275–88.

———. "Philosophical Pluralism and Philosophical Truth." *Philosophy Today* 10, nos. 1–4.(1966): 3–16.

———. "Philosophy of Religion and the Redefinition of Philosophy." In *The Challenge of Religion Today,* edited by Frederick Ferre, Joseph Kockelmans, and John E. Smith. New York: Seabury, 1982.

———. "Postmodern or Modern-plus?" *Communio: International Catholic Review* 17 (1990): 152–66.

———. "Postmodernism and the Catholic Tradition." *American Catholic Philosophical Quarterly* 73 (1999), 233–52.

———. "Purity of Soul and Immortality." *Monist* 69 (1986): 396–415.

———. *The Recovery of Wonder: The New Freedom and the Asceticism of Power.* Montreal and Kingston: McGill–Queen's University Press, 2005.

———. "The Redemptive Role of the Knowledge of Nature." *Franciscan Studies* 24 (1964): 223–60.

———. "Ritual Elements in Community." *Religious Studies* 17 (1981): 163–77.

———. "The Root and Branch of St. Thomas's Thought." In *Thomas Aquinas and His Legacy,* edited by David M. Gallagher, 1–15. Studies in the Philosophy and the History of Philosophy 28. Washington, D.C.: The Catholic University of America Press, 1994.

———. "The Roots of Catholic Intellectuality." In *Catholic Commission on Intellectual and Cultural Affairs Annual* 1984. Washington, D.C.: Catholic Commission on Intellectual and Cultural Affairs, 1984.

———. "Scrutinizing the Inscrutable." *Review of Metaphysics* 27 (1973), 346–70.

———. "Selves and Persons: A Difference in Loves?" *Communio: International Catholic Review* 18 (1991): 181–206.

———. "Shapes of Evil in Mediaeval Epics: A Philosophical Analysis." In *The Epic in Mediaeval Society: Aesthetic and Moral Values,* edited by Harald Scholler, 37–63. Tübingen: Max Niemeyer, 1977.

———. "The Solidarity of Personalism and the Metaphysics of Existential Act." *Fides Quaerens Intellectum* 1 (2001): 183–99. Republished in *The Texture of Being*, edited by Paul O'Herron, 132–45. Studies in Philosophy and the History of Philosophy 46. Washington, D.C.: The Catholic University of America Press, 2007.

———. "St. Thomas and the Appeal to Experience." *Catholic Theological Society of America* 47 (1992): 1–20.

———. *The Texture of Being: Essays in First Philosophy*. Edited by Paul O'Herron. Studies in Philosophy and the History of Philosophy 46. Washington, D.C.: The Catholic University of America Press, 2007.

———."Theological Clearances: Foreground to a Rational Recovery of God." In *Prospects for Natural Theology*, edited by Eugene T. Long. Studies in the Philosophy and the History of Philosophy 25. Washington, D.C.: The Catholic University of America Press, 1992.

———. "Towards a Metaphysical Restoration of Natural Things." In *An Etienne Gilson Tribute*, edited by Charles O'Neill. Milwaukee: Marquette University Press, 1959.

———. "Traces of Eternity." *Communio: International Catholic Review* 15 (1988): 294–304.

———."Transcendental and Empirical Pressures in Human Subjectivity." *Thought: Hegel Commemorative Issue* 56 (1981): 272–86.

———. "The Transfiguration of Gnosis in Late Enlightenment German Thought." *Communio: International Catholic Review* 24 (1997): 691–712.

———. "*Was heißt Philosophie?* One Hundred Years of German Catholic Thought." In *One Hundred Years of Philosophy*, edited by Brian Shanley, 133–55, 142–43n30. Studies in Philosophy and the History of Philosophy 36. Washington, D.C.: The Catholic University of America Press, 2001.

———. "Weiss and Creation." *Review of Metaphysics* 18 (1964): 147–69.

———."What Happens to Tradition when History Overtakes It?" *Reason in History: Proceedings of the American Catholic Philosophical Association* 68 (1994): 59–72.

———. *What Has Clio to Do with Athena? Etienne Gilson: Historian and Philosopher*. The Etienne Gilson Series 10. Toronto: Pontifical Institute of Mediaeval Studies, 1987.

———. "The Witness of Beauty: The Profile of God." In *The Texture of Being*, edited by Paul O'Herron, 300–15. Studies in Philosophy and the History of Philosophy 46. Washington, D.C.: The Catholic University of America Press, 2007.

———. "World and Word in Theophany." *Faith and Philosophy* 1 (1984): 50–70.

Seager, Sara. "Head Games." *Popular Science* (October 2007): 66.

Searle, John. *The Rediscovery of Mind*. Cambridge, Mass.: MIT Press, 1992.

Second Vatican Council. "Dogmatic Constitution on Divine Revelation," *Dei Verbum*. In *Vatican II: The Conciliar and Post Conciliar Documents*. New rev. ed. Edited by Austin Flannery, O.P. Boston: St. Paul Books and Media, 1992.

Shakespeare. William. *The Tragedy of King Lear* (The Conflated Text). In *The Norton Shakespeare*. Based on the Oxford Edition, edited by Stephen Greenblatt, Walter Cohen, Jean E. Howard, and Katharine Eisaman Maus, 2479–553. New York and London: W. W. Norton, 1997.

Smith, Gerard. *The Philosophy of Being*. New York: MacMillan, 1961.

Sokolowski, Robert. *Christian Faith and Human Understanding*. Washington, D.C.: The Catholic University of America Press; South Bend, Ind.: Notre Dame University Press, 2007.

———. *The God of Faith and Reason: Foundations of Christian Theology*. South Bend, Ind.: University of Notre Dame Press, 1982. Reprint, Washington, D.C.: The Catholic University of America Press, 1995.

Spedding, James, Robert Leslie Ellis, and Douglas Denon Heath, eds. *The Works of Francis Bacon*. Vol. 2. London: Longman, 1859.

Steenbergen, Fernand van. *La philosophie au xiiie siècle*. Louvain: Publications universitaires, 1966.

Strasser, Stephan. *Phenomenology of Feeling: An Essay on the Phenomena of the Heart*. Translated with Introduction by Robert Wood. Preface to the English edition by Paul Ricoeur. Pittsburgh: Duquesne University Press; New York: Humanities Press, 1977.

Theunissen, Michael. *Sein und Schein: Die kritische Funktion der Hegelschen Logik*. Frankfurt am Main: Suhrkamp Verlag, 1980.

Thorburn, William. "The Myth of Occam's Razor." *Mind* 27 (1918): 345–53.

Thorndike, Lynn. *A History of Magic and Experimental Science*. 8 vols. New York: Columbia University Press, 1923–58.

Todorov, Tzvetan. "La naissance de la sémiotique occidentale." In *Théories du symbole*, 13–58. Paris: Éditions du Seuil, 1977. Translated as "The Birth of Occidental Semiotics," trans. Daphne Swabey and Judith Mullen.

———. *The Sign*. Edited by Richard W. Bailey, Ladislav Matejka, and P. Steiner. Ann Arbor, Mich.: Michigan Slavic Publications, 1978.

Tornay, Stephen. *Ockham: Studies and Sketches*. La Salle, Ill.: Franciscan Institute, 1938.

Uexküll, Jacob von. "Bedeutungslehre," *Bios* 10 (Leipzig, 1940). Translated by Barry Stone and Herbert Weiner as "The Theory of Meaning." *Semiotica* Special Issue 42, no. 1 (1982): 25–82.

———. *Streifzuge durch die Umwelten von Tieren und Menschen* (Berlin, 1934). Translated and edited by Claire H. Schiller as "A Stroll through the Worlds of Animals and Men." In *Instinctive Behavior: The Development of a Modern Concept*. New York: International Universities Press, 1957, 5–80.

Vacant, Jean-Michel-Alfred. *Études Théologiques sur les Constitutions du Concile du Vatican d'après les actes du Concile*. Vol. 1. Paris and Lyon: Delhomme et Briguet, 1895.

Vernon, James. *Hegel's Philosophy of Language*. New York: Continuum, 2007.

Vico, Giambattista. *The New Science of Giambattista Vico*. Translated by Thomas Goddard Bergin and Max Harold Fisch. Ithaca: Cornell University Press, 1984.

Vignaux, Paul. "Nominalisme." In *Dictionnaire de théologie catholique* 11. Paris: 1909–1950.

von Balthasar, Hans Urs. "On the Tasks of Catholic Philosophy in our Time." *Communio: International Catholic Review* 20 (1993): 148–87.

———. "A Résumé of My Thought." *Communio: International Catholic Review* 15 (1988): 468–73.

———. "Retrieving the Tradition: *Communio*—A Program." *Communio: International Catholic Review* 33 (2006): 153–69.

———. *The Theology of Henri de Lubac*. Translated by Susan Clements. San Francisco: Ignatius, 1983.

———. *The Theology of Karl Barth: Exposition and Interpretation*. Translated by Edward T. Oakes, S.J. San Francisco: Ignatius Press, 1992.

Wallace, William A. "Philosophical Setting of Medieval Science." In *Science in the Middle Ages*, edited by David C. Lindberg, 105–6. Chicago: University of Chicago Press, 1978.

Warminski, Andrzej. *Readings in Interpretation: Hölderlin, Hegel, Heidegger*. Minneapolis: University of Minnesota Press, 1987.

White, Lynn, Jr., ed. "The Changing Past." In *Frontiers of Knowledge in the Study of Man*, edited by Lynn White, Jr., 68. New York: Greenwood Press, 1969.

———. "The Dynamo and the Virgin Reconsidered." *American Scholar* 27 (1958).

———. *Frontiers of Knowledge in the Study of Man*. New York: Greenwood Press, l969.

———. "Technology and Invention in the Middle Ages." *Speculum* 15 (1940): 141–56.

Whitehead, Alfred North. *Science and the Modern World*. New York: Macmillan, 1925.

Wieland, Wolfgang. "Bemerkungen zum Anfang von Hegels Logik." In *Seminar: Dialektik in der Philosophie Hegels*, edited by Rolf-Peter Horstmann, 194–212. Frankfurt am Main: Suhrkamp Verlag, 1978.

Williams, Bernard. *Ethics and the Limits of Philosophy*. London: Fontana, 1985.

Williams, George. *The Mind of John Paul II*. New York: Seabury, 1981.

Winthrop-Young, Geoffrey. "Silicon Sociology, or, Two Kings on Hegel's Throne? Kittler, Luhmann, and the Posthuman Merger of German Media Theory." *Yale Journal of Criticism* 13, no. 2 (2000): 391–420.

Wippel, John F. "The Condemnations of 1270 and 1277 in Paris." *Journal of Medieval and Renaissance Studies* 7 (1977): 169–201.

———. "Thomas Aquinas and the Condemnation of 1277." *Modern Schoolman* 72 (1955): 233–72.

Wood, Allen W. *Hegel's Ethical Thought*. Cambridge and New York: Cambridge University Press, 1990.

Wood, Robert E. "Hegel on the Heart." *International Philosophical Quarterly* 41 (2001): 131–44.

———. *A Path into Metaphysics*. Albany: SUNY Press, 1991.

———. "Philosophy, Aesthetics, and Theology: A Review of Hans Urs von Balthasar's *The Glory of the Lord*." *American Catholic Philosophical Quarterly* 47 (1993): 355–82.

———. *Placing Aesthetics: Reflections on the Philosophic Tradition*. Athens: Ohio University Press, 1999.

———. "Potentiality, Creativity, and Relationality: Creative Power as a 'New' Transcendental?" *The Review of Metaphysics* 59 (2005).

Wojtyla, Karol. *The Acting Person*. Translated by Andrzej Potocki. Dordrecht: Reidel, 1979.

Žižek, Slavoj. *For They Know Not What They Do: Enjoyment as a Political Factor.* New York and London: Verso, 1991.

———. "Hegel's "Logic of Essence" as a Theory of Ideology." In *Tarrying with the Negative: Kant, Hegel and the Critique of Ideology,* 130–31. Durham, N.C.: Duke University Press, 1993.

———. *The Sublime Object of Ideology.* London: Verso, 1989.

———. *Tarrying with the Negative: Kant, Hegel and the Critique of Ideology.* Durham, N.C.: Duke University Press, 1993.

CONTRIBUTORS

Thomas C. Anderson is professor emeritus in the Philosophy Department at Marquette University, Milwaukee, Wisconsin, where he also served as chair. He is the author of *The Foundation and Structure of Sartrean Ethics; Sartre's Two Ethics: From Authenticity to Integral Humanity;* and, most recently, *A Commentary on Gabriel Marcel's "The Mystery of Being,"* as well as many articles on Marcel, Sartre, and Søren Kierkegaard. He also edited an issue of the *American Catholic Philosophical Quarterly* devoted to Jean-Paul Sartre. He is past president of the American Catholic Philosophical Association and was the founder and first president of the Gabriel Marcel Society in North America.

Jennifer Bates is associate professor of philosophy at Duquesne University. She is the author of *Hegel's Theory of Imagination* and *Hegel and Shakespeare on Moral Imagination.* Her expertise is in nineteenth-century continental philosophy, with an emphasis on Hegel. Her publications also include interdisciplinary articles such as "Stevens, Hegel and the Palm at the End of the Mind" in the *Wallace Stevens Journal* and "An Inquiry Into the Nature of Environmentally Sound Thinking" in *Environmental Ethics.* She has research interests in Buddhist philosophy and is currently writing on the works of Søren Kierkegaard.

Michael Baur is associate professor of philosophy and adjunct professor of law at Fordham University. He holds a Ph.D. in philosophy from the University of Toronto and a J.D. from Harvard Law School. He is the translator of J. G. Fichte's *Foundations of Natural Right* and series editor of "Cambridge Hegel Translations." His areas of research include the philosophy of law, Thomism, German Idealism, and contemporary continental thought. He has edited numerous books and has published articles and book chapters on a wide range of thinkers, including Aristotle, Aquinas, Kant, Fichte, Hegel, Heidegger, Adorno, Gadamer, Lonergan, and John Henry Newman.

John W. Burbidge is professor emeritus at Trent University, Peterborough, Ontario, Canada, and honorary president of the Hegel Society of Great Britain. He is author of eight books, including *Being and Will: An Essay in Philosophical Theology, On Hegel's Logic,* and *Hegel's Systematic Contingency.*

Thomas W. Busch is professor of philosophy at Villanova University and is the author of *The Power of Consciousness and the Force of Circumstances in Sartre's Philosophy* and *Circulating Being: From Embodiment to Incorporation: Essays in Late Existentialism,* as well as a number of articles on phenomenology and existentialism.

James Crooks is professor of philosophy and dean of arts and science at Bishop's University in Sherbrooke, Quebec. His principal interests lie in the ancient world (Heraclitus, Plato), but he has also published on Hegel, Kierkegaard, Nietzsche, and Heidegger. His most recent article is "Inventing Socrates: Truth, Jest and Care in Plato's *Apology*" in *Reexamining Socrates in the Apology,* edited by Patricia Fagan and John Russon.

Daniel O. Dahlstrom, chair and professor of philosophy at Boston University, is the author of *Philosophical Legacies* and editor of *Interpreting Heidegger: New Essays.* His recent articles include "*Continentia,* Self-possession, and Resoluteness: What Is the Good of *Being and Time?*" *Research in Phenomenology* 39, no. 2 (2009): 248–65 and "The *Critique of Pure Reason* and Continental Philosophy," in *Cambridge Companion to Kant's Critique of Pure Reason,* edited by Paul Guyer.

John Deely is professor and holder of the Rudman Chair at the University of St Thomas, Houston, and an editor of *The American Journal of Semiotics.* In early and late October of 2008 he received, respectively, the scholarly award of the International Étienne Gilson Association and the American Maritain Association. His most recent books are *Medieval Philosophy Redefined* and *Semiotics Seen Synchronically: the View as of 2010.* Of many articles, his most recent is "The Essays in Paralipsis," an overview of the 26 essays comprising the "Four Ages Special Issue" of *Semiotica* 178, nos. 1–4 (2010): 329–36, guest-edited by Susan Petrilli and John Hittinger, based on Deely's 2001 opus published by the University of Toronto Press, *Four Ages of Understanding: The First Postmodern Survey of Philosophy from Ancient Times to the Turn of the Twenty-First Century.*

Martin Donougho was educated in Sussex, England, and Toronto, Canada, and currently teaches philosophy at the University of South Carolina, Columbia, where he is cross-appointed in Comparative Literature and in Film

Studies. He has published widely on Hegel, continental thought, and the philosophy of art. Recent articles by him include an exploration of Heideggerian traces in Terry Malick's *The New World* and a piece on Hegel and abstract art. His current project is on the "genealogy" of art, as institution and as concept, using some of Niklas Luhmann's ideas.

Jude P. Dougherty is professor emeritus and dean emeritus of the School of Philosophy, The Catholic University of America. His most recent books include *The Logic of Religion, Jacques Maritain: An Intellectual Profile,* and *Wretched Aristotle.* He is a member of the Pontifical Academy of St. Thomas and of the European Academy of Science.

Louis Dupré was from 1973 until 1998 the T. Lawrason Riggs Professor in the Philosophy of Religion at Yale University. He is now professor emeritus in Yale's Department of Religious Studies. He has previously served as president of the American Catholic Philosophical Association and as president of the Hegel Society of America. His many published books include: *Kierkegaard as Theologian; Contraception and Catholics; The Philosophical Foundations of Marxism; The Other Dimension; Transcendent Selfhood; A Dubious Heritage: Studies in the Philosophy of Religion after Kant; The Deeper Life; Marx's Social Critique of Culture; The Common Life; Passage to Modernity: An Essay in the Hermeneutics of Nature and Culture; Metaphysics and Culture; Religious Mystery and Rational Reflection;* and *Symbols of the Sacred.*

James Kow is an associate professor of philosophy in the Department of Philosophy and Religious Studies at King's University College, University of Western Ontario, London, Ontario, Canada. His published work has appeared in *Communio: International Catholic Review,* the *International Philosophical Quarterly,* the *Proceedings of the American Catholic Philosophical Association,* and *Philosophy, Tradition, and Culture.*

Jay Lampert is associate professor of philosophy at the University of Guelph, Ontario, Canada. His books include *Synthesis and Backward Reference in Husserl's* Logical Investigations, *Deleuze and Guattari's Philosophy of History,* and the forthcoming *Simultaneity and Delay.* He has published articles on Hegel, Derrida, Balibar, Marion, and others, usually on topics related to time and history. The graduate courses he took from Professor Schmitz are among his greatest influences and inspirations.

John C. McCarthy is associate professor of philosophy and associate dean of the School of Philosophy, The Catholic University of America. For the last several years, early modern philosophy has been the primary focus of his teaching, writing, and study. Along those lines, he recently completed "Bacon's Third Sailing: The 'Pre–Socratic' Origins of Modern Philosophy," which will appear in *Early Greek Philosophy: Reason at the Beginning of Philosophy*, edited by Joe McCoy (The Catholic University of America Press, forthcoming).

†***Ralph McInerny*** was professor of philosophy, director of the Jacques Maritain Center, and Michael P. Grace Professor of Medieval Studies at the University of Notre Dame. He died on January 29, 2010. He was author of numerous books on philosophy and the history of philosophy, including: *New Themes in Christian Philosophy; Thomism in an Age of Renewal; St. Thomas Aquinas; Ethica Thomistica: The Moral Philosophy of Thomas Aquinas; A First Glance at St. Thomas Aquinas: A Handbook for Peeping Thomists; Aquinas on Human Action: A Theory of Practice; The Question of Christian Ethics; Aquinas and Analogy;* and *Praeambula Fidei: Thomism and the God of the Philosophers.*

John Russon is professor of philosophy at the University of Guelph, Ontario, Canada, and director of the Toronto Summer Seminar in Philosophy. He is the author of *Human Experience: Philosophy, Neurosis and the Elements of Everyday Life; Bearing Witness to Epiphany: Persons, Things, and the Nature of Erotic Life; Reading Hegel's Phenomenology;* and *The Self and Its Body in Hegel's Phenomenology of Spirit*. His most recent of many articles is "Emotional Subjects: Mood and Articulation in Hegel's *Philosophy of Mind*," *International Philosophical Quarterly* 49 (2009).

Daniel E. Shannon is a professor of philosophy at DePauw University, Greencastle, Indiana. He is editor of the translation, G. W. F. Hegel, *"Spirit": Chapter Six of the Phenomenology of Spirit* and co-editor of the volume *The Challenges of Globalization: Rethinking Nature, Culture, and Freedom*. His latest published article is "Justifying Atonement: An Anselmian Response to Modern Critics," *St. Anselm Journal* 6, no. 2 (Spring 2009).

Robert E. Wood is professor of philosophy in the Institute of Philosophic Studies at the University of Dallas. From 1989 to 2009 he was editor of the *American Catholic Philosophical Quarterly*. He has published three books and 70 articles on aesthetics, anthropology, and metaphysics developed through studies in the history of thought.

INDEX

Person, Being, & History: Essays in Honor of Kenneth L. Schmitz was designed and typeset in Dante by Kachergis Book Design of Pittsboro, North Carolina. It was printed on 60-pound House Natural Smooth and bound by Sheridan Books of Ann Arbor, Michigan.